Writing the Novel
From Plot to Print

Lawrence Block

Writer's Digest Books, Cincinnati, Ohio

Library of Congress Cataloging in Publication Data

Block, Lawrence.
    Writing the novel from plot to print.

    1. Fiction—Authorship. I. Title.
PN3365.B54   808'.025   79-10677
ISBN 0-911654-67-4

Books by Lawrence Block

NOVELS
After the First Death
Deadly Honeymoon
Death Pulls a Doublecross
The Girl with the Long Green Heart
Mona
Ronald Rabbit is a Dirty Old Man
The Specialists

BOOKS ABOUT EVAN TANNER
The Thief Who Couldn't Sleep
The Canceled Czech
Tanner's Twelve Swingers
Two for Tanner
Tanner's Tiger
Here Comes a Hero
Me Tanner, You Jane

BOOKS ABOUT MATTHEW SCUDDER
The Sins of the Fathers
Time to Murder and Create
In the Midst of Death

BOOKS ABOUT BERNIE RHODENBARR
Burglars Can't Be Choosers
The Burglar in the Closet
The Burglar who Liked to Quote Kipling

NOVELS BY PAUL KAVANAGH
Such Men Are Dangerous
The Triumph of Evil
Not Comin' Home to You

NONFICTION
Writing the Novel: From Plot to Print

For Miss May Jepson, my 11th Grade English teacher at Bennett High School in Buffalo, New York, who first encouraged me to become a writer;

For my mother and father, whose support toward that end was unflagging;

For John O'Hara, Evan Hunter, Fredric Brown, W. Somerset Maugham, Rex Stout, Dashiell Hammett, James T. Farrell, Thomas Wolfe, and so many more writers from whom I've learned so much of what I know;

For Nolan Miller, whose writing workshop at Antioch College was my nursery;

For John Brady, who encouraged me to write about writing;

For my daughters, Amy and Jill and Alison, who can be whatever they want in this world;

For Bill and all his friends, who have shared their experience, strength and hope;

And for Mary Pat, with all my love.

Acknowledgments

Before this present volume was in the planning stages, I circulated a questionnaire on writing methods with the intention of doing a magazine piece on the subject. A large number of writers of fiction and nonfiction alike were kind enough to reply at some length. While my article was not ultimately published, the replies to my questionnaire were of inestimable value to me when it came time to write this book on the novel. I've had occasion to quote from several of the replies I received; all of them in one way or another enlarged my understanding of how writers do whatever it is that we do.

This book's defects are mine alone. For its strengths, I should like to acknowledge the assistance of all those who replied to my questionnaire, to wit:

Mary Amlaw, Poul Anderson, Mel Arrighi, Isaac Asimov, Michael Avallone, Jean L. Backus, Eugene Franklin Bandy, D.R. Benson, Robert Bloch, Murray Teigh Bloom, Barbara Bonham, Jon L. Breen, William Brittain, Barbara Callahan, William E. Chambers, Thomas Chastain, John Cheever, Mary Higgins Clark, Virginia Coffman, George Harmon Coxe, Linda Crawford, Clive Cussler, Dorothy Salisbury Davis, Richard Deming, F.M. Esfandiary, Stanley Ellin, Harlan Ellison, Robert L. Fish, Patricia Fox-Sheinwold, Lucy Freeman, Anne Freemantle, Tonita S. Gardner, Brian Garfield, Herbert Gold, Arthur Goldstein, Joe Gores, Marilyn Granbeck, Russell H. Girran, Irving A. Greenfield, Isidore Haiblum, Joseph Hansen, Joyce Harrington, Tony Hillerman, Edward D. Hoch, Peter Hochstein, James Holding, Hans

Holzer, Dorothy B. Hughes, Beatrice Trum Hunter, Bel Kaufman, Richard Kostelanetz, Eda J. LeShan, Elizabeth Levy, Robert Ludlum, John Lutz, Arthur Lyons, Arthur Maling, Harold Q. Masur, John D. MacDonald, Ross Macdonald, Gregory McDonald, Thomas M. McDade, Patricia McGerr, William P. McGivern, James McKimmey, Francis M. Nevins, Donald Newlove, Stephen R. Novak, Al Nussbaum, Dennis O'Neil, Robert B. Parker, Don Pendleton, Judson Philips, Richard S. Prather, Bill Pronzini, Tom Purdom, Robert J. Randisi, Malcolm Robinson, Willo Davis Roberts, Sam Ross, Sandra Scoppettone, Justin Scott, Henry Slesar, Martin Cruz Smith, Jerry Sohl, Jane Speed, Aaron Marc Stein, Richard Martin Stern, Ross Thomas, Lawrence Treat, Louis Trimble, Thomas Walsh, Stephen Wasylyk, Hillary Waugh, Sol Weinstein, Edward Wellen, Helen Wells, David Westheimer, Donald E. Westlake, Collin Wilcox and Chelsea Quinn Yarbro.

Contents

Introduction

This is a book designed to help you write a novel. It contains the distillation of my own experience of twenty years as a published novelist, plus a considerable amount that I've learned from other writers. My goal throughout has been to produce the sort of book I might have found useful when I set out to write my own first novel.

But there are no guarantees. Just because you've bought this book, just because you've studied it diligently, does not mean for a moment that your success as a novelist is a foregone conclusion. You may never write so much as the first paragraph of a novel. You may begin work on a book and find yourself unable to complete it. Or you may labor long and hard on a book, working your way through outline and first draft and final polish, only to discover that you've turned a perfectly good ream of paper into something commercially unviable and artistically indefensible.

These things happen. That they happen constantly to neophyte writers should hardly be surprising news. What may be more of a surprise is that they happen to seasoned professional novelists as well.

They even happen to me. Over the years, I've published, at last count, twenty novels under my own name, plus perhaps five times that number under various pseudonyms. You would think that all that furious typing would have resulted in my having learned something, that while I might not know how to tie my shoes or cross the street I ought certainly to have the mechanics of writing a novel down cold by now.

But in the past two or three years I've had perhaps half a dozen ideas for novels that got no further than the first chapter. I've written three novels that died after I'd written over a hundred pages; they repose in my file cabinet at this very moment, like out-of-gas cars on a highway, waiting for someone to start them up again. I very much doubt they'll ever be completed.

That's not all. During that same stretch of time I've seen two novels through to completion and succeeded only in producing books that no one has wanted to publish—and, I've come to believe, for good and sufficient reason. Both were books I probably shouldn't have tried writing in the first place. Both failures constituted learning experiences that will almost certainly prove beneficial in future work. While I could by no means afford the time spent on these books, neither can I properly write that time off as altogether wasted.

But how could an established professional write an unpublishable book? If he's written a dozen or two dozen or five dozen publishable ones in a row, wouldn't you think he'd have the formula down pat?

The answer, of course, is that there's no such thing as a formula. Except in the genuinely rare instances of writers who tend to write the same book over and over, every novel is a wholly new experience.

In *Some Thoughts I Have in Mind When I Teach,* Wendell Berry makes the point that

> No good book was ever written according to a recipe. Every good book is to a considerable extent a unique discovery. And so one can say with plenty of justification that nobody knows "how to

write." Certainly nobody knows how other people ought to. For myself, though I think I know how to write the books I have already written—and though I guess, wrongly no doubt, that I could now write them better than I did—I am discomforted by the knowledge that I don't know how to write the books that I have not yet written. But that discomfort has an excitement about it, and it is the necessary antecedent of one of the best kinds of happiness.

Some of the books I write involve series characters. I've done three books, for example, about a burglar named Bernie Rhodenbarr; in each of them he becomes the prime suspect in a homicide investigation because of his activities as a burglar, and in order to get himself out of the jam he has to solve the murder himself. There is, clearly, a similarity to the structure of all three of these books which at a cursory glance might well look like a formula.

But each plot is significantly different and each book, let me assure you, has presented its own specific problems. You might think the books would become easier to write. The third, just recently completed as I write these lines, was by a fair margin the most difficult of the three.

As a noun, *novel* means a book-length prose narrative. As an adjective, it means "of a new kind or nature." The dual definition is historic, of course, deriving from a time when the novel was a new fictional form. Still, I see it as a happy accident, for every novel *is* novel.

I would suppose that a majority of this book's readers have yet to write a book-length work of fiction. It is commonplace to hear that the first novel presents special problems to author and publisher alike. But in a larger sense every novel is a first novel, presenting no end of unique problems, carrying enormous risks, and offering immense excitement and other rewards.

If you're unprepared for the risks, perhaps you'd like to rethink this whole business of novel-writing. If you're unwilling to live with the possibility of failure, perhaps you'd be more comfortable writing laundry lists and letters to the editor.

If you really want to write a novel, stick around.

* * *

One thing you won't find in this book is an explanation of *the* way to write a novel.

Because I don't believe there is one. Just as every novel is unique, so too is every novelist. The study I've made of the writing methods of others has led me to the belief that everybody in this business spends a lifetime finding the method that suits him best, changing it over the years as he himself evolves, adapting it again and again to suit the special requirements of each particular book. What works for one person won't necessarily work for another; what works with one book won't necessarily work with another.

Some novelists outline briefly, some in great detail, and a few produce full-fledged treatments that run half the length of the final book itself. Others don't outline at all. Some of us revise as we go along. Others do separate drafts. Some of us write sprawling first drafts and wind up cutting them to the bone. Others rarely cut three paragraphs overall.

Some months before I wrote my own first novel—of which there will be more later—I read a book which purported to tell how to write a novel. The author taught writing at one of America's leading universities and had written a couple of well-received historical novels, and he had set out to tell the great audience of would-be novelists how to go and do likewise.

His method was a dilly. What you did if you wanted to write a novel, I was given to understand, was to trot down to the nearest stationery store and pick up several packs of three-by-five file cards. Then you sat at a desk with the cards and a trayful of sharp pencils and got down to business.

First you went to work on your character cards. You wrote out one or more of those for each and every character to appear in the book, from the several leads to the most minor bit players. For the major characters, you might use several cards, devoting one to a physical description of the character, another to his background, another to his personal habits, and a fourth, say, to the astrological aspects at the moment of his birth.

Then you prepared your scene cards. Having used some other cards to rough out the plot, you set about working up a file card for every scene which would take place in your novel. If one character was going to buy a newspaper somewhere around page 384, you'd write out a scene card explaining how the scene would play, and what the lead would say to the newsdealer, and what the weather was like.

There was, as I recall, rather more to this method. By the time you were ready to write the book you had innumerable shoeboxes filled with three-by-five cards and all you had to do was turn them into a novel—which, now that I think of it, sounds rather more of a challenge than converting a sow's ear into a silk purse, or base metal into gold.

I read this book all the way through, finding myself drawing closer to despair with every passing chapter. Two things were crystal clear to me. First of all, this man knew how to write a novel, and his method was the right method. Secondly, I couldn't possibly manage it.

I finished the book, heaved a sigh, and gave myself up to feelings of inadequacy. I decided I'd have to stick to short stories for the time being, if not forever. Maybe someday I'd be sufficiently organized and disciplined and all to get those file cards and dig in. Maybe not.

Couple of months later I got out of bed one morning and sat down and wrote a two-page outline of a novel. About a month after that I sat down to the typewriter with my two-page outline at hand and a ream of white bond paper at the ready. I felt a little guilty without a shoebox full of file cards, but like the bumblebee who goes on flying in happy ignorance of the immutable laws of physics, I persisted in my folly and wrote the book in a couple of weeks.

Shows what a jerk that other writer was, doesn't it? Wrong. It shows nothing of the sort. The extraordinarily elaborate method he described, while no more inviting in my eyes than disembowelment, was obviously one that worked like a charm—*for him*.

Perhaps he said as much. Perhaps he qualified things by explaining that his method was not *the* way to write a novel but merely *his* way to write a novel. It's been a long time since I read his book—and it'll be donkey's years until I read it again—so I can't trust my memory on the point. But I do know that I was left with the distinct impression that his method was the right method, that all other methods were the wrong method, and that by finding my own way to write my own novel I was proceeding at my own peril. It's unlikely that he put things so strongly, and my interpretation doubtless owes a good deal to the anxiety and insecurity with which I approached the whole prospect of writing a book-length work of fiction.

Nevertheless, I would hate to leave anyone with the impression that the following pages will tell you everything to know about how to write a novel. All I'll be doing—all I really can do—is share my own experience. If nothing else, that experience has been extensive enough to furnish me with the beginnings of a sense of my own ignorance. After twenty years and a hundred books, I at least realize that I don't *know* how to write a novel, that nobody does, that there *is* no right way to do it. Whatever method works—for you, for me, for whoever's sitting in the chair and poking away at the typewriter keys—is the right way to do it.

Chapter 1

Why Write a Novel?

If you want to write fiction, the best thing you can do is take two aspirins, lie down in a dark room, and wait for the feeling to pass.

If it persists, you probably ought to write a novel. Interestingly, most embryonic fiction writers accept the notion that they ought to write a novel sooner or later. It's not terribly difficult to see that the world of short fiction is a world of limited opportunity. Both commercially and artistically, the short-story writer is quite strictly circumscribed.

This has not always been the case. Half a century ago, the magazine story was important in a way it has never been since. During the twenties, a prominent writer typically earned several thousand dollars for the sale of a short story to a top slick magazine. These stories were apt to be talked about at parties and social gatherings, and the reputation a writer might establish in this fashion helped gain attention for any novel he might ultimately publish.

The change since those days has been remarkable. In virtually all areas, the short fiction market has shrunk in size and significance. Fewer magazines publish fiction, and every year they publish less of it. The handful of top markets pay less in today's dollars than they did in the much harder currency of fifty or sixty years ago. Pulp magazines have virtually disappeared as a market; a handful of confession magazines and a scanter handful of mystery and science-fiction magazines are all that remain of a market once numbered in the hundreds. Whole categories of popular fiction have categorically vanished; the western, the sports story, the light romance—these were once published in considerable quantity, twelve or fifteen stories per magazine, and now they have simply gone the way of the dodo and the passenger pigeon.

The remaining pulps are scarcely worth writing for. Consider the plight, for example, of the writer of detective fiction. Twenty years ago, the two leading magazines in the field paid five cents a word for material, and their rejects sold quite readily to any of a batch of lesser markets. Now, at a time when the erstwhile nickel candy bar has gone to twenty cents, those two magazines still pay the same nickel a word—and only a single cent-a-word publication exists to skim the cream of the stories they reject.

The outlook is not much more promising for writers of "quality" fiction. Very few magazines publish stories of literary distinction and pay a decent price for the privilege. After a piece has made the rounds of *The New Yorker, Atlantic, Harper's,* and a few others, its author is reduced to submitting it to the small literary magazines that pay off in contributor's copies or, at best, token payment. It is not merely impossible to make a living in this fashion; it is very nearly impossible, over the course of a year, to cover one's mailing expenses.

On the other hand, one can make a living writing novels.

I'm not going to make you drool by rattling on about the stratospheric sums certain writers have received of late for their novels. The earnings of best sellers, the fortunes paid for film and paperback rights, have relatively little to do with the average writer, be he neophyte or veteran. James Michener once remarked that America is a country in which a writer can make a fortune but not a living—i.e., a handful of successful writers get rich while the rest of us can't even get by. There's some truth in this—the gap between success and survival is, I submit, an unhealthily yawning one—but there's some hyperbole in it as well. A writer can indeed make a living in America; if he's a reasonably productive novelist, he can make a living verging on comfortability.

Financial considerations aside, I have always felt there are satisfactions in the novel which are not to be found in shorter fiction. I began as a writer of short stories, and to have written and published a short story was an accomplishment in which I took an inordinate amount of pride. But genuine literary achievement, as far as I was concerned, lay in being able to hold in my own hands a book with my own name on the cover. (I was to hold a dozen of my own books before one of them was to bear my own name, as it turned out, but that's by the way.)

Short-story writing, as I saw it, was estimable. One required skill and cleverness to carry it off. But to have written a novel was to have achieved something of substance. You could swing a short story on a cute idea backed up by a modicum of verbal agility. You could, when the creative juices were flowing, knock it off start-to-finish on a slow afternoon.

A novel, on the other hand, took real work. You had to spend months on the thing, fighting it out in the trenches, line by line and page by page and chapter by chapter. It had to have plot and characters of sufficient depth and complexity to support a structure of sixty or a hundred thousand words. It wasn't an anecdote, or a finger exercise, or a trip to the moon on gossamer wings. It was a *book*.

The short-story writer, as I saw it, was a sprinter; he deserved praise to the extent that his stories were meritorious. But the novelist was a long-distance runner, and you don't have to come in first in a marathon in order to deserve the plaudits of the crowd. It is enough merely to have finished on one's feet.

* * *

These arguments presented above would all seem to urge the writer to turn eventually to the novel. But it's my contention that the beginner at fiction ought to focus his attention on the novel not sooner or later but right away. The novel, I submit, is not merely the ultimate goal. It is also the place to start.

At first, this may well seem illogical. We've just seen the short story likened to a sprint, the novel to a marathon. Shouldn't a marathon runner work up to that distance gradually? Shouldn't a writer develop his abilities in the short story before attempting the more challenging work of the novel?

Certainly a great many of us do begin that way. I did myself, as far as that goes. In my earliest efforts, it was extremely difficult for me to sustain a prose narrative for the fifteen hundred words necessary to constitute a proper short-short. Over a period of time I became increasingly at ease writing full-length short stories, and then I finally wrote my first novel. Other writers have followed a similar path, but perhaps as many have leaped directly into the novel without any serious effort at short stories. There doesn't seem to be any traditional path to follow in becoming a writer. Whatever road leads to the destination turns out to have been the right road for that particular traveler.

With the understanding, then, that all roads lead to Rome, here are some of the reasons why I believe a writer is best advised to begin with a novel.

Skill is less at a premium. This may seem paradoxical—why should a novel require less skill than a short story? You'd think it would be the other way around.

Don't you have to be a better craftsman to manage a novel? I don't think so. Often a novelist can get away with stylistic crudity that would cripple a shorter piece of fiction.

Remember, what a novel affords you as a writer is *room*. You have space to move around in, space to let your characters develop and come to life, space for your story line to get itself in motion and carry the day. While a way with words never hurts, it's of less overwhelming importance to the novelist than the sheer ability to grab ahold of the reader and make him care what happens next.

The best seller list abounds with the work of writers whom no one would want to call polished stylists. While I wouldn't care to name them, I can think offhand of half a dozen writers whose first chapters are very hard going for me. I'm perhaps overly conscious of style—writing does radically change one's perceptions as a reader—and I find their dialogue mechanical, their transitions awkward, their scene construction clumsy, their descriptions imprecise. But if I can make myself hang on for the first twenty or thirty or forty pages, I'll lose my excessive awareness of the trees and start to perceive the forest. The author's pure storytelling ability grips me and I no longer notice the defects of his style.

In shorter fiction, the storyline wouldn't have this chance to take over. The story would have run its course before I ceased to notice the author's style.

Similarly, some novels triumph over the style in which they are written because of the grandeur of their themes or the fascination of their subject matter. The epic novel, presenting in fictional form the whole history of a nation, catches the reader up because of the sheer power of its scope. Leon Uris's *Exodus* is a good example of this type of book. And Arthur Hailey's books exemplify the novel that conveys an enormous amount of information to the reader, telling him almost more than he cares to know about a particular industry. This is not to say that these novels, or others of their ilk, are stylistically clumsy, but merely to point out that style becomes a considerably less vital consideration than it must be in short fiction.

The idea is less important. I've known any number of writers who have postponed writing a novel because they felt they lacked a sufficiently strong or fresh or provocative idea for one. I can understand this, because similar feelings delayed my own first novel. Logic would seem to suggest that a novel, by virtue of its length, would require more in the way of an idea than a short story.

If you're having trouble coming up with ideas, you may well be better off with a novel than with short stories. Because each short story absolutely demands either a new idea or a new slant on an old one. Often the short story amounts to very little more than an idea fleshed out and polished into a piece of fiction. This is particularly likely to be the case with the short-short, which is typically not much more than a fifteen-hundred-word preamble leading up to a surprise ending, an idea thinly cloaked in the fabric of fiction.

Novels, on the other hand, are time and again written with no original central idea to be found. Every month sees the publication of new gothic novels, for example, and the overwhelming majority of them hew quite closely to a single plotline—a young woman is in peril in a forbidding house, probably on the moors; she is drawn to two men, one of whom turns out to be a hero, the other a villain. Another category, the historical romance of the *Love's Tender Fury* variety, has an initially innocent heroine getting ravished in various historical periods and with varying degrees of enjoyment.

Westerns typically adhere to one of five or six standard plotlines. Similarly, there are a handful of basic book types in the mystery and science-fiction fields. And, in the world of mainstream fiction, consider how many novels each year deal with nothing more original than the loss of innocence.

This is not to say that the novel does not demand ingenuity. It is this quality which enables the novelist to take a standard theme and hang upon it a book which will seem quite fresh and new to everyone who reads it. As he writes, characters come to life, scenes acquire dimension upon the page, and a wealth of original incident serves to make this particular book significantly different from all those other novels to which it is thematically identical.

Sometimes these elements of characterization and incident

which make a novel unique exist in the forefront of the author's mind when he sits down to the typewriter. Sometimes they emerge from his creative unconscious as he goes along.

* * *

I enjoy writing short stories myself. They offer me considerable satisfaction, for all that their production is economically unsound. I very much enjoy being able to sit down at the typewriter with an idea fully formed in my head and devote myself to a day's work of transforming that idea into a finished piece of fiction.

The enjoyment's so keen that I'd do this sort of thing more often—except that each story requires a reasonably strong central idea, and the idea itself gets used up in the space of a couple of thousand words. I simply don't get that many ideas that I find all that appealing.

Ed Hoch makes a living writing nothing but short stories, and he manages this superhuman feat because he seems to be a never-ending fount of ideas. The development of short story ideas and their speedy metamorphosis into fiction is what gives him personal satisfaction as a writer. I sometimes find myself envying him, but I know I couldn't possibly come up with half a dozen viable short story ideas every month the way he does. So I take the easy way out and write novels.

You can learn more. Writing has this in common with most other skills: we develop it best by practicing it. Whatever writing we do helps us to become better writers.

It has been my observation, however, that there is no better way to learn how to write than by writing a novel. I learned quite a bit by writing short stories. I learned much much more when I wrote my first novel, and I have continued to learn something or other with virtually every novel I have written since.

Short story writing taught me quite a bit about effective use of the language. I learned, too, how to construct a scene and how to handle dialogue. Everything I learned in this fashion was valuable.

When I wrote a novel, it was as if I were working out now with heavy weights; I felt growth in muscles I had not previously been called upon to use at all.

Characterization was at once a very different matter. Before my characters had existed to perform specific functions and speak specific lines. Some were well drawn, some were not, but none had the sort of fictive life that transcended their role on the page. When I wrote a novel, the characters came to life for me. They had backgrounds, they had families, they had quirks and attitudes that added up to more than the broad lines of caricature. I had to know more about them in order to make them maintain vitality over a couple of hundred pages, and thus there was more substance to them. This not to say that my characterization in my earliest novels was particularly good. It was not. But I learned immeasurably from it.

I learned, too, how to deal with time in fiction. My short stories had often consisted of a single scene, and rarely of more than three or four scenes. The novels I wrote seemed to cover a matter of days or weeks, and of course consisted of a great many scenes. I learned to deal with any number of technical matters—viewpoint shifts, flashbacks, internal monologues, etc.

You can earn while you learn. It's curious how many writers tend to expect instant gratification. We've barely rolled a sheet of paper into the typewriter than we expect to see our efforts on the best seller list.

It seems to me that other artists are rather less impatient of tangible success. What painter expects to sell the first canvas he covers? More often than not he plans to paint over it once it's dried. What singer counts on being booked into Carnegie Hall the first day he hits a high note? Every other artistic career is assumed to have an extended and arduous period of study and apprenticeship, yet all too many writers think they ought to be able to write professionally on their first attempt, and mail off their first stories before the ink is dry.

There must be reasons for this. I suppose the whole idea of communication is so intrinsic a part of what we do that a piece of writing which goes unread by others is like Bishop Berkeley's tree falling where no human ear can hear it. If nobody reads it, it's as if we hadn't even written it.

Then too, unpublished writing strikes us as unfinished writing. An artist can hang a canvas on his own wall. A singer can croon in the shower. A manuscript, though, is not complete until it is in print.

At first glance this desire to receive money and recognition for early work would look like the height of egotistic arrogance. It seems to me, however, that what it best illustrates is the profound insecurity of the new writer. We yearn to be in print because without this recognition we have no way of establishing to our own satisfaction that our work is of any value.

I would not for a moment advise a new writer to expect to get any recognition or financial gain out of a first novel. Unless you are fully prepared to spend months writing a book with no greater reward than the doing of it, you would very likely be better off getting rid of your typewriter and taking up some leisure pastime which places less of a premium on achievement.

This notwithstanding, there is no gainsaying the fact that any number of first novels are published every year. Publishers typically bitch about the difficulty of breaking even on a first novel, conveniently ignoring the several first novels per season to achieve best seller status. True, most first novels are not published. True too, most that are sell very poorly. The wonder is that any are published at all.

Thus it is possible to make certain gains, in money and in

recognition, while acquiring those skills which can only be acquired through experience. And this sort of paid apprenticeship is far more readily accessible to the novelist than the short story writer.

It wasn't always this way. When the newsstands teemed with pulp magazines, the pulps were precisely where the new writer earned a living—albeit a precarious one—while developing his skills and refining his technique. A similar kind of magazine apprenticeship is standard procedure to this day in the field of nonfiction; article writers earn while they learn by writing for house organs and trade journals before they are ready to write either nonfiction books or articles for more prestigious magazines.

Some of the surviving fiction magazines are certainly open to new writers—*Ellery Queen's Mystery Magazine,* for example, makes a special point of publishing first stories, having printed over five hundred maiden efforts to date. But ever since the decline of the pulps in the 1950s, there has not been sufficient depth to the magazine fiction market for a writer to serve out his apprenticeship there.

In contrast, the market for original paperback fiction continues to be quite strong, and quite receptive to the work of beginners. The relative viability of the various categories of category fiction—suspense, adventure, western, science fiction, gothic, light romance, historical romance—runs a cyclical course, but there are always several categories which constitute a healthy market.

I served my own novelistic apprenticeship in the field of paperback sex novels. In the summer of '58, I had just finished my first novel and was wondering what to do next. My agent was marketing the book; I had no idea whether it would sell or fail completely.

The agent got in touch with me to say that a new publisher was entering the field of sex novels. Did I know what these books were? Could I read a few and try one of my own?

I bought and skimmed several representative examples in the field. (If I had all of this to do over again, I'd spend more time on this analysis, as detailed in Chapter Three.) I then sat down at the typewriter with the assurance of youth and batted out three chapters and an outline of what turned out to be the start of a career.

I didn't know how many sex novels I was to write in the years to follow. For quite a while I was doing a book a month for one publisher with occasional books for other houses as well, along with a certain amount of more ambitious writing. I suppose I must have turned out a hundred of them. Maybe not—I really don't know, and my copies of most of the books were lost in the course of a move some years ago. Let's just agree that I wrote a lot of them and let it go at that.

I learned an immeasurable amount from doing this. Bear in mind that these books were written in more innocent times; while they were the most inflammatory reading matter then on the market, they can barely qualify as soft-core pornography by contemporary standards. Unprintable words were not to be found, and descriptive passages were airbrushed like an old-fashioned *Playboy* centerfold.

The books had a sex scene per chapter, but the scene couldn't take up the whole chapter. There was plenty of room left for incident and characterization, for dialogue and con-flict and plot development, room in short for a story to be told with periodic interruptions for sexual titillation. Without the sex, surely, the books would have had no reason for existence; the stories in the main were not strong enough to carry the books unassisted. (Though I can think of one or two excep-tions, books where a character took over and came to life, so that the sexual episodes seemed almost like annoying interrup-tions. But this was rare indeed.)

This was a wonderful apprenticeship for me. I was by nature a fast writer, gifted with the ability to write smooth copy in a first draft; thus I could produce these books rapidly enough to make a satisfactory living. (They did not pay much, nor were there royalties to be had or subsidiary income to anticipate; it was indeed like working for the pulp magazines, with all sales outright.)

I learned a tremendous amount about how to write fiction, learning by the irreproachable method of trial and error. I could fool around with multiple viewpoint, with various sorts of plot structure, could in fact try whatever I wanted as long as I continued to write the books in English and keep the action coming. I got any number of auctorial bad habits out of my system. And, as I've said, I earned while I learned.

I'm acquainted with quite a few writers who started out by cultivating this particular secret garden. There were a number who never went on to anything else; they earned some easy money at sex novels until the novelty wore off but lacked the particular combination of talent and drive which it evidently takes to establish a writing career. The rest of us moved on, sooner or later, to other things. I don't know anyone who doesn't regard the experience as valuable.

In my own case, I suspect I found the sex-novel groove too comfortable and stayed with it too long, past the point where it was able to teach me much. I probably should have tried stretching my literary muscles a little sooner. On the other hand, I was painfully young then in virtually every possible way. The sex books put bread on the table and gave me the satisfaction of regular production and regular publication at a stage when I was incapable of writing anything much more ambitious. I can hardly regret the time I devoted to them.

Is the sex novel field a good starting place for a beginner today? I'm afraid not. Their equivalent in today's market is the mechanical, plotless, hard-core porn novel, written with neither imagination nor craft and composed of one overblown sex scene after another. The books I wrote were quite devoid of merit—let there be no mistake about that—but by some sort of Gresham's Law of Obscenity they've been driven off the market by a product that is indisputably worse. Any dolt with a typewriter and a properly dirty mind could write them; accordingly, the payment is too low to make the task worth performing. Finally, the books are published by the sort of men who own massage parlors and peep shows. You meet a better class of people on the subway.

There's no need, though, to be nostalgic for the old days, be they the old days of pulp magazines or the old days of soft-core sex novels. There always seems to be an area in which to serve out a writer's apprenticeship. We'll see how to choose your own particular area in the next chapter; meanwhile, let it be said that for the foreseeable future it's almost certain to be a novel of some sort.

The suggestion that a beginner ought to begin as a novelist is a radical one. The natural response is to offer some immediate objections. Let's consider some of the most obvious ones.

Isn't it harder to write a novel than a short story?

No. Novels aren't harder. What they are is longer.

That may be a very obvious answer, but that doesn't make it any less true. It's the sheer length of a novel that the beginning writer is apt to find intimidating.

As a matter of fact, you don't have to be a beginner to be intimidated in this fashion. My suspense novels generally stop at two hundred pages or thereabouts. On the several occasions when I've begun books I knew would run two or three times that length, I had a lot of trouble getting started. The very vastness of the projects put me off.

What's required, I think, is a change in attitude. To write a novel you have to resign yourself to the fact that you simply can't prime yourself and knock it all out in a single extended session at the typewriter. The process of writing the book is going to occupy you for weeks or months—perhaps for years.

But each day's stint at the typewriter is simply that—one day's work. And that's every bit as true whether you're writing short stories or an epic trilogy. If you're writing three or six or ten pages a day, you'll get a certain amount of work accomplished in a certain span of time—whatever it is you're working on.

I remember the first really long book I wrote. When I sat down to begin it I knew I was starting something that had to run at least five hundred pages in manuscript. I got a good day's work down and wound up knocking out fourteen pages. I got up from the typewriter and said, "Well, just 486 pages to go"—and went directly into nervous prostration at the thought.

The thing to remember is that a novel's not going to take forever. All the old clichés actually apply—a journey of a thousand miles begins with a single step, and slow and steady honestly does win the race.

Consider this: If you write one page a day, you will produce a substantial novel in a year's time. The writer who turns out one book a year, year in and year out, is generally acknowledged to be quite prolific. And don't you figure you could produce one measly little page, even on a bad day? Even on a *rotten* day?

When I write a short story I can hold the whole thing in my head when I sit down at my desk. I know exactly where I'm going and it's just a matter of writing it down. I don't have that kind of grasp on a novel.

Of course you don't. Nobody does.

The chapter on outlining will offer some suggestions in this regard. Meanwhile, there are two things to keep in mind.

First of all, recognize that the total control you have over short stories may be largely illusory. What you really have is confidence—because you *think* you know everything about the story by the time you set out to write it.

But, if you're like me, you keep surprising yourself at the typewriter. Characters take on a life of their own and insist upon supplying their own dialogue. Scenes that looked necessary at the outset turn out to be superfluous, while other scenes take a form other than that you'd originally intended for them. As often as not, midway through the story you'll think of a way to improve elements of the plot itself.

This happens to a much greater extent in novels. And it should. A work of fiction ought to be an organic entity. It's alive, and it grows as it goes. Even the most elaborately outlined novel, even the product of those authors who write outlines half the length of the final book, must have this life to it if it is going to live for the reader. The writing of fiction is never purely mechanical, never just a matter of filling in the blanks and tapping the typewriter keys.

A second thing to realize is that you do not have to grasp the whole book at once because you are not going to be writing the whole book at once. Novels are written—as life is lived—One Day At A Time. I've found that all I really have to know about a book in order to put in a day's work on it is what I want to have happen during that day's writing.

I get in trouble when I find myself starting to project. As soon as I step back and try to envision the novel as a whole, I'm likely to be paralyzed with terror. I become convinced that the whole thing is impossible, that there are structural flaws which doom the entire project, that the book can't conceivably resolve itself successfully. But as long as I can get up each morning and concentrate exclusively on what's going to happen during that particular day's stint at the typewriter, I seem to do all right—and the book takes shape, page by page and chapter by chapter.

Many of the books I write are mystery novels of one sort or another. Books of this type have two storylines which unfold simultaneously. First, there's what happens before the reader's eyes from the first page to the last, the record of action as perceived by the viewpoint character or characters. Underlying this plot is the mystery storyline itself, that which is happening (or has happened previously) and is withheld from the reader until the book's climax.

Years ago, I took it for granted that a writer had to have both of these storylines fully worked out in his head before puting a word on paper. I've since learned that it's occasionally possible to write an elaborately complicated mystery novel without knowing the identity of the villain until the story is almost at an end. In *Burglars Can't Be Choosers,* I was within two or three chapters of the finish before a friend's chance remark enabled me to figure out whodunnit; I had to do some rewriting to tie off all the loose ends, but the book worked out fine.

Suppose I spend a year writing a novel and it proves to be unsalable. I can't risk wasting that much time, so wouldn't it be safer to stick to short stories?

Would it? Let's assume that you could write twelve or twenty short stories in the time it would take you to write a novel. What makes you think you'd have a better chance of selling them? The nature of the market is such that you'd probably have a better chance placing one novel for publication than one out of twenty short stories. And, assuming you wouldn't sell either the novel or the short stories, why would a batch of unsalable short stories feel less like a waste of time than an equally unsalable novel?

Nevertheless, the fear of wasting one's time keeps a lot of people from writing novels. But I don't think the fear is justified even when it proves true.

So what if a first novel's unsalable? For heaven's sake, most of them are, and why on earth should they be otherwise?

Any of several things may happen to the person who produces an unsalable first novel. He may discover, in the course of writing the book, that he was not cut out to be a novelist, that he doesn't like the work or doesn't possess the talent.

I don't know that it's a waste of time to make this sort of discovery.

On the other hand, the author of an unpublishable first novel may learn that writing is his métier, that he has a burning desire to continue with it, and that the weaknesses and flaws which characterized his first book need not appear in the ones to follow. You might be surprised to know how many successful writers produced hopelessly incompetent first books. They were not wasting their time. They were learning their trade.

Consider Justin Scott, whose first novel I read in manuscript several years ago. It was embarrassingly bad in almost every respect, and hopelessly unpublishable. But it did him some good to write it, and his second novel—also unsalable, as it happened—was a vast improvement over the first.

He remained undiscouraged. His third novel, a mystery, was published. Several more mysteries followed. Then he spent over a year writing *The Shipkiller,* a nautical adventure story on a grand scale which brought a six-figure paperback advance, sold to the movies for a handsome sum, and did well enough in the stores to land on several of the bestseller lists.

Do you suppose Justin regrets the time he "wasted" on that first novel?

Maybe I haven't started a novel because I'm afraid I wouldn't finish it.

Maybe so. And maybe you wouldn't finish it. There's no law that says you have to.

Please understand that I'm not advocating abandoning a novel halfway through. I've done this far too often myself and it's something I've never managed to feel good about. But you do have every right in the world to give up on a book if it's just not working, or if you simply discover that writing novels is not for you.

As much as we'd all prefer to pretend our calling is a noble one, it's salutary to bear in mind that the last thing this poor old planet needs is another book. The only reason to write anything more extensive than a shopping list is because it's something you want to do. If that ceases to be the case you're entirely free to do something else instead.

I'm inclined to hope you *will* complete your first novel, whatever its merits and defects, whatever your ultimate potential as a novelist. I think the writing of a novel is a very valuable life experience for those who carry it through. It's a great teacher, and I'm talking now about its ability to teach you not about writing but about yourself. The novel, I submit, is an unparalleled vehicle for self-discovery.

But whether you finish it or not remains your choice. And failing to begin a task for fear of failing to complete it doesn't make abundant sense, does it?

Okay, I'm convinced. I'm going to sit down and write a novel. After all, short stuff isn't significant, is it?

It isn't, huh? Who says?

I'll grant that commercial significance singles out the novel, and that long novels are automatically considered to be of more importance than short ones. I'll admit that, with a handful of exceptions, short story writers don't get much attention from literary critics. And I won't deny that your neighbors will take you more seriously as a writer if you tell them you've written a novel. (Of course if that's the main concern, just go ahead and tell them. You don't have to write anything. Lie a little. Don't worry—they won't beg to read the manuscript.)

But as far as intrinsic merit is concerned, length is hardly a factor. You've probably heard of the writer who apologized for having written a long letter, explaining that he didn't have the time to make it shorter. And you may be familiar with Faulkner's comment that every short-story writer is a failed poet, and every novelist a failed short-story writer.

I'm not sure the desire to be significant is a particularly useful motive for writing anything. But length is no guarantee of significance and brevity no hallmark of the trivial. Sonnet, short story, thousand-page novel—write whatever it is you want to write, and that's the long and short of it.

All right. Significant or otherwise, what I want to write is a novel. But what novel should I write? All I've got is a desk and a typewriter and a ream of paper and an empty head. What do I do now, coach?

Well, for openers, why don't you turn the page?

Chapter 2

Deciding Which Novel to Write

You may not need this chapter. A certain proportion of novelists start off knowing pretty much what book they want to write, and you may very well be one of them. Although the precise shape of the plot and the structure of the book may be vague in your mind, it's possible that you know certain things about the book. You know that it is a novel, for example, and you know what it's about.

Perhaps the book you have decided to write is based upon your own life experience. Maybe you've endured something that strikes you as the raw material for a novel—a hitch in the military, a stretch in the slammer, or four years in a coed dormitory, say. Colorful or bland, anyone's life can be turned into arresting fiction if it is incisively perceived and dramatically portrayed.

Similarly, you may be caught up in the notion of a novel that has nothing whatever to do with your visible life experience. Something from your reading or fantasy may have stimulated your creative imagination in such a way that you have a book to write firmly in mind. Perhaps your lead is a member of the Children's Crusade, or an intergalactic explorer, or a contemporary private detective with a taste for Armagnac and a collector's passion for oriental snuffboxes. Or your central character might as easily be a realistic contemporary figure with whom you identify on some inner plane—an abused child, an ex-athlete recovering from a failed marriage, a nun breathless with adoration. The possibilities are quite literally infinite; the only requisite is that there's a character or conflict or fundamental situation somewhere along the line that makes you want to write a novel about it.

If this is the case, you have a slight advantage; you at least know what you want to write about, and the knowledge puts you one important step closer to the act. Skip ahead to the next chapter, if you're so inclined.

* * *

During the first of my several vexingly undistinguished years as a college student, a cartoon hung for months on the English Department bulletin board. I returned to that campus twenty years after my precipitous departure from it, a prodigal son come home to teach a writing seminar, and as I walked across the greensward that cartoon came vividly back to me.

It showed a sullen eight-year-old boy staring down an earnest school principal. "It's not enough to be a genius, Arnold," the man was saying. "You have to be a genius *at* something."

I recall identifying very strongly with Arnold. I had known several years before college that I wanted to be a writer. But it seemed it wasn't enough merely to *be* a writer.

You had to be a writer *of* something.

Some people get the whole package as a gift. Not only are they endowed with writing talent but they seem to have been born knowing what to write about. Equipped at the onset with stories to tell, they have only to get on to the business of telling them.

Some people, in short, have it easy.

But some of us don't. We know *that* we want to write without knowing *what* we want to write.

It's encouraging to note that we're in the majority, that most writers have been obsessed with the idea of becoming writers before the nature of what they might write about revealed itself to them. It's easy to accept this premise about the nuts-and-bolts commercial writer, but the same initial uncertainty is every bit as likely to characterize the early years of writers with impeccable critical reputations. The identification of self as writer comes for most of us before we know what sort of writer we'll be or what we'll write about, and that seems to be just as true whether our ultimate literary product is *Moby Dick* or *Trailer Trollop*.

(This might be a good place to suggest, incidentally, that fiction writers of every stripe have a great deal more in common that the disparity of our work might suggest. The fact that we write unites us far more than the nature of what we write separates us.)

*   *   *

Let's suppose, then, that all you know at this point is that you want to write a novel. Why you have this curious urge is not terribly important. It's enough that you have it in good measure. Whether you'll prove to have other elements essential to novelistic success—talent, perseverance, resourcefulness—is not something you have to know at this stage. Indeed, it's not something you're in a position to know. You'll find out in due course.

How do you decide what novel to write?

It seems to me that this question can best be answered by asking a few others. First of all, what kind of novel do you like to read? I would not go so far as to say that we can only produce the sort of fiction that we most enjoy reading ourselves.

I've known of too many instances where this is simply untrue. When I was knocking out soft-core sex novels, for instance, I did not commonly spend my free hours reading other people's soft-core sex novels. And I've observed that a substantial number of people who write westerns are very much averse to reading in the genre. Contrariwise, most mystery and science-fiction writers seem to enjoy reading in their respective fields.

When I was starting out, confession magazines constituted the most receptive market for new writers. They paid fairly well, too. Their numbers have shrunk since then and their rates of payment have actually declined, illustrating once more how the short story writer's lot has gotten worse over the years, but back then they were an excellent place for a neophyte to get started.

I think, because I read a lot of them, I understood what a confession story was, the basic structure of its plot, and what made one story good and another unacceptable. During the year I spent working for a literary agent, the two confessions I yanked out of the slush pile both sold on their initial submissions, and the author of one of them came to be a leader in the field, ultimately going on to make a name for herself in the field of romantic fiction.

Well, I was game. Confessions back then paid several times what I was earning for suspense short stories, so on several occasions I went out and bought or borrowed confession magazines and set about reading my way through them. I never quite made it. I could not read one of the damned things all the way through without skimming. I couldn't concentrate on what I was reading. And I couldn't shake the conviction that the entire magazine, from front to back and including the bust-developer ads, was nothing but mind-rotting swill.

Nor, consequently, could I produce a confession story. The ideas my mind came up with were either mind-numbingly trite or at odds with the market's requirements. I never did turn one of these ideas into a story that I stayed with beyond a couple of tentative pages, never completed a confession until one bizarre weekend when I wrote three of them to order for a publisher with a couple holes to fill and a deadline fast approaching. I wrote them somehow because I'd accepted the assignment, and he printed them because he had to, and that was not the easiest money I ever made in my life, let me tell you.

How much do you have to like a type of novel in order to have a chance of success at it yourself? Well, let's suppose you sit down one weekend with a stack of gothics or male adventure novels or light romances or whatever. If you have to flail yourself with a whip or whip yourself with a flail in order to get them read, fighting a constant urge to hurl the books across the room, and if your ultimate response is something along the lines of "This stuff is garbage and I hate it," I think you might want to look a little further.

On the other hand, if you find the stories reasonably riveting even though you never lose sight of the fact that you're not reading *War and Peace,* and if your final reaction is more in the vein of "This stuff's garbage, all right, but it's not *bad* garbage, and while I might not want word to get around I've got to admit that I sort of like it," then perhaps you've found a place to start.

* * *

There are other questions to ask yourself. Here's one—how important is it for you to be rewarded for your work? And what sort of reward's most important? Money? Recognition? Or simply seeing your work in print? While the three are by no means mutually exclusive, and while the great majority of us want all three—in large portions, thank you—each of us is likely to find one of the three of maximum importance.

When I was fifteen or sixteen years old, and secure in the

knowledge that I'd been placed on this planet to be a writer, it didn't even occur to me to wonder what sort of thing I would write. I was at the time furiously busy reading my way through the great novels of the century, the works of Steinbeck and Hemingway and Wolfe and Dos Passos and Fitzgerald and all their friends and relations, and it was ever so clear to me that I would in due course produce a Great Novel of my own.

I'd go to college first, naturally, where I might get a somewhat clearer notion of just what constituted a Great Novel. Then I'd emerge into the real world where I would Live. (I wasn't quite certain what all this capital-L Living entailed, but I figured there would be a touch of squalor in there somewhere, along with generous dollops of booze and sex.) All of this Living would ultimately distill itself into the Meaningful Experiences out of which I would eventually produce any number of Worthwhile Books.

Now there's nothing necessarily wrong with this approach. Any number of important novels are produced in this approximate fashion, and the method has the added advantage that, should you wind up writing nothing at all, you'll at least have treated yourself to plenty of booze and sex en route.

In my own case, though, I learned quickly that my self-image as a writer was stronger than my self-image as a potential great novelist. I didn't really care all that deeply about artistic achievement, nor did I aspire to wealth beyond the dreams of avarice. I wanted to write something and see it in print. I don't know that that's the noblest of motives for doing anything, but it was at the very core of my being.

Let's suppose, for a moment, that you regard yourself as similarly motivated. While you'd certainly like to write something in which you can take great personal pride, something that might win you a measure of critical recognition, something that might lead stockbrokers and accountants to vie for your custom, your primary purpose as a writer is to get something published.

If that's the case, you would probably be best advised to

find a place for yourself in the field of category fiction, a term which covers the broad group of novels—generally paperback originals—which lend themselves readily to categorization as mysteries, adventure, romance, gothic, science fiction, historical saga, western, or whatever. These categories change slightly over the years; too, they go hot and cold, with one year's hot ticket next year's drug on the market. Every once in a while a novel achieves overwhelming success, to the point where its imitators quickly come to constitute a brand-new category. Kyle Onstott's *Mandingo* went through printing after printing before other writers began to work the same vein; in due course the slave novel defined itself as a staple category of paperback fiction. Similarly, but far more rapidly, the first two steamy historical romances—Kathleen Woodiwiss' *The Flame and the Flower* and Rosemary Rogers' *Sweet Savage Love*—rolled up impressive instant sales and sparked a new category overnight.

Some writers move with no apparent effort from one category to another over the years, furnishing a steady supply of whatever the market demands. When gothics are hot they write gothics; when a publisher calls with a demand for war stories or romantic intrigue, they shift gears and maintain full production. Typically, these jacks-of-all-trades meet minimal standards in every genre they take up without really distinguishing themselves in any one area. They are always competent but never inspired.

Which, come to think of it, is not terribly surprising. Professional competence is too rare a jewel to be dismissed summarily as hack work. Nevertheless, the writer who can do every type of novel with equal facility is a writer who has not managed to zero in on a type of novel that is uniquely his own. While you may prove to be this variety of writer, and while you may be happiest covering a wide range of fictional categories, I think you would do well first to determine if there's a particular kind of novel that appeals to you more than the others.

We've established that the novel you set out to write ought to be of a type you would not find yourself unable to read had someone else written it. The converse of this argument is not necessarily true. Just because you can enjoy reading a particular sort of novel doesn't mean you'd be well advised to try writing it.

Take me, for example; there was a time when I read a great deal of science fiction. I liked most S-F stories, and I liked the good ones a lot. Furthermore, I used to hang out with several established science fiction writers. I found them a congenial bunch, fellows of infinite jest and an engagingly quirky turn of mind. I liked the way they grabbed hold of ideas and turned them into stories.

But I couldn't write science fiction. No matter how much of the stuff I read, no matter how much I enjoyed what I read, my mind simply did not yield up workable S-F ideas. I might read those stories with a fan's intense enjoyment, but what I couldn't do was get the sort of handle on what I read that left me saying to myself, "*I* could have written that. I could have come up with that idea, and I could have developed it along those lines. I might even have improved it by doing thus and so. By gum, I could have been the writer of that story."

I've enjoyed a good many historical novels over the years, and I've been deeply interested in history for as long as I can remember. There was a period of several years during which a fair percentage of my leisure-time reading consisted of works of English and Irish history. One might think I'd do well to combine business and pleasure and turn my sights on the historical novel, trying my hand at a novel the theme and background of which might suggest itself from my reading.

I wouldn't dream of it. One of the innumerable unpleasant facts I have to face about myself is that I'm a sluggard when it comes to research. I don't enjoy it and I don't do a very good job of it. I force myself when I have to, and I've become better about this in recent years, less given to slipshod fakery, but the idea of deliberately setting out to write a book which requires a vast amount of academic research is anathema to me.

Beyond that, I'm not comfortable with the idea of writing something set in a time other than my own. I wasn't around then, so how could I presume to know how people talked? How could I expect to get their dialogue right, or to have the faintest idea what it felt like to be around in eighteenth-century Ireland, say, or Renaissance Italy? The fact that no one else knows how people talked or felt back then does nothing to put my mind at rest. I have to be able to believe in the fictive reality of what I'm doing in order to make it work.

This is not to say that I'm comfortable only when I write out of my own experience. I probably know as much about eighteenth-century Ireland as I do about contemporary Yugoslavia, yet I've blithely set several books in that country without doing more than cursory research. I've never killed anyone—yet—but I've written a great deal about murderers. I wrote a book from the point of view of a professional burglar and found the voice so natural that the book became the first of a series. I've written several books from a woman's point of view. It's a matter of identification, I suppose, of one's ability to project oneself into certain environments and situations and not into others.

More simply, it's a matter of identifying with an author. One of the things that makes fiction work is one's identification with the characters. And one of the things that makes it writable, if you will, is identification with the person who wrote it.

I can remember the first time I felt it. It was the summer after my first year at college. I picked up a paperback anthology of short stories entitled *The Jungle Kids*. The author was Evan Hunter, who had recently made a name for himself with *The Blackboard Jungle*—hence the book's title, not to mention the fact of its publication. The dozen or so stories in the book all dealt with juvenile delinquents and virtually all of them had been originally published in *Manhunt*. I identified, not so much with the characters in these stories, but with Evan Hunter himself.

I was genuinely excited when I reached the end of the book. Here was someone writing and publishing well-written stories that I could respect and enjoy—and, most important, I could see myself doing what he had done. I felt it was within my abilities, and I felt plots and characters of this sort could engage and stimulate my creative imagination. And I also felt that the whole thing was eminently worth doing.

I ultimately did make my first short story sale to *Manhunt,* but that's another story. More to the point, my first novel grew directly out of a similar case of identification with the author.

I had at the time been writing and publishing crime stories for a year and felt it was time to write a novel. A senior colleague at the literary agency where I was working had suggested I try a light romance of the type Avalon was then publishing; because the rate of payment was awful, this was an easy market for the beginner to hit. I read one, and it was confessions all over again. I couldn't get through the thing and knew I'd be incapable of coming up with an idea for one, let alone writing it.

What I really wanted to do was a detective novel. I'd read hundreds, liked the form very much, and made a couple of stabs at knocking out one of my own. But for one reason or another I couldn't get a handle on a suspense novel.

During this time I had read perhaps a dozen lesbian novels. The sensitive novel of female homosexuality constituted a small but quite popular category in the fifties. I probably read the books more for information and titillation than anything else. I wasn't personally acquainted with any lesbians at the time, nor did my knowledge of their lives go beyond what I read in those novels or witnessed on Bleecker Street in Greenwich Village.

For whatever reason, I did find the books compulsively readable, and one day I finished one and realized that I could have written it myself. Or one quite like it. Possibly, by Georgia, one a shade *better* than what I'd just read.

In the name of research, I promptly read every lesbian novel

I could get my hands on. Elements of a novel of my own began percolating in my mind—fragments of a character, a scene, a setting. Then one morning I awakened with the plot ready to happen, and I sat down and typed up a two or three page outline. After a gestation period of perhaps another month I sat down and wrote the thing in two weeks flat.

It sold first time out to Fawcett, then the leading market for that sort of book, and I was a published novelist just like that. I was not an overnight success, nor did I find an immediate identity for myself as a writer of lesbian novels; curiously enough, it was years before I wrote another. But I learned a tremendous amount writing the book, as one does writing any first novel, and it was that jolting realization of I-could-do-this that got me going.

*　　*　　*

This sort of identification with the writer, this recognition of one's own capacity to write a certain type of book, is not limited to category fiction. Whatever makes you want to become a novelist, whatever sort of novelist you want to become, the process I've described is a basic starting point for finding your own first novel.

If you've decided that money is the spur that goads you and that you want to reach for the brass ring right away rather than work your way up to it, you would do well to have a broad acquaintance with the sorts of books that have made their authors rich. By regularly reading best-selling novels, and especially by concentrating on the works of those authors who consistently hit the best seller list, you'll develop a sense of the sorts of books which tend to earn big money.

Some books make the best seller lists by happy accident. Perhaps they are category novels which have acquired a greater than usual readership because of increasingly widespread recognition of the author's particular excellences. John D. MacDonald and Ross Macdonald are two cases in point; both continue to write the excellent hard-boiled suspense novels they've been writing for years, but their audience has swelled to the point where the books they write are best sellers.

Other books on the list are novels of considerable literary merit which have enough breadth of appeal to make them best sellers. E. L. Doctorow's *Ragtime* is a good example of this phenomenon, as are *The World According to Garp,* by John Irving, and *Final Payments,* by Mary Gordon. Similarly, a few highly esteemed authors hit the best seller list routinely, not because of the type of books they write but because of the prominence they have achieved and the size of their personal following among readers. John Updike's an example. So are Gore Vidal and John Cheever.

The remainder of the best seller list is chiefly composed of books with certain qualities common to best sellers—and here we find ourselves on marshy terrain indeed, because I don't feel it's proper to think in terms of a best seller class or category. Certainly there's no magic formula, and certainly these books differ enormously from one another. By familiarizing yourself with best-selling fiction, you'll get a sense of what qualities they have in common.

Perhaps more important, you'll find that you like best sellers of one sort while disliking others. And, somewhere along the line, you'll find one or more best-selling novels that spark that identification with the author we've talked about. You'll realize you could have written a particular book, or one a good deal like it. When this happens, you will have found a direction for your writing which holds the promise of the rewards you seek while remaining compatible with your own literary inclinations.

* * *

That last point is worth a digression.

A great many people seem to believe that all it takes for a talented writer to produce a best-selling novel is a sound idea and the will to carry it out. Writers frequently make the mistake of believing this themselves, and the results can be markedly unsuccessful.

The writers who consistently produce best-selling fiction are not writing down to their audience. They are not making deliberate compromises between the books they'd like to write and what the public wants. On the contrary, they are turning out precisely the books they were born to write, working at the top of their form, and while they may wistfully wish they were geared to write the kind of thing that wins awards and sparks doctoral theses, just as Norman Rockwell occasionally expressed regret that he didn't paint like Picasso, they have become successes by being themselves.

Best sellers are occasionally written cynically. William Faulkner batted out *Sanctuary* with the intention of producing a potboiler that would make him rich; he remained an artist in spite of himself, and while *Sanctuary* did sell impressively it remained quintessential Faulkner. On the other hand, it's probably safe to assume that John Updike wrote *Couples* out of comparable cupidity. *Couples* did sell very well, but it's hardly vintage Updike, and the author's own detachment from it is evident throughout.

I've known several writers of category fiction who have tried to break through into the world of bestsellerdom, a natural ambition in a world where success is largely measured in dollars and cents. Some writers manage this rather neatly; they'd written category fiction as an apprenticeship, or their development carried them to a point where they are comfortable working on a broader canvas—for one reason or another, their books work. Others of us have found ourselves trying to be something we're not in order to attain a goal to which we unwisely aspire. The result, more often than not, is a book which is satisfying to neither its authors nor its readers, a financial and artistic failure. The Peter Principle seems to apply; we extend our literary horizons until we reach our level of incompetence.

I'm sorry to say that I know whereof I speak, and the knowledge was not gained painlessly. What I have learned to my cost is that I do my best work when all I am trying to do is my best work. And it is when I do this that I incidentally achieve the most critical and financial success in the bargain.

There's a moral there somewhere, and I have a hunch it shouldn't be too hard to spot.

* * *

Suppose I don't want to write category fiction? I want to write a serious mainstream novel. But I don't know what I want to write about. I don't have a setting or a plot or a character. I just know that I want to write a serious novel. How do I get started?

Maybe you're not ready yet.

Give yourself time. Read the sorts of novels you enjoy and admire, and try to spot those which afford a measure of the author-identification we've discussed. You may not want to write books which specifically resemble what you've read, but this identification process, this reading from the writer's point of view, may help your subconscious mind to begin formulating ideas for your own book.

Sooner or later, you'll begin to get ideas—out of your own background and experience, out of your imagination, out of some well of story material within yourself. This process will happen when the time is right. Until it does, there's not very much you can do.

Chapter 3

Read...Study...Analyze

Let's suppose that you've managed to zoom in on a type of novel you think might make for comfortable writing. You don't know that you're ready to embark on a lifelong career as a writer of sweet savage romances, say, or shoot-'em-up westerns, but you feel it might be worthwhile to take a shot at writing one of them. You've found something you enjoy reading and it's also something you can see yourself writing. The talent you perceive yourself having seems likely to lend itself to this particular sort of book.

Now what do you do?

Well, it's possible you're ready to sit down and go to work at the typewriter. Maybe you've already got your book firmly in mind, plot and characters and all. If that's the case, by all means sit down and start hitting the keys. The book may or may not work, depending on the extent of your readiness, but in any event you'll learn a great deal from the experience.

It's very likely, though, that you'd do well to take another step before plunging in. This step consists of subjecting your chosen field to a detailed analysis by reading extensively and submerging yourself in what you read. The analytical process is such that you wind up with both an ingrained gut-level understanding of what constitutes a successful novel of your chosen type and a mind trained to conceive, produce and develop the ideas for such a novel.

I can't think of a better name for this process than *"market analysis,"* yet something in me recoils at the term. It's too clinical, for one thing, and it seems to imply that writing a salable gothic novel lends itself to the Harvard Business School case-study approach. We're talking about *writing,* for Pete's sake. We're dealing with creativity. We're artists, aren't we? Market analysis is something they do in Wall Street offices, not Greenwich Village garrets.

Besides, the process I'm talking about is oriented more to the work than to the market. What we study here is the individual novel, and our concern is in discovering what makes it work, not what has induced some particular editor to publish it or some group of readers to buy it.

Okay. Whatever you call it, I want to do it. What do I do first?

Good question.

As I said, what you do is you read.

When you picked a type of book to write, one of the criteria was that it was one you were capable of reading with a certain degree of pleasure. This had better be the case, because you're going to have to do some intensive reading. Fortunately, the odds are that reading is a habit for you from the start. That's true for most people who want to write, and it's especially true for most of those who wind up successful at it. Some of us find ourselves reading less fiction as time passes, and many of us are inclined to avoid reading other people's novels while writing our own, but I rarely encounter a writer who's not a pretty enthusiastic reader by nature.

So there's a fair chance that you've been reading books in your chosen field for some time now, beginning long before you selected this field for your own novelistic endeavors. I'd had this sort of prior experience with suspense novels, for example, before I seriously attempted one of my own. On the other hand, I had not read widely in the soft-core sex novel field when the opportunity arose for me to write one. Few people had; the genre was just beginning to emerge.

Makes no difference. Either way, you have fresh reading to do. You have to read not as a normally perceptive reader, but with the special insight of a writer.

My first venture into this sort of reading came when I first began writing stories for the crime fiction magazines, but the process is pretty much the same for both short stories and novels. What I did, having made my first short story sale to *Manhunt,* was to study that magazine and every other crime fiction magazine far more intensively than I have ever studied anything before or since. I bought every magazine in the field the instant it appeared on the stands. In addition, I made regular visits to back-magazine shops, where I picked up every back issue of the leading magazines that I could find. I carried check lists of these publications in my wallet to avoid buying the same issue twice, and I carted the magazines home and arranged them in orderly fashion on my shelves. At night when I got home from the office I read magazine after magazine, going through every last one of them from cover to cover.

Understand, please, that I did not learn any formulae. I don't know that such things exist. What I did learn, in a manner I cannot entirely explain, is a sense of the possible variations that could be worked upon the crime story, a sense of what worked and what didn't.

Does this mean I have to read hundreds and hundreds of novels? I'll be spending eternity in the library.

You won't have to read as many novels as I read short stories. You'll probably read hundreds of them over the years—I think it's vital to continue reading in one's field, even when one's established oneself as a writer in the field. Remember, though, a distinction we observed earlier between the short story and the novel. The short-story writer has to come up with a constant supply of ideas. The novelist, on the other hand, deals with a smaller number of ideas but must be far more concerned with their extensive development.

So you won't have to read so many novels. Eight or ten or a dozen should give you a sufficient reading background for your own first attempt. But you'll have to read them far more exhaustively than the beginning short-story writer has to read examples in his field. It's not enough simply to read these books. You'll have to take them apart and see what makes them work.

How do you go about that?

Well, let's say you've decided to take aim at the gothic novel. Chances are you've read more than a few of them in reaching this decision, but maybe not; perhaps you read one and knew in a flash it was your kind of thing. Whatever the case, you'll want to have half a dozen books on hand in order to launch this project of analyzing the gothic novel. You may elect to use your favorites among the books you've already read or make a trip to the newsstand for some new material. I'd suggest that you pick books by six different writers, choosing a mixture of established names in the field and neophytes, but that's not necessary. I've heard tell of a writer, for example, who sat down and pored over the gothic novels of Dorothy Daniels as if they were holy writ. Then he turned out a book that was described by the editor who bought it as an absolutely perfect example of second-rate Dorothy Daniels. Second-rate Dorothy Daniels is still good enough to sell, and sell it did.

I wouldn't recommend so limited an approach. While it may not be the worst way in the world to break into print, it can't do much to bring out the writer within oneself. What we're trying to achieve by this market analysis is not slavish imitation but synthesis. By digesting a genre and absorbing its parameters into one's system, one prepares oneself to write one's own books within the particular confines of that genre.

That's theoretical. Let's get down to practical matters. Having bought a half-dozen suitable gothics, what do I do?

Read them, for openers. Read them one after the other, without reading anything else in between. And don't rush this reading process. Forget any speedreading courses you may have taken. If you've gotten in the habit of skimming, break it. Slow yourself down. You want to find out more than what happens and who's the bad guy and whether or not the girl gets to keep the house at the end. You want to find out what the author's doing and how he's doing it, and you can only manage that feat by spending plenty of time with the book.

Reading slowly and deliberately is something that's come on me over the years, and I can relate it directly to my own development as a writer. Before I got into this business, and during my early years in it, I raced through books. The more I have come to read *like a writer,* the more deliberate the pace of my reading.

Once you've read all of the books at a thoughtful pace, it's time to take them apart and see how they work. First, try summing up each book in a couple of sentences, like so:

> A young widow is hired to catalogue the antique furniture in a house on the moors in Devon. The chauffeur-handyman tries to warn her off and she knows he's up to something. She's drawn to the son and heir, whose wife is coughing her lungs out in an attic bedchamber. Turns out the son has been selling off the good furniture, replacing it with reproductions and junk, and slowly poisoning his wife. He tries to kill our heroine when she uncovers the truth but she's saved by the handyman, who's actually the disguised second son of the Earl of Dorset, and . . . .

Well, you get the idea. I don't write gothics myself, and I see no reason why I should squander my creativity plotting this one just as an example of what a summary is. Boil each of the six novels into a paragraph. The length doesn't matter terribly much. No one else is going to read these things. The object is to reduce the sprawl of a novel to something you can grasp in a hundred words or so.

This method is useful in analyzing short fiction, too. A

short-story writer would do well to write out brief summaries of dozens of short stories, paring away the writer's facility with prose and dialogue and characterization and reducing each story to its basic plot. The novelist-to-be works with a smaller number of examples and winds up studying them rather more intensively.

By this I don't mean you have to examine the plot summaries you've prepared like a paleontologist studying old dinosaur bones. Instead, you'll return to the books you've summarized and go through them again, this time outlining them chapter by chapter. For each chapter you'll write down what happens in a couple of sentences. To return to our mythical gothic, we might see something like this:

Chapter One—Ellen arrives at Greystokes. Liam meets her at the train and tells her the legend of the ghost in the potting shed. She is interviewed by Mrs. Hallburton who explains her duties and shows her to her room. She lies down on her bed and hears a woman coughing and sobbing on the floor above.

Chapter Two—Flashback. The cough triggers her recollection of her husband's death. She remembers their meeting, tender moments in their courtship, the discovery of his illness, and his final days. She recalls her determination to resume her life and the circumstances that brought her to Greystokes.

Chapter Three—Dinner the first night. She meets Tirrell Hallburton, whose wife is coughing in the room above her own. After dinner she goes to the attic to look in on Glacia, the invalid. Glacia tells her that Death is on his way to Greystokes. "Someone will die soon—take care it isn't you!" Ellen leaves, certain Glacia has a premonition of her own death . . . .

Maybe I ought to write this thing after all. It's beginning to come to life for me in spite of myself.

I think you see how the process works. The outline may be as sketchy or as comprehensive as you want it to be—and the same rules will apply when you prepare an outline for your own novel. Because these outlines, like the outline you create for your own book, are designed to be tools. You'll use them to get a grasp on what a novel is.

Although they're often easier to write than short stories, for reasons we've already discussed at sufficient length, novels are often harder to master. So much more goes on in them that it's difficult to see their structure. Just as our summaries served to give us a clear picture of what these several novels are *about,* so will our outlines show us their structure, their component parts. Stripped to outline form, the novel is like a forest in winter; with their branches bare, the individual trees become visible where once the eye saw nothing but a mass of green.

To repeat, your outlines may be as detailed as you wish. I would suggest that you make them as complete as possible in terms of including a scene-by-scene report of what is actually taking place. There's no need in this sort of outline for explanation—why the characters do what they do, or how they feel about it—so much as there's a need to put down everything that goes on, every scene that exists as a part of the whole.

In this fashion, you'll develop a sense of the novel as a collection of scenes. God knows it's not necessary to do this in order to write a novel, or even to understand how novels are constructed, but I think it helps.

It helps in an even more obvious fashion when you set out to outline your own novel. We'll discuss this point at more length in Chapter Six; meanwhile, suffice it to say that the best way to prepare yourself to outline your own book is by outlining someone else's book first.

Question—with all this reading and analyzing and outlining, all this mechanical swill, aren't we stifling creativity? I have a feeling I'll be trying to duplicate what's been written rather than write my own novel.

That's not how it works. But it's easy to understand the anxiety. I've heard young would-be writers explain that they want to avoid reading fiction altogether in order to avoid being influenced by what's already been done. They use phrases like "natural creativity" a lot. What happens, more often than not, is that such writers unwittingly produce trite stories because they haven't read widely enough to know what's been done to death already. An isolated tribesman who spontaneously invents the bicycle in 1982 may be displaying enormous natural creativity, but one wouldn't expect the world to beat a path to his door.

The outlining process I've discussed doesn't stifle creativity. At least it shouldn't. I suppose a person could copy a character here and a plot line there and a setting from somewhere else, jumbling things up and putting together a novel from the chopped-up corpses of the novels he's read. But that's certainly not what we're trying to do, and it's not the best way to write something that will be commercially and artistically successful. Our object is to learn how to cast our own stories within the framework of a particular kind of novel, to stimulate our unconscious to produce plot and character ideas which lend themselves to this chosen type of novel so that it will be natural for our minds to think in these terms.

The best defense I can offer is the following exchange which appeared in an interview in the *New York Times Book Review* for December 24, 1978. The interviewer is Steve Oney; the writer interviewed is Harry Crews, the highly regarded author of *A Feast of Snakes* and several other novels noted for their imagination, originality, and technical proficiency:

Q. For someone who had been exposed to very little literature, how did you actually learn how to write?

A. I guess I really learned, seriously learned, how to write just after I got out of college when I pretty much literally ate Graham Greene's "The End of the Affair." My wife and I were living in a little trailer . . . in Jacksonville, Fla., where I was teaching seventh grade . . . I wrote a novel that year, and here's how I did it. I took "The End of the Affair," and I pretty much reduced the thing to numbers. I found out how many characters were in it, how much time was in it—and that's hard to do as there is not only present time in a book but past time as well. I found out how many cities were in the book, how many rooms, where the climaxes were and how long it took Greene to get to them.

And there were a lot of other things I reduced to numbers. I read that book until it was dog-eared and was coming apart in my hands. And then I said, "I'm going to write me a damn novel and do everything he did." I knew I was going to waste—but it wasn't a waste—a year of my time. And I knew that the end result was going to be a mechanical, unreadable novel. But I was trying to find out how in the hell you did it. So I wrote the novel, and it had to have this many rooms, this many transitions, etc. It was the bad novel I knew it would be. But by doing it I learned more about writing fiction and writing a novel and about the importance of time and place—Greene is a freak about time and place—than I had from any class or anything I'd done before. I really, literally, ate that book. And that's how I learned to write.

I have no trouble believing the method Crews describes was every bit as instructive as he says it was. I don't know that I would care to write a book in this fashion, or that I would be able to discipline myself sufficiently to complete a book I knew would be unsalable by definition, but I would surely imagine that the educational potential of the process is considerable. Even without going so far as to write an imitative novel of one's own, a writer could greatly increase his understanding of what novels are and how they work by following the first stages of Crews' system—i.e., by taking an admired novel apart, reducing it to numbers, and learning how the author handles such matters as time and place and action and pace and so forth.

Getting back to the question you asked a couple of pages ago, it's evident that Crews' approach did stifle creativity in the particular novel he describes. His purpose was not creative development but technical progress—he wanted to learn what made a novel tick so he took one apart to find out, then tried putting it back together again. But you'll be studying not one but half a dozen books, books which may have the common features of their genre but which differ considerably each from the other. The book you write will in turn differ from each of them while presumably retaining those elements which make them a satisfying experience for the people who read them. That's not a matter of stifling creativity but one of finding the right frame for it and lighting it properly.

This outlining sounds like a WPA project. I can see doing some extensive reading, sort of soaking up the market that way, but I hate the idea of purposeless work. Is it absolutely essential to do this?

Of course not.

I think outlining other people's novels as I've described it is as effective and expedient a way as I know to learn what a particular sort of novel is and how it works. But it's not the only way, and it's certainly no prerequisite for writing your own novel. If you find it tedious to such an extent that it seems counter-productive, by all means give it up.

You don't even have to read widely in your chosen field, as far as that goes. The only thing you absolutely *have* to do to produce a novel is sit down and write the thing. Some people profit greatly by such preparatory work as I've described. Others get along just fine without it.

I wouldn't be so sure, though, that outlining is purposeless work, or a waste of time. On the contrary, I'd be inclined to guess it saves time for most of the people who do it—time spent repairing mistakes and reworking false starts that might not have occurred had they laid the groundwork properly before starting their own novels.

But pick the approach that feels right for you as a writer. That, ultimately, is the most important thing you can do.

Chapter 4

Developing Plot Ideas

"Where do you get your ideas?" is one of the questions writers get asked all the time. What's galling about it, in addition to its banality, is the questioner's implicit assumption that coming up with a clever idea is all there really is to the business of being a writer. Turning that idea into a book—well, that's just a matter of typing, isn't it?

But of course not. Were that the case, I'd run books through my typewriter at seventy or eighty words per minute, not four or five agonizing pages per day.

While ideas are not the *sine qua non* in the novel that they often are in the short story, they are nevertheless essential.

A handful of writers can produce books that are not specifically *about* something and make them work. It scarcely matters what *Finnegan's Wake* is about, for example. For the rest of us, a strong central idea is basic to our novels. How we are to get these ideas, and how we can best develop them into strong plots, is something with which we might well concern ourselves.

* * *

It's my own conviction that we do not *get* our ideas. They

are given to us, bubbling up out of our own subconscious minds as if from some dark and murky ferment. When the conditions are right, it is neither more nor less than the natural condition of things for a writer's imagination to produce those ideas which constitute the raw material of his fiction.

I don't know that I have much control over this process of generating ideas. This is not to say that I don't *want* to control the process, or even that I don't *try* to control it. But I've gradually come to see that I can't stimulate ideas by hitting myself in the forehead with a two-by-four.

This does not mean that there's nothing the writer can do to foster the development of novelistic ideas. Note, please, my argument that the process occurs of its own accord *when the conditions are right.*

My job, when I want ideas to bubble up, is to make sure the conditions are right. Then I can let go of the controls and pick ideas like plums when they come along.

That's a little hazy. Can't we get a bit more specific? How do I adjust the conditions?

We can get a whole lot more specific. And as far as adjusting the conditions is concerned, you've already been doing that. The reading and studying and analysis we talked about in the preceding chapter has as one of its functions the development of fictional ideas. By immersing ourselves in these books and turning them inside out, we come to know them on a gut level, so that our imaginations are encouraged to toy with the kinds of plot material which will be useful to us.

There are other things we can do as well. For instance:

Pay attention. The little atoms of fact and attitude which can link up into the molecules of an idea are all over the damn place. Each of us sees and hears and reads a dozen things a day that we could feed into the idea hopper—if we were paying attention.

Back in the early sixties I was reading one of the newsmagazines when I happened on an article on sleep. I learned no end of things, all of which I promptly forgot except for one delicious nugget of information—there seems to be a certain number of cases in medical literature of human beings who do not sleep at all. They get along somehow, leading lives of permanent insomnia, but otherwise not demonstrably the worse for wear.

Fortunately, I wasn't sleeping when I read that item. I rolled it around in my brain, filed it for cocktail-party conversation, and never dreamed I'd wind up writing seven books about a character named Evan Tanner, a free-lance secret agent whose sleep center had been destroyed during the Korean War.

A few million people probably read that article without writing a book about an insomniac. Conversely, I've undoubtedly come up against a few million facts which might have sparked a character or a setting or a plot, but didn't. What made the difference, I think, is that I happened to find this particular fact oddly provocative. My unconscious mind was eager to play with it, to add it to the murky ferment we talked about earlier. That my mind ultimately made Tanner the particular character he is is very likely attributable to the particular character *I* am—as we'll observe when we look at the process of character development more closely in another chapter. That the plot in which I put Tanner took the shape it did is attributable to two things. First, I'd schooled myself and/or had been inclined by nature to develop plots that lent themselves to suspense fiction. Second, another key principle operated, to wit:

Two and two makes five. Which is to say that synergy is very much at work in the process of plot development. The whole is ever so much greater than its parts. The writer, in possession of one fact or anecdote or notion or concept or whatever, suddenly gifted with another apparently unrelated fact or anecdote or et cetera, takes one in each hand and automatically turns them this way and that, playing with the purposefulness of a child, trying to see if they'll fit together.

Let's get back to Tanner. A full three years after that news-magazine item, I spent an evening with a numismatic journalist just back from Turkey, where he'd spent a couple of years earning a very precarious living smuggling ancient coins and Roman glass out of the country. Among the stories on which he was dining out was one about a rumor he'd heard of a cache of gold coins secreted in the front stoop of a house in Balekisir, where the Armenian community had presumably hidden its wealth at the time of the Smyrna massacres. He and some associates actually located the house as described by a survivor, broke into the stoop in the dead of night, established that the gold had been there, but also established, alas, that someone had beat them to it by a couple of decades.

Now I hadn't consciously been carrying my insomniac character around in the forefront of my mind, waiting for a plot to materialize for him. But I must have been carrying him around subconsciously, because shortly after my evening with the journalist I began a book about a young man, his sleep center destroyed by shrapnel, who goes to Turkey and finds that elusive Armenian gold.

Fawcett published that book as *The Thief Who Couldn't Sleep*. For my part, I decided to write more books about Tanner, and there was a point when I could barely pick up a news-paper without running across something that would turn into plot material. Tanner was a devotee of political lost causes and national irredentist movements, and it seemed as though every other story in the first section of the daily *New York Times* was grist for my mill. By perceiving news stories this way, picking them up and seeing what I could do with them, I was following yet another principle:

Remember what you're looking for. Here's an example that happened just a couple of weeks ago. I was with a group of people, and one woman complained about a problem she was having with her upstairs neighbor. He was evidently a drunk, and was given periodically to turning his radio on at top volume and then either leaving the apartment or passing out cold on the floor. Efforts to reach him invariably failed, and the radio blared all night, keeping the woman awake and doing very little for her peace of mind.

People suggested a variety of things—that she call the police, kick the door in, report him to the landlord, and so on. "Get a flashlight," I told her, "and go down to the basement and find the fuse box and remove the fuse for his apartment. Just turn him off altogether. Pull the plug on the clown."

I don't know if she did this. That's her problem, not mine. But after the conversation shifted, I was left to think about the basic problem and let my mind wander with it. That I'd thought of the fuse box ploy was not inconsistent with my choosing burglars and such types as viewpoint characters; I'm blessed or cursed, as you prefer, with that type of mind. I thought of that, and I thought that my burglar hero, Bernie Rhodenbarr, would certainly offer the same suggestion if a friend called him in the middle of the night with that particular problem.

And then, because I've learned not to walk away from thoughts along these lines, I asked myself what Bernie would do if, for some reason or other, his friend couldn't pull the fuse, or get access to the fuse box, or whatever. Some fuse boxes in New York apartments are located within the individual apartment, for instance. Suppose Bernie's sidekick Carolyn Kaiser called him because of this blaring radio, and suppose Bernie was obliging enough to trot over with his burglar's tools, and suppose he did what he does best, letting himself into the offending apartment just to turn off the radio, and suppose there was a dead body spread out on the living room rug, and suppose . . . .

I may or may not use it. But a few minutes of rumination had provided me with the opening for a novel. It's not a plot. It's not enough for me to sit down and start writing. I'm not ready to write another book about Bernie just now and won't be for six or eight months. By then, if I remember who I am and what I'm looking for, I'll very likely have picked up other stray facts and thoughts and bits and pieces, and I'll have played with them and tried fitting them together, and if two and two makes five I may have a book to write.

Stay awake. I heard very early on that a writer works twenty-four hours a day, that the mind is busy sifting notions and possibilities during every waking hour and, in a less demonstrable manner, while the writer sleeps as well. I liked the sound of this from the start—it was a nice rejoinder to my then wife if she said anything about my putting in only two hours a day at the typewriter, or skipping work altogether and going to the friendly neighborhood pool hall for the afternoon. But I'm not sure I believed it.

I believe it now, but with one qualification. I believe we *can* be on the job twenty-four hours a day. I believe we can also choose not to, and those of us who make this choice severely limit ourselves.

A great many writers use alcohol and drugs, ostensibly to stimulate their creativity. This very often seems to work in the beginning; the mind, jarred out of its usual channels by this unaccustomed chemical onslaught, may respond by digging new channels for itself. Similarly, some artists early in their careers find hangovers a creative if hardly comfortable time. The process of withdrawal from the drug evidently has a stimulating effect.

Eventually, these same writers commonly use alcohol and drugs to unwind, to turn off the spinning brain after the day's work is finished. The process is not true relaxation, of course, but anesthesia. One systematically shuts off the thinking and feeling apparatus for the night. For those who ultimately become drug- or alcohol-dependent—and a disheartening proportion of the members of our profession wind up in this category—the results are devastating. One reaches a stage wherein work is impossible without the drug or the drink, and this stage is in turn succeeded by one in which work is impossible with or without the substance. Alcoholism and drug dependency have ended too many successful careers prematurely, while they've nipped no end of promising careers in the bud.

It's hardly revolutionary to advise an alcoholic writer not to drink, anymore than it's a controversial stance to urge diabetics not to binge on sugar. But I'd suggest further that heavy drinking or drug use is severely detrimental even to the writer who does *not* become alcoholic or drug-dependent, simply because it shuts off his mind.

For years I drank when my day's work was done, convinced that it helped me relax. One thing it indisputably did was take my mind off my work. This, to be sure, was one of the things I wanted it to do; I felt I ought to be able to leave the work behind when I left the typewriter.

But writing, and especially novel writing, just doesn't work that way. Writing the novel is an ongoing organic process, and we carry the book with us wherever we go. It's during the period between one day's work and the next that our minds play, both consciously and subconsciously, with the ideas that will enable us to perform creatively when we resume writing. We may rest the mind during these times but we hurt ourselves creatively if we shut our minds off completely. Later on we'll talk about the value of daily writing. It's similarly related to the notion of keeping oneself present in one's book, day in and day out. Extended breaks in the writing interrupt this continuity, and so do those interruptions of consciousness or attentiveness or awareness caused by heavy drinking and drug use.

More recently, marijuana has been touted as a creative stimulant, presumably nonaddictive, harmless, etc. Its addictive properties and harmlessness aside, I have found that its potential for creative stimulation is largely illusory. The common marijuana experience consists of making marvelous seminal mental breakthroughs which, hard to grasp as the smoke itself, are gone the next morning. If only one could remember, if only one could hold onto those fantastic inspired insights. . . .

Well, one can. The story's been told of the fellow who kept paper and pencil at the ready, determined to write down his brilliant insights before they were lost. He awoke the following morning, recollected that he'd had a fantastic insight and that for once he'd managed to write it down. He wasn't sure that it contained the absolute secret of the universe, but he knew it was dynamite.

He looked, and there on the bedside table was his pad of paper, and on it he had written, "This room smells funny."

Whether to smoke or drink or pop pills is an individual decision, as is the extent to which you may care to employ these substances. I would suggest, though, that if you do elect to drink or drug heavily, you do so between novels, not during them. And recognize that whatever excellence your work has is in spite of the substances that you're using, not because of them.

Stay hungry. Some time ago a friend of mine was on a television talk show with several other mystery writers, Mickey Spillane among them. After the program ended, Spillane announced that they'd neglected to talk about the most important topic. "We didn't say anything about money," he said.

He went on to explain that he'd spent several years on an offshore island in South Carolina, where he did nothing too much more taxing than swim and sunbathe and walk the beach for hours at a time. "Every once in a while it would come to me that it'd be fun to get started on a book," he said. "I thought I'd keep my mind in shape and I'd enjoy doing it. But I could never get a single idea for a story. I'd sit and sit, I'd walk for miles, but I couldn't get an idea.

"Then one day I got a call from my accountant to say that the money was starting to get low. Nothing serious, but I should start thinking about ways to bring in some dough. And boy, did I get ideas for books!"

Money makes the mare go. It's very often the spur for what we might prefer to think of as pure creativity. I don't believe for a moment that financial insecurity is essential to a writer's imagination. In my own case, really severe money problems have occasionally kept me from thinking of anything beyond the desperate nature of the situation, leading to a vicious circle verging on writer's block. Money doesn't have to be the spur or the genuinely rich members of our profession would not continue to write productively and well. A man like James Michener, who consistently gives away most of what he earns writing best sellers, is certainly not driven by the desire for cash.

But he's spurred on by something. There is a hunger at the root of all our creative work, whether it is for wealth or recognition or a sense of accomplishment or some tangible proof that we are not worthless human beings after all. To return to an earlier metaphor, we might call that hunger the yeast that starts that dark ferment working down in the unconscious.

If we can stay in touch with that hunger, the pot will keep bubbling—and ideas that engage us will continue rising to the surface.

* * *

When an idea does come along, make quite sure you don't forget it.

I would recommend carrying a notebook around as routinely as you carry your house key or wallet. Whenever an idea turns up, make a note of it. The simple act of writing down a few words will help to fix the idea in your mind so your subconscious can get hold of it.

Before you go to bed at night, make a point of glancing through the notebook. If you have the wrong attitude, this process can simply load you up with guilt over all the fiction ideas you've left undeveloped. Don't let this happen. Those scribbles and scraps in your notebook aren't things you *have* to do, and they're certainly not projects which must be undertaken right away. The notebook's a tool. It's there to make sure you don't lose sight of things that might turn out to be worth remembering; by referring to it frequently, you use it to give your memory a jog and stimulate the unconscious development of the idea over a period of time.

For some writers, a notebook comes close to being an end in itself. They approach the notebook as an art form, using it as a sort of creative journal and devoting an hour or so at the end of the day to ruminating therein. I've never been able to do this, perhaps because of a constitutional incapacity for sustained work at something without at least the possibility that what I'm doing will be publishable. Then too, it's my own feeling that the writer who puts too much energy into notebook entries is like the athlete who overtrains, like the boxer who leaves his fight in the gym.

That's just personal prejudice. Once again, writing is an utterly individual matter, and your notebook ought to be whatever you want it to be. Whatever works is what is right.

It's generally better, if rumination is your thing, to confine it to a notebook rather than to discuss your plot notion with friends. Sometimes this sort of discussion is useful, especially if the friends are writers themselves. When people in the business bat plot material around, the brainstorming process often results in clarifying and strengthening the ideas. All too often, though, talking about an idea winds up serving as an alternative to writing about it, especially if the people you talk to are not writers. I can lose enthusiasm for ideas if I talk them out at length. Perhaps the ideas I've gone stale on in this fashion are ideas that would have withered on the vine regardless, but my experience in this area has made me superstitious and secretive on the subject. I tend now to sit on my better ideas like a broody hen, letting them hatch as they will in their own good time.

* * *

One thing that I've learned, occasionally to my chagrin, is that it's not enough for an idea to be a good one. It has to be a good one *for me.*

It's easy to fool oneself in this area. Just because I've thought of an idea for a novel, and just because it's the sort of idea that could be developed into a viable book, is no reason in and of itself for me to write that particular book. It may not be my type of book at all. But sometimes, overawed by the commercial potential of the project, I lose sight of this fact.

I recently had a painful lesson in this regard, and it was a long time coming. Some years ago I was reading something about Case Barbarossa, the Nazi invasion of Russia that was the beginning of the end for Hitler's Germany. I got an idea—specifically, that Hitler had been manipulated into attacking Russia by a British agent who had penetrated the Berlin government. I thought that was a neat premise to hang a novel on, and discussed it with my friend, novelist Brian Garfield, figuring it was the sort of book he could do a nice job with.

Brian was intrigued, but not quite captivated enough to do anything with the notion. Time passed, and the idea lingered in my subconscious, and two or three years later on a flight to Jamaica an idea struck me out of the blue, tying the original notion I'd dreamed up with Rudolf Hess's inexplicable flight to Scotland. A whole bunch of quirky historical elements would not fit themselves into the context of my little fiction, and the book which might result might just have the stuff of which best sellers are made.

There was only one problem. It still wasn't my kind of book. It wasn't really the kind of book I'd be terribly likely to read, let alone write. I might have recognized this, had I not had my judgment clouded by pure and simple greed. (Then too, I didn't have anything else to write, and there were no other ideas hanging fire that did much for me.)

I had a terrible time with the book, and the first draft of it, certainly, was at least as terrible as the time I had. The whole project may well turn out to be salvageable, and I may indeed wind up entering this particular book on the profit side of my ledger, but I hope I never lose sight of the fact that it was a mistake for me to write this book. If I've learned that, and if the lesson sticks, then I'll really have profited from the experience regardless of how it turns out financially.

For the beginner, a certain amount of experimentation in this regard is both inevitable and desirable. It takes a lot of writing to know with any degree of assurance what you are and are not capable of doing. Furthermore, at the start of a writing career any writing experience is valuable in and of itself. But as you grow to develop a surer sense of your individual strengths and weaknesses, you'll be better able to decide what ideas to develop, what ones to give away, and what ones to forget about altogether.

*   *   *

Some ideas come from other people. I've had both good and bad experiences writing books based on the ideas of others.

Years ago Donald E. Westlake got an idea for a suspense

novel—a bride is raped on her wedding night and the bridal couple take direct revenge on the bad guys. He wrote an opening chapter, found it didn't seem to go anywhere, and he put it away and forgot about it.

A year or so after that I called him up and asked if he had any plans for the idea. When he said no, I requested permission to steal the notion—it had been percolating on a back burner of my mind ever since he first mentioned it to me. He graciously told me to go ahead, and *Deadly Honeymoon* became my first hardcover novel, a fair success in book form and ultimately the basis of a film, called *Nightmare Honeymoon* for reasons I wouldn't presume to guess.

Agents and publishers have come up with other ideas and given them to me. Sometimes I've written the books their ideas sparked, and sometimes they've turned out well.

On the other hand, I've had several experiences where ideas originated by other persons led me to books that proved ultimately unwritable, or books which gave me a great deal of trouble, or books which simply failed for one reason or another.

It can be quite difficult, for example, working from a publisher's idea. The temptation to do so can be considerable, since one is not working on speculation; the publisher, along with the idea, generally dangles a contract and an advance in front of one's eyes, and the more attractive the contract and the larger the advance, why, the better the idea is going to look. Thus you find yourself bound to an idea you might have dismissed out of hand if you'd thought it up all by yourself.

Sometimes—and I've had this experience—the publisher has only a vague idea of what he wants. In order to produce a book you'll be able to write effectively, you have to transform this idea and make it your own. If the publisher's got an open mind, that's no problem. Occasionally, however, he'll be struck by the discrepancy between what you've produced and the sublime if hazy vision with which he started. If the book's good enough in its own right you'll sell it somewhere sooner or later, but it doesn't make for the best feelings all around.

What it boils down to, then, is that you really have to be sure you like another person's idea before you use it. Remember, your own ideas bubble up from your own mind; when you work on them, that bubbling process will continue and the idea will develop. When you're working on another person's idea, you're adopting it. It has to be the sort you can love as if it were your own or you won't be able to bring your subconscious fully to bear upon it. It won't grow organically the way an idea must if it is to become a fully realized book.

* * *

How well developed does an idea have to be before you can start writing the book?

It depends.

The Thief Who Couldn't Sleep took a couple of years gestating until various plot components fitted themselves together. By the time I sat down to write the book, I had a very strong sense of the character of Tanner and a pretty good grasp of the book's plot. I didn't know everything else that was going to happen by any means, but I had the general outline of the book pretty clear in my mind.

With *Deadly Honeymoon,* I could fit the book's premise into one sentence, and that was as much of a handle as I had on the book when I sat down and wrote the first chapter. I think now that I might have written a better book if I'd known more about the various characters and had given the plot more thought before I started, but I was impatient to get on with it, and it's possible the book gained by the impatient enthusiasm that gripped its author.

One night Brian Garfield parked his car on the street in

Manhattan and returned to it to find the convertible top slashed by some archfiend in human form who wanted to steal a coat from the back seat. Brian's first reaction was murderous rage. He realized he couldn't find the villain and kill him, but he could find some other villain and kill him, couldn't he? Because Brian is a writer rather than a homicidal maniac—although admittedly the two classes are not mutually exclusive—he decided to write a book about someone so motivated rather than act out his anger directly.

He might have begun work immediately upon a book about a vigilante who goes around killing people after someone slashes his convertible top—and that's not the worst premise for a book I've ever heard. But Brian gave the book plenty of time to take shape, let the character of accountant Paul Benjamin emerge from wherever our ideas grow, made the motivating experience the rape and beating of Benjamin's wife and daughter by a trio of hoodlums, with the wife dying and the daughter shocked into madness, and let the story grow from there. The result, *Death Wish,* was an artistic success as a novel and an enormous commercial triumph as a film.

Don Westlake, on the other hand, once wrote a first chapter in which a surly fellow walks across the George Washington Bridge into New York, snarling at motorists who offer him rides. Don didn't know where he was going with that one but found out as he went along. The result was the lengthy series of novels Don wrote under the pen name Richard Stark, all of them featuring Parker, a professional heist man and as unobliging a chap as he was the day he walked across the bridge.

As the years go by, which is something they do with increasing rapidity lately, I find myself giving ideas more rather than less time to take shape. I'm no longer so anxious to rush Chapter One through the typewriter if I have no idea what'll happen in Chapter Two. One learns from experience, and I've had the experience of watching far too many first chapters wither on the vine to dismiss the possibility of its happening again. I'm less inclined to worry that an idea will evaporate if I don't get it into production as quickly as possible. If I make a note of it so I won't forget it, and if I read through my notebook from time to time and make it a point to think about what I find there, the good ideas will survive and grow. The bad ones will drop out along the way, and that's fine; I don't feel compelled to add to my stack of first-chapters-of-books-destined-never-to-have-a-second-chapter.

On the other hand, the next book I intend to write is one I've been thinking about for several months now, getting more and more of a sense of the lead character, considering and rejecting any number of geographical settings, changing my mind over and over again about the nature of the plot.

I got the idea, incidentally, by the serendipitous process that yields so many ideas. I was at the library, doing research on patron saints for the sake of a bit of conversational by-play in a light mystery novel, *The Burglar Who Liked to Quote Kipling*. This led me to a passage from Aquinas that amounted to a marvelous moral justification for larceny. Then, because I was tired of saints, patron or otherwise, I started browsing magazines, something I rarely do, and came across an interview with Dennis Hopper. I felt I really ought to go home and get to work, but I felt self-indulgent that day and read the Hopper interview, and there was the idea for my next novel, just waiting there for me to find it. (I won't tell you what it is—I don't want to leave my fight in the gym.)

Anyway, I expect I'll start writing the book in a couple of months. I know the book will have benefited greatly from the time I've spent thinking about it off and on ever since I read that interview. But I'm quite certain that I won't know very much about the direction the plot will take. I'll have my first chapter pretty well worked out in my mind, and I'll know a lot about the characters, and I'll have a variety of possible directions for the book to go, but . . . .

But I won't be able to sit down and paint the thing by numbers. That's what makes it hard, no matter how much plotting time you give a book, but it's also what keeps it exciting.

Chapter 5

Developing Characters

The chief reason for almost any reader to go on turning the pages of almost any novel is to find out what happens next. The reason the reader *cares* what happens next is because of the author's skill at characterization. When the characters in a novel are sufficiently well drawn, and when they've been so constructed as to engage the reader's capacities for sympathy and identification, he wants to see how their lives turn out and is deeply concerned that they turn out well.

The books that I don't finish reading—and their numbers increase with the years—are generally abandoned along the way for one of two reasons. Sometimes the writer's style puts me off; because I'm a writer myself I've become increasingly aware of literary technique, much as a professional musician will notice sour notes and technical flaws that would escape my attention. Unless theme or story line or characters have a great hold upon me, I'll lose interest in an inexpertly written novel.

If the writing's competent, my interest may flag nevertheless if I find that I just don't give a damn whether the characters live or die, marry or burn, go to the Devil or come out the other side. This may happen because I just don't believe in the characters the author has created. They don't act like real people, they don't sound like real people, and they don't seem to have the emotions or thoughts of real people. Thus they're unreal as far as I'm concerned, and I say they're spinach and the hell with them.

Note, please, that my complaint is that these wooden characters don't seem like *real* people, not that they aren't *ordinary* people. Some of the most engaging characters in fiction, clutching my attention as the Wedding Guest hung on to the Ancient Mariner, have been the farthest thing from ordinary. Nothing about Sherlock Holmes is ordinary, yet the character's appeal has been such as to keep the Conan Doyle stories in print to this day, and to have Holmes resuscitated and brought back to life in several novels by contemporary authors, novels which owe their success almost entirely to public enthusiasm for Conan Doyle's eternally fascinating character.

Similarly, I've found Rex Stout's books about Nero Wolfe endlessly rereadable. There's nothing ordinary about Wolfe, and it's not only his corpulence that makes him larger than life. I don't reread the books because their plots are so compelling, certainly not the second or third time around. Nor am I dazzled by Stout's sheer writing ability; while it was considerable, I never got interested in his non-Wolfe books, either the mysteries starring other detectives or the several straight novels he wrote before creating Wolfe. No, I read him as I suspect most people do, for the sheer pleasure of watching the interplay between Nero Wolfe and Archie Goodwin, of seeing these two men react to different situations and stimuli, and of participating vicariously in the life of that legendary brownstone on West Thirty-fifth Street.

Ordinary? Scarcely that. But so real that I sometimes have to remind myself that Wolfe and Goodwin are the creations of a writer's mind, that no matter how many doorbells I ring in the West Thirties, I'll never find the right house.

That's characterization. It was the ability to create characters readers could care about, too, that made Charles Dickens a monumental popular success. While Oscar Wilde might have remarked that only a man with a heart of stone could read of the death of Little Nell without laughing, the truth of the matter is that readers did not laugh when they read that scene. They wept.

Some novels depend rather more on characterization than do others. In the novel of ideas, the characters often exist as mouthpieces for various philosophical positions; while the writer may have taken the trouble to describe them and give them diverse individual attributes, they often have little real life outside of their specific argumentative role in the novel.

Some whodunits rely on the clever intricacy of their plotting to hold the reader's attention, stinting on characterization in the process. Erle Stanley Gardner's Perry Mason mysteries can be compulsively readable, but does Mason himself ever emerge as anything more than a forceful courtroom presence and a keen legal mind? Agatha Christie supplied her Hercule Poirot with a variety of attitudes and pet expressions, but I've never found that the little Belgian added up to anything more than the sum of these quirks and phrases. He serves admirably as a vehicle for the solution of brilliant mystery puzzles but does not interest me much as a character.

On reflection, it seems to me that even in these categories— the novel of ideas, the plot-heavy whodunit—my favorite novels are those in which the author has created characters to whom I am capable of responding strongly. Arthur Koestler's *Darkness at Noon* is a brilliant novel of political and philosophical argument; I find it ever so much more effective because the lead character, Rubashov, is so absorbing a human being. And, while one of Ms. Christie's Poirot mysteries will always do to fill an idle hour, I'm a passionate fan of her Jane Marple stories, not because their plots are appreciably different from the Poirots but because Marple herself is such a fascinating character, warm and human and alive.

*   *   *

So characterization is important in fiction, and especially so in the novel. The argument is hardly a controversial one. With that much established, how does one go about creating characters with whom the reader can identify, characters he'll want to spend time with, characters whose fate will be a matter of concern to him?

A first principle of characterization may seem fairly obvious, but I think it's worth stating. Characters are most effective when they are so drawn that the author can identify with them, sympathize with them, care about them, and enjoy their company.

At the risk of sounding like an armchair psychoanalyst, I would suggest that all characters are to a greater or lesser extent a projection of the author's own personality. I know this is true in my own writing. While all my characters are not like me by any means, they are each and every one the people I would be were I clothed in their particular skins. In other words, when I create a character I work very much in the manner of an actor playing a role. I play that character's part, improvising his dialogue on the page, slipping into his role as I go along.

This is most obviously the case with viewpoint characters; indeed, it's commonplace for readers to make the mistake of too closely identifying an author with the attitudes and opinions of his novel's narrator. But I know that in my own writing, this identification is true too for the subordinate characters, the villains, the bit players, for everyone who puts in an appearance. I do most of the work of characterization from the inside out, playing all the parts myself, writing all the dialogue, and walking all the characters through their paces. Naturally, in any given novel there will be some characters with whom I can more readily identify than others; it's generally true those are the characters I do a better job with.

It's important, I think, to play around with the idea of a character before plunging into a book. Occasionally in the past I've rushed to get a first chapter written without taking the time to figure out who the people were, letting the characters define themselves on the page. This was the case with *Deadly Honeymoon;* I was concerned with a plot and incident and dramatic effect, and so I began writing the book with no clear picture of the bridal couple who served as the book's joint leads. I think the book might have been a good deal better had I known more about my characters before I began.

With Tanner, I had an abundance of time. After I'd first been taken with the notion of writing about a permanent insomniac, as I explained in the preceding chapter, I read something in an encyclopedia indicating that the British royal house of Stuart survived to the present time, with the current pretender some sort of Bavarian princeling. I thought this was splendid, and decided my insomniac could be plotting the restoration of the House of Stuart to the British throne.

That didn't go anywhere, but it gave me this image of Tanner as a devotee of political lost causes. I thought of him from time to time and figured out other things about his character. I decided he'd have lots of time on his hands, not having to spend eight hours a day sleeping, and I thought he could put that time to use by compulsively learning one language after another. This sort of scholarly devotion seemed to fit the occupation I decided to give him—I had him write theses and examination papers to order for students with more money than industry.

Tanner's gradual evolution over a period of a couple of years was such that, when Providence provided me with a plot, my character was all set to go. It was easy to plot the book to suit the particular character I had already created in my mind. And that character, quirky and highly individualistic, was one with whom I could identify profoundly, because for all our differences Tanner was very clearly a projection of the author.

He was precisely the person I would have been had I been wearing his skin and living his life.

* * *

Another series character of mine illustrates the manner in which one can adapt and define a character to suit the requirement of author-identification.

Two things inspired the creation of Matt Scudder. First, it was an opportune time for me to do a detective series for Dell Books. Second, I'd just read *On the Pad,* Leonard Shecter's excellent book with and about Bill Phillips, the New York City cop, admittedly corrupt, who'd collected evidence for an investigative commission and who had been tried and found guilty of the murder of a call girl and her pimp. What struck me was the notion of a corrupt cop, living with and on corruption, running his own hustles, and functioning all the while as a very effective policeman, breaking cases and putting criminals in jail.

As I began working on the character, I realized that the cop I had in mind might make an absorbing character, that I might very well enjoy reading someone else's interpretation of such a character, but that he was not a character with whom I could identify sufficiently in order to write books about him myself. I'm not comfortable using viewpoint characters who function within a bureaucracy. For one reason or another, I've always felt more comfortable from the point of view of an outsider. I didn't feel at all sanguine about my ability to render a crooked cop believable, let alone sympathetic.

So I let my imagination play around with Scudder, and then I sat down at a typewriter and began writing a long memo to myself *about* the man. I decided he was something of a burnt-out case; he had been a cop, had lived with wife and children in the suburbs, and had been both a proficient detective and a man to whom small-scale corruption was a way of life. Then, while thwarting a tavern holdup while off-duty, his ricocheting bullet killed a small child. This led poor Scudder to an agonizing reappraisal of his own life and enough existential angst to drown a litter of kittens. He left his wife and kids, moved into a monastic hotel room in Manhattan, quit the police force, picked up the habit of visiting churches and lighting candles, and became a serious drinker. Occasionally he would earn money as an unofficial and unlicensed private detective, using his contacts in the NYPD and investigating cases with the special sensibilities of a hip and hard-nosed cop.

I wrote three novels and two novelettes about Scudder and took enormous satisfaction in them: I like the books as well as anything I've written. They worked, and Scudder worked, because I was able to take a generally sound character idea and transform it into a character who came to life as a projection of the author. I identified strongly with Scudder. For all the apparent difference of our lives and our selves, he and I had any number of underlying aspects in common.

All characters in this book are fictional, and any resemblance to persons living or dead is purely coincidental. The earth is flat.

The above disclaimer notice, which appeared in the front of *Ronald Rabbit is a Dirty Old Man,* brought me an invitation— eagerly accepted, I might add—to join the Flat Earth Society of Canada. My purpose in including the notice was not to proselytize against the globularist heresy, as we Flat Earthers are wont to call it, but to make a point about the disclaimer notices that appear so routinely in so many novels. The statements are generally palpable nonsense; resemblance to persons living or dead is often quite intentional.

Many of the characters with whom we people our fiction are drawn from life, and how could it be otherwise? One way or another, all our writing comes from experience, and it is our experience of our fellow human beings that enables us to create characters that look and act and sound like human beings.

The average reader often seems to think that writers go about snatching people off the streets and bundling them into books with the rapacious fervor of an old-fashioned white slaver. It is as if the characters were stolen from the real world and transplanted bodily into a novel.

Once in a while it very nearly amounts to that. In the genuine *roman à clef,* where the author presumes to render real events in the guise of fiction, the characters are portrayed as much like their real life prototypes as the author can manage. Thomas Wolfe wrote in this fashion, telling his own story in *Look Homeward, Angel* and *Of Time and the River,* casting himself as Eugene Gant and his own family as the Gant family. Even so, the Gants inevitably became fictional characters; Wolfe had to invent, to devise. Even a character like Eliza Gant, modeled so faithfully upon his own mother, emerges finally as Wolfe's interpretation of the woman, as the person *he* would have been had he been her.

Furthermore, the novelist's imagination and the novelist's sense of order work changes upon characters drawn from life. In his autobiographical work, *Christopher and His Kind,* Christopher Isherwood tells of various persons with whom he was acquainted over the years, some of whom appeared previously as characters in his largely autobiographical novels. Here's how he discusses a friend and the way the man appeared in a novel:

> In *Down There on a Visit,* Francis appears as a character called Ambrose and is described as follows:
>
> "His figure was slim and erect and there was a boyishness in his quick movements. But his darkskinned face was quite shockingly lined, as if Life had mauled him with its claws. His hair fell picturesquely about his face in wavy black locks which were already

streaked with grey. There was a gentle surprise in the expression of his dark brown eyes. He could become frantically nervous at an instant's notice—I saw that; with his sensitive nostrils and fine-drawn cheekbones, he had the look of a horse which may bolt without warning. And yet there was a kind of inner contemplative response in the midst of him. It made him touchingly beautiful. He could have posed for the portrait of a saint."

This is true to life, more or less, except for the last three sentences, which relate only to the fictitious part of Ambrose. Photographs of Francis at that time show that he was beautiful, certainly, but that he had the face of a self-indulgent aristocrat, not a contemplative ascetic. I can't detect the inner response. . . .

Isherwood goes on to recount several other aspects of Francis's character which he did not incorporate in the fictional Ambrose. However unmistakably the one may have been modeled upon the other, the writing process has clearly made them different personalities.

Another popular sort of novel specializes in holding up a fun-house mirror to life. This is the generally tacky type of book in which the story line is largely a matter of sheer invention, occasionally incorporating bits of rumor and scandal, and with several of the characters so obviously based on prominent persons as to make the reader regard the book almost as an unauthorized biography. Someone remarked not long ago that Frank Sinatra, for one, has been pressed into service in so many novels over the years, whether as the lead or in a cameo role, that he really deserves to collect a royalty. And any number of novels have similarly "starred" Elizabeth Taylor, Jackie Onassis, and more other celebrities than I would care to name or number.

More often, the characters we create are drawn in part from people we have known or observed, without our in any sense attempting to recreate the person on the page. I may borrow a bit of physical description, for example, or a mannerism, or an oddity of speech. I may take an incident in the life of someone

I know and use it as an item of background data in the life of one of my characters. Little touches of this sort from my own life experience get threaded into my characters much as bits of ribbon and cloth are woven into a songbird's nest—for color, to tighten things up, and because they caught my eye and seemed to belong there.

The first time I consciously transferred an aspect of a real person into a novel was when I wrote a book called *After the First Death*, a murder mystery set in the half-world of Times Square streetwalkers. I had at the time a nodding acquaintance with one such woman—and on one occasion she told me about a relationship she'd had of some duration with a married man from Scarsdale. She'd evidently been off drugs at the time, and seeing him exclusively, but after he'd cancelled a planned European trip with her and took his wife to the Caribbean instead, she ended the relationship and returned to prostitution and heroin addiction.

I don't know that the character of Jackie in my novel had much in common with the woman who told me this story. Jackie was certainly a romanticized character; if she didn't have a heart of gold, she had at the very least a soft spot in her heart of brass. Nor did I know the real-life hooker well enough to haul her off the streets and plunk her down on the printed page. But certainly the portrayal of Jackie owed a lot to my impression of her, and the story about her Scarsdale Galahad found its way almost word for word into print.

Some years later I wrote a pseudonymous novel in the manner of *Peyton Place*—sensational doings in a small town, that sort of thing. I very deliberately set the book in a particular town with which I was personally familiar, and several of the characters owed something to real people who lived in the town. For one character, I borrowed the physical description of a local actor, not intending to ape him too closely; only to find that the character I'd created had a will of his own and insisted upon speaking and behaving precisely as his real-life prototype spoke and behaved. I couldn't write the character's dialogue without hearing my friend's voice booming in my ears. Now I suppose it's possible to fight that sort of thing, but what writer in his right mind would presume to do so? The best possible thing had happened. A character had come to life. I might be inviting a lawsuit or a public thrashing by allowing him to play out his part, but I'd have been false to my art to do otherwise.

For me, the most exhilarating moment at the typewriter is when a character takes on a life of his own. It's not an easy thing to describe. But it happens. One can scarcely avoid playing God when writing a novel, creating one's own imaginary universe and arranging the destinies of the characters as one sees fit. When the magic happens, however, and a character speaks and breathes and sweats and sighs apparently of his own accord, one feels for a moment that one has created life.

It's a heady experience, and so satisfying that you'd want it to happen all the time. Unfortunately, it doesn't—at least not for me. Some of my characters live for me as I've described. Others walk around like empty suits, doing what's required of them but never coming to life. They may work well enough for the reader—craft can disguise the fact that certain characters are just walking through their roles—but not for me.

This was the case with the war novel I talked about in the last chapter. The lead character in my first draft had a lot of interesting things about him. He was a former stunt pilot, the survivor of an unhappy love affair, an American of Irish and Jewish heritage who had enlisted in the RAF. Who could fail to make such a man interesting?

Who indeed? I could, and did. I carried the poor clown through five hundred pages of tedious manuscript and never had the feeling that he could stand up without my support. He remained a two-dimensional cardboard cutout, mouthing the lines required to fit a situation, going places and doing things, acting and reacting and doing it all like a brainwashed zombie.

Why didn't he come to life? I don't know. It wasn't because there was anything fundamentally unsympathetic about the sort of person he was or the acts he performed. A few minor characters in the same novel did verge on animation, including a few whom I found distinctly unpleasant, but my lead remained dead and hollow at the core. Perhaps my inability to breathe life into him owed something to my own negative feelings about the novel itself. Perhaps I couldn't get past seeing him as an instrument rather than a person.

* * *

In contrast, Bernie Rhodenbarr came to life on the very first page of the first draft of the first novel in which he made an appearance.

Previously, I'd written a couple of chapters of a Scudder novel in which a burglar's suspected of murder because he knocks off an apartment with a dead body in it. That particular burglar was a sort of gentle oaf, and Scudder was going to come to his rescue, but the book never got off the ground.

Later I decided to revive that plot notion, eliminate the detective, change the tone entirely from downbeat to sprightly, and let the burglar himself solve the crime and go on to tell the tale.

I decided to open with the initial burglary, so I sat down and typed out the following:

A handful of minutes after nine I hoisted my Bloomingdale's shopping bag and moved out of a doorway and into step with a tall blond fellow with a faintly equine cast to his face. He was carrying an attaché case that looked too thin to be of much use. Like a high-fashion model, you might say. His topcoat was one of those new plaid ones and his hair, a little longer than my own, had been cut a strand at a time.

"We meet again," I said, which was an out-and-out lie. "Turned out to be a pretty fair day after all."

He smiled, perfectly willing to believe that we were neighbors who exchanged a friendly word now and then. "Little brisk this evening," he said.

I agreed that it was brisk. There wasn't much he might have said that I wouldn't have gladly agreed with. He looked respectable and he was walking east on Sixty-seventh Street and that was all I required of him. I didn't want to befriend him or play handball with him or learn the name of his barber or coax him into swapping shortbread recipes. I just wanted him to help me get past a doorman.

By the time I had that much written, I knew who Bernie Rhodenbarr was. More important, he'd already begun to take on a life of his own. I didn't have to stop and think how he would phrase something; it was simply a matter of shifting gears and speaking in his voice—or, if you will, of letting go and allowing him to recite his own lines spontaneously.

I don't want to make this sound too mystical. Books don't write themselves and characters don't relieve their creators of the necessity of getting the right words on the page. But when a character does come to life in this fashion, when you find yourself knowing him from the inside out, you are then able to bring to the process of literary creation the assurance of the natural athlete.

*　　*　　*

How does one manage to make characters distinct and memorable? Is it a matter of little traits—pet expressions, a perpetually untied shoelace, a drooping eyelid? These are the little tricks of caricature, to be sure, and they are more or less effective depending on the skill with which they are managed.

In *Time to Murder and Create,* for instance, I made use of a character named Spinner Jablon. He's not onstage long; he's a stool pigeon turned blackmailer who hires Scudder to hold an envelope for him, said envelope to be opened in the event of his death, which in turn happens early in the book.

I had this to say about Spinner:

> They called him the Spinner because of a habit he had. He carried an old silver dollar as a good-luck charm, and he would haul it out of his pants pocket all the time, prop it up on a table top with his left forefinger, then cock his right middle finger and give the edge of the coin a flick. If he was talking to you, his eyes would stay on the spinning coin while he spoke, and he seemed to be directing his words as much to the dollar as to you.

This spin-a-silver-dollar bit was a handy character tag; it gave Spinner something memorable to do, made for an interesting bit of business to go on during Spinner's conversation with Scudder, and later in the book provided a way for Scudder to underscore Spinner's death—he purchases a silver dollar from a coin dealer and takes to carrying it around himself and spinning it on tabletops.

This isn't characterization. It's gimmickry, but sometimes for me it's the first step in the process of characterization. It gives me a tag, a handle, and the actual character evolves in due course through a process that seems to be largely intuitive.

The sort of handle you get on a character varies with the kind of writer you are and the particular character you're dealing with. I find I'm most likely to latch onto characters by the way they sound, the manner in which they use language. It's often through their dialogue that they become real for me, and I frequently fasten onto this while having a less concrete notion of what they look like physically. Sometimes, though, I start with a particular visual picture of a character and all the rest follows.

I still remember a line that popped into my head a few years ago after I caught a glimpse of a woman in a Los Angeles restaurant. *"She had the pinched face of someone who'd grown up on a hardscrabble hillside farm and would do anything to keep from going back."*

I didn't write down those imperishable words but they stayed in my mind, along with not only an image of the woman I'd seen but a whole set of attitudes. I knew who the woman was and how she would sound and what her reactions would be to various phenomena. I didn't know what use I might one day make of her, whether she'd be a heroine or a villain, a protagonist or a spear carrier. So far the only use I've gotten out of her is here and now, to illustrate where characters come from and how they evolve, and it's possible that's all the use I'll ever get out of her.

If you keep a notebook, character sketches are a logical item to include. Maugham's *Writer's Notebook* makes fascinating reading because of the character sketches it contains, many of which ultimately found their way into his short stories and novels. You can jot down whatever you want—your actual observations of a real person, some bits and pieces of gimmickry you've thought up or observed and might eventually want to use for a character of your own creation, or any sort of tag or impression that might blossom into a full-blown character.

* * *

Which comes first, the plot or the character?
There's no answer for that one. A book may start with either the plot or the characters more fully grasped, but both aspects generally take shape side by side as the book itself is formed. Even in books where I think I know pretty much what's going to happen before I start writing, unplanned incidents crop up in the plotting and invariably call for the creation of new

minor characters on the spot. My lead, say, goes looking for someone at a hotel. His quarry's out, but a conversation ensues with the hotel clerk, either to develop certain information or just because such a conversation would be part of the natural order of things. I can make that clerk as much or as little an individual as I want. He can be tall or short, young or old, fat or thin. He can have something or nothing much to say.

Is he doing something when my lead approaches him? Looking at a girlie magazine? Filling in a crossword puzzle in ink? Dozing? Sucking on a bottle of bourbon?

These are all decisions you make as a writer. You may make them quickly and spontaneously and intuitively. You may elect to tell a lot or a little about this sort of bit player. The success of your novel will not stand or fall upon the way you handle him, as it well may hinge on your treatment of major characters, but all characterization plays an important part in the overall impact of your fiction.

Chapter 6

Outlining

An outline is a tool which a writer uses to simplify the task of writing a novel and to improve the ultimate quality of that novel by giving himself more of a grasp on its overall structure.

And that's about as specifically as one can define an outline, beyond adding that it's almost invariably shorter than the book will turn out to be. What length it will run, what form it will take, how detailed it will be, and what sort of novel components it will or will not include, is and ought to be a wholly individual matter. Because the outline is prepared solely for the benefit of the writer himself, it quite properly varies from one author to another and from one novel to another. Some writers never use an outline. Others would be uncomfortable writing anything more ambitious than a shopping list without outlining it first. Some outlines, deemed very useful by their authors, run a scant page. Others, considered equally indispensable by *their* authors, run a hundred pages or more and include a detailed description of every scene that is going to take place in every chapter of the book. Neither of these extremes, nor any of the infinite gradations between the two poles, represents the right way to prepare an outline. There is no right way to do this—or, more correctly, there is no wrong way. Whatever works best for the particular writer on the particular book is demonstrably the right way.

I've written quite a few novels without employing any outline whatsoever. The advantage of eschewing outlines is quite simple. With no predetermined course, the novel is free to evolve as it goes along, with the plot growing naturally out of what has been written rather than being bound artificially to the skeletal structure of an outline like a rosebush espaliered to a trellis.

The writer who does not use an outline says that to do so would gut the book of its spontaneity and would make the writing process itself a matter of filling in the blanks of a printed form. At the root of this school of thought is the argument first propounded, I believe, by science-fiction author Theodore Sturgeon. If the writer doesn't know what's going to happen next, he argued, the reader can't possibly know what's going to happen next.

There's logic in that argument, certainly, but I'm not sure it holds up. Just because a writer worked things out as he went along is no guarantee that the book he's produced won't be obvious and predictable. Conversely, the use of an extremely detailed outline does not preclude the possibility that the book will read as though it had been written effortlessly and spontaneously by a wholly freewheeling author.

Some time ago I queried a hundred or so authors on their writing methods. A considerable number explained that they didn't outline at all, or prepared minimal outlines at most. Here's Willo Davis Roberts echoing Sturgeon's Principle:

> I seldom outline, except insofar as I have to come up with enough to interest an editor if I want a contract before I do the book. Often I do not know how a suspense novel will turn out until I get to the last chapter, which is more fun than having the end all planned beforehand.

Tony Hillerman takes the same position, not because it's

more fun necessarily but because it's what comes naturally for him:

> I have never been able to outline a book. I work from a basic general idea, a couple of clearly understood characters, a couple of thematic and plot ideas, and a rough conception of where I'm going with it all. I also work with a clear idea of place. I tend to write in scenes—getting one vividly in mind, then putting it quickly on paper.

In marked contrast, consider this from Richard S. Prather, author of forty suspense novels, most of them lighthearted frothy chronicles of the doings of private eye Shell Scott:

> I spend considerable time on plot development, typing roughly 100,000 or more words of scene fragments, gimmicks, "what if?" possibilities, alternative actions or solutions, until the overall story line satisfies me. I boil all of this down to a couple of pages, then from these prepare a detailed chapter-by-chapter synopsis, using a separate page (or more) for each of, say, twenty chapters, and expanding in those pages upon characters, motivations, scenes, action, whenever such expansion seems a natural development. When the synopsis is done, I start the first draft of the book and bang away as speedily as possible until the end.

If I ever tried the method Prather describes, I'm sure what I produced would have all the freshness and appeal of week-old mashed potatoes; it would certainly not possess the sparkle of his Shell Scott books—which only serves to underscore the highly individual nature of outlines in particular and writing methods in general. If writing *with* an outline is for some people like filling in a printed form, writing *without* an outline is for others like playing tennis without a net—as Robert Frost said of free verse. In some instances, it's even more like walking a tightrope without a net.

It's all up to you. If you feel comfortable beginning your book without an outline—or even without all that firm an idea where it's going—by all means go ahead. If you'll feel more confident of your ability to finish the book with an outline in front of you, by all means construct and employ one. As you go along, you'll learn what works best for the particular writer you turn out to be.

And that's all that matters. No one ever bought a book because it was written with an outline, or because it wasn't.

*   *   *

I want to use an outline. Now what?

The first step is to find out what an outline is. And the easiest way to do that is to write one. Not of your book but of somebody else's.

In an earlier chapter, we discussed this method of preparing an outline of someone else's book as a means of understanding how novels work. The process is similarly valuable as an aid to learning what an outline is.

Some years back I decided in a weak moment that I wanted to write movies. I was bright enough to recognize that film is an infinitely different medium from prose, and reasoned that I had to familiarize myself with it before I could expect to produce anything that would fly. First thing I did was start going to movies day after day.

This was fun, and it wasn't all that bad an idea, but it didn't teach me a hell of a lot about screenwriting. I came to realize somewhere along the way that I was taking the wrong approach. I wouldn't be writing *movies,* after all. I would be writing *screenplays.* So, instead of studying the films themselves, I ought to be reading their scripts.

If it sounds like a small distinction, I suggest you give it some thought. What I wanted to write was a script, and in order to do that I had to learn what a script was, how it worked not on the screen but on the page. I had to be able to see a film as words on paper, not images on a screen, because I would be writing that script by putting words on paper.

So I read scripts, quite a few of them, and what a difference it made! In the first place, I began to understand what scripts were, how they were written, and how I could write one of my own. In the second place and at least as important, my reading of film scripts made a significant change in my perception when I looked at a film in a theater. My perspective was changed, and I'd look at the movie and mentally translate it back into the script it had come from.

This didn't make me a screenwriter. I did write a movie script, and a treatment for another movie, and in the course of doing this I learned that I wasn't really cut out to be a screenwriter and didn't really want to be one, for any of a variety of perfectly sound reasons. But I still watch films with a heightened awareness of the underlying screenplay, and I wouldn't be surprised if this has paid some dividends in my prose writing.

In the same fashion, the best preparation for writing an outline is reading outlines, not reading novels. By studying the outlines themselves you will see how an outline looks on a typed page; as important, you will develop the ability to see other novels—and, ultimately, your own novel—with x-ray eyes; i.e., you'll see through the prose and dialogue to the bare bones beneath.

How do you outline another person's novel? Whatever way you wish. Your outline of somebody else's book can be as sketchy or as detailed as you like, just as the outline you eventually work up for your own novel may be sketchy or detailed, brief or lengthy. Do whatever seems most natural to you.

* * *

Once you've familiarized yourself with outlines of other writers' novels—or once you've decided not to bother with that step—it's time to get to work on your own outline. At this point some warm-up exercises and wind sprints can be useful. Few of us would care to do as much pre-outline work as Richard S. Prather describes, with preparatory writing running to almost double the length of the finished book, but one can do as much as seems useful.

Character sketches are handy, for example. In the preceding chapter I mentioned how the evolution of my Matthew Scudder character was facilitated by the memo I wrote to myself, in which I discussed Scudder at some length, talking about his background, his habits, his current way of life, his likes and dislikes, and how he likes his eggs for breakfast. In his journals, Chekhov suggests that a writer ought to know everything he can about a character—his shoe size, the condition of his liver, lungs, clothes, habits, and intestinal track. You may not *mention* the greater portion of this in your writing, but the better you know your characters the more effectively you'll be able to write about them. I always keep learning new things about my characters as I go along; I'm still learning about Scudder and Bernie Rhodenbarr, even after several books about each of them—but the better I know them in advance, the better equipped I am for outlining and, later, for writing the novel.

It's also occasionally helpful to write an answer to the question "What is this book about?" In the early days of Hollywood, the conventional wisdom held that a story line ought to be capable of being conveyed in a single sentence. While I suspect this theory was originally propounded by illiterates who couldn't hold more than one sentence in their heads at a time, and while it unquestionably overstates the case, there's some merit to the argument. If nothing else, one feels more confident about approaching a book when one is able to say, if only to oneself, what the thing is *about.*

Burglars Can't Be Choosers is about a cheeky professional burglar who steals an object to order, and the cops walk in on him and catch him in the act, and there's a dead body in the apartment and he escapes and has to clear himself by solving the crime, which he does.

That's what one novel is about, all in one sentence, cumbersome though that sentence be. Explaining what your book is to be about may take several sentences or paragraphs. It's possible, certainly, to write a book without consciously knowing in advance what it's to be about; sometimes we write the books in order to answer that very question. And it's possible to know what the book's about without spelling it out on paper. But sometimes getting it down improves one's grasp on the whole thing.

The next step is to write the outline itself, in as much or as little detail as you wish. I have frequently found it useful to make this a chapter outline, with a paragraph given to describe the action that will take place in each chapter. If you take this approach, don't be unduly concerned with just how you'll divide your narrative into chapters. When you do the actual writing, you may very well discover that the breaks come naturally in different places than the outline indicated. You'll simply ignore the division in the outline and do them whatever way seems best. This is just one way in which you'll ultimately feel free to deviate from the outline, as we'll see in due course. Writing the outline chapter by chapter, whether or not the book will correspond to this division, introduces a sense of order; I think that's why I've found it valuable.

How detailed should the outline be? Given the premise that this is an individual matter, infinitely variable from one author to another and from one book to the next, we might go on to say that there ought to be enough detail so that the story line makes sense. Outlining rarely amounts to more than putting on paper a plot that is already completely formed in your head. As you write things out, chapter by chapter, scene by scene, you'll be working out the details of the story as you go. Problems that wouldn't occur to you otherwise will present themselves.

You'll work out the solutions to some of these problems in the course of completing the outline. But you won't work out *all* of them this way, and it's important to recognize that you don't *have* to. Simply by spotting and defining a problem you have taken a step toward its solution. From then on, your unconscious mind (and your conscious mind as well, for that matter) will be able to play with the problem. While you write the early chapters, you'll have the plot and structure problems of future chapters somewhere in the back of your mind. In other words, the outlining process is part of the whole organic evolution of the book. The book grows and takes shape during it, and the book will continue to grow and shape itself as a result of it.

It's possible, I think, for an outline to be *too* detailed. And it's also possible to waste time and words in an outline explaining motives and background excessively. One thing to remember, in this sort of outline, is that you're writing this for your own benefit, not for anybody else to read. That being the case, you don't have to explain and justify things to yourself when you already have a sufficient grasp of them. Writing is liveliest when it's interesting to the person doing it. Purposeless elaboration in an outline is one way to kill your own interest in what you will later have to sit down and write.

> "When *I* use a word," Humpty Dumpty said, in a rather scornful tone, "it means just what I choose it to mean—neither more nor less."
>
> "The question is," said Alice, "Whether you *can* make words mean so many different things."
>
> *"The question is,"* said Humpty Dumpty, *"which is to be master—that's all."*

I don't really know that that's the question with words; it seems to me that words work best for me if I take care to employ them more or less in accordance with accepted English usage. With outlines, however, it's important that the writer be the master of the situation.

That, I think, is the chief danger of outlines—that one can

feel bound by them. Remember, the book continues to grow and define itself after the outline has been written, and this process continues during the writing itself. It's important that you feel free to give your imagination its head. If you can think of a more interesting development, a sounder resolution for Chapter Six, or even a wholly different course for the book to take somewhere along the way, you have to be able to chuck the outline and do whatever's best for the book.

Some writers avoid putting their plots down on paper because an outline confines them in this fashion. I lean in this direction myself, and rarely write an outline nowadays unless I'm using it to nail down a contract. Other writers do write out an outline but then put it in a drawer and avoid referring to it during the actual writing of the book.

Robert Ludlum takes this approach. As he explained in an interview published in *Writer's Digest,*

> While working as a producer I learned to break a play down so that I developed a sense of its dimensions, where it was going, what made it work dramatically. Outlining a novel is a way to break down a book in much the same way. It gives me an understanding of the theme, the material, the main characters. I'm able to see the story in terms of beginning and middle and ending. Then, once I have a handle on the story, I don't need the outline any more. The book itself will differ in plot specifics from the outline, but it'll be the same in thrust.

So far we have been talking about an outline strictly as an author's aid—something you write before you write the book itself, for the purpose of making the book stronger and the writing easier. Along the way, however, I've alluded a couple of times to an outline which has another purpose, that of persuading a publisher to offer a contract for a book which has not yet been written.

Writers who have established themselves professionally rarely write a complete book without having made arrangements for its publication somewhere along the line. When one is of sufficient stature, it's not even necessary to have a specific idea for a novel in order to get a publisher's signature on a contract; when one has no track record whatsoever, most publishers would prefer to have a completed manuscript in hand before making any commitment.

I would strongly advise a first novelist to finish at the very least the first draft of his book before making any attempt to sell it. Almost any publisher will look at a neophyte's chapters and outline, but he's unlikely to offer a contract on that basis. Why should he? He has no reason to assume the unproven writer has the capacity to finish the book, to sustain whatever strengths the chapters and outline display. If he is sufficiently attracted by what he sees, he may gamble to the extent of offering far less generous terms than he would for a completed manuscript.

But that's not the main reason why I would recommend writing the whole book first. More often than not, any interruption in the writing of a novel is a mistake. A loss of momentum can sometimes be fatal. If the book's going well, for heaven's sake stay with it. If it's not going well, figure out what's wrong and deal with it; bundling it off to a publisher isn't going to solve your problems. A couple of times, when I had sent chapters and outline to a publisher, I kept right on with the writing of the book while awaiting word on the portion I'd submitted. In some instances that I can recall, I had the book completed before the publisher made up his mind.

When you do reach a point in your career where it's advantageous to submit an outline, the document you will want to produce is a rather different proposition from the sort you write solely for your own benefit. Your object in this submitted outline is to convince another person—the editor or publisher—that you have a sound grasp of the book and will be able to complete a novel which will fulfill the promise of its opening chapters. A successful outline of this sort gives whoever reads it the impression that the book's already there in your mind, fully realized, just waiting for you to tap it out on the typewriter keys.

When it comes to clinching a sale, long, detailed outlines are best. There are two reasons for this, one logical and the other human. The logical one is that the more substance and detail you include in an outline, the more the editor is able to know about what you intend to do in the material to come, and thus the better able he is to judge whether the book you will write will be a book he would want to publish.

The other reason is rather less firmly rooted in logic. Editors are people, too—hard as I occasionally find it to admit this. If they are going to commit their firm to the purchase of a novel in progress, and if they are going to lay substantial cash on the table as an advance to bind the deal, they like to feel they are getting something tangible for their money. A fifty-page outline, comprehensive enough to be what the film industry delights in calling a "treatment," has some heft to it. You don't even have to read it to know there's something there; just weighing it in your hand will get that message across. And, by George, you can tell that the author put in some time writing it. It's infinitely different from a one-page synopsis that he could have batted out in eighteen-and-a-half minutes on a rainy afternoon. Never mind that the one-page synopsis might be as much as he'd need to have a firm grasp on the remainder of the novel—anyone would be more comfortable dealing on the basis of a fifty-page treatment.

Just how long and detailed an "outline-for-submission" must be varies greatly with circumstances. Random House contracted for my third mystery novel about burglar Bernie Rhodenbarr on the basis of a one-page letter to my editor, Barbé Hammer. In the letter I told her the book's basic premise and some of the general avenues I intended to explore. There was nothing in the letter to show that I knew how to resolve the plot complications I intended to develop, and there was considerable vagueness even in the opening premise—I said, for instance, that Bernie was going to be hired to steal a particular collector's item, from one enthusiast for another's benefit, but I didn't say what the gimcrack would be because I admittedly hadn't yet decided.

I got by with this rather cavalier approach because of the particular circumstances that were operating. Barbé knew and liked my work. Random House had already published two books about Bernie and folks there were pleased with them aesthetically and commercially. All I really had to do to get a contract was indicate that I had a sound idea for a book, that it was sufficiently "the same only different" to continue the series, and that I at least was confident of my ability to tie everything up neatly by the end of the book.

In contrast, my outline for my World War II novel ran a dozen or so pages and was as detailed as I could comfortably arrange. In this instance I was offering to write a book of a sort with which I had no real prior experience, and a more substantial outline was necessary not only to convince a publisher that I knew what I was setting out to do but to make *me* similarly confident. Before I began a 500-page monster of a novel, I wanted to assure myself that I wouldn't wind up somewhere around page 374 having painted myself into some plotting corner. In retrospect, I wish I'd written this particular outline two or three or four times as long; had I done so, I might have had an easier time of writing the book.

* * *

To sum up:

An outline is a tool, the equivalent of a painter's preliminary sketches. Use it to whatever extent it is helpful. Don't be a slave to it; if the book begins to grow away from the outline, let the book chart its own course.

Above all, remember there's no one right way to do it. You can sit down with no outline whatsoever and write the whole book from first page to last. Or you can write a one-page synopsis, expand it into a chapter outline, expand *that* into a detailed chapter outline with each scene sketched in, and even expand that outline into a super-treatment with bits of dialogue included and point-of-view changes indicated. Some writers operate this way, blowing up the balloon of their novel one breath at a time, until the writing of the novel's actual first draft is just a matter of doubling the length of the final outline. If that's what works for them, then that's the right way to do it—for them.

Finally, for anyone interested in the best illustration I can recall of what an outline is and how it all works, I would recommend Donald E. Westlake's hilarious novel, *Adios, Scheherazade.* The narrator is a hapless hack who has written a sex novel a month for the past twenty-eight months and who confronts a massive writer's block when he attempts to write Opus Twenty-Nine. At one point he produces an outline for the book, an outline that's very instructive to any apprentice novelist while it finds its way to one of the funniest punchlines I ever read. I can't reproduce it here, but I earnestly commend the book to your attention.

Chapter 7

Using What You Know...
and What You Don't Know

Write about what you know.

That's the conventional wisdom, and it seems as sensible now as it did when I first heard it back around the time when the idea of becoming a writer first occurred to me. Several writers whom I greatly admire—Thomas Wolfe for one, James T. Farrell for another—had written whole series of novels which I recognized as frankly autobiographical. Others wrote books that clearly derived from their own life experience. One dust jacket blurb after another would recount the author's background, and each of those writers seemed to have the sort of job résumé that would strike terror into the heart of a personnel manager. A writer, I quickly learned, was someone who grew up on an Indian reservation before running off with a circus. Then over a period of years he worked as an itinerant fruit picker, a gandy dancer on the railroads, a fry cook in a lumber camp, and a teacher in ghetto schools. He saw combat in an infantry division and spent a few years as a merchant seaman. He wrestled a grizzly bear and made love to an Eskimo woman—or was it the other way around?

Never mind. In any event, it was evident to me that I had

two choices. I could ramble around the world gathering up subject matter for stories and novels or I could probe the depths of my life to date, telling an eager world just what it was like to grow up in Buffalo, New York, in one of those happy families that Tolstoy has assured us are all alike.

I recognized at a very early date that I was not temperamentally equipped to write the conventional autobiographical novel. While I would not argue that my family and childhood contain nothing of the stuff of which novels are wrought, I was neither sufficiently perceptive nor of the right emotional bent to turn that background into fiction, though many writers have done that successfully.

Nor did I seem inclined to stride adventurously into the world, ready to take on whatever grizzly bears and grizzlier women presented themselves. I was in a hell of a hurry—not to amass experience but to get busy with the actual business of writing. As I've recounted, I wound up writing for a living at rather a tender age; I couldn't write out of my own experience because I hadn't had any, for heaven's sake.

One way or another, this is the case with a great many of us. While a few of us actually have the adventures first and then learn how to type, that's not usually the way it goes. In actual practice most real-life adventurers never get around to writing; there's always another grizzly bear in their future, and they're too much inclined to pursue fresh experience to bother with emotion recollected in tranquility, as Wordsworth characterized the origin of poetry. Even when we start out with a background of extensive life experience, adventurous or otherwise, we generally tend to use up our past in our fiction and find ourselves stranded like an overzealous general who has outrun his supply lines. It doesn't take too many books for most of us to exhaust the experiences we've piled up before we started writing. And how are we to gather fresh experience after that point? We've just been sitting in rooms, staring into space and banging away at typewriter keys, and how are we to fashion *that* experience into a novel?

* * *

The difficulty of writing out of one's experience can be vividly demonstrated in the field of genre fiction. In my own bailiwick of crime fiction, for example, I'm at a loss from the standpoint of experience. I have never been a private detective like Joe Gores, a cop like Joseph Wambaugh, or a district attorney like George V. Higgins. Neither have I worked the other side of the street and spent time in the clink like Malcolm Braly and Al Nussbaum—not yet, anyway.

All the same, I find myself using my own background and experience every time I go to work. Just as often, I find myself using what I *don't* know—putting to work a combination of research and fakery to furnish what my own background and experience cannot supply.

Let's take them in turn. How can you put your own presumably ordinary background and experience to work for you? Here are a few ways to make use of what you already know.

Shape your story line to fit your personal knowledge and experience. Let's hearken back for a moment to the gothic novel we examined in outline form in an earlier chapter. Remember the premise? "A young widow is hired to catalogue the antique furniture in a house on the moors in Devon. . . ." Perhaps you might have come up with just that plot after having done some studying of the gothic category. There's only one trouble. You don't know Louis Quinze from Weird Louie the Plumber, you don't know moors from marshmallows, and the closest you've been to Devon is St. Joe, Mo.

It might seem as though the obvious answer is to write about a weird Missouri plumber with a passion for marshmallows, but the resultant manuscript might be tricky to place with an editor of gothics. A less radical solution calls for examining your plot line and seeing how you can adapt it to fit what you've got going for you.

You say you don't know zip about antique furniture? Well,

that's okay, but what *do* you know about? Rare books? Maybe your heroine has been hired to catalogue the ancestral library. Have you got some background in fine art? Maybe she was hired to clean and restore paintings, or to evaluate them or something. Is there some sort of collectible with which you have a fair degree of familiarity? Rare stamps or coins? Old porcelain? Nineteenth-century patent medicine bottles? Roman glass? Oceanic art? A good many plots are almost infinitely adaptable in this fashion, and it doesn't take too much in the way of ingenuity to discover a means of channeling such a story to fit whatever expertise you can furnish.

Use familiar settings for your material. Let's say you haven't wandered far afield from St. Joe, Mo. Or Butte or Buffalo or Bensonhurst. How are you going to write this story about the young widow on the Devonshire moors and make it authentic?

First thing you can do is decide whether or not your story really has to take place in Devon. Maybe there's a lonely house on the outskirts of St. Joseph that could serve as the setting for your story as well as any creaking windswept old manse in the West of England. Maybe there's no such place in reality, but you can build one in your imagination readily enough. Maybe you can readily figure out how people living in such a house, and warped by the strains and stresses built into your basic plot, would relate to and interact with the local people in St. Joseph, much as those moor dwellers in your original outline would relate to the townspeople in Devon. In short, maybe you can transplant all the significant elements of your plot into your own native soil.

If you can manage this, you won't be cheating; on the contrary, you'll simply be making the story that much more your own, one that derives from your own experience and reflects your own perceptions. Perhaps any of a hundred writers could turn out an acceptable book about an imagined Devon moor, but how many could write your story of an old farmhouse on the outskirts of your own town, occupied now by the descendants of the original inhabitants, the farm acreage sold off piece by piece over the years, the house itself surrounded by suburban tract houses, but still awesome and forbidding, and. . . .

See?

On the other hand, maybe there's a reason why your book has to take place in Devon, because of some particular plot component which you regard as intrinsic to the story you want to write. Just as a writer of westerns is locked into setting his books in the old west, you must set this book in Devon.

Fine. As we'll see shortly, there's a great deal you can do by way of research to make your setting authentic. But there's also a way in which you can exploit your own background in order to construct a setting halfway around the world.

You may not know moors from marshmallows, but if you've crossed the Central Plains you may recall the sense of infinite space, the loneliness, the uninterrupted flatness. You may have had a similar feeling in the desert. Or you may have experienced a comparable sense of isolation in terrain that has no similarity whatsoever to the moors—the North Woods, say, or smack in the middle of a milling Times Square crowd, or sealed into your own car on a high-speed freeway. The location itself doesn't matter much. Search into your own bag of past experience, using your past like a Method actor, selecting something that will supply you not with circumstances identical to what you're writing about but with equivalent feelings.

Similarly, you can pick a house you know and plunk it down on the moors. Your research may have told you that you need a beamed Tudor dwelling, and indeed you may so describe the house in your narrative. Once you get past the beams, however, you can fill in with details of that house down the road that all the kids were scared of when you were in grade school.

Explore your background and experience as a source for story ideas. Earlier, when we talked about reading and analysis, we saw how familiarity with a genre trains the mind to come up with plot ideas suitable for that genre. Similarly, the study you do and the perception you have of yourself as a writer should result in your sifting your background for elements that will prove useful in your writing.

Once when I was in high school I came home one afternoon to find that my mother had left the place locked. I went around and crawled in through the milk chute, an accomplishment which looked to be as likely as slipping a camel through the eye of a needle, given the tiny dimensions of the milk chute and the unpleasantly plump dimensions of the embryonic author. I was to repeat this procedure on numerous occasions when the door was unlocked, for the entertainment of friends and relatives, and I can still recall squirming through that hole in the wall and landing upside down in a confusion of mops and brooms and scrub buckets; the milk chute, unused since the war, opened into a cluttered broom closet.

Nowadays I write books about a burglar. (Perhaps the seed was planted all those many years ago, when I first discovered the thrill of illicit entry.) I've written three novels to date about Bernie Rhodenbarr without making use of that milk-chute entrance, but I recalled it a week or so ago, and this time I saw it from the stance of one who writes about burglary. I immediately saw any number of ways such a bit of business could fit into a novel about a burglar, and I let my mind play with the possibilities, and I filed them all away in the cluttered broom closet I call a mind; someday I'll quite probably get some use out of it.

In the same fashion, ongoing experience becomes grist for the mill. I can't seem to enter a building without pondering how Bernie would enter it illegally. When I visit a museum I see not merely objects of artistic and historical significance, but things for him to steal. On a recent trip to London, a visit to the Sir John Soane's Museum in Lincoln's Inn Fields turned up a display of the photograph of a pistol which Soane purchased in the belief that it had belonged to Napoleon. It was actually an utter fake and the whole story about its provenance a pawnbroker's fabrication; however, only the photo was on display because the actual pistol, fake or no, had been stolen from the museum in 1969.

I think I'd like that story even if I wrote nothing but stories about kittens and bunny rabbits for preschoolers. Given the kind of writing I do, I immediately thought of six different ways to work that item into fiction. I may never use it at all, but my writer's eye and my writer's imagination have taken a museum exhibit and turned it into the raw material out of which fiction may someday be fashioned.

Cultivating this habit becomes increasingly important the more time you spend in this business. Consider the paradox of the full-time professional writer: He writes out of his experience, using up his past, and the greater his success the less likely he is to store up useful new experiences. I don't get a hell of a lot of fresh input sitting at a desk with a typewriter for company. And, while I derive enormous essential stimulation from the company of other writers, I don't often get source material from them.

Happily, my inclinations are such that I spend a great deal of time away from my desk. My circle of friends includes people of all sorts, and their conversation puts me in worlds I'd never explore otherwise. Just the other day a policeman friend of mine told three or four stories that will very likely turn up in my work sooner or later; more important, his company sharpens and deepens my sense of what a cop's life is like.

Some years ago a friend told me of an evening his father, then the manager of a Miami Beach hotel, had spent in the company of John D. MacDonald. As a long-time fan of MacDonald, I was very interested in knowing what he was like and what he'd had to say.

"Well, he didn't have much to say at all," my friend reported. "He got my father talking, and evidently he's the world's best listener. By the time the evening was done, my father didn't know too much about John D. MacDonald, but MacDonald sure learned a lot about hotel management and the life history of Seymour Dresner."

And that's how it works. A lot of us enjoy holding court, sitting back and talking expansively about our work. It's hearty fare for the ego, to be sure. But if instead we make a real effort to draw out other people's stories, we'll be using the time to good advantage, providing ourselves in due course with stories of our own.

* * *

The use of conversation just described is another example of the manner in which the writer is always working, even if he doesn't know for certain what he's working on or what he'll ultimately wind up doing with it. Every conversation, every book read, every new place visited, is a part of the endless and all-encompassing business of nonspecific research.

Which in turn leads us—and I hope you're paying attention to the facility with which I'm making these transitions—which leads us, then, to the business of specific research. We've seen a few of the ways to use what we know. How do we cover ourselves when it comes to something we don't know?

Let's go back to our hypothetical gothic novel, our widow's tale of furniture appraisal on the moors of Devon. Having examined some of the ways we could change that story to fit our own areas of knowledge and experience, let's suppose that for one reason or another we've considered them and ruled them out. Because of particular plot elements we like too much to sacrifice, we're locked to the antique furniture business and the Devon location.

The obvious answer is research. Before you start to write,

you have to learn enough about Devon and the antique trade to allow you to feel confident writing about them.

You do not have to become an expert. I'm italicizing this because it's worth stressing. Research is invaluable, but it's important that you keep it in proportion. You are not writing *The Encyclopedia of Antique Furniture.* Neither are you writing *A Traveller's Comprehensive Guide to Devon and Cornwall.* You may well consult both of these books, and any number of others, but you're not going to be tested on their contents.

On the whole, I don't doubt for a moment that too much research is better than too little. Sometimes, though, research becomes a very seductive way to avoid writing.

Ages ago, before I began the first novel I've mentioned earlier, I decided that a historical novel set during the 1916 Easter Rising in Dublin would be a good first book for me to write. I knew nothing about Ireland in general or the Rising in particular, so I read several books on the subject. These made it clear to me that I lacked the necessary background. I decided it was important to begin at the beginning, and I decided further that I couldn't properly grasp Irish history without a thorough knowledge of English history, whereupon I set about amassing an impressive library of books on the subject. You might well ask what a six-volume history of Britain before the Norman Conquest had to do with the purported subject of my novel; I can reply now, in retrospect, that I evidently found reading history a more congenial prospect than writing that novel, and that I found buying books an even more attractive occupation than reading them.

Over the years I did do considerable reading in English and Irish history, for recreational purposes rather than research, and I don't doubt that it enriched my writing in various subtle ways. But I never did write that Irish novel and I doubt I ever shall. I didn't really want to write it in the first place and used research as a way out.

George Washington Hill, the legendary tobacco company

president, used to say that half the money he spent on advertising was a flat-out waste. "The trouble is," he added, "there's no way of telling which half it is."

Research is a lot like that. For the mythical book we've been discussing, you would want to browse extensively in books on antique furniture, nibbling here and there, trying to get a sense of the antique business while deciding what type of furniture to deal with in the novel and picking up here and there some specific facts and labels and bits of jargon to give your writing the flavor of authenticity.

Some general reading along these lines, perhaps coupled with a few visits to antique shops and auction galleries, ought to precede the full-scale plotting of your novel, whether such plotting will involve a formal written outline or not. In this way the perspective of your research will very likely enrich the actual plot of the book. Then, having plotted the book in detail, you can return for the pinpoint research, picking up the specific fact that you now know to be necessary for the book.

This is what I did with *The Burglar Who Liked to Quote Kipling.* In the original proposal for the book, I supplied a vague outline, explaining that Bernie Rhodenbarr, now operating a bookstore as a cover occupation, is engaged to steal an unidentified whatsit from one collector for another. During the idea's gestation period, I decided to make the stolen item a book of some sort, figuring this would go nicely with Bernie's cover as bookstore proprietor.

Because I envisioned the man who hired him as a pukka sahib type, the thought came to me of making the elusive volume one of Rudyard Kipling's. I accordingly availed myself of an armload of rare book catalogues to find out where Kipling stood in the antiquarian book market. I also got hold of a biography of the author and read it.

My research and my vaunted writer's imagination worked hand in hand. I figured out that the particular book in question would be the sole surviving copy of a privately printed edition which Kipling saw fit to destroy; my copy would be one he'd already presented to his great good friend, writer H. Rider Haggard. I plotted the book accordingly, then went back to the research desk to learn more about Kipling now that I knew what I was looking for. I read a collection of his poems. I sifted some anecdotal material.

Then I started writing the book. And, intermittently, I stopped for some specific spot-research when points came up during the writing that required it.

I could have done more research. I could have read everything Rudyard Kipling wrote instead of limiting myself to the poetry collection and the *Just So Stories*. I can't see that it would have hurt the book had I known more, because there's always the possibility I would have stumbled on something that would have enriched my novel.

By the same token, I could have managed to write this book with considerably *less* research than I did. I could have invented an item of rare Kiplingana without taking pains to root it in the facts of his life. It would have been *good enough* with less research, I suspect, but it would not have been as good a book as it is now (whatever its overall merits may be).

How much or how little research any area demands is very definitely a subjective judgment. If the Kipling book played a less central role in the mystery, I'd have been wasting time to delve into the subject so deeply. If it played a greater role—if, say, the whole puzzle hinged on various events in the great man's life—then more extensive research might well have been indicated.

If you substitute antique furniture for Rudyard Kipling in what I've just recounted, you'll see how the same principles would apply in our gothic novel. And if you'll substitute whatever unfamiliar subject matter plays a role in your own novel, you'll be able to see to what extent research is required.

What about geographical research? How much do you have to know about a place in order to set a novel there?

Once again, the amount of research advisable is both subjective and relative. Feasibility is a consideration here. I spent an afternoon in Forest Hills Gardens walking around the neighborhood where Bernie was to steal *The Deliverance of Fort Bucklow,* but Forest Hills Gardens is only a fifty-cent subway ride from my door. If I were writing that gothic novel we've been talking about—and I'm beginning to feel as though I am—I could hardly afford to go winging off to Devon for the sake of local color.

On the other hand, if I felt this gothic had enough going for it so that it might transcend its genre and be a candidate for "bestsellerdom," then it might indeed be worth a trip to Devon to give it that added dimension. But if my plot's nothing more than a good honest sow's ear, in no way transmutable into silk-purse status, I don't want to spend as much on research as I can legitimately expect to earn on the finished book.

When I wrote the Tanner books, my hero commonly visited eight or ten countries in a single novel, zipping sleeplessly if not tirelessly all over the globe. Equipped with a decent atlas and a library of travel guides, it's not all that difficult to do an acceptable job of faking a location. A few details and deft touches in the right places can do more to make your book *appear* authentic then you might manage via months of expensive and painstaking on-the-spot research.

I don't want to suggest that such research would be detrimental to a book, just that it's often too costly in time and money to be undertaken. It's worth noting, too, that in certain instances a smattering of ignorance can be useful. In the Tanner books, I'm quite sure my Balkan settings bore little relationship to reality. Then again, I'm equally certain the overwhelming majority of my readers weren't aware of the discrepancy between my version of Yugoslavia and the real one. I was free to make Yugoslavia as I wished it to be for the purpose of the story I wanted to tell, as if I were a science-fiction writer shaping an uncharted planet to my fictive purpose.

I don't know how comfortable I'd be working this way now; I've become a more meticulous writer, sacrificing brash self-confidence in the process. I know, too, that the cavalier attitude I showed would have been a mistake if I had been writing for a market composed of readers who knew Yugoslavia firsthand. One thing a reader will not abide is glaring evidence that the writer doesn't know what he's talking about.

The work of James Hadley Chase is a good example of this. Chase writes hard-boiled suspense novels set in the United States, and while he may have visited here briefly he certainly never spent substantial time on these shores. His American locations never ring true and his American slang is wildly off the mark, the American equivalent of having a dutchess drop her "aitches" like a Cockney costermonger. Because of this, his novels have never sold terribly well in the U.S. and most of them are not published over here.

But this doesn't hurt him in England. Some of his readers may realize that the United States of James Hadley Chase bears about as much resemblance to reality as the Africa of Edgar Rice Burroughs, but the false notes don't constantly hit them between the eyes—and they're reading the books for action and suspense, not for their travelogue value. So Chase continues to sell very well over there, year in and year out.

Is Chase a poorer writer because the United States of his fiction differs so greatly from the real United States? I don't think so. It's worth remembering, I think, that fakery is the very heart and soul of fiction. Unless your writing is pure autobiography in the guise of a novel, you will continually find yourself practicing the dark arts of the illusionist and the trade of the counterfeiter. All our stories are nothing but a pack of lies. Research is one of the tools we use to veil this deception from our readers, but this is not to say that the purpose of research is to make our stories real. It's to make them *look* real, and there's a big difference.

Sometimes a few little details will turn the trick, doing far more to provide the illusion of reality than a mind-numbing assortment of empty facts and figures. Sometimes a phony detail works as well as a real one. Bernie Rhodenbarr talks admiringly of the Rabson lock, making me sound quite the expert; there is no Rabson lock—I borrowed the name from Rex Stout's novels. Archie Goodwin always has things to say about the Rabson lock.

Sometimes these little "authentic touches" can happen quite by accident. When I read galleys of *Two For Tanner,* I was startled when a CIA agent in Bangkok pointed out "drops and meeting places and fronts—a travel agency, a tobbo shop, a cocktail lounge, a restaurant. . . ."

A tobbo shop?

What on earth was a tobbo shop?

I checked my manuscript. I'd written "a tobacco shop" and a creative linotypist had vastly improved on it. I decided a tobbo shop would be the perfect CIA front, adding a cracker-jack bit of local color.

So I left it like that.

And now I look forward to the day when I spot in someone else's fiction a reference to the notorious tobbo shops of Thailand. And who's to say that the day will never come when some enterprising Thai opens a tobbo shop of his own? Stranger things have happened.

* * *

A very important part of research consists of making use of acquaintances and friends. You'll learn more about what it's like to be a sandhog or a scrap dealer or a bond salesman by hanging out with one than by reading books on the subject. Friends with an expert's knowledge of an area can frequently help you work out bits of plot business; if you present them with a problem, they may be able to think of a solution which would never occur to you.

I've found people even more useful after the book is written. They can read the manuscript and may spot the sort of howlers that, once in print, will draw you no end of angry letters from outraged readers. I don't know much about guns, for instance, and I doubt I ever will; the subject is of limited fascination to me. But I've learned to check points occasionally with a friend of mine who's a gun enthusiast; otherwise the mailman gets tired of bringing me letters from indignant gun nuts.

I wouldn't worry too much over imposing upon acquaintances in this fashion. People like to help writers in their own areas of expertise. I suppose it's ego food. Then too, it gives them a brief role in the writing world, a world which appears to those outside of it to be somehow touched with glamour and romance. I don't know what they think is glamourous about it, but I do know that an astonishing percentage of people go out of their way to help writers, and it makes sense to take advantage of this help when you can use it.

Chapter 8

Getting Started

Every novel has a beginning, a middle, and an ending.

I picked up this nugget of information when I first studied writing in college, and I've heard it restated no end of times since then. I pass it on to you because I've never been able to challenge the essential truth of the statement.

I've been trying to think of one solitary instance over the past twenty years when it's helped me to know that a novel has a beginning, a middle and an ending. And I can't come up with a one. I learned at about the same time that in 1938 the state of Wyoming produced one-third of a pound of dry edible beans for every man, woman and child in the nation, and that fact too has lingered in my mind for all these many years, and it hasn't done me a whole hell of a lot of good either. But I pass it on, too, for whatever it's worth.

A beginning, a middle and an ending?

Let's start with the beginning.

* * *

Openings are important. In a more leisurely world—a couple of centuries ago, say—the novelist had things pretty much to himself. There was no competition from radio and television, nor were there very many other novelists around. The form was new. Furthermore, life as a whole moved at a gentler pace. There were no cars, let alone moon rockets. One took one's time, and one expected others to take their time—in life or in print.

Accordingly, a novel could move off sedately from a standing start. A long first chapter might be given over to a thoroughgoing summary of events which we are told took place *before* our story gets underway. It is not uncommon to encounter a Georgian or Victorian novel in which the first chapter constitutes little more than an extended family tree; the story's protagonist doesn't even land in the cradle until Chapter Two.

Things are different now. Novels, crowded together like subway riders at rush hour, stand on tiptoe shouting "Read me! Read me!" They compete with each other and with the myriad other leisure-time activities clamoring for public favor. The reader, however prepared he may be for a long leisurely perusal, is not of a mind to spend a first chapter pruning a family tree. He expects a book to catch his interest right away; if it doesn't, it's the easiest thing in the world for him to reach for another.

"The first chapter sells the book," Mickey Spillane says. "And the last chapter sells the next book."

Spillane, I'm told, also claims to write a book's final chapter first. His entire book is geared to build up to the impact of the finale, he theorizes, so he can best achieve a powerful climax by writing that last scene first, then writing the rest of the book as prelude. I can see the logic in this, but we'll go with the premise for now that you're going to write your book more or less in order, beginning with page one. If nothing else, it makes numbering the pages ever so much simpler.

To return to the point, the first chapter does indeed sell the book. If it is to do so successfully, the reader must be caught up in the story as quickly as possible. Things must be going on in which he can become immediately involved. If you can open with action, physical or otherwise, so much the better.

Beginners frequently have trouble managing this. I know I did. My first chapters tended to introduce characters. I would have them arriving in town, or moving into a new apartment, or otherwise embarking on a new chapter in their lives even as I embarked upon the first chapter of a new book. They would meet people and have exploratory conversations. What kind of a way is that to grab the reader's attention in a grip of steel?

There's a trick I'm going to share with you. I learned it almost twenty years ago and I've never forgotten it, and it's yours for $10.95. If I were you and that were all I got for the price of this book, I don't think I'd have cause to complain. So pay attention.

Don't begin at the beginning.

Let me tell you how I first came to hear those five precious words. I had written a mystery novel, the second to be published under my own name; Gold Medal issued it under the eminently forgettable title of *Death Pulls a Doublecross*. The book was a reasonably straightforward detective story in the Chandler-Macdonald mode featuring one Ed London, an amiable private eye who drank a lot of brandy and smoked a pipe incessantly and otherwise had no distinguishing traits. I don't recall that he was hit on the head during the book, nor did he fall down a flight of stairs. Those were the only two clichés I managed to avoid.

My original version of the book opened with London being visited by his rat of a brother-in-law, whose mistress has recently been slain in such a way as to leave the brother-in-law holding the bag, or the baby, or the bathwater, or whatever. In the second chapter London wraps the young lady's remains in an oriental rug, takes her to Central Park, unrolls the rug and leaves her to heaven. Then he sets about solving the case.

I showed the book to Henry Morrison, who was then my agent. He read it all the way through without gagging, then called me to discuss it.

"Switch your first two chapters around," he said.

"Huh?" I said.

"Put your second chapter first," he said patiently. "And put your first chapter second. You'll have to run them through the typewriter so the transitions work smoothly but the rewriting should be minimal. The idea is to start in the middle of the action, with London carting the corpse around, and then go back and explain what he's doing and just what he's got in mind."

"Oh," I said. And glanced up quickly to see if a lightbulb had taken form above my head. I guess it only happens that way in comic strips.

Now this change, which was a cinch to make, didn't turn *Death Pulls a Doublecross* into an Edgar candidate. All the perfumes of Arabia wouldn't have turned the trick. But it did improve the book immeasurably. By beginning with Chapter Two, I opened the book with the action in progress. There was movement. Something was happening. The reader had no idea who Ed London was or why this young lady was wrapped in her Bokhara like cheese in a blintz, but he had plenty of time later to dope out the whys and wherefores. After he'd been hooked by the action.

(The reader may have further wondered where Ed London got the muscles to manhandle a rug with a corpse rolled in it; oriental rugs are pretty heavy, even without bodies in them. This whole question never occurred to me until years later.)

Ever since Death pulled that doublecross, I've used this opening gambit more often than not. All seven Tanner books employed this device. In some of them I wrote a single chapter before doubling back to explain the book's premise, while in others I let the story line run on for two or three chapters before flashing back and explaining who these people were and what they were doing and why. In the Tanner books, a secondary purpose was served by this technique. The opening chapter or chapters generally left Tanner up against the wall—suspended in a bamboo cage in northern Thailand in *Two For Tanner,* and informed that he's to be executed at sunrise; on a train in Czechoslovakia in *The Canceled Czech,* with a cop asking him for his papers; and literally buried alive in Modonoland in *Me Tanner, You Jane.* This tension was maintained and even heightened by forcing the reader to pause for a flashback; the effect was that of a cliffhanger in an old-fashioned serial.

This business of beginning after the beginning is a natural for novels of suspense and adventure and action. But it works as well in the sort of novel in which characters do not get tossed off Czech trains or buried alive or shot at sunrise. If your story is one of a young man's loss of innocence in the big city, you don't have to begin with him arriving in town. You can choose instead to open with a scene involving him and a girl he's taken up with some weeks after his arrival. They're at a party, or in bed, or having a fight, or whatever—you're writing this, not me. Then in the next chapter you can fill in whatever background has to be filled in. The point, remember, is to involve the reader, to make him care what happens next. You do this by showing your characters in action, in conflict, in motion, not sitting on a park bench musing about the meaning of life.

Innumerable examples of mainstream fiction of the highest order are structured along these lines. They open with a scene designed to get things off to a good start. Indeed, I've read a slew of novels in which the first chapter poses a crisis, the ensuing thirty chapters recount the hero's entire life up to the moment of that crisis, and the final chapter resolves it. Jerome Weidman's *The Enemy Camp* is a vivid example of this approach. By and large this strikes me as too much of a good thing; if the problem is such that it can be stated and resolved in two chapters, why must we wade through a hundred thousand words of background between the statement and the resolution?

Is it always a mistake to begin at the beginning?

Of course not. Always is a word we're trying to stay away from, remember? There are very few absolutes in this business of novel writing, and the First-Things-Second Principle is definitely not one of them. It's extremely useful, and it's always worth considering, but there are times when the best way to start a novel is the most natural way—i.e., at the beginning.

Here are some examples from my own work:

Deadly Honeymoon features a newlywed couple. On their wedding night thugs kill a man at a nearby lakeside cabin. Almost as an afterthought, the bad guys beat up the husband and rape the bride. Our leads do not report this to the cops but hunt down the villains themselves. Here I felt the rape scene was of paramount importance, supplying the motive for everything that follows and making the vigilante activity acceptable and even laudable. Furthermore, there's more action and involvement in that rape scene than in the rather plodding chapters which follow, in which Dave and Jill set about the nuts-and-bolts work of tracking the killers. To open with them making phone calls and checking city directories and then flash back to the rape scene would be spectacularly senseless.

Such Men Are Dangerous—written under the pen name of Paul Kavanagh—concerns a burnt-out ex-Green Beret on the verge of a breakdown who hies himself off to an island in the Florida Keys and lives a hermit's existence. Then a CIA type drops in and involves him in a caper. This would have been a natural for the First-Things-Second approach, but I was more interested in establishing the lead's character at the beginning since I saw that as the most important single element in the book. Moreover, I wanted to show the character going through the process of personality disintegration before he found his way to the Keys, then show the contrast achieved through some months of solitude and self-sufficiency.

The Sins of the Fathers, the first of three books about Matthew Scudder, begins with his being hired by the father of a murder victim. The action which follows is gradual and I felt the book would build more effectively if events were dealt with in chronological order. The two succeeding Scudder books, however, open First-Things-Second.

* * *

There are two schools of thought about the opening of a novel. One holds that the important thing is to get it written, the other that the important thing is to get it right. Both of them are quite valid, of course; the distinction is one of emphasis, and it will vary with the writer and with the particular novel.

In my own case, a book is never entirely real for me until I begin putting words on paper. The words of an outline or treatment somehow don't count. I have to be doing the actual writing, pulling finished pages of prose and dialogue from my typewriter. The pages may not be finished in any true sense; I may throw them out, or rewrite them any number of times, before the book is in final form. But they have the look of finished pages, and when they begin to accumulate to the left of my machine, I know I'm really engaged in the curious process of writing a book.

Because of this, I probably start some books prematurely, before they're as well thought out as they might be. My first drafts of my first several chapters are frequently a part of this thinking-out process. It's in the course of writing them that I find out a lot of essential information about my characters and the plot in which they're caught up.

This happened in *The Burglar Who Liked to Quote Kipling.*

Having already written two books about Bernie Rhodenbarr, I probably didn't have to type out fifty pages of first draft in order to make his acquaintance. Nor was I running blind as far as plot was concerned; I already had a pretty clear view of the plot for at least the first hundred pages when I sat down to write page one.

Even so, fifty pages in I decided I didn't like what I'd done. The pace felt wrong to me. There were some characters I wanted to drop, some scenes I wanted to compress. There was a relationship between Bernie and his sidekick Carolyn Kaiser which I knew more about for having written the fifty pages; as a result I wanted to do them over so I could redefine it in the early pages. There were some things I knew about the plot that I hadn't known when I started, and I wanted to lay the groundwork for them in my opening.

On the other hand, I wrote a book called *After The First Death* knowing a great deal about the opening and not too much about what would happen later on. The premise is simple enough: a man has spent time in prison for killing a prostitute during an alcoholic blackout. He wins his release via one of those landmark decisions of the early sixties—Miranda, Escobedo, Gideon, one of those cases. The book opens First-Things-Second style, with Alex waking slowly, coming out of blackout in a Times Square hotel room, seeing a dead woman on the floor in a pool of blood and rocked with the thought that he'd done it again. In the second chapter he decides not to turn himself in, as he did the first time, but becomes a fugitive from justice. Then we're at last told who he is and what it is that he seems to have done again, and then, the flashback completed, he searches his memory and gets a tiny flash of the moment just before he went into blackout, enough of a flash to convince him that he didn't kill the hooker after all and that he has to find out who did. The rest of the book concerns his attempts to do so.

I didn't know who the killer was when I started the book. I

didn't even have a clue who the various suspects would be. All I really knew was how I wanted the book to open. That scene was vivid in my mind, and during the writing of it I got enough of an idea who the lead was to write the second chapter. After that point I largely plotted the book as I went along. For all of that, I never did have to rewrite the first two chapters. They were sufficiently well realized to hold up fine despite the fact that I wrote them without knowing what would follow them.

By and large, though, first chapters are more apt to need rewriting than subsequent chapters, at least in my own novels. When this proves to be the case, I have the choice of rewriting my opening immediately or pushing on with the book and redoing the opening after I've completed the first draft.

Again, the decision is individual and arbitrary. Do you get it written first or do you first get it right? I've come to the conclusion that I'm more comfortable with a book if I rewrite this sort of thing as I go along; otherwise my concentration on Chapter Fifteen, say, is diffused by the nagging awareness that Chapters One through Three have to make another trip through the typewriter. We'll discuss this general dilemma again in a chapter on revision, but it seems worth a brief mention here because beginning sections are so often apt to be out of synch with the rest of the book.

Knowing that an opening may very well need to be rewritten can make you sloppy. For this reason, I always proceed on the premise that what I'm writing is what will one day be set in type, word for imperishable word.

But that's just my approach. For another writer, that sort of sloppiness might be worth encouraging; he might be infinitely less inhibited typing an unabashedly rudimentary first draft on yellow second sheets than if he felt his words were being carved on stone tablets.

The important thing, as I've said before, is neither to get it written nor to get it right. The important thing is to do what works.

Chapter 9

Getting It Written

Writing a novel is hard work.

Now writing anything well is work, whether it's an epic trilogy or the last line of a limerick for a deodorant contest. But when it comes to the novel you have to work long and hard even to produce a bad one. This may help explain why there are so many more bad amateur poets around than there are bad amateur novelists. Writing a good poem may be as difficult as writing a good novel. It may even be harder. But any clown with a sharp pencil can write out a dozen lines of verse and call them a poem. Not just any clown can fill 200 pages with prose and call it a novel. Only the more determined clowns can get the job done.

"I could never be a writer," countless acquaintances have told me, "because I just don't have the necessary self-discipline. I'd keep finding other things to do. I'd never get around to working on the book. I wouldn't get anything accomplished."

Let's not kid ourselves. It does take self-discipline. On the dullest day imaginable, I can always find something to do besides writing. I have innumerable choices. I can read, I can watch television, I can pick up the phone and call somebody, I can hit the refrigerator—or I can decide instead to sit at a typewriter, pick words out of the air, put them in order, and spread them on the page.

Unless I can consistently choose to work, I'm not going to get books written.

* * *

Self-discipline takes a variety of forms. In this regard we might consider two of the most prolific novelists the world has ever known, Georges Simenon and John Creasey. Each wrote several hundred books, and each achieved considerable prominence in the field of crime fiction.

John Creasey wrote every day. He worked seven days a week, fifty-two weeks a year, producing approximately 2,000 words each morning before breakfast. His routine never varied; at home or abroad, tired or bursting with energy, he got up, brushed his teeth, and started writing. He admitted his behavior was compulsive, explaining that he couldn't relax and enjoy the rest of the day unless he'd first tended to his writing chores. If you write 2,000 words a day, you are going to turn out close to a dozen books a year, and Creasey did just that for most of his lifetime.

Georges Simenon's approach was altogether different. You may have seen a television documentary on his writing habits; it has had considerable exposure over the educational channels. Typically, he would pack a bag and a typewriter and travel to one European city or another where he would check into a hotel. There he would work in the most intense manner imaginable, immersing himself utterly in his work, avoiding human contact for the duration, and producing a finished manuscript in ten or twelve days. The book finished, he would return home and resume his everyday life, letting the plot gradually develop for his next novel, and ultimately heading off to another city and repeating the process once again.

My own writing methods have changed constantly over the past twenty years, forever shaping themselves to fit my state of mind, time of life, and various special circumstances. In the early years, the Simenon approach had a tremendous appeal for me. I can still see something to be said for the idea of completing a book in as short a total span of time as possible; that way one remains very much in the book during the term of its production, and one's involvement can be very intense indeed.

I have on occasion written books in as little as three days; I've written a couple that took only seven or eight days that are probably as good as anything I've done. I can't argue that I made a mistake writing those books as rapidly as I did. Nor am I at all inclined to attempt to do that sort of thing now.

Nowadays I try to write not twenty or thirty pages in a day's time but five or six or seven. Age may very well be a factor, but I rather doubt that it's the only one, or even the major one. It's at least as significant, I think, that I've become a more careful writer and a more flexible one. When I was a brash and cocky young scribbler I was blessed with a very useful sort of tunnel vision; i.e., I could just see one way to do something in a book, and so I lowered my head and charged right in and did it. Now my vision has widened. I'm apt to be more aware of possibilities, of the multiplicity of options available to me as a writer. I'm able to see any number of ways to structure a scene. A slower pace helps me choose among them, selecting the one I'm most comfortable with.

Years ago I was apt to work late at night, and that's something else I don't do any more. I'm sure part of the appeal of the midnight oil lay in the image that went with it—the lonely toiler, fortifying himself with endless cups of coffee, smoking endless cigarettes, and fighting the good fight while the rest of the world slept. There was also a practical element involved; with the rest of my family (like the rest of the world) asleep, I could work without interruption, a consummation devoutly to be wished if ever there was one.

Then too, at that stage in my life I appeared to be more of a night person. I felt the wise thing to do with mornings was to sleep through them, and that a sunrise was a marvelous thing to look at immediately before going to bed.

Ah, well, The only constant is change, and now I almost always make work the thing I do at the beginning of the day, not the end. My work is done most frequently in the morning, immediately after breakfast. When I try to work considerably later in the day, I find my mind's not up to it. I'm fresher first thing in the morning, when I've had six or eight hours of sleep to clear the garbage out of my head.

A majority of professional writers seem to have found this to be true. Quite a few report that they used to work in the evening, or late at night, but that they gradually found themselves becoming morning writers. Others work at night still, and find it's the only time they can work. Others work any old time, whenever they can get it together.

There's no magic answer, and there are certainly more exceptions than there are rules, so I would not dream of advocating that anyone abandon a system that seems to be working just fine. However, for someone trying to decide at what point of the day to schedule writing time, I would very strongly recommend working first thing in the morning, especially for those writers with nonwriting jobs. It's easier to write, and to write well, after a night's sleep than after a hard day's work. It's also a sounder policy to write after morning coffee than after the post-ratrace martini.

*   *   *

More important than what hours you spend at the typewriter are how often you choose to spend them. If there's one thing I'm convinced of, on the basis of my own experience and the experience of others, it is the desirability of steady production. There are exceptions—there are always exceptions—but as a rule the people who make a success of novel writing work regularly and consistently. They may take time off between books, or between drafts of a book, but when they're working they damn well work—five or six or even seven days a week until it's done.

There are two reasons why this is important. Obviously, the more steadily you work the sooner you'll be done with this monumental task. If you write two pages a day, a two hundred-page book is going to take you one hundred days. If you write every day, you'll complete that book in a little over three months. If you only average three writing days a week, the same book will take the better part of a year.

More important, I believe, is that steady day-in-day-out work on a book keeps you *in* the book from start to finish, and keeps the book very much in your mind during those hours you're at the typewriter and during those hours you're doing something else—playing, reading, sleeping. You and the book become part of one another for the duration. Your unconscious mind can bring its resources to bear upon plot problems as they present themselves. You don't have to stop at the beginning of the day's work to read over what you've already written and try to remember what you had in mind when you left off last week.

"A novelist," Herbert Gold says, "has to think/dream his story every day. Poets and story writers can go for the inspired midnight with quill dipped in ink-filled skull." And Joseph Hansen adds, "I have made a number of young novelists angry by saying that writing is something you do when you get up in the morning, like eating breakfast or brushing your teeth. And it is. Or it had better be."

* * *

After you've determined when to write and how often to write, there's something else you have to work out. That's how much you'll write each day, or how many hours you'll spend doing it.

Some writers put in a certain number of hours each working day. I've never worked that way, and research leads me to believe that most pros pace themselves more by the amount they produce than the time it takes to produce it.

I'm certainly more comfortable making a contract with myself to produce five pages of copy, than to spend three hours at the typewriter. For one thing, the amount of time I spend working doesn't seem particularly relevant. Nobody's paying me by the hour, and nobody's checking to see if I punched the old time clock at the appointed hour. The idea of spending a set number of hours working may help to allay one's conscience, but I don't think it has much to do with the business of writing.

Some days the writing flows and I can do my five pages in one glorious hour. When that happens, I'm free to do as I wish with the rest of the day. I've learned to stop writing then and there, because my mind's tired after five pages, whether it took me one hour or three hours to get them written.

Other days, the writing pours like January molasses. Maybe I'll take five hours to do as many usable pages. Those days aren't much fun, but I've learned to keep at it for as long as it takes, because for all the agony of their composition, those pages are apt to read just as smoothly as the ones that came with no effort. If I threw in the sponge after three hours, those pages wouldn't get written.

I had much the same system at the beginning of my career, when I wrote soft-core sex novels in two weeks' time, five days on, a weekend off, then five days to finish the book. Then I wrote twenty pages a day where now I write five, but the basic principle was the same.

The number of pages you shoot for is for you to decide. My pace changes depending on the book I'm writing. Some novels seem to demand a more intense level of concentration, and a smaller number of pages will tire me. Others, for whatever reason, move at a faster natural pace.

You may find that one page a day is as much as you can easily manage. That's fine. Work six days a week and you'll produce a book in a year. You may find that it's no strain for you to turn out ten or twenty or thirty pages at a stretch. That's fine, too—enjoy yourself. My questionnaire responses suggest that a preponderance of pros do four or five pages a day, but that doesn't mean you'll be less than professional by shooting for a higher or lower number. They settled on that figure because they found out it seemed to be right for them, just as you'll find out what's the right pace for your own novel.

One thing you might try to avoid, in this connection, is attempting to extend your productivity. This sort of overload principle works fine in weightlifting, where one's ability to manage more weight increases as one lifts more weight, but it doesn't work that way in writing. It's tempting to try to do a little more each day than we did the day before, and I still find myself intermittently struggling to resist this particular temptation, even after lo these many years. If I can do five pages today, why can't I do six tomorrow? And seven the day after? For that matter, if I really catch fire and do seven today, that proves I can definitely do a minimum of seven tomorrow. Doesn't it?

No, it doesn't.

What does happen, in point of fact, is that this sort of overload generally leads to exhaustion. Then I can rationalize taking a couple days off—after all, I'm ahead of schedule, aren't I?—and the next thing I know I'm not producing consistently at all. I'm writing in fits and starts, stealing days off and then trying to make up for them by doubling up on my work. The book suffers, the manuscript takes longer than it would have taken otherwise, and once again the tortoise nips the hare at the finish line.

The motto is "Easy does it." Find your right pace, make sure it's one that's not going to be a strain, and then stick with it. If you do have a day when you write an extra page or two, don't waste time thinking about it. Regard it as a freak occurrence, nothing to be deplored but nothing you should make an effort to repeat. When the next day dawns, resume your regular pace and go on writing the book one day at a time.

* * *

For years I proofread my manuscripts after they were finished. I hated doing this. When I wrote "The End" in the middle of the last page I felt like a marathon runner crossing the finish line. I wanted to lie down, not jog back over the route and see if I'd dropped my keys somewhere along the way.

As a result, I tended to give my scripts a rather slipshod proofing. That wasn't disastrous—I tend to turn out a reasonably clean script anyway—but after a number of years I found a way to avoid being confronted with that unpleasant postwriting chore, and it paid unanticipated dividends. So I'll share it with you.

I proofread the book as I go along. Not a page at a time, certainly, but either a chapter at a time or a day's work at a time. I perform this little chore either at the end of the day's work or before beginning work the following day.

The effect of this ongoing proofreading is threefold. First, it keeps me very much in the book, especially if I do the job immediately before beginning the next day's work. In the course of proofreading, I'm picking up where I left off and getting my mind set for resuming the narrative.

Second, I do a much more thorough job of proofing when I have a molehill to deal with instead of a mountain. I'm able to take the time to notice changes I want to make. I can spot stylistic irregularities and change them then and there.

Third, I'm more comfortable with what I've done because those pages stacked to the left of my typewriter are in more finished form. True, I may wind up rewriting the whole damned thing—but that's immaterial at this stage. As far as I'm concerned while I'm writing, those neatly stacked pages are what the linotype operator is going to set type from.

Another stray word about proofreading, while we're on the subject. While I'm writing, I tend to xxxxxx out mistyped words and failed phrases. I obliterate these xxxxxx'd out passages with a thick marking pen when I proofread. To expedite matters, I go through the pages once just dealing with the xxxxxx'd out portions; then I can concentrate more deliberately on the actual text when I go through it a second time with a fine-tipped pen.

* * *

Seems to me you're making a pretty broad assumption. You seem to take it for granted that all I have to do is put my body in front of my typewriter and everything will follow. What about the days when my mind's a blank?

There are a couple of ways to answer that question. For openers, I'd have to say that the most important step I can take to assure that I'll get work done today is to plant my behind in my desk chair and face the typewriter. While it may not be absolutely true that if you bring the body the mind will follow, the reverse is indisputable; if I don't show up for work I'm not going to get work done. Period.

When in spite of this my mind doesn't seem to be doing its job, it usually means one of two things. Either I'm paralyzed by an inability to figure out What Happens Next, or my mental attitude is keeping my fingers off the keys, making me dissatisfied with my sentences even as I try to form them in my mind.

The first problem, being unable to decide What Happens Next, is one that turns out to be projection a good nine-tenths of the time. Most frequently I know what's going to happen in the five pages I intend to write today; I'm paralyzed because I'm worrying about what's going to happen tomorrow, or the day after, or sometime in early April.

That way lies madness. The better I'm able to focus only on what I'm going to write today, the better equipped I find myself to do a good job with today's writing.

And tomorrow generally takes care of itself. Understand, I'm not denigrating the value of true and proper planning. That's why outlining can be so useful, whether your outline is formal or unwritten. And planning continues to be useful on a day by day basis. I often find myself looking up from a magazine of an evening and letting my mind ruminate upon some plot problem a few days in the book's future.

But when I'm writing, I do best if I concern myself only with that day's writing. Because that's all I'm in a position to deal with at the time. I can no more write tomorrow's pages today than I can breathe tomorrow's air today. The fact that I don't know what I'm going to write tomorrow doesn't matter much today. I don't have to know until tomorrow. And, when tomorrow comes, I'll probably have the answer when I need it. It'll grow out of what I manage to write today and whatever processes my unconscious mind sets in motion between now and then.

Sometimes, however, I know what's going to happen next, both today and tomorrow. What stops me in my tracks is that the words just don't seem to come out right. Nothing seems to work and I begin to have dark suspicions of organic brain damage.

That brings us to our second problem: There are days when all you can do is go to the movies. But there aren't really very many days like that. What I've learned to do on those headful-of-cotton-candy mornings is to sit down and write my daily quota of pages anyway.

I make a bargain with myself. I give myself full permission to decide after the fact that the five pages read as though they were typed by an orangutan. If I hate them the following morning, I can throw them out with a clear conscience. But in the meantime I'm going to sit down and get them written, for better or for worse.

You'd be surprised how often I wind up with five pages of perfectly acceptable copy this way. I may yank a lot of sheets out of the typewriter en route, crumpling them up, hurling them at the wastebasket, and shattering the air with colorful imprecations. But I generally get five pages written that prove to be, if not divinely inspired, nevertheless as good as my prose is apt to get. And, on those genuinely rare occasions when I throw out the five pages on the morning after, I've nonetheless gained from the ordeal; the struggle will have jarred something loose, and I can approach with a clear vision the task that had been so impossibly muddled the day before.

Here's where it's so important that your daily quota is not too great a burden. For my part, I can always manage to squeeze five pages out of my typewriter. It's a manageable burden. If I set my goals higher, I might have no trouble fulfilling them on good days, but on bad ones I'd be awed by having to produce ten or twelve pages. So I'd do none at all, and instead of making progress I'd sacrifice momentum.

Now and then a book grinds to a halt not because of projection or muddleheadedness but because something has Gone Wrong. We'll deal with that in the next chapter.

Chapter 10

Snags, Dead Ends and False Trails

Sometimes a book just plain runs into a wall. It moves merrily along, lulling you into a false sense of security—is there any other kind?—and then a wheel comes off and there you are, knowing only that it's your fault and that there ought to be something you can do about it.

If I had a magic answer, I would not be writing this book. Not because I'd be unwilling to share such divinely-inspired insight with you. Nothing would give me more pleasure. But I'd be too busy finishing up the dozen or more books of mine that ran into walls over the years, and that have languished unfinished in drawers and cardboard boxes ever since.

I'm not talking about those false starts where I knocked out one or two chapters of a book, then gave it up as a bad job. Those were just ideas I ran up the flagpole; when nobody saluted I hauled 'em down without a second thought. No, I'm talking about books that I stayed with for fifty or a hundred or a hundred fifty pages before something went curiously wrong, with them or with their author, and nothing more ever happened with them.

In some instances, this has happened to me because of my propensity for writing books without having a terribly clear idea where I'm going. I'm sure that if I always worked from a reasonably detailed outline I would run into dead ends far less frequently. On the other hand, my willingness to take a well-realized opening sequence and follow it to see where it leads has enabled me to write several of my most successful novels. If a trunkful of false starts is part of the price I've had to pay along the way, I can't argue that it hasn't been worth it.

All the same, it's never fun investing substantial time and effort, not to mention mental and emotional involvement, in a never-to-be-finished book. Schubert's "Unfinished Symphony" is part of every symphony orchestra's repertoire, and *The Mystery of Edwin Drood* has remained in print since Dickens left it unfinished at his death, but this doesn't mean any of my stillborn literary offspring will ever get anywhere. While regretting them is a waste of time, I'd certainly like to have as few of those abortive efforts as possible in my future.

One thing I've come to recognize is that I tend to run into a wall at a certain point in almost all of my books. I've been given to understand that marathon runners experience this sort of exhaustion somewhere around the twenty-mile mark when their glycogen stores run out. They keep going anyway and generally finish the race on their feet.

Most of my suspense novels run a shade over two hundred pages in manuscript, which probably comes to something like sixty thousand words. More often than not, these books hit the wall somewhere around page 120. It's around that point that I find myself losing confidence in the book—or, more precisely, in my ability to make it work. The plot seems to be either too simple and straightforward to hold the reader's interest or too complicated to be neatly resolved. I find myself worrying that there's not enough action, that the lead's situation is not sufficiently desperate, that the book has been struck boring while my attention was directed elsewhere.

I have come to realize that this conviction is largely illusory. I don't know what causes this misperception of mine, but I would suspect it reflects attitudes of my own that have nothing much to do with the book. In any event, I know from experience that there's very likely nothing wrong with the book, and that if I push on and get over the hump I'll probably have a relatively easy time with the final third of the manuscript, and that the book itself will be fine.

If I put it aside, however, and wait for something wonderful to happen, I'll very likely never get back to it.

It may not work this way for everyone, but I've learned to my cost that it works this way for me. The temptation to take a break from a novel when it runs out of gas is overwhelming. It seems so logical that such a break will have a favorable effect; phrases like "recharging one's batteries" come readily to mind. The wish, I'm afraid, is father to the thought; struggling with a difficult book is unpleasant, and one very naturally wishes to be doing something else—anything else!—instead. But such a move is generally undertaken at the cost of completing the book.

I hardly ever go back to the books I abandon. Maybe that's as well, maybe they're better off rusting out on the side of the road, but I don't think so. It seems to me that some of the ones I let go of had just run into that wall around page 120; if I'd stayed with them they'd have worked out fine. By taking a break from them I sacrificed all the momentum I'd built up. In addition, I let my grasp of the characters and settings loosen up. The book drew away from my consciousness and from my unconscious as well.

Understand, please, that I'm not referring to an occasional break of a day or two. That may be useful for me when I've been working too hard for too long and I need to relax. But when I put a book aside for a week or a month, when I deliberately elect to shelve it while I work on something else, I'm really laying it aside forever.

* * *

This said, the fact remains that many books do hit snags, run into dead ends, or wander off down false trails. Having established that the thing to do is press on with them, the question arises as to how best to manage this.

Frequently the trouble is plot. If you outline as I generally do, with a more comprehensive picture of the early portion of the book and blind faith that the latter chapters will take care of themselves, the problem is often one of planning what will occur next. In mysteries, where the unfolding of action occurs simultaneously with the gradual discovery of what's really been happening, this business of figuring out what's going on is doubly problematic.

But people who outline carefully can have the same sort of plot trouble. For them—or for me, with those books in which I use a detailed outline—the problem comes when the book grows apart from its outline. Perhaps a certain character has taken shape in such a way as to make what's scheduled to happen no longer viable. We spoke earlier of the need for flexibility, stressing that you have to be willing to adapt your outline to allow for the organic growth of your novel. When this happens, you're in the same place as the person writing without an outline to start with. You have to figure out what happens next.

The image that comes to mind when I think of this sort of snag is that of a log jam. I've generally got enough ideas in my mind but they're snarled up like floating timber in a river, pinning each other down, getting in each other's way. If I could just shake things loose the book would flow downstream with no trouble at all.

The best way I've found to jar thoughts loose is to talk to myself at the typewriter, babbling away at myself without regard to style or sense, producing something that's a combination of stream-of-consciousness, letter to self, and outline of the remainder of the book. I usually throw these things away when they've ceased to be useful—I've never seen the point in saving remnants for posterity, figuring it's unlikely enough that posterity will be interested in my books, let alone my literary fingernail clippings. With my most recent book, however, I ran headlong into what looked at the time to be a serious plotting problem. I resolved it by chattering to myself at the typewriter, and I haven't yet discarded the gibberish I produced, having realized at the time that it might come in handy to illustrate a point in this present volume. Here, then, is how I talked to myself during a difficult stage of *The Burglar Who Liked to Quote Kipling:*

All right, where's the book going? Bernie stole the book from Arkwright on Whelkin's orders. Then went to meet Whelkin at Porlock's apartment. She drugged him, and when he woke he was framed for her murder. Meanwhile, a Sikh tried to get the book from Bernie and went off with the wrong book.

Okay. Say the Sikh worked for the Maharajah of Jaipur. Madeleine Porlock was being kept by somebody, stole the book and sold it to Arkwright. Suppose Porlock was sleeping with Arkwright, kept by him. Bernie could know this from fur labels in her closet. She and Whelkin knew each other—that's why she wore the wig to the bookstore—and she managed to learn that Whelkin was going to try to steal the book via Bernie.

Suppose Arkwright wanted the book to swing an import-export deal with a Saudi Arabian big shot who collects anti-Semitic material. The book would be a sweetener. Arkwright's enough of a collector to have gotten into a book discussion with the Saudi.

Suppose there were a couple of dozens of these books. Whelkin got hold of the cache in England and faked the Haggard inscription on all of them, selling them one at a time to rich book collectors with the proviso that they keep it a secret. He's sold a copy to Arkwright. Then he finds out Arkwright is going to show his copy to the Saudi. He has to get the Arkwright copy back or the Saudi will know there's been fraud committed.

Who killed Porlock?

Could be Whelkin. Say Whelkin worked through Porlock to get Arkwright to buy the book. Porlock was trying to recover the book herself to sell it elsewhere. Whelkin entered the apartment after she drugged Bernie and killed her, framing Bernie for it.

Or suppose it was Arkwright? When he found the book missing he suspected Porlock engineered the theft. He figured she played him for a sucker and shot her and left the gun in Bernie's hand to get rid of the disloyal mistress and the actual burglar in one swoop. Bernie could half-recognize the gun from having seen it in Arkwright's den.

What about the Sikh? He works for somebody, the Saudi or the Maharajah, who cares?, and he learned that Bernie had stolen the book. . . .

This process of talking out loud goes on for another couple of hundred words, with more possibilities brought up and discussed and set out for inspection. Then I wrote an outline of the next three chapters to be written, and then, unblocked and a little bit clearer, I sat down and wrote them.

That wasn't the end of my problems with *The Burglar Who Liked To Quote Kipling*. The plot was a complicated affair and it continued to work itself out as it went along, and twice more I rolled a sheet of paper into the typewriter and did some thinking on the keys. Both times I managed in this fashion to shake something loose and I was able to continue plotting and writing the book, carrying it through to completion. I not only finished a book that at one point looked unworkable, but I wound up producing a novel I'm pleased with.

If instead I had put it on the shelf to sort itself out, I'm certain it would still be there, gathering dust and serving as the source of monumental guilt. Snags and dead ends don't sort themselves out, I've come to believe. They get sorted out, and it takes work, and you have to do it yourself.

You don't have to do this sort of thing on paper. Some writers find it useful to talk this sort of a problem into a tape recorder. Later they play back the tape and find out what they've got in mind. Others work things out by discussing things with a friend. Not every friend will do for this process, and you have to experiment to determine which of your acquaintances serves you best as a sounding board. Some people—well-meaning, certainly, and often creative themselves—serve only to stifle your imagination. Others prove enormously helpful, perhaps because they're capable of listening so attentively. The person you select may be an agent or an editor. It may as easily be someone unconnected with the business, someone who doesn't even read much. You can try different people to see who does you some good, bearing in mind the distinct possibility that this is a process you can only handle on your own.

Sometimes my difficulty in writing Chapter Eleven is directly attributable to the way I wrote Chapter Ten. If I take a wrong turn in a book, that can fence me in further down the line.

The answer's clear enough. You drop back fifteen yards and punt. In other words, I go back to where things took that wrong turn and start rewriting at that point.

The problem lies in knowing when that's what's hanging you up. Happily enough, the solution sometimes works even when this isn't the real problem. Maybe you're blocked because of atmospheric conditions, or phases of the moon, or what you had for dinner last night. Even so, redoing a chapter you've already written may start the juices flowing and unblock you all the same.

* * *

When John D. MacDonald goes stale, he props open somebody else's book and starts copy typing. After a few paragraphs or pages, he finds himself changing a word here and a phrase there, improving what he's copying. Pretty soon he's ready to get back to work on something of his own.

Perhaps you'll find this approach useful should you go stale in the course of writing your novel. There are a few other suggestions that may or may not prove helpful.

Read what you've written. Suppose you've had to spend a week or two away from the manuscript, not because you've been avoiding it but because something else came up. The danger here is not just loss of momentum but that the book slips out of mind. Take your time and read it over before plunging back into it. You may even want to read it more than once. Remember that, important as it is for us to stay in the now while we write a book, a portion of our mind deals with the past and the future—i.e., what we've already written and what we'll be writing next. Reading the manuscript recharges those batteries.

Retype the last few pages. This is a good way to get back into the rhythm of your writing, whether you've been away from it for a short or long period of time. I've heard of writers who make it a practice to begin each day's work by retyping the last page they wrote the day before. The habit may have started when they left off in the middle of the page and wanted to start in on a clean page; it endured when they found it helped them recapture the flow of the previous day's writing.

Break in the middle of a sentence. I've read this advice in various forms over the years. Some people advocate stopping at the bottom of the fifth page of the day, say, even if it's smack in the middle of a hyphenated word. Others are less compulsive about where you stop but merely suggest that it be at a point where you know precisely what sentence you're going to write next.

The theory here is that you'll have an easier time picking the book up the next day because you already know what your first sentence or two will be. I offer this suggestion because it evidently works for some people, but I'm not going to tout it too strongly because I've really made some grim mornings for myself this way.

Imagine, for instance, sitting down to the typewriter and seeing this looking back at you. "She looked up at me, bright-eyed, and her smile was like. . . ."

Like *what,* for the love of God? I obviously had a simile in mind when I wrote what I wrote, and I'll never come up with a new simile and believe it to be as good as the lost one, and in the meantime I may spend half an hour scratching my head and trying to recall what I was thinking of. If I've got a good sentence in mind, the best thing I can do with it is commit it to paper before I lose it. So my own advice would be more along the lines of this:

Find a logical place to break off. At the end of a chapter, or the end of a scene, or the end of a paragraph, or at the very least at the end of a sentence. Not only does this avoid the sort of minor aggravation described above, but I believe it helps focus the attention of the subconscious mind upon the new chapter or scene or whatever to be tackled next.

* * *

You've abandoned books—quite a few of them, from the sound of it. And you've already said there's a strong possibility that my first novel won't prove publishable, that its main function may be as a learning experience. Suppose I reach a point where I'm sure it's not going to succeed. Wouldn't I be justified in abandoning it?

No.

Oh, you *can* abandon the book. For that matter, you don't have to start writing it in the first place.

But if you do undertake to write a first novel, I strongly urge you to finish it. Whether or not you lose faith in it along the way. Whether or not you're convinced it stinks. No matter what, stay with it a day at a time and see it through to completion. If its chief function is to be educational, rest assured that you'll learn infinitely more by finishing a first novel than by casting it aside.

I'd suggest further that you complete a first draft from beginning to end before getting involved with substantial revision. There's one exception—if you want to go back and start over after you've done forty or fifty pages, feel free to do so. But after you've passed the fifty-page mark, I would recommend that you push onward to the end before giving any through to rewriting.

I have a reason for this stance. I've observed that most of the people who start first novels never finish them, and I've come to believe that actually seeing a book through to the finish line is the most important thing you can do in your first essay at the novel. This to my mind is what separates the sheep from the goats and the ribbon from the clerks: the determination to stay with a book until it's done, for better or for worse.

If you abandon a first novel, the chances of your ever writing and completing a second novel are rather slim. If you pause in the course of a first novel for substantial revision, the chances of your finishing the book are lessened. Finishing a novel isn't a cinch, even if you've done it a dozen times already. When you're making your initial attempt, I would suggest that other considerations be kept in the background. In this case, the first thing is to get it written. Later on you can worry more about getting it right.

Chapter 11

Matters of Style

> In stating as fully as I could how things really were, it was often very difficult and I wrote awkwardly and the awkwardness is what they called my style. All mistakes and awkwardnesses are easy to see, and they called it style.
>
> —Ernest Hemingway

I've often wondered, when contemplating the passage quoted above, whether or not the author wasn't being a trifle disingenuous. We certainly regard Hemingway as a highly stylized writer. Passages from his works, taken out of context, are unmistakably his, and the Hemingway style is as inviting a target for the parodist as is the Bogart lisp for an impressionist. It's hard to believe a man could develop a style at once so individualized and so influential without having the slightest suspicion of what he was doing.

Be that as it may, I have no quarrel with the implied message—i.e., that the best way to develop a style is to make every effort to write as naturally and honestly as possible. It is not intentionally mannered writing that adds up to style, or richly poetic paragraphs, or the frenetic pursuit of novel prose rhythms. The writer's own style emerges when he makes no deliberate attempt to have any style at all. Through his efforts to create characters, describe settings, and tell a story, elements of his literary personality will fashion his style, imposing an individual stamp on his material.

There are a handful of writers we read as much for style as for content. John Updike is one example who comes quickly to mind. The manner in which he expresses himself is often interesting in and of itself. It is occasionally said of a particularly effective actor that one would gladly pay money to hear him read the telephone directory. Similarly, there are readers who would gladly *read* the phone book—if someone like Updike had written it.

The flip side of this sort of style is that it sometimes gets in the way of content in the sense that it blunts the impact of the narrative. Remember, fiction works upon us largely because we are able to choose to believe in its reality. Hence we care about the characters and how their problems are resolved. Just as a poor style gets in our way, making us constantly aware that we are reading a work of the imagination, so does an overly elaborate and refined style set up roadblocks to the voluntary suspension of our disbelief. From this standpoint, one may argue that the very best style is that which looks for all the world like no style at all.

* * *

Style, along with the various technical matters that come under that heading, is difficult for me to write about, very possibly because my own approach has always been instinctive rather than methodical. From my earliest beginnings as a writer, it was always a relatively easy matter for me to write smoothly. My prose rhythms and dialogue were good. Just as there are natural athletes, so was I—from the standpoint of technique, at least—a natural writer.

This gave me a considerable advantage in breaking into

print. I can see now that a lot of my early pulp stories had rather little to recommend them in terms of plot and characterization, but the fact that they were relatively well-written in comparison to the efforts of other tyros got me sales I wouldn't have had otherwise. But a smooth style in and of itself is no guarantee of true success. For years I was accustomed to a particular message in letters of rejection. "The author writes well," my agent would be advised. "This book didn't work for us, but we'd be very interested in seeing something else he's written." That sort of response is encouraging the first few times you receive it. When it becomes a common refrain, all it sparks is frustration.

I know several writers who were similarly gifted stylistically and who report similar early experiences. Over the years we've worked to develop our abilities at plotting and characterization, though for some of us the disparity is still in evidence. In my own case, it hasn't been all that long since an editor last explained how much he liked my writing—but that he didn't like my book.

Other writers have the opposite problem. A friend of mine has an extraordinary natural sense of story, coupled with an enthusiasm for his plots and characters which communicates itself in the drive of his narrative. From a technical standpoint, however, he's almost numbingly maladroit. His first novel was rewritten several times prior to publication, and received extensive textual editing from his publisher; even so, it remained a crude book. He has improved considerably since then, but to this day, ten books later, he is still very much the heavy-handed writer. Nevertheless, his books are almost invariably best sellers because of the particular strengths they do possess.

My point here is that someone like my friend, who has had to teach himself so much about the nuts-and-bolts side of writing, might well be better equipped than I to discuss the subject. It's harder to discourse effectively upon something when one's approach to it has always been intuitive.

That said, perhaps we can have a look at a handful of subjects which fit under the general umbrella of style. Perhaps you'll find something here of some value, whether you yourself are a natural literary athlete or whether you have to work very hard to make it look easy.

Grammar, Diction and Usage

A fiction writer doesn't have to be the strictest grammarian around. He can get by without a clear understanding of the subjunctive. Indeed, the sort of slavish devotion to the rules of grammar that might gladden the heart of an old-fashioned English teacher can get in the way of the novelist, giving his prose a stilted quality and leading his characters to talk not as people speak but as they ought to.

In my own case, I'm aware that I make certain grammatical errors, some of them deliberate, others through sheer ignorance. I have a copy of Fowler's *Modern English Usage,* a book I unhesitatingly recommend, and yet months pass without my referring to it. When I'm hammering away a the typewriter keys, trying to get a scene written and to get it right, I'm not remotely inclined to interrupt the flow for the sake of what Churchill called "the sort of errant pedantry up with which I will not put."

In first-person writing, I would maintain that the writer is fully justified in breaking grammatical rules and regulations at will. How the narrator expresses himself, the words he uses and the way he puts them together, is part of the manner in which his character is defined. I will argue further that a first-person narrator may follow a particular precept on one page and violate it on another. If our characters are to be lifelike, we can hardly demand absolute consistency of them.

The same principle applies, and rather more obviously, in dialogue. Most people don't express themselves the way

English teachers wish they would, and it's part of the novelist's license to make their speech as grammatical or ungrammatical as suits his purpose.

You'd think this would go without saying. I've far too often had my characters' grammar corrected by overzealous copyeditors to believe that *anything* in this area goes without saying.

Copyeditors are even more of a nuisance when it comes to punctuation. Various rules for punctuation have grown up over the years, but it's a moot point whether they apply to fiction, where punctuation may be properly regarded as a device the writer can use to obtain the effect he desires. You can choose to write this sentence:

She was angry, and not a little frightened.

Or you can write it this way:

She was angry and not a little frightened.

The decision, I maintain, is personal. The presence or absence of a comma in this sentence determines the rhythm of its reading, and that's a choice the author is fully entitled to make. It will hinge on the rhythm of the sentences which precede and follow it, on the author's natural style, on the effect he's trying to achieve, and on such intangibles as the weather and the astrological aspects. It should not hinge on what someone with a red pencil was taught in English Comp 101.

I get rather emotional on this subject. For years copyeditors have gone through my manuscripts, arbitrarily deleting commas of mine and inserting commas of their own. I don't put up with this sort of thing anymore. Brian Garfield, similarly infuriated, has taken to writing before-the-fact memos to copyeditors, explaining that he's been in this line for a few years now and knows the rules of punctuation sufficiently well to break them at will.

And yet, and yet . . . .

I remember, back in school, a student's inquiring of a teacher as to whether spelling errors would lower one's grade on a particular examination.

"That depends," the teacher explained. "If you spell cat with two t's, I might let it pass. If you spell it D-O-G, it's a mistake."

Some writers approach grammar and usage and punctuation like the kid who spelled cat D-O-G. I've been trying lately to read what is either a memoir of Hollywood or a novel in the form of a memoir—the publisher's blurb leaves the question open—and the author's cavalier disregard for matters of usage makes the book sporadically unreadable, for all that's interesting in the material.

Consider this sentence, a personal favorite of mine: *They didn't even say "Presbyterian Church"—they called it "the First Pres," that's how the texture of even as innocuous as watered-down Protestantism was watered down.*

Now the trouble with that sentence is that you can read it three times trying to figure out what it means and you won't get anywhere. I can't even figure out how to fix it. The whole book is full of stuff like this, and it's enough to give you a headache.

A reputable publisher issued this one, and I can only assume the author had strong feelings about the integrity of her prose. Otherwise a copyeditor would have made any number of changes, most of which could only have been for the better. When a writer's style is at the expense of clarity, when the prose obscures the meaning, something's wrong.

Dialogue

When you're looking for something to read at a library or bookstore, do you ever flip through books to see how much dialogue they have? I do, and I gather I'm not alone.

There's a reason. Dialogue, more than anything else, increases a book's readability. Readers have an easier and more enjoyable time with those books in which the characters do a lot of talking to one another than those in which the author spends all his time telling what's happening. Nothing conveys the nature of a character more effectively than overhearing that character's conversation. Nothing draws a reader into a story line better than listening to a couple of characters talking it over.

A good ear for dialogue, like a sense of prose rhythms, can be a gift. *Ear* is the right word here, I believe, because I think it's the ability one has to hear what's distinctive in people's speech that expresses itself in the ability to create vivid dialogue in print. (Likewise, I think it's the ear that enables some people to mimic regional accents better than others; the acuity with which you perceive these things largely determines your ability to reproduce them.)

I think a writer can improve his ear by learning to keep it open—i.e., by making a conscious effort to listen not only to what people say but to the way they say it.

It's worth noting that the best dialogue does not consist of the verbatim reproduction of the way people talk. Most people, you'll notice, speak in fits and starts, in phrases and half-sentences, with "uh" and "er" and "you know" tossed in like commas. "I was, see, like the other day I was goin' to the store, see, and uh, and like I was, you know, like, walkin' down the street, and . . . ."

People do talk this way, but who the hell would want to read it? It's tedious. This doesn't mean that you can't have a character express himself in this fashion, but that you would do so not by holding a tape recorder in front of him but by *suggesting* his conversational manner: "Like the other day I was goin' to the store, see, and I was like walkin' down the street . . . ."

A little goes a long way. Same thing with phonetic spelling of dialogue. There was a great vogue for that sort of thing a while back, when regional fiction was in its heyday, and there are still people who are crazy about it. Most people find it off-putting. There's no question that it slows things down for the reader; he has to translate everything before going on.

Here again, the answer lies in suggestion, in picking a couple of key words and using them to illustrate the character's unorthodox speech patterns. You might indicate a West Indian accent by spelling man *M-O-N,* for example, or a Puerto Rican inflection by rendering don't *doan* or affixing an *E* to the front of a word like *study.* A light sprinkling of this sort of thing reminds the reader that the speaker has a particular accent; he'll then be able to supply the rest of the accent, hearing it in his mind as he reads the character's dialogue, even though the rest of the words are spelled in the traditional manner.

Remember, less is better, and when in doubt, forget it.

Richard Price handles dialogue brilliantly. His first book, *The Wanderers,* traces the lives of members of a Bronx street gang. Their speech patterns are faithfully rendered and add greatly to the book's impact. Recently, though, I happened on a back issue of a literary quarterly in which a chapter of *The Wanderers* appeared prior to the book's publication. In that version, Price made extensive use of phonetic spelling, and while other elements of the story were identical, the spelling put me off. Evidently the book's editor reacted similarly. Whether Price or his editor made the actual changes is immaterial. The book gained greatly by them.

Good dialogue differs from real-life dialogue in another respect. It's written out. The reader gets the words without the inflection. If you just put down the words, the result can be ambiguous. You can italicize a word to show that it's being *stressed* by the speaker, or you can include the occasional notation that a given sentence was said lightly or seriously or heavily or archy or whateverly, but sometimes you have to restructure a sentence so that the reader will not have trouble getting your meaning.

Another thing you have to do in dialogue is compress

things. People generally have more time for conversation in real life than in books. You have to speed things up in the actual dialogue, cutting out a certain amount of the normal volleying, and you also have to do a certain amount of summing up. In my Scudder novels, for example, Scudder receives the bulk of his information by going around and talking to people, and the reader overhears much of this in the form of dialogue. But from time to time Scudder will break off reporting exactly what was said in dialogue form and simply give the gist of a conversation in a sentence or two.

When this isn't done, when a book's all dialogue, it feels puffy and padded. It moves fast and it's easy to read, but it's ultimately unsatisfying. One's left with the feeling that nothing has happened at great length.

Past versus Present Tense

The great majority of fiction is written in the past tense. The effect is that one is being told a story which has taken place. Even if the story is set in future time, as in most science fiction, either the narrator or the disembodied voice recounting the story is presumably speaking at a later time than the action occurred.

There is an alternative to this which is achieved through the use of what is known as the historical present tense. Those who prefer this tense argue that it makes the story a more immediate experience for the reader; it is going on as he reads it.

They are also apt to take the position that it is more contemporary, less old-fashioned. There is, as it happens, nothing particularly new about the historical present. Offhand, I can recall that the Marquis de Sade used it in his novels in the eighteenth century, and it may for all I know go back halfway to Homer. In our own time, there is something distinctly cinematic about writing in the present tense. It has a screenplay feel to it.

There's rather more to the use of the historical present than a simple change of tense. This becomes clear when you take a patch of prose written in the past tense and change it to the present. It will very likely be stiff and awkward, unnatural. In order for the historical present to be effective, the whole narrative attitude changes in subtle ways.

Whether or not to employ the historical present is entirely a matter of choice. In genre fiction I would consider it a poor idea, if only because category novels are hardly ever written in present tense. I wouldn't care for the job of trying to sell a gothic or a western, say, written in the historical present, though I do not doubt for a moment that such a novel could be written effectively and might even find its way into print.

My own personal bias against the historical present is a very strong one, so much so that, when I'm browsing paperback racks looking for something to read, I'm inclined to pass up books written in present tense. The one time I tried to write a novel in the present tense I found myself incapable of sustaining the voice past a couple of pages. But that's my personal reaction, and has nothing much to do with the relative merits of the two tenses.

First versus Third Person

Correspondingly, I've noticed in my paperback rack browsing that I'm distinctly biased in favor of books written in the first person. Perhaps this is not surprising in view of the fact that a majority of my own novels have been first-person narratives.

The conventional advice to beginning writers of fiction is to abjure the first person. It's allegedly full of pitfalls for the tyro, serves as a distancing mechanism between the reader and the story, limits the scope of the narrative, and causes dental caries in children and skin tumors in laboratory mice.

For my part, I find I'm more likely to enjoy a novel by an unfamiliar writer if it's written in the first than the third person because the writing itself is more likely to have a natural flow to it. The first-person voice is, after all, the one we all grow up using. First-person novels have an immediacy to them that helps close the gap between writer and reader. It's as if the writer, clothed in the flesh of his narrator, is holding me by the elbow and telling me the story.

Some novels, to be sure, cannot be written in the first person. It's only an option when your novel is to be told from a single point of view, and it becomes a sensible choice in direct proportion to your ability to identify with that particular character. If your lead's larger than life—the President of the United States, a glamorous movie star, Al Capone, or whoever—the third person might be a wiser choice; you might be more comfortable writing the character from the outside, and the reader might be more comfortable reading about him that way.

Single versus Multiple Viewpoint

It's probably easiest, in a first novel, to show everything through the eyes of a single lead character—whether the voice you choose is first or third person. Single viewpoint keeps a novel on a true course. It limits options and cuts down the opportunity for diffusion of the force of the narrative.

This does not mean that it's perforce the right choice for your novel. Some books depend upon a broad scope for a measure of their strength. The story you choose to tell will very often dictate whether it is to be told from one or several points of view.

Whether you select single or multiple viewpoint for your novel, you would probably do well to avoid changing point of view within a scene, switching back and forth from one character's mind to another's. In a book in which the author maintains a consistent overview, never really getting inside the skins of his characters but describing all their actions from without, it may be permissible to move around the room within a scene, telling what the various characters in turn are thinking or feeling. But when you make this sort of viewpoint switch within a scene in a book where characters are shown from within, the result is apt to be confusion—the reader can't remember who's thinking what—and a slowdown in the book's pace. I was most recently made aware of this while reading *True Confessions,* John Gregory Dunne's generally successful novel of clerical and police political machinations.

An advantage of multiple viewpoint lies in the fact that the author is not stuck with a single character for the duration of the book. When a scene winds to a close, and when there's nothing further to be said about the viewpoint character for the time being, you simply skip two spaces and pick up one of the other principals.

In any novel of this sort, it makes good sense to keep your number of principal characters down to a manageable figure. When you pass the half dozen mark, it becomes a little more difficult for the reader to remember what's going on and who's doing what and why. You can, however, have any number of additional *minor* viewpoint characters, from whose vantage point an occasional scene or two is portrayed. This can add a sense of richness to a novel without diluting the reader's attention to the main characters.

More important than learning a multitude of rules on the subject of viewpoint is that you be aware of the question of the point of view in your own reading. Your perceptions of the way other writers handle viewpoint changes, your sense of what works and what doesn't, will teach you more about the subject than you can learn by reading *about* it.

I doubt that many readers are aware of point of view. They're interested in characters and story. It's possible, too, that I tend to pay more attention to consistency in this area than I need to.

Some years ago, for example, I wrote *The Triumph of Evil* under the pen name of Paul Kavanagh. The entire novel, written in the third person, was told from the point of view of

Miles Dorn, assassin and agent provocateur. The entire novel, that is, with the exception of a single chapter which dealt with an assassination at which Dorn was not physically present. He was over a thousand miles away at the time, and it seemed essential to me that the scene be viewed from close up.

After considerable soul-searching, I shrugged heroically and wrote the scene from the point of view of the young man used as a pawn by Dorn. I felt this was a jarring inconsistency but couldn't think of a better way to deal with it.

As far as I know, no one was ever bothered by this inconsistency, or even aware of it. No editor or writer who read the book mentioned it. Rereading the section preparatory to writing this chapter, it seemed to me unlikely that I would have noticed it myself—had I not been the book's author. We who write these books are inevitably more aware of their essential structure than are the people who read them.

Don Westlake employs an interesting original framework for his Richard Stark novels about Parker, and I wonder if many of his faithful readers are aware of it. In almost every Parker novel, the first two quarters of the book are told exclusively from Parker's point of view. The third quarter is told from the individual points of view of all of the other principal characters. Then, in the fourth section, once again Parker is the viewpoint character throughout.

I think this serves Westlake superbly. But I doubt that very many Parker fans pay much mind to the almost symphonic structure of these books. I suspect they're interested in the plot and the characters, and they want to find out how the heist turns out and who winds up alive and dead when it's over. I don't think they care how the author does it.

It's useful for us as writers to care, and to pay attention. But an excessive preoccupation may be more liability than asset. The main thing is always the story.

Transitions

When I first started writing, I had a certain amount of

difficulty getting from one scene to the next. I also had trouble getting my characters on and off stage, or in and out of the room.

This difficulty was most pronounced in first-person novels. If I had a character in conversation at a bar one night, and then I had something for him to do the next morning, I wasn't sure how to get him through the intervening hours. I figured I had to explain where he went and what he did at all times.

I found out that's not necessary. I could let the bar conversation run its course. Then I could skip an extra space, and then I could write, "At ten the next morning I showed up at Waldron's office. I was wearing my blue pinstripe and his secretary seemed to like the looks of it."

They learned some years ago in the film business that the best transitions are nice clean abrupt ones. Remember the slow dissolves you used to see in movies? Remember how they would indicate the passage of time by showing different shots of a clock, or pages flipping on some dumb calendar? They don't do that any more, and that's largely because they realized that they don't have to. Comtemporary audiences are hip enough to put two and two together.

So can readers. I learned a lot about transitions by reading Mickey Spillane. In the early Mike Hammer books, he hardly ever explained how Hammer got from one place to another, or wasted time setting scenes up elaborately. There were no slow dissolves in those books. They were all fast cuts, with each scene beginning right on the heels of the one before it. Since the books had enormous appeal to a generally unsophisticated audience, I would assume few readers had trouble following the action line, for all the abruptness of the transitions.

* * *

Temporal transitions—jumps back and forth in time—can

be handled most expeditiously simply by crediting the reader with the intelligence to figure out what you're doing without over-explaining yourself. In this area, too, I suspect the techniques of the visual media, including not only the cinema but especially television commercials with their intricate crosscutting in a thirty- or sixty-second span, have contributed greatly to the sophistication of the public.

I can recall seeing *Two For The Road,* a film with Audrey Hepburn and Albert Finney, sometime in the late sixties. Director Stanley Donen salted the film wih flashbacks, providing no special indication of the temporal changes, simply cutting from one present-time sequence to one in past time. I was as interested in the audience as in the film. Some older viewers, I noticed, were utterly confounded; their frame of reference was too rigidly linear for them to know what the hell was going on. But the majority of the audience, including all of its younger members, seemed perfectly at ease.

For a particularly well-crafted example of a novel in which several temporal phases of a story are simultaneously related, you might have a look at *Some Unknown Person,* by Sandra Scoppettone. The book is based on the life and death of Starr Faithfull, the star-crossed girl-about-town who served as a model for Gloria Wandrous in John O'Hara's *Butterfield Eight.* Scoppettone interweaves her lead character's early years, the life story of a man instrumental in her death, the events leading up to her death, the last days years later of the aforementioned man, and several other aspects of the story, cutting back and forth through time in a most instructive fashion.

Chapter 12

Length

In *Threesome,* one of Jill Emerson's characters wants to
know how long a chapter ought to be. As long as Abraham
Lincoln's legs, another character assures her. (Lincoln, you
may recall, informed a heckler that a man's legs ought to be
long enough to extend from his body to the ground.)

A chapter, then, should be long enough to reach from the
one before it to the one that follows it. In other words, there is
no fit and proper length for a chapter.

When I wrote sex novels, I tended to be compulsive about
chapter length. Originally my books were two hundred pages
long, and were written in the form of ten twenty-page chapters.
Then, when my publisher complained that they were running a
wee bit short, I upped the length to 205 pages, alternating
twenty-one page chapters with twenty-page chapters and stopping when I had written five of each. In retrospect, I can see
readily enough that this rigidity was pointless insofar as the
reader was concerned. I'm positive my average fan, busy turning the pages with one hand and panting over the lurid innuen-
do, barely realized that the book was divided into chapters in
the first place. In his mind, it was more conveniently divided
into hot parts and dull stretches.

Now that the books I write no longer contain hot parts, I'm
a good deal more flexible in dividing the dull stretches into

chapters. In a series of four novels written about (and ostensibly by) Chip Harrison, I furnished each book with one chapter a single sentence in length. *"The gun jammed,"* for instance, was an entire chapter in *No Score; "Chip, I'm Pregnant"* was a similarly complete chapter in *Chip Harrison Scores Again.* The two other books each contained an equally terse chapter. I did this sort of thing for the fun of it, not for any particular effect.

If I'm less compulsive about chapter length nowadays, I still tend to keep the chapters of a particular book roughly the same length. An occasional chapter shorter than its fellows provides a sort of staccato effect that is not without dramatic value. When you break for a chapter you're slamming a door on the action. The reader has to pause and think for a moment, if only for the length of time it takes him to turn the page.

Some books aren't divided into chapters at all. The author just skips an extra space between scenes and lets it go at that. An advantage of chapter breaks—that they provide a convenient place for the reader to stop—is also their disadvantage, in that the reader may elect not to pick the book up again. Some writers avoid chapter breaks because they don't want to encourage the reader to pause in the course of their heart-pounding narrative. One might argue in reply that a story that's all that gripping will hold its readers through a chapter break. In my own reading, I've found that chapterization tends to keep me reading. I tell myself I can stop in a few minutes, at the end of the next chapter, and I keep telling myself that until I've finished the book.

One function of chapters is that they reduce the book in the writer's own eyes to manageable dimensions. If your prior experience is with short stories, you may find it easier to imagine yourself writing a three or four or five thousand-word chapter than a full-length novel. By parcelling your book into such bite-sized portions the task of writing it may seem within your abilities. A chapter can be grasped all at once as a book frequently cannot, and of course when you've written twenty or thirty chapters of this sort, you'll have produced a novel.

Another use of chapters is for viewpoint shifts—which is not to say that every change in point of view calls for a new chapter. In *Not Comin' Home To You,* written under the Paul Kavanagh pen name, the viewpoint shifts back and forth between the two leads, who see the emerging story very differently. Breaking chapters for these viewpoint shifts prepares the reader better than simple double spacing.

Finally, it's worth noting that the manner in which you do or don't divide your novel into chapters is not something that will have any discernible effect upon a publisher's decision to accept or reject your book. It's not too likely he'll care one way or the other, but if he does it's the easiest sort of change for him to suggest, and the easiest change for you to make. For this reason, whether you use chapters and how long you make them is a minor point at most and one you should arrange to suit yourself while you write the book.

* * *

The length of your chapters may not be important. The length of your novel is.

From a purely aesthetic standpoint, a novel's like a chapter. It should be long enough to get from the beginning to the end. But length is rather more rigidly determined on the basis of various commercial considerations which a novelist neglects at his peril.

As far as category fiction is concerned, length is largely predetermined. If you want to write a light romance for Harlequin, let's say, you'll probably have noticed that all the Harlequin romances on the newsstands run the same number of pages and have the same number of words on a page. If the books all run fifty-five thousand words and you submit an eighty thousand-word manuscript, the likelihood of their accepting your novel is considerably diminished.

Not all length requirements in category novels are equally strict. Most houses might try a longer-than-usual gothic mystery or western if they felt its strengths were such as to offset the disadvantage of its unusual length. But you're swimming against the tide when you try this sort of thing. It's hard to sell a first novel without increasing the difficulty by failing to conform to market requirements in this area.

If your book's too long, an editor may still like it enough to suggest cuts. If it's too short, you've really got a problem. With a handful of very obvious exceptions, really short books really don't sell. It may not be impossible to write a novel in less than fifty thousand words, but it's evidently very tricky to convince the reader that he's getting his money's worth. Nor is an editor as likely to feel comfortable suggesting ways to beef up a book as he may feel suggesting deletions.

How do you make sure your book's the right length? We'll assume that your market study has led you to select an ideal length. You want to write a mystery, say, and a study of the type of mystery you intend to write indicates that the most successful books tend to run in the neighborhood of sixty-five to seventy thousand words. You've calculated that, given the way you set your margins and other quirks of style, you'll need to write 225 pages to come in at the optimum length.

Outlining's a help in giving you a sense of the relationship between your plot and your predetermined length. It makes it easier for you to see how much should happen within the first fifty or hundred pages in order for things to be working out on schedule. Even without an outline, it's frequently possible to sense as you go along whether you're running long or short.

If you're running short, you have several choices. You can reexamine your plot and see if there's a way to add scenes and complications to it that will give the book more bulk. You can decide that the problem is not in the plot but in the writing, and can accordingly write your scenes so that they run longer, furnishing rather more in the way of dialogue and description. Finally, you can just press on to the end in the manner that seems most comfortable, figuring you'll add substance one way or another in your second draft.

Your choices are essentially the same if you find your book running long, but here you'd probably be best advised to pick the last option and let the first draft run its course at whatever wordage seems natural. A great many writers do this as a matter of course and produce their best work in this fashion.

Robert Ludlum, for example, almost invariably trims his first draft by a third when he rewrites it. Sidney Sheldon has said that he puts everything he can think of into his first draft, giving his imagination free rein; he commonly cuts more than half of what he has written.

I'm not happy working this way. As I've said, I do my best work when I'm operating under the assumption that what I'm writing is going to be set in type as soon as I've got the last page written. (One writer, Noel Loomis, was a skilled linotypist, and could compose faster on that machine than on a typewriter; he wrote his westerns on a linotype, pulled galley proofs from the chases of set type, and submitted galleys to his publishers. I'd do that myself if I could.)

I can see, though, a great advantage in writing long and cutting afterward. If you work that way, your first draft contains all the possibilities your creative imagination hands you. Then, when you rewrite, you're able to skim the cream.

* * *

There's another advantage in writing long. If your book simply works best at a greater length than you had in mind for it, it may have greater commercial value than you planned.

There's a paradox here that requires a word of explanation. On the one hand, the average thriller runs somewhere around sixty or seventy thousand words, and a book that runs substantially longer than that is going to present problems to a publisher of category fiction.

On the other hand, those occasional thrillers that turn up on the best seller list are generally a hundred to a hundred fifty thousand words long. The same length that would preclude their sale as paperback originals serves to swing them right up onto the hardcover sales counter.

The conventional explanation holds that longer books have more to them, that they have greater depth and stronger story values, that they are more to be taken seriously on account of their length. Because of these factors, such books are said to transcend their categories and appeal to readers who do not ordinarily read that type of novel.

Very often this is demonstrably true. Brian Garfield's *Hard Times* is an epic novel of the Old West, with only its setting to link it with standard westerns. Any best seller list will yield similar examples.

Even so, other books turn up on the lists with nothing remarkable about them but their bulk. I read one recently, a detective novel by a writer who has produced some best-selling thrillers over the years. Unlike his other books, this had nothing special going for it; it was a standard straight-line detective plot told from a single point of view and overblown to a hundred fifty thousand words. It was a poorer book for its length, but a better seller because of it.

What it comes down to, I'm afraid, is that readers of best sellers—which is to say the majority of readers in this country—prefer long books. This is their right, certainly, and it is only sensible for the writer who wants to sell to this best seller audience to provide them with what they're looking for.

It almost seems to be true that there's no such thing as a book that's too long to be commercially viable. For years publishers resisted overlong first novels, saying that higher production costs made such books even more unprofitable than trimmer first novels. Nowadays the trend is in the other direction. If a first novel is sufficiently substantial—and of course if it satisfies other commercial considerations as well— then it can be promoted and ballyhooed and even *sold.*

James Clavell's novel *Shogun* had a long run as a best seller a couple of years back. While it was an engrossing reading experience for me all the way through, I could not avoid applying to it Dr. Johnson's observation regarding *Paradise Lost*— i.e., no one ever wished it were longer. For all its 1,400 pages, and for all that more readers started it than finished it, the book was a literary and commercial success. Not too many years ago a publisher might have hesitated to bring out quite so long a novel, especially one set in medieval Japan. Clavell's track record helped, certainly, but equally helpful I suspect was the growing recognition that great length helps more books than it hinders.

* * *

Does this mean you should aim from the beginning at long books?

No, not necessarily. It may mean that you shouldn't try to hit the best seller list with a short book, any more than you should try to peddle a quarter of a million words as a paperback.

But your first object, remember, is to write your own kind of book. You'll learn, from your own reading and as you begin writing, what sort of book suits you best. I've come to see that I myself am most comfortable writing relatively lean, spare volumes. This no doubt limits my potential from a commercial standpoint, but I'd be limiting myself rather more severely were I to force myself to write books that suited me less for purely commercial motives.

That said, it's worth noting that a great many writers find themselves producing longer books as time goes by. This does not mean that they are attempting to respond to the dictates of the marketplace. While that may be a factor, it's at least as likely that this extension of their range has simply come about naturally. An intimidating length becomes less intimidating after one has written a batch of short novels.

I could go on. But this chapter, like Abraham Lincoln's legs, is plenty long enough as it is.

And that's the long and short of it.

Chapter 13

Rewriting

I rewrite constantly. For every page that gets printed there must be five that go into the wastebasket. One of the hardest aspects of writing is accepting this squandering of labor, but it is essential. I doubt if there is one page in a thousand, throughout the whole of literature, that wouldn't have been improved by the author's redoing it.

—*Russell H. Greenan*

Professional writers vary considerably in their approach to rewriting. Some would endorse the observation quoted above while others would dismiss it as nonsense. Some regard rewriting as the genuinely enjoyable side of their occupation, the stage in which one sees the book taking its final form. Others hate rewriting but do it anyway. Some do one complete draft after another until the book satisfies them. Others polish each page before moving on to the next one. Some write five or more drafts of a book before they feel they've got it right. Others submit their first drafts.

I don't believe there's any right or wrong way to approach rewriting, not with so many pros having so much success with so many widely divergent methods. As with so many aspects of writing, each writer must determine what works best in his own particular case—what method produces the best work and makes him most comfortable.

* * *

I myself have always been the sort of writer who loathes revision. Looking back over the years, I can see a couple of factors which tend to explain this attitude. I was always more concerned with the accomplishment than the act; I was interested less in writing, you might say, than in having written. Once I finished writing a short story or a novel I wanted to consider myself done with it for all time. Indeed, the minute I typed "The End" I wanted to be able to take a deep breath, walk around the corner, and see my work in print at the newsstand. The last thing I desired at such a moment was to sit down, take an even deeper breath, and commence feeding the whole thing through the typewriter a second time.

Because I was a naturally smooth stylist, as I mentioned a couple of chapters back, I could get away with submitting first drafts. They didn't look rough. And, because I had a sort of fictive tunnel vision, I was unlikely to see more than one way that a book could be written.

When I was writing the soft-core sex novels, economic considerations largely ruled out rewriting. Who could afford it? Who had time for it? When you're turning out somewhere between twelve and twenty books a year, you may cheerfully agree with Greenan's point and still never rewrite a line. So what if every last one of your pages could be improved by making another trip through your typewriter? There's no time to polish each page to perfection, and no incentive, either. The readers won't notice the difference. The publisher probably won't notice either, and wouldn't care if he did.

There's even an argument *against* revision, and it may have applied to those early sex novels. Jack Kerouac advanced it when he spoke of his writing as "spontaneous bop prosody," equating his manner of composition to a jazz musician's creative improvisation. More cynically, the lead character in Barry

N. Malzberg's *Herovit's World,* a hack science-fiction writer enormously contemptuous of his own work, argues that rewriting would rob his crap of the only thing it has going for it, its freshness. Once you start rewriting, Herovit holds, you're not able to stop. With each draft the fundamental banality and worthlessness of the material becomes more evident even as its vitality and spontaneity are drained from it. All you wind up doing is what William Goldman, discussing the agony of rewriting an inadequate play prior to its opening, called "washing garbage."

I never washed my garbage in those days. Thinking back, I'm astonished at the sangfroid with which I presumed to forego revision altogether. I scarcely ever retyped a page.

There was one time I well remember when, checking the pages at the end of the day's work, I discovered that I'd written pages 31 through 45 but had somehow jumped in my page numbering from 38 to 40. Rather than renumber the pages, I simply sat down and wrote page 39 to fit. Since page 38 ended in the middle of a sentence, a sentence which then resumed on page 40, it took a little fancy footwork to slide page 39 in there, but the brash self-assurance of youth was evidently up to that sort of challenge.

* * *

Jacqueline Susann used to tell talk show audiences how she rewrote every book four or five times, using yellow paper for one draft, green for a second, pink for a third, blue for a fourth, and finally producing finished copy on white bond. I don't seem to recall the point of this rainbow approach to revision, nor am I sure I believe Susann actually did this; anyone as accomplished as she at self-promotion might well have been capable of embroidery.

But that hardly matters. What's relevant, I think, is that Susann knew her audience. The public evidently likes the idea of reading books over which writers have labored endlessly. Perhaps readers find it galling to shell out upwards of $8.95 for a book that flowed from its author's typewriter like water from a cleft rock. The stuff's supposed to *read* as though it came naturally and effortlessly, but one wants to be assured that a soul-satisfying amount of hard work went into it.

That's nice to know when Dick Cavett holds your book up and asks you how you did it, but in the meantime you're naturally more concerned with producing the best possible novel than with figuring out how best to push it on the tube. Is revision necessary? And what's the proper approach to it?

For me, the best approach involves a sort of doublethink. If I take it for granted while writing a book that I'm going to have to sit down and do it over, I'm encouraging myself to be sloppy. I don't have to find the right word or phrase. I don't have to think a scene through and decide which way I want to tackle it. I can just slap any old thing on the page, telling myself that the important thing is to get words on paper, that I can always clean up my act in the rewrite.

Now this may be precisely what you require in order to conquer your inhibitions at the typewriter. Earlier I mentioned a couple of writers who produce lengthy first drafts, throwing in everything that occurs to them, then pruning ruthlessly in their second drafts.

I find, though, that unless I regard what I'm writing as final copy, I don't take it seriously enough to give it my best shot. For this reason I proofread as I go along, do my first drafts on damnably expensive high-rag-content white bond, and get each page right before I go on to the next one. I don't necessarily rewrite as I go along, but neither do I leave anything standing if it bothers me. Sometimes I'll have twenty or thirty crumpled pages in or around my wastebasket by the time I've produced my daily five pages of finished copy. Other times I won't have to throw out a single page, but even then I'll be doing what you might call rewriting-in-advance in that I'll try sentences and paragraphs a few different ways in my mind before committing them to the page.

In the chapter on starting your novel, I mentioned that I frequently rewrite the opening chapters of a book. Aside from that, I usually push on all the way through to the end without any substantial rewriting other than the polish-as-you-go business just described. Now and then, however, upon proofreading yesterday's work prior to beginning today's production, I'll find something bothersome in the last couple of pages. This may happen because the unconscious mind, laboring during the night with what's to be written next, will have come up with something that calls for changes in the section immediately preceding it. It may happen, too, because I was tired when I reached the end of yesterday's work, and the results of fatigue are evident in the light of dawn. When this occurs, I'll naturally redo the offending pages; this serves the dual purpose of getting me into the swing of my narrative even as I'm improving yesterday's work.

Some writers elaborate on this method, rewriting their whole manuscript as they go along. They begin each day by rewriting *in toto* the first draft they produced the day before, then go on to churn out fresh first-draft copy which they will in turn revise the following morning, and so on a day at a time until the book is finished. There's a lot to be said for this method. If your first drafts are stylistically choppy enough to require revision as a matter of course, and if the idea of being faced with a top-to-bottom rewrite all in one chunk is unattractive, this sort of pay-as-you-go revision policy has much to recommend it. Among other things, you don't encourage yourself to be slipshod in your first draft, since your day of reckoning isn't that far in the future.

This won't work, incidentally, if you produce the sort of first drafts that require substantial structural revision, with lots of cutting and splicing.

* * *

A couple of pages back I described my present approach to writing and rewriting as a sort of doublethink. By this I mean that, although I work with the intention of producing final copy the first time around, I keep myself open to the possibility that a full second draft will be required. If I determine that this is the case, the fact that my first draft is neatly typed on crisp white bond paper doesn't alter the fact that I have to redo it from top to bottom.

When I wrote *Burglars Can't Be Choosers,* I stopped one chapter from the end and rewrote the whole thing. I suppose I could have written the final chapter of the first draft before starting the rewrite, but I didn't see the point; I knew that my final chapter would be affected by the revisions I'd make in earlier chapters, so that I'd only wind up redoing it entirely later on.

Burglars Can't Be Choosers got a complete rewrite for a couple of reasons. One stemmed from the fact that I didn't know the identity of the murderer until I was almost three-quarters of the way through the book. The solution I hit on necessitated a certain amount of changes along the way. I wanted to push on to the end—or almost to the end, as it turned out—before making them, but they did have to be made in order for the book to hold up.

In addition, I was dissatisfied with the pace of the novel. While most of the scenes worked well enough, I felt there was too much wasted time in the story line. A rereading convinced me that I could eliminate a day from the plot, tightening things up a good deal in the process.

I could have tried making these changes by cutting and pasting, redoing selected pages here and there. I considered this but couldn't avoid the conclusion that the book would profit considerably from a complete rewrite. While it seemed to me that some portions of the book didn't require any changes beyond an occasional sentence here and there, I decided to retype everything.

By doing this, I made an incalculable number of changes. It's virtually impossible for me to retype a page of my own work without changing something. Sometimes it was clear to me that these changes constituted a substantial improvement, although this improvement might not have been apparent to most of the book's audience. In other cases it's moot whether the changes I made were for better or worse; I occasionally had the feeling I was changing phrasing solely as a respite from the boredom of pure copy typing.

I would never have rewritten *Burglars Can't Be Choosers* for stylistic reasons alone. The book was written smoothly enough the first time around, and if I hadn't had to make structural changes I would have submitted my first draft as it stood. In retrospect, I'm glad I was forced to rewrite it; it's a better book for the extra work it received.

* * *

It's possible you'll produce a first draft which looks to be submittable without a major rewrite. You may find, however, that the manuscript needs to be retyped before you send it off.

If so, I have a suggestion. Unless you absolutely can't stand the idea, do the final typescript yourself.

You can probably guess the reason from my discussion of the revision of *Burglars Can't Be Choosers*. No matter how much editing you do in pen or pencil, no matter how thoroughly you rework your material before having it typed, you'll find more little changes to make when you actually hammer away at the keys yourself.

A friend of mind used to do this. Then she started to get

higher advances and her books began earning more subsidiary income, and she decided she could afford the luxury of hiring somebody to type her final drafts for her. She works very hard over them, making innumerable pencil corrections before bundling them off to the typist, but her style's not as polished in her latest books because she's not doing her own typing. She's omitting what was always a set stage in her personal process of revision, and while her books are still well written, I think they used to be smoother.

* * *

Earlier, in the chapter on snags and dead ends, I advised against setting a book aside when you run into trouble with it. Although it may seem like a good idea, it rarely lets you develop a fresh slant on your novel. The books I abandon in midstream invariably float off out of my life and are never seen again.

When you finish a first draft, however, I think you should give yourself breathing space before plunging into a rewrite. There's a reason for this beyond the very real fact that you're likely to be tired and deserving of a break.

The writer who has just completed a book cannot usually be sufficiently objective about it to appraise it properly with an eye toward revision. In my own case, it's hard enough to be objective about my work ten years after it's been published, let alone when the pages are still warm and the ink still wet. At that stage I'm not only too close to the book, I'm still *inside* it. A break of a couple of weeks lets me unwind, and when I sit down and read the thing from start to finish I just might have a certain amount of perspective on it.

During this cooling-off period, you might want to have someone else read the book—but only if you've got someone around whose judgment you trust. If a negative reaction might paralyze you, don't take any chances. Wait until you've done your rewriting before you show the book to anybody.

Now's the time to have the book read by a knowledgeable acquaintance if you're concerned about your lack of expertise in a certain area. Suppose the book has a background in coin collecting, for instance. You've done a ton of research on the subject but you're no numismatist and you can't be certain you've got the lingo right. Maybe you've committed the sort of glaring error that'll get you snotty letters from your readers.

Show the book to someone with the right background, explaining your uncertainty to him and asking him to read it with that consideration in mind. Make it clear to him that you want him to spot errors, that you're not showing him the book in the hope that he'll praise it. (It's necessary to state this out front, because most people assume that most authors want not criticism but praise. And most of the time, incidentally, they're absolutely right.) When he tells you what's wrong and how to fix it, you can incorporate the information you get from him in your rewrite. If he tells you everything's fine and your book is numismatically accurate, you can stop worrying about that aspect of it while you rewrite.

And, if he offers a lot of nonnumismatic criticisms of your story and characters and writing style, you can thank him politely and pay him no more attention in this respect than you see fit. Remember, you showed him the book because of his knowledge about rare coins, not because you figured him as the most perceptive editor since Maxwell Perkins.

* * *

Which leads us, neatly enough, into another area of the question of rewriting. So far we've dealt with the matter of the revision work that you do or don't perform before submitting the manuscript. Of another sort altogether are those changes you make at the suggestion of an agent or publisher.

Most new writers will change almost anything to get a book published, and that's probably as it should be. Just as the first law of nature is quite properly self-preservation, so is the first commandment of the first novelist to get published if it is at all possible. If you can accomplish this simply by revising your manuscript as an editor suggests, you would probably be foolish to do otherwise.

Hopeful writers have a fairly common fantasy in this area. It usually involves a hard-boiled editor trying to seduce them into making crass commercial changes to the book's artistic detriment. The author either makes the changes only to discover the hollowness of great financial success at the cost of his soul, or he stands up for what he believes, tells the editor to go climb a tree, and (a) finds a more understanding publisher through whose efforts his book brings him wealth and glory beyond his wildest imaginings or (b) drinks himself to death in righteous indignation.

It all makes alluring fantasy, but it's not too well grounded in reality. An agent or editor suggests changes because he thinks the changes will improve the book, not because he's anxious to louse it up. His point of view may be in part the result of his commercial orientation, and if that's not somewhat true he's probably limited in his effectiveness in the business. But I've never known an editor to ask for a change that he didn't believe would result in a stronger book.

Beliefs, however, are not facts. Agents and editors are wrong often enough. And in the world of fiction, rightness and wrongness are often subjective matters.

To get to the point, what do you do when an editor wants changes with which you disagree? Do you bite the bullet and make the changes? Do you stand up for what you believe in? Come to think of it, how do you *know* what you believe in?

How much significance can you attach to your own feelings? After all, you only wrote the thing.

It's a tricky question, and you can spend years in this business and still have occasional trouble answering it. One thing that's certain is that the decision is yours to make. It's your book, it's going to have your name on it, and only you can decide how strongly you feel about what's between the covers. If you refuse to make certain changes, you may be saying "no" to publication, and another opportunity for publication may not ever come along. You can't assume no one else will ever take the book, but you may have to acknowledge the possibility, especially with a first novel.

Generally speaking, writers gain confidence with increased experience. I made some changes at an editor's suggestion in my own first book, the lesbian novel I discussed earlier. One of those changes was a bad idea and I disliked making it, but it didn't really occur to me to demur. I was twenty years old, delirious at the thought of having a book published, and awestruck at the two-thousand-dollar advance they were handing me. I know now that I could have talked my way clear of the one change I really hated making, but I didn't even try.

That was minor. A friend of mine cut a long novel drastically some years ago at the suggestion of a respected editor. He felt at the time that the book would be weaker, both commercially and artistically, as a result of the cuts; however, he also felt the editor's opinion was worth more than his. Perhaps it might have been in most cases but in this one it manifestly was not. He now regrets making those cuts. With the experience he now has under his belt, and with the track record he has since amassed as a successful commercial novelist, he would be far more likely to resist making similar changes.

Experience, the very factor that supplies confidence and self-assurance, can also deepen one's humility and enable one to recognize and admit flaws in one's work. In my own case, I know I've become more open to suggestions regarding revision than I was a number of years ago, although I'm apt to be unyielding when I'm convinced my position is right.

I'm sure I was inclined to take a stand against revision on some prior occasions because of simple laziness. I didn't want to do the work, so my mind obligingly supplied reasons why the indicated changes were not a good idea. I still have a tendency to think this way, but I'm more inclined to see it now for what it is, and thus have trouble mistaking it for artistic integrity.

Your own decision, then, is your own decision. You'll have to make it yourself when the time comes. It may help you to know that almost all novels require some work after they've caught an editor's eye, and a great many of them require considerable rewriting. While John O'Hara might snarl that the only way to improve a story after you've written it is by telling an editor to go to hell, you probably won't want to be quite that quick to suggest travel plans to the editor who asks you to make changes. And a look at O'Hara's correspondence shows that he wasn't either—not until he was so well established that he could afford to.

But this is all cart-before-horse stuff, isn't it? First you have to find a publisher who's interested enough to want changes in the first place.

Which, conveniently enough, brings us to our next chapter.

Chapter 14

Getting Published

Once you've written your novel, you're probably going to want to get it published.

It's a curious fact about this whole business of writing that the preceding sentence almost goes without saying. The great majority of us write with the absolute intention of publishing what we have written.

This isn't generally true with other artistic pursuits. The man who paints as a hobby doesn't necessarily aspire to gallery showings. The woman who plays the cello once a week in an amateur string quartet doesn't call herself a failure because she's not on her way to Carnegie Hall.

The writer's different. For him, publication is seen as part of the process that begins with an idea. His manuscript, unlike an artist's finished canvas, is not in final form; his novel will only be in that condition when it has been set in type, printed, and bound.

This is unfortunate. While writing is unquestionably a profession, it is also a hobby, and functions very nicely in that capacity. Of those who write, I suspect it will always be the case that a relatively small percentage will be able to produce salable, publishable work, while the greater majority will be writing essentially for their own amusement. There's nothing wrong with this; about the same ratio obtains in all artistic occupations. What's tragic is that the amateur writer is so likely to consider himself a failure because of his inability to publish.

I elaborated on these thoughts a while ago in a *Writer's Digest* column on Sunday writers, suggesting that we needn't publish in order to consider ourselves successful writers. A heartening number of readers wrote to say they'd drawn encouragement from my observations. Suffice it to say now that I feel anyone who manages to complete the task of writing a novel ought to consider himself a success whatever its merits or publishability. If you've written a novel, you're already a winner. Whether you try to publish it, whether you succeed or fail in your efforts, you've run a marathon and finished on your feet.

Congratulations.

* * *

That said, let's suppose you've decided to make a few tries for the brass ring before stuffing your manuscript in a trunk. What are your chances of success? And what can you do to improve them?

Let's not kid ourselves. It's not going to be ice cream and cake all the way. Like a dime-novel hero, you're going to need luck and pluck—and plenty of both.

I might be tempted to offer the bromidic message that every novel will get published sooner or later if it's good enough and if you work hard enough at the business of offering it to publishers. It's the conventional wisdom, and it's the sort of thing one likes to hear and would prefer to say.

I'm beginning to doubt that it's true.

A case in point: In 1977 a fellow named Chuck Ross set out to establish the difficulties faced by new novelists. He submitted a novel to fourteen publishers and thirteen literary agents.

And the novel he submitted wasn't one of his own but a freshly-typed copy of Jersy Kosinski's *Steps,* the National Book Award winner for 1969.

No one recognized the manuscript, although one editor compared the author's style to Kosinski. Neither did any publisher want to issue the book or any agent offer to represent it. Admittedly, Kosinski's novel is an experimental work, and not the sort of item that has best seller written all over it when it comes in the guise of an unknown writer's work. The experiment doesn't prove that agents and publishers are all idiots, or that the emperor has no clothes, or anything of the sort.

But it should give you an idea of what you're up against.

And just what am I up against? The wall? Is it safe to say that the new writer is facing impossible odds, that I'd be better off putting my book in a dresser drawer, or not writing it in the first place? Should I take up Sunday painting instead? Start taking cello lessons?

You can do any or all of those things if you want. I told you before that nobody ever said you had to write a novel. Nobody's saying now that you have to publish one, or try to publish one. It's your novel, for heaven's sake. You can circulate copies among your friends, lock it away in a safe deposit box, or use it to insulate your attic. You can submit it to fourteen publishers and thirteen agents, and then, satisfied that you've made the effort, you can put it in the outhouse next to the Monkey Ward catalog, so that it won't be wasted.

Or you can bundle it off to a fifteenth publisher or a fourteenth agent.

If you want something badly enough, Fredric Brown pointed out in *The Screaming Mimi,* you'll get it. If you don't get it, that only goes to show you didn't want it badly enough.

* * *

This is no place for specific advice on marketing your novel. Market conditions change constantly. Annual editions of *Writer's Market* and marketing columns in *Writer's Digest* will keep you in touch with these changes as they occur. If you're writing category fiction, your own day-by-day research at bookstores and newsstands will let you know just who's publishing exactly what.

A few marketing observations, however, might be useful.

It's been a trend of late for publishers to adopt a policy of declining to read unsolicited manuscripts. This doesn't mean they're all a bunch of flint-hearted old dogs. It simply means that more and more of them are finding that the cost of reading over-the-transom submissions is unaffordably high, given the infinitesimal number of such submissions that wind up getting published. By limiting their reading to agented manuscripts and others that have come recommended, publishers can save thousands of dollars a year.

What does this mean to you? First, let me say that it's not as disastrous as it looks. It certainly doesn't transform the business of novel writing into a closed shop. You don't need a track record, or an agent, or even a membership card in Author's League in order to have your novel considered for publication.

What you do need is permission to submit your novel, and what I would suggest is a query letter. Let's suppose you've written that gothic novel of the windswept moors of Devon and your market research has led you to believe that it would have its best chance of acceptance at any of six paperback houses. You've checked *Writer's Market* and learned the name of the editor at each house who's likely to be in charge of gothics. Now you sit down and write each of the six editors a letter, something like this:

Dear Ms. Wimpole,
    I have recently completed a gothic novel with the working title of *Trefillian House.* Its setting is Devon, its heroine a young Ameri-

can widow hired to appraise antique furniture in a creaky old mansion on the lonely windswept moors.

Would you be willing to look at a copy of the manuscript? I'm enclosing herewith a self-addressed stamped envelope for your reply, and I'll look forward to hearing from you.

I would suggest you write a letter of this sort whether or not the house in question reads unsolicited manuscripts. You'll get a reply, and a much faster reply than if you submitted a complete manuscript, as it takes rather less time to read a letter than a novel. If the reply tells you thanks but no thanks, that they're no longer an active market for gothics, that they're overinventoried with books set in Devon, or any other sort of negative reply, you'll have saved the cost of submitting your novel to them and the time they'd take returning it.

If the editor agrees to consider the manuscript, you've cleared a hurdle. *Trefillian House* is no longer an over-the-transom submission, no longer pure slush. It's instead a manuscript an editor has agreed to read.

This doesn't mean Ms. Wimpole's going to buy your book. It doesn't mean you should get your hopes up, only to be deflated when the manuscript comes winging back to you. But it does mean that you've improved your odds a little bit.

* * *

Your query letter will have served another purpose. In it you've already described what you're sending—not the nature of your novel, but the nature of your submission. You've labelled it not *the manuscript* but a *a copy of the manuscript,* and that's precisely what you're going to submit.

To several publishers. Simultaneously.

Publishers, like everybody else in this imperfect world, like to have things their own way. For years they managed this by somehow getting the word out that it would be unethical for an author to submit his work to more than one publisher at a time. Never mind the fact that a manuscript could languish on a publisher's desk for months on end. Multiple submission, one was given to understand, was underhanded and unfair.

The hell with that noise. The only possible argument against simultaneous submission is that it's improper to lead someone to believe he's the only person considering a novel if this is not in fact the case. By describing what you're sending as a copy, both in your query letter and in the covering letter that accompanies your manuscript, you eliminate this possible source of unpleasantness, and you do this without displaying an unpleasantly aggressive manner. You wouldn't want to say, "I'm sending this novel to ten other guys at the same time, so you better hop to it if you want to get there fustest with the mostest." That just might rub Ms. Wimpole the wrong way.

It should go without saying that we're talking about a clean legible copy of the manuscript, a photocopy equal in quality to the original. Not a carbon copy. Not one of those old-fashioned photocopies on smelly purplish plasticized paper. If that's the best you can do, you'll have to do better.

I would suggest that you have between four and six copies of your novel in circulation. More than that gets confusing. When you submit the novel, describe it again as a copy and make it clear that the editor has encouraged you to send it. Don't take it for granted that she'll recall your name or anything else about you. It may be hard for you to grasp this, but at this stage of the game Ms. Wimpole plays rather more of a role in your life than you do in hers.

You might write something like this:

Dear Ms. Wimpole,
    Thanks very much for your letter of February 19th. As you suggested, I'm enclosing herewith a copy of my gothic novel, *Trefillian House*. I hope you like it and that it will fit your publishing requirements.
    SASE enclosed.

It's virtually impossible, when submitting to more than one publisher at a time, not to project a fantasy in which two or more of them accept the book the same day. There are three things to keep in mind when this fantasy strikes:

(1) It won't happen.
(2) It should be your biggest problem.
(3) Your agent will handle it.

*   *   *

Speaking of agents, do you need one? And, if you do, how do you get one?

It's possible, certainly, to represent yourself, just as it's possible for you to act as your own attorney or remove your own appendix. And there's less potential hazard than you'd face in the courtroom or the hospital.

Some very successful authors act as their own agents, making their own deals and doing quite well at it. They let their publishers act as their representatives in the foreign market (usually at a higher commission than most agents charge) and generally remain with one publisher for many years.

Personally, I think they cost themselves money, but it's hard to prove it to them. They see the 10 percent commission they're saving and they don't see the money they're *not* earning by going it alone. They don't see the clauses in their contracts that a decent agent would insist be changed. They don't see the higher advances and better rates they might be receiving. But that's their business. My business is writing, and I'm pleased to leave the dollars-and-cents side of it to my agent.

For a novice writer, it would seem that an agent would be all the more desirable. He's in daily contact with the market, knows what editor is looking for what sort of material, and can pick up a phone and set wheels in motion. What he can't do—and this is worth stressing—is get an editor to buy a book he wouldn't want in the first place. He can lead the horse to water or carry water to the horse, but that's as far as it goes.

How do you get such a person? The same way you bring your manuscript to the attention of an editor. By writing a query letter of the sort you wrote to Ms. Wimpole, explaining a little about your book, detailing whatever previous writing experience you've had, and asking if the agent would be willing to have a look at what you've got. *And,* let me remind you, enclosing a stamped self-addressed envelope.

The agent may already have a full house. He may not have any interest in representing the type of material you've written. If he's willing to look at the script, send him a copy. If he reads it and expresses a willingness to represent your work, you've got an agent.

Let's suppose you've managed to connect with an editor all by yourself. You've submitted a novel to Ms. Wimpole and she writes back that she'd like to publish it. Perhaps she presents terms. Perhaps she encloses a contract. Perhaps she asks for revisions without saying anything about terms or a contract. Perhaps . . . .

Perhaps you need an agent *now.*

You may feel it goes against the grain to seek representation now that you've already done the hard part of finding a publisher. But it's at this stage of the game that not having an agent can really screw you up. Before you sign anything, before you do any further work on speculation, in short before you make any conclusive move, you should have professional counsel. The commission you'll pay is a small price.

Sounds like a good idea. But won't Ms. Wimpole get steamed if I tell her I don't want to do anything without an agent?

She shouldn't. If she's a competent editor working for a respectable publisher, she'll probably welcome the news; she knows it's easier to deal with a professional agent than with an unknowledgeable and perhaps scatterbrained amateur writer. She may even suggest of her accord that you avail yourself of an agent.

Even if she doesn't, she'd be a good person to ask advice from on the subject. I know any number of writers who selected agents largely on the basis of their publishers' recommendations.

It's true, though, that some publishers are more reputable than others. While all the major houses play it straight, you might wind up breaking into the business writing for some graduate of the Ring Around The Collar School of Business Ethics. You may be assured that you don't need an agent, that the publisher's more comfortable not dealing through agents, and you may be given the impression that insisting on an agent may blow the whole deal.

If that costs you the deal, you're better off without it.

Where do I find an agent—assuming I don't have an editor to recommend one?

There's a list of them in *Writer's Market.* That's one sensible place to start.

If you know anybody who knows an agent, so much the better. The agents I've known have always gotten a large number of new clients through referrals from other clients. Any third party whose name you can conveniently use can make it easier for you to get a positive reply to your query—and that's all connections can ever do for you. After that, the book has to sell itself.

What about reading fees?

Forget about reading fees.

Some agents charge prospective clients a fee to cover the cost of reading and evaluating their work. The rationale here is that the agent has to be compensated for his time, but more often than not the tail winds up wagging the dog. The great majority of agents who solicit reading fees barely have a professional client list worthy of the name; without reading fees, they'd have trouble swinging the monthly light bill.

As a result, you wind up paying a fee in the hope that you'll be represented by a man who, if anything, has negative clout with the publishing industry. Furthermore, the criticism he gives you can't be trusted, because he has a vested interest in encouraging you to keep on writing—and to keep on sending in manuscripts with checks attached.

In some instances, the fee agent is in the editing business as well. The fee's not all he wants from you. He'll also offer to rewrite the manuscript, for a price.

Not all agents who charge fees are quite so venal about it, and I suppose there are a few who are really just trying to cover the overhead while assembling a list of professional clients. Even so, why pay an agent when you can find another agent to perform the same task for free?

The fee agent, of course, is a sure bet. You won't have to write him a query letter and wait with bated breath for his reply. And, after he's read your book, you can be fairly sure of a courteous letter praising various aspects of your writing. An agent who reads your work at no charge may send it back with a brief not-for-us note.

Think about it. Do you want to pay fifty or a hundred bucks so someone'll write you a nice letter? We're supposed to get paid for what *we* write, not to pay for what other people write to us. Remember?

I suppose you feel the same way about subsidy publishers?
You bet.

There is some justification for paying to have your work published if you are a poet or a writer of nonfiction. For most poets, that's the only available avenue for publication. And, since poetry doesn't make money anyway, there's no particular stigma attached to paying for publication.

Some nonfiction deserves publication and can be commercially viable, but it may be too highly specialized to interest a commercial publisher. This is particularly likely with regional material.

In such cases, there's no reason why an author would be ill advised to underwrite the cost of publishing his book. I personally believe that self-publishing is a much better plan than paying a subsidy publisher to do the job for you, but that's by the way. We're talking about novels, and it just doesn't make sense for a novelist to pay for publication of his book. The only possible reason for it is vanity.

The novel you publish with a subsidy publisher will not do much of anything but cost you money. It will not get reviewed in any significant media. It will not be handled by stores. It will not sell enough copies to amount to anything. It will not even do much for your vanity, really, because knowledgeable people will look at the book, note the subsidy house's imprint, recognize it for what it is, and know that your novel is one you had to pay to have published.

You can avoid the last pitfall by publishing the book yourself, using some *ad hoc* imprint. And, if you want to have a small edition of books made up in this fashion so that you can pass out copies to friends, there's really nothing wrong with that. Writing's a fine hobby, and if the novel you produce turns out not to be commercial, there's no reason why you can't indulge yourself a little and see your work in print. You'll still spend considerably less annually than an amateur photographer, say, would part with for equipment and film.

Self-publication's okay, then, if you can afford it. And if you know that it's not the road to wealth, fame or professional status.

And what is the road to all those good things?

You just keep punching. You must submit your manuscript relentlessly, shrugging off rejection and sending it on to another publisher the day it comes back. You simply cannot let rejection get you down, whether it comes in the form of a printed slip, a personal note, or a refusal to read your book in the first place. You can remind yourself that all a rejection means is that one particular person decided against publishing your book. It doesn't mean your book stinks. It doesn't even mean that particular editor *thinks* it stinks. And it certainly doesn't mean *you* stink.

You can remind yourself, too, that most novels have taken awhile to find a publisher, that many smash best sellers were turned down by ten or twenty or thirty publishers before someone recognized their potential. And you can tell yourself that success doesn't hinge upon merit alone, that the determination to keep marketing your book is equally essential if you're going to get anywhere.

You already showed you've got determination. It takes plenty of it to get a novel written from the first page to the last. You're not going to quit now, are you?

No trick, then? No handy household hints to make it easier?

One trick.

One way of taking your mind off rejection.

Get busy on another book. Get deeply involved in another book, so much so that the rejections the first one piles up won't hurt nearly as much. You'll be amazed, I think, by how much easier the second book is to write—and by how much you've grown as a result of the work that went into the first one.

One of the functions of an agent is to spare you the hassle of marketing your own work, not only because he's better at it than you are but so that you don't have to concentrate on two things at once. Until you acquire an agent, you'll be wearing two hats, an agent's peaked cap and a writer's pith helmet. To keep the marketing process from taking your mind off your writing, make the business of getting your manuscript in the mail as automatic as possible. And, to take the sting out of the rejections your novel accumulates along the way, throw yourself into your second novel as completely as you can.

Chapter 15

Doing It Again

It's a lot easier to begin work on a second book if some eager publisher snapped up the first one ten minutes after it left your typewriter. But it doesn't happen that way very often. As I suggested earlier, a great many of us write first novels that turn out to be unsalable. And many who do go on to produce salable second novels—but that only happens if we get that second novel written.

There's no reason to assume that your first novel will turn out to be unpublishable. But there's every reason in the world to expect that it will take a long time finding its way into a publisher's heart and onto his spring list. That time will pass much faster and be put to far better use if you spend it writing your next book.

Among other things, plunging into your next book may help you deal with the old My-Novel's-Finished-And-I-Wish-I-Were-Dead Blues.

I almost hesitate to mention the depression that so frequently follows the completion of a novel for fear of making it a matter of self-fulfilling prophecy. I'd hate to think that, having finished your book in high spirits, you'll now go sit in the corner and sulk so you can be just like the pros. I think it's better overall, though, to be able to allow for this sort of thing. We writers tend to regard ourselves as unique specimens of humanity, so it may be reassuring to know that one is not the first person in the world to have finished a novel and wanted to throw up.

It does indeed happen to most of us, and I'm sure it's not limited to writers. This sort of after-work depression seems to be the typical aftermath of any arduous long-term creative endeavor. Indeed, it's quite obviously equivalent to the syndrome known as Post-Partum Depression, the feeling of emptiness and purposelessness so many mothers go through immediately after childbirth. For nine months they've defined themselves in terms of this life growing inside of them. Their whole purpose has been to carry their child to term. Now the child's born and the mother's chore is completed, and what's she supposed to do for an encore?

Sound familiar?

It's a little worse for a writer. The mother's got a cute little baby to play with, and if changing him's a bore, there's still a certain amount of satisfaction in having him around the house. If nothing else, everybody who sees him is going to make admiring noises. Even if the kid looks like a monkey, nobody's going to hand him a banana. They'll all assure the mother that her kid's a handsome devil.

Pity the poor novelist. Nobody comes over to visit his book and bring it a squeaky toy or a cuddly stuffed animal. His friends read it out of a sense of obligation, and what praise they offer has a suspiciously hollow ring to it. Agents and editors, meanwhile, have the effrontery to tell him thanks but no thanks. His child doesn't fit their needs at the moment, he's assured, although this is not to say that the little brat lacks merit.

My book's no good, the novelist concludes. *Therefore I'm no good. Therefore I'm a failure, and therefore I'll be a failure forever, and if I had any brains I'd blow them out. If I had the guts to do it, which I don't, because I'm worthless. So I guess I'll drink myself to death, or go eat worms, or really get into daytime television watching.*

There's not much point in attacking this position logically. Logic doesn't have a whole lot to do with it. Post-novel depression is just as likely to strike when the book's a hit, and it's absolutely devastating when the novel scores a really impressive success.

Does that seem strange? Here's how the writer's mind adds it all up:

The book's a success. Gee, that's terrific. But wait a minute. It can't really be that good. I know it can't be that good, because I'm the guy who wrote it, and I'm not that good, so how good can it be, huh? Now sooner or later they're gonna find out it's not as good as they think it is, and where'll I be then? And anyway, what difference does it make if it's good or not? Because one thing's sure. I couldn't possibly write anything that good again. Matter of fact, I don't think I could write anything halfway decent again. Come to reflect on it, I'm pretty sure I couldn't write anything again, decent or otherwise. I think I'll throw my typewriter out the window. I think I'll throw myself out the window. I think . . . .

I think you get the idea.

Does this really happen? You bet it does. I've written more novels than I can shake a stick at—though some of them deserve it—and I still experience a letdown when I finish a book, one composed of many of the thoughts presented above. After all this time, I recognize what I feel as symptomatic of Post-Novel Depression. You would think this recognition would help, and once in awhile it does, but often it doesn't.

Some years ago, finishing a book was a signal for me to reach for a bottle. I put myself under considerable pressure in my work and felt that alcohol would do a good job of relieving that pressure when the work was done. What booze does, of course, is not so much relieve tension as mask its symptoms. When post-novel depression set in, I'd go on drinking in an attempt to alleviate the depression.

This wasn't wise. Alcohol is clinically a depressant, and pouring it into a depressed writer is like pouring oil on troubled fires. It does exactly the opposite of what you hope it will do, deepening and exacerbating the underlying depression. A few celebratory "Hey-the-book's done" drinks may be a great idea, but the kind of medicinal drinking some of us get into can be ruinous.

I don't drink any more, and that helps. Another thing that makes my post-novel depressions easier to bear is that I don't have as much of a high to crash from these days. I don't write as intensively as I used to, having settled down to a steady and comfortable pace of five pages or so per day. I'm not panting when I get to the finish line, and that seems to make a difference.

When I finish a book nowadays, I take good care of myself. For a couple of weeks I take plenty of time off. I read fiction— something I often can't do while I'm writing it. I take long exploratory walks, recharging my batteries for the next book. I buy myself a present. If I can afford it, I try to get away for a week.

During this period, I recognize my own emotional frailty. I've learned not to be surprised if my eyes begin to tear while I'm watching reruns of the Mary Tyler Moore show, I make it a point to eat properly, to get plenty of exercise, to keep reasonably regular hours. Sometimes I even try fasting for a few days.

Before very long, my mind begins to remember that I'm a writer. It starts sending up signals, playing games of What If?, knitting little plot fragments like a subtle wife turning out tiny garments. I can't avoid knowing that, to strain the metaphor, the honeymoon is over. It's time to get back to work on the next one.

*   *   *

You write the second book the same way you wrote the first

one—hatching an idea, shaping it into a plot, outlining or not outlining as you prefer, and turning out the book itself one day at a time. In a sense, every novel's a first novel—because you haven't written it before. You'll be ever so much more at ease the second time around, and you'll probably display considerable technical proficiency compared to your maiden effort, but that doesn't mean it's going to be a piece of cake. Listen, it's *never* a piece of cake. No matter how many books you've done.

Should your second book be similar in type to your first? Having written *Trefillian House,* would you be wise to embark on another gothic while Ms. Wimpole's reading your first one?

That's your decision to make. And it's possible your unconscious mind will make it for you. After I wrote my first novel, years passed before I was to write another lesbian novel—not because I wouldn't have been delighted to do so, but because my mind didn't produce any ideas in that vein. If I hadn't been so goddam young and stupid I might have cudgeled it some, but I guess I just figured I'd exhausted the subject and ought to go on to other things—which may have been the right decision for me at the time.

You may find that *Trefillian House* was your ultimate statement in the world of gothic novels. Or you may decide that you're simply ready for something else; while you had fun writing the book, you now regard it as a warm-up exercise for something more ambitious and artistically satisfying. On the other hand, you may have found your metier, and your mind may be teeming with ways to write the same book different— and better this time around.

Remember that the choice is yours, and that it doesn't involve signing any long-term contracts. You can try something else with your second book, then return to gothics at a later date. Conversely, you can write a second gothic without typing yourself irreversibly as a writer of gothics and nothing else. Your second book is just a second book. It's not a career.

* * *

Even if you do write a second gothic, it's not too likely that we'll be seeing more of *Trefillian House*'s young widow. Gothic novels don't run to series heroines. Their lead characters are generally well supplied with house and husband by the time the book is over.

Series characters, however, are frequently met with in some other fiction categories—suspense novels, first and foremost, but westerns and science-fiction novels as well.

I've worked with three series characters over the years— Evan Tanner, Matt Scudder and Bernie Rhodenbarr. Obviously, I enjoy doing this sort of thing, developing a character over several books, learning more about him as he makes his way through plot after plot. When I get hold of a character who really engages me, I'm loathe to let go of him.

Should your second novel feature the same character as your first? Again, that's up to you. If you find that the lead of your first book has a sufficiently strong hold upon your imagination so that you want to write a second book about him, by all means go ahead and do it. Bear in mind, though, that you can always write your second book about some other character and come back to the first one in a later book. You may want a change of pace.

It's important, if you do embark on a series, that you not presuppose the reader's acquaintance with any previous books. Your second novel—indeed, each of your series novels—ought to be complete in and of itself. You're writing a second book about a particular character, not Volume Two of a trilogy; the reader shouldn't have to have read your first book in order to appreciate your second.

At the same time, there shouldn't be so much duplication in the second book that someone who has read the first will be bored. Don't worry overmuch about this last, however. It's been my observation that the sort of reader who likes series books doesn't mind being reminded of certain things. The sense of the familiar evidently appeals to him; he gets the feeling that he's an insider, already acquainted with characters who must be described for noninsiders.

One problem with a series is that you have to remember who's who and what's what. The same readers who most enjoy series novels are most insistent that the writer avoid inconsistencies. It may be no particular problem remembering that your lead has blue eyes, but what color are his girlfriend's? And where did I mention the names and ages of Scudder's kids?

Arthur Maling has a particular dilemma along these lines, and one that serves to illustrate just how complicated the business of series novels can be:

> The Price, Potter and Petacque books have given me particular problems. Instead of having just one series character, I have a cast of fifteen or sixteen major and minor characters that move from book to book—Brock Potter and everyone in the company—and I have a hell of a time remembering the color of everyone's eyes, the names and ages of everyone's kids, etc. A fellow mystery writer and friend of mine, James McClure, made a chart for me, listing all the Price, Potter and Petacque characters and their relationships, and it's been helpful; but I keep forgetting to enter the pertinent details, which means that I frequently have to dig through several finished books or a couple of hundred pages of manuscript to find what I said about one or another of the characters a year or two or four previously.

A problem with a series, albeit one you're not terribly likely to face in the second book, is boredom. Most series writers run into this sooner or later. Dorothy Sayers is supposed to have told Agatha Christie how sick and tired she was of writing about Lord Peter Wimsey; Christie in turn confessed to a deep-seated desire to kill off Hercule Poirot, and proved it by doing precisely that in the "final" Poirot novel, written in the forties and not published until after the author's own death.

I stopped writing the Tanner series not because I grew tired of the character but because the books themselves seemed to have a deadening sameness about them. It seemed to me that Tanner kept going to the same kinds of places, meeting the same sorts of people, having the same kinds of conversations, and dealing with the same kinds of plot problems. I've since come to realize that there's nothing necessarily wrong with that. My awareness of this sameness was inevitably more acute than a reader's would be, since I was spending a couple of months writing something he would read in as many hours. Besides, readers want a series book to be pretty much like the last one; if they hadn't liked the last one in the first place they wouldn't have bought the second, or the third, or the fortieth.

The fact that you've created a strong character doesn't mean you should write a second book about him. It seems as though some writers are geared to write series books and others are not. Sometimes success will tend to force a series upon a writer. That sort of thing has been happening ever since Shakespeare wrote *The Merry Wives of Windsor* because Queen Elizabeth wanted to see another play about Falstaff. At this stage of the game, however, it's not too likely that you'll have to launch a series as a command performance for royalty. With one unpublished novel to your credit, you still have the freedom to make your own decisions.

The journeyman novelist occasionally has the opportunity to produce books of a sort we haven't yet discussed—tie-ins, novelizations, and books in someone else's series.

I haven't mentioned them previously because they're the sort of thing a publisher is likely to hand out as an assignment, and it's highly unlikely your first novel will be assigned to you. Later on, though, when publishers are familiar with you and your work, or when you have an agent who can recommend you for assignments, some of this work may come your way.

Books of this sort aren't much fun to write. You can't display a hell of a lot of creativity, nor are you likely to earn substantial sums from them. Writing paperback novels about the Brady Bunch will not make you rich. Turning Grade "B" movie scripts into Grade "C" novels won't make your name a household word. And there's a limit to how much pride you can take in having been one of fifty people to write under the umbrella pen name of Nick Carter.

All the same, any assignment that brings the novice novelist money for writing fiction is not all bad. And writing the books can sharpen your craft considerably, whatever the ultimate merits of what you write. There's a point, certainly, when you should stop accepting these assignments and concentrate instead on your own work, but you can burn that bridge when you come to it.

The tie-in is a book based on someone else's characters. You generally furnish your own plot, although the publisher or someone from the network may have suggestions to throw into the hopper—which is probably the right place for them.

I wrote my first detective novel this way. Belmont Books had a deal set for a tie-in novel based on *Markham,* a series starring Ray Milland. The book I wrote turned out rather well, and my agent agreed it was a shame to waste it as a tie-in so he showed it to Knox Burger, then at Gold Medal. Knox liked it, whereupon I had to redo the book, changing Roy Markham to Ed London and otherwise altering the character. That done, I had to go write yet another book about Markham, which Belmont did indeed publish.

Novelizations are easier in that the whole plot is laid out for you, scene by scene. You've got a movie script in front of you and your job is to turn it into prose. It's very rare that this is anything more than a purely mechanical task, which explains why knowledgeable readers shun those paperbacks that carry notices indicating they were based upon a screenplay. They're almost invariably lifeless.

The fact that the books sell so well all the same indicates too how few readers are all that knowledgeable, or all that sensitive to writing quality. Sad to say.

Some writers are better at novelizations than others. A pro who can turn out solid acceptable novelizations regularly can count on a decent steady income. A handful have acquired reputations; Leonore Fleischer, for one, is able to demand high advances and preferential royalty rates because of her reputation for delivering a quality product.

Writing books in somebody else's series is just what it sounds like. I couldn't say how many people have launched literary careers by being Nick Carter for a couple of books. Here again, the work is thankless and ill-paying, but it's a way to learn your craft while you get paid for it, and that's not the worst thing that ever happened to a writer.

You wouldn't want to spend a career writing this sort of swill, but one book does not a career make. As to whether this sort of hack work is lower than you care to stoop, that's for you to decide.

If you figure it'll make you blind, you can always quit when you need glasses.

*   *   *

A second novel, whatever sort you choose, is the best thing to do after you've done your first novel. You'll learn from it, even as you have learned from the first. You'll be able to see your own increased facility. You'll be doing the best thing possible to cure the post-novel blahs. And, once you've finished it, you'll have two manuscripts out to market. While this may bring rejections at double your usual rate, so too will it more than double your chances of eventual acceptance.

Finally, there's one more argument for writing a second novel. If you don't, how can reviewers complain that it doesn't fulfill the promise of your first novel?

*   *   *

Has this helped any?

I wonder, looking over what I've written, whether I've done what I set out to do. I'm often similarly uncertain when I write the last words of a novel, skip a few spaces, and type "The End" in the center of the page. Does the story hold up? Are the characters interesting? Is the book I've written the book I wanted to write in the first place? It never quite is, perhaps because one's reach exceeds one's grasp, but is it at least a good book?

Maybe you'll get something out of it. I don't know. In the final analysis, you can no more learn the gentle art of novel writing from a book than you can learn how to ride a bicycle. The only way you really learn is by doing it yourself, and you may fall off a lot before you get the hang of it.

I wish you luck.

I won't read your manuscript, or recommend an agent, or put you in touch with a publisher. I'll answer letters—if I can make the time, and if you enclose a stamped self-addressed envelope. But that's as much as I'll do. You have to do the rest yourself. That, I'm afraid is how it works in this business.

I hope you write your novel. I hope you write a lot of them, and that they're very good books indeed. Not because I would presume to regard your work as a sort of literary grandchild of mine—let's face it, you'd write it whether or not you read this book.

But simply because, while there are far too many books in this world, there are far too few good ones.

And I don't ever want to run out of things to read.

Books of Interest From Writer's Digest

Artist's Market, edited by Cathy Bruce and Betsy Wones. Contains over 3,000 commercial art buyers. Listings tell you who to contact and where, pay rates, special requirements and more. 423 pp. $10.95.

The Beginning Writer's Answer Book, edited by Kirk Polking, Jean Chimsky, and Rose Adkins. "What is a query letter?" "If I use a pen name, how can I cash the check?" These are among 567 questions most frequently asked by beginning writers—and expertly answered in this down-to-earth handbook. Cross-indexed. 270 pp. $8.95.

The Cartoonist's and Gag Writer's Handbook, by Jack Markow. Longtime cartoonist with thousands of sales, reveals the secrets of successful cartooning—step by step. Richly illustrated. 157 pp. $8.95.

A Complete Guide to Marketing Magazine Articles, by Duane Newcomb. "Anyone who can write a clear sentence can learn to write and sell articles on a consistent basis." says Newcomb (who has published well over 3,000 articles). Here's how. 248 pp. $8.95.

The Confession Writer's Handbook, by Florence K. Palmer. A stylish and informative guide to getting started and getting ahead in the confessions. How to start a confession and carry it through. How to take an insignificant event and make it significant. 171 pp. $7.95.

The Craft of Interviewing, by John Brady. Everything you always wanted to know about asking questions, but were afraid to ask—from an experienced interviewer and editor of *Writer's Digest*. The most comprehensive guide to interviewing on the market. 244 pp. $9.95.

Craftworker's Market, edited by Lynne Lapin. Over 3,500 places for you to sell and exhibit your work. Listings include names and addresses, payment rates, special requirements and other information you need to sell your crafts. 696 pp. $11.95.

The Creative Writer, edited by Aron Mathieu. This book opens the door to the real world of publishing. Inspiration, techniques, and ideas, plus inside tips from Maugham, Caldwell, Purdy, others. 416 pp. $8.95.

A Guide to Writing History, by Doris Ricker Marston. How to track down Big Foot—or your family Civil War letters, or your hometown's last century—for publication and profit. A timely handbook for history buffs and writers. 258 pp. $8.50.

Handbook of Short Story Writing, edited by Frank A. Dickson and Sandra Smythe. You provide the pencil, paper, and sweat—and this book will provide the expert guidance. Features include James Hilton on creating a lovable character: R.V. Cassill on plotting a short story. 238 pp. $9.95.

How to be a Successful Housewife/Writer, by Elaine Fantle Shimberg. The art of being a successful housewife/writer. 256 pp. $10.95.

How to Make $20,000 a Year Writing (no matter where you live), by Nancy Edmonds Hanson. This covers the waterfront of writing opportunities. Discover how you can capitalize on your talent to earn more money than you ever dreamed possible. 256 pp. $10.95.

How To Write and Sell Your Personal Experiences, by Lois Duncan. How to turn everything that happens to you into writing that sells. 256 pp. $10.95.

How to Write and Sell Your Travel Experiences, by Louise Purwin Zobel. Turn your travels into cash. All the secrets of travel writing are shared by this much-published author. 256 pp. $11.95.

How to Write Short Stories That Sell, by Louise Boggess. Here's an over-the-shoulder look at how successful writers develop a short story. You'll learn how to create a salable idea and expand it step-by-step into a completed short story. 185 pp. $8.95.

Law and the Writer, edited by Kirk Polking and Leonard S. Meranus. Don't let legal hassles slow down your progress as a writer. Now you can find good counsel on libel, invasion of privacy, fair use, taxes, contracts, social security, and more—all in one volume. 249 pp. $9.95.

Magazine Writing: The Inside Angle, by Art Spikol. Successful editor and writer reveals inside secrets of getting your mss. published. 288 pp. $10.95.

Magazine Writing Today, by Jerome E. Kelley. If you sometimes feel like a mouse in a maze of magazines, with a fat manuscript check at the end of the line, don't fret. Kelley tells you how to get a piece of the action. Covers ideas, research, interviewing, organization, the writing process, and ways to get photos. Plus advice on getting started. 220 pp. $9.95.

Mystery Writer's Handbook, by the Mystery Writers of America. A howtheydunit to the whodunit, written and revised by members of the Mystery Writers of America. Includes the four elements essential to the classic mystery. A comprehensive handbook that takes the mystery out of mystery writing. 273 pp. $8.95.

1001 Article Ideas, by Frank A. Dickson. A compendium of ideas plus formulas to generate more of your own! 256 pp. $10.95.

One Way to Write Your Novel, by Dick Perry. For Perry, a novel is 200 pages. Or, two pages a day for 100 days. You can start and finish your novel, with the help of this step-by-step guide taking you from blank sheet to polished page. 138 pp. $8.95.

Photographer's Market, edited by Melissa Milar. Contains what you need to know to be a successful freelance photographer. Names, addresses, photo requirements, and payment rates for 3,000 markets. 624 pp. $12.95.

The Poet and the Poem, by Judson Jerome. A rare journey into the night of the poem—the mechanics, the mystery, the craft and sullen art. Written by the most widely read authority on poetry in America, and a major contemporary poet in his own right. 400 pp. $11.95.

Sell Copy, by Webster Kuswa. Tells the secrets of successful business writing. How to write it. How to sell it. How to buy it. 224 pp. $11.95.

Songwriter's Market, edited by William Brohaugh. Lists 2,000 places where you can sell your songs. Included are the people and companies who work daily with songwriters and musicians. Features names and addresses, pay rates and other valuable information you need to sell your work. 432 pp. $10.95.

Stalking the Feature Story, by William Ruehlmann. Besides a nose for news, the newspaper feature writer needs an ear for dialog and an eye for detail. He must also be adept at handling off-the-record remarks, organization, grammar, and the investigative story. Here's the "scoop" on newspaper feature writing. 314 pp. $9.95.

Successful Outdoor Writing, by Jack Samson. Longtime editor of *Field & Stream* covers this market in depth. Illustrated. 288 pp. $11.95.

A Treasury of Tips for Writers, edited by Marvin Weisbord. Everything from Vance Packard's system of organizing notes to tips on how to get research done free, by 86 magazine writers. 174 pp. $7.95.

Writer's Digest. The world's leading magazine for writers. Monthly issues include timely interviews, columns, tips to keep writers informed on where and how to sell their work. One year subscription, $18.

The Writer's Digest Diary. Plan your year in it, note appointments, log manuscript sales, be prepared for the IRS. It will become a permanent annual record of writing activity. Durable cloth cover. 144 pp. $9.95.

Writer's Market, edited by William Brohaugh. The freelancer's bible, containing 4,500 places to sell what you write. Includes the name, address and phone number of the buyer, a description of material wanted and rates of payment. 912 pp. $14.95.

The Writer's Resource Guide, edited by William Brohaugh. Over 2,000 research sources for information on anything you write about. 488 pp. $12.95.

Writer's Yearbook, edited by John Brady. This large annual magazine contains how-to-articles, interviews and special features, along with analyses of 500 major markets for writers. 128 pp. $2.95.

Writing and Selling Non-Fiction, by Hayes B. Jacobs. Explores with style and know-how the book market, organization and research, finding new markets, interviewing, humor, agents, writer's fatigue and more. 317 pp. $10.95.

Writing and Selling Science Fiction, compiled by the Science Fiction Writers of America. A comprehensive handbook to an exciting but oft-misunderstood genre. Eleven articles by top-flight sf writers on markets, characters, dialog, "crazy" ideas, world-building, alien-building, money and more. 197 pp. $8.95.

Writing for Children and Teenagers, by Lee Wyndham. Newly revised edition shares secrets for selling to this large, lucrative market. Features: the 12-point recipe for plotting, and the Ten Commandments for Writers. 253 pp. $9.95.

Writing for Regional Publications, by Brian Vachon. How to write for this growing market. 256 pp. $11.95.

Writing Popular Fiction, by Dean R. Koontz. How to write mysteries, suspense, thrillers, science fiction, Gothic romances, adult fantasy, Westerns and erotica. Here's an inside guide to lively fiction, by a lively novelist. 232 pp. $8.95.

DATE DUE

MY 28 '93			
NO 19 93			
DE 17 '93			
FE 9 00			

DEMCO 38-296

BORIS YELTSIN

BORIS YELTSIN

FROM BOLSHEVIK TO DEMOCRAT

JOHN MORRISON

A DUTTON BOOK

DUTTON
Published by the Penguin Group
Penguin Books USA Inc., 375 Hudson Street,
New York, New York 10014, U.S.A.
Penguin Books Ltd, 27 Wrights Lane,
London W8 5TZ, England
Penguin Books Australia Ltd, Ringwood,
Victoria, Australia
Penguin Books Canada Ltd, 10 Alcorn Avenue,
Toronto, Ontario, Canada M4V 3B2
Penguin Books (N.Z.) Ltd, 182–190 Wairau Road,
Auckland 10, New Zealand

Penguin Books Ltd, Registered Offices:
Harmondsworth, Middlesex, England

First published by Dutton, an imprint of New American
Library, a division of Penguin Books USA Inc.
Distributed in Canada by McClelland & Stewart Inc.

First Printing, October, 1991
10 9 8 7 6 5 4 3 2 1

ISBN: 0-525-93431-6

Printed in the United States of America
Set in Aster

Contents

CONTENTS

Acknowledgments

This book is the product of a sabbatical year, funded by Reuters, as a Mid-Career Fellow at the Russian Research Center, Harvard University. Needless to say, the judgments expressed here are mine alone, and not those of my employers. I would like to thank Mark Wood and Graham Williams of Reuters for the wholehearted support which made my sabbatical and the publication of this book possible.

At the Russian Research Center I benefited from the help and encouragement of many scholars, including Adam Ulam, Marshall Goldman, Edward Keenan, and Lubomyr Hajda. My thanks go in particular to librarian Susan Gardos Bleich.

Colleagues at Harvard, in Moscow, and elsewhere, who took time to read all or part of the manuscript and offer their comments, deserve special thanks: Meg Bortin, Vladimir Brovkin, Virginie Coulloudon, Ralph and Leyla Boulton, and Jonathan Lyons.

This is in no sense an authorized biography: it was completed without the cooperation of Boris Yeltsin or his staff. I do however owe special gratitude to three of his close political collaborators who found time to give me interviews in May 1991: Mikhail Poltoranin, Sergei Shakhrai, and Arkady Murashev. I would also like to thank ethnologist Nikolai Rudensky, for a stimulating discussion on problems of Russian nationality, and writers Eduard Volodin and Alexander Prokhanov, for giving me the Russian nationalist perspective on Yeltsin.

For Ralph and Leyla Boulton and for my sister-in-law Jane Martineau, who housed, fed, and watered me during the researching and writing of this book, a special note of appreciation is due.

Finally, a word of thanks to my family: my parents, who first sent me to Russia twenty-five years ago—a journey that awoke a lifetime's curiosity; my sons Alexander and Nicholas, who put up with an unsociable father hunched over his computer; and most of all my wife, Penny, who has done her best for twenty years to prevent me becoming a Dead Soul.

John Morrison
September 1991

Introduction

When Sir Walter Raleigh wrote his *History of the World* in the early seventeenth century, he apologized to his readers for staying clear of contemporary events and sticking to the ancient Greeks and Romans: "I know that it will be said by many, That I might have been more pleasing to the reader if I had written the Story of mine own times; having been permitted to draw Water as near the Well-head as another. To this I answer, That whosoever in writing a modern history, shall follow truth too near the Heels, it may happily strike out his Teeth."

Raleigh may not have had Russia in mind, but his warning should be heeded by all who write about events in a land where generations of Western experts have risked having their teeth metaphorically struck out. As visitors discover to their cost, things are often not what they seem.

A further problem is that, since 1985, Russian political vocabulary has changed radically. Old words have been re-born with new meanings, while new borrowings from English and other Western languages have crept in but with their meanings subtly changed. Because language is so fundamental to the art of politics, I have tried to avoid the pitfall of expecting Russian words to mean the same as their Western equivalents. Some words, such as *perestroika* and *glasnost*, have been so overused as to become meaningless, and in the interests of clarity are better avoided. To some extent, uncertainty in the use of language is a natural phenomenon at a time of major upheaval such as the present.

One such uncertainty is over the use of the words "Russian" and "Soviet." In this book I shall use "Russian" as a historical term covering the period both before and after the Bolshevik revolution. When discussing the period 1917 to 1989, the term "Soviet" is preferable. From 1989 to the present, "Russian" is used to denote the territory and institutions of the Russian Republic or RSFSR, while "Soviet" refers to all-Union institutions and the territory of the Soviet Union as a whole.

For centuries, making sense of political events in Russia has been a risky business for outsiders. As Harvard professor Edward Keenan has written, "It [is] one of the system-preserving features of the Russian political culture to deprive nonparticipants of crucial information about the rules of the system itself."[1]

Before 1985, the system appeared frozen in immobility. For those on the outside, this had certain advantages and disadvantages. While individual politicians came and went according to the iron laws of biology, the structures in which they operated were stable. Like astronomers looking at the night sky, Kremlinologists who looked long enough could build up a picture of the stars, the planets, and the fixed patterns in which they moved. It was a world where the rules of the game were predictable, but where the celestial speed of change made it hard to spot long-term trends.

"Along came a man and woke up the sleeping kingdom of stagnation," the Kirgiz writer Chingiz Aitmatov recalled in 1989.[2] The man, of course, was Mikhail Gorbachev. Astronomers found the stars no longer moved in fixed patterns. As the Russian nationalist writer Alexander Prokhanov put it, "We are a galaxy that has exploded."[3]

For most analysts who have tried to disentangle events in the Soviet Union since Gorbachev's appointment as General Secretary of the Communist Party in 1985, Gorbachev himself has inevitably been at the center of the picture. It was right to emphasize his personal role in a process of reform which he did so much to start. From 1989 onward, however, the Soviet political picture began to change at a giddying speed, and Gorbachev was forced to share the stage with a number of other figures. By 1990, he was more a spectator than an actor in the increasingly turbulent world of domestic politics. In August 1991, the coup against Gorbachev and its aftermath revealed to the world what many in the Soviet Union had understood for months—that his dominance was over.

This book attempts a different approach. Instead of Gorbachev, it looks at the career of Boris Yeltsin, the only political leader to have survived from 1985 into the 1990s with his position not only intact, but greatly strengthened. While Gorbachev's popularity has slumped, Yeltsin's has soared. His spectacular expulsion from the leadership at the end of

1987 was the first real crisis of Gorbachev's time in office and was to prove a pivotal event: it was simultaneously the last of the old Stalinist show trials and the first glimmering of a new pluralist style of politics. While it was Gorbachev who changed the rules of the game by introducing the principle of free elections, it was Yeltsin rather than Gorbachev himself who proved the principal beneficiary. Cast into near total political disgrace, he fought his way back to power through the ballot box, to become a member of the Soviet parliament in 1989, chairman of the Russian parliament in 1990, and the first freely elected president of Russia in 1991.

The man who clambered onto a tank outside his parliament building and defied the coup plotters on August 19, 1991, had been ignored and snubbed by many of the Western politicians who lined up to offer him their congratulations when his defiance proved successful. He had been told by Gorbachev himself that he would never be allowed back into politics. It was the ultimate irony that Gorbachev was to be saved from oblivion by a man he had himself helped to drive into the wilderness.

Yeltsin's unique political trajectory—so different from that of Gorbachev—is important not only for its own sake but for the light it sheds on how Soviet politics has changed since 1985. Like Gorbachev, he has both shaped events and been shaped by them. His stormy relationship with his mentor and rival goes far beyond a simple clash of personalities. It has roots deep in Russian history, in the tension between different concepts of the Russian state. But here again, as so often in Russia, things are not always what they seem. It is a paradox that Gorbachev, the ruler of the supposedly internationalist Soviet Union, is closer to traditional Russian nationalism than Yeltsin, the ruler of Russia.

This book will not attempt to displace Gorbachev from his central position in the story of the last few years; he cannot be written out of the story, like Hamlet in Tom Stoppard's play *Rosencrantz and Guildenstern Are Dead*. But by putting Yeltsin at the center of the picture, I have chosen a different perspective which may in the long run prove more helpful in understanding the turbulent events of the past few years.

One of the things that has changed most in Soviet politics since 1985 is the relaxation of the old patterns of secrecy. The problem for Western observers is now no longer one of too little information, but of too much. *Pravda* has been joined in the newspaper kiosks by hundreds of new publications, all of which repay careful reading.

Journalists, when seized with feelings of shame at the ephemeral nature of their profession, often like to claim that they are writing the first draft of history. Only a future generation of historians will be able to look clearly at the events described here and draw parallels with Russia's earlier *"smutnoe vremya,"* the "Time of Troubles" of the early seventeenth century, or with the revolutionary year of 1917.

With the long lens of hindsight they will probably notice not so much the things that changed under Gorbachev— freedom of speech, free elections, and democratic debate—as the things that stayed the same. They will notice fundamental continuities in Russian political culture and hunt for the patterns of what Keenan calls "Muscovite Political Folkways." In any country's political culture, there are deeper unchanging structures hidden behind the changing words: the way a civil service bureaucracy operates, or the way individuals form groups and clans to conduct politics. There are moments in history such as the August coup of 1991 during which it looks at first glimpse as though everything has changed with extraordinary suddenness. As Gorbachev told the Soviet parliament, when he returned to Moscow from his captivity by the Black Sea, he was returning to a different country.

But such moments often merely accelerate a course of events that is already under way. When they take place, it is like a sudden flash of lightning that illuminates a darkened landscape. How, we ask ourselves, did we never see it before?

Despite Sir Walter Raleigh's warning, this book has been inspired by the conviction that close analysis of the written record, while not providing all the answers, can shed some light on the landscape of Soviet politics. The facts are mostly there—for those who have the patience to look for them. The most important thing is to ask the right questions. As Lenin put it in his most famous two-word sentence, *"Kto kovo?"*— "Who is beating whom?"

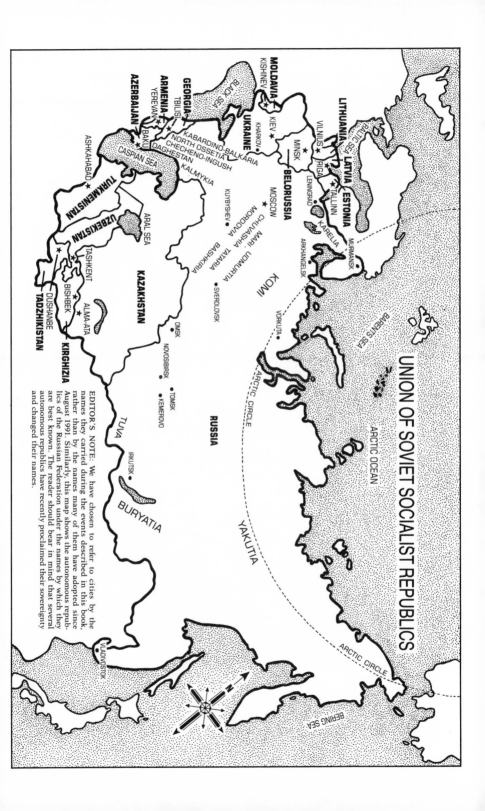

UNION OF SOVIET SOCIALIST REPUBLICS

EDITOR'S NOTE: We have chosen to refer to cities by the names they carried during the events described in this book, rather than by the names many of them have adopted since August 1991. Similarly, this map shows the autonomous republics of the Russian Federation under the names by which they are best known. The reader should bear in mind that several autonomous republics have recently proclaimed their sovereignty and changed their names.

The Emperor With No Clothes

Moscow, May 1991. My first arrival at Sheremetyevo airport in four years.

"You have sex pictures?"

"No sex pictures, sorry."

"Why no sex pictures?" The Moscow airport customs officer looks disappointed. "Okay."

He hands back my passport. I am free to rediscover the Soviet Union.

For some reason, I feel cheated by this anticlimax. What happened to *Bditelnost* ("Vigilance"), that great virtue of the Brezhnev era? What happened to the customs officer who once spent half a day picking through my luggage at the Polish border? Entering the Soviet Union used to be a rite of passage, a grim ceremony in which the uniformed actors would play their parts, and I would play mine. It was a game with trivial victories or defeats—a letter successfully hidden, a Russian émigré magazine successfully found and confiscated. When the game was over, I would pass as through a mirror into another world. Like the three travelers in Andrei Tarkovsky's haunting science fiction film *Stalker*, I would enter a mysterious zone where things would not be quite what they seemed, where people would never say what they really thought. It was a world where an airport customs officer whose real interest was in getting his hands on a copy of *Penthouse* would pretend with every sign of sincerity to be searching for anti-Soviet literature.

Rediscovering the Soviet Union after an absence always used to be easy; it was like buying a ticket to a long-running stage show—something like Agatha Christie's *Mousetrap*. When the curtain went up, a quick look at the stage would show that the sets had been repainted and the costumes brought up to date. But the actors were the same and the script never changed. Of course, once they left the stage and took off their make-up, the actors would become real people again. But when they were onstage, the illusion was complete.

This was what bothered me about the customs officer—he had forgotten his lines. Perhaps he was a recent addition to the cast or too young to have ever learned them? How could this be the Soviet Union, if everybody was now suddenly obliged by some new theatrical convention to throw away the script and say what they really thought? Some subversive new Brechtian director was now telling the actors to come onstage without make-up and play themselves.

Walking through Moscow's potholed and rubbish-strewn streets, the theatrical analogy kept coming back. The decor and costumes were looking distinctly shabby, but the people were different from those of the Brezhnev era.

I remembered a yawning gulf of dishonesty between private and public discourse. With rare exceptions, like Andrei Sakharov and a few other brave dissidents, nobody ever dared to say in public what they thought. As in the world of Orwell, public speech and private thought inhabited two separate levels of the personality. It was quite logical that dissidents who tried to overcome this split personality by saying what they thought should have been diagnosed as schizophrenics. After all, anybody who challenged the system by signing a protest letter or demonstrating in the street must have been a little crazy, given the likely consequences. The Brezhnev period was one of shared hypocrisy, ritual, and pretense, in which the rulers and the ruled conspired together to perform a play. Offstage, around a million kitchen tables, the actors removed their masks and said the truth, but only in front of close friends.

Ten years later, the private and the public worlds seem to have merged in a compulsive orgy of truth-telling. Truths once kept for the kitchen are now shouted in the middle of Red Square.

Red Square has always had a special role in the public rituals of Soviet life as the meeting place between the leadership and the people. Inside the Kremlin, Moscow's "Forbidden City," members of the Politburo kept their secret counsels. Big black ZIL limousines purred in and out of the gates, the passengers hidden by curtains and smoked glass. Intrigues, plots, and disagreements were ever present but were carefully kept within the Kremlin walls. Like the boyars of old Muscovy who surrounded the Tsar, they followed the old Russian maxim: *Iz izby soru ne vynesi* ("Don't carry the dirt outside the hut").

The cobbled square outside was an antechamber to the place of secrets. A notice proclaimed that "Smoking in Red Square Is Forbidden," reinforcing the impression of a holy space enclosed in an invisible envelope rather than open to the skies. In the center of the square stood the temple: the red marble mausoleum of Lenin, with its strutting KGB guards and the long winding line of pilgrims waiting to pay homage to the dead leader. At the entry to the shrine, watchful guards reminded visitors to keep silent and to take their hands out of their pockets. On top of the mausoleum, twice a year, on May 1 and November 7, the rulers would appear to accept the obeisance of the ruled, in a ritual codified by Stalin, the former seminarian. By invitation only, the masses would assemble under a forest of red banners, bearing portraits of Marx, Engels, and Lenin, and of those in the Politburo, and then march through the square in orderly columns. Standing on the marble mausoleum, Brezhnev and the other elder statesmen watched their portraits file past, like so many holy icons. Having displayed their "monolithic unity" to the world, they returned to their intrigues. Foreign Kremlin-watchers, unbelievers in the state religion, looked closely at the line-up for clues as to who was rising in the hierarchy.

These high feast days had their own atmosphere, neither particularly joyful nor particularly gloomy, just reassuringly familiar, like an Orthodox service. On one particularly wintry November day, a heavy snowfall forced the elderly Politburo team to beat an early retreat from the mausoleum before all the columns had filed through the square. Instead of showing an empty mausoleum, however, the live telecast continued to repeat a recording of the leadership at the start of the parade, with only a light dusting of snow on their fur hats. If television had simply rerun the recording of the previous year's ceremonies from beginning to end, nobody except a few sharp-eyed foreigners would have noticed.

On ordinary days, Red Square was at first glance a normal

place for strollers and tourists, just like St. Mark's Square in
Venice, but the appearance was deceptive. In 1968, when a
handful of dissidents unfurled a banner protesting against
the Warsaw Pact invasion of Czechoslovakia, they were seized
in seconds by plainclothes security men. Red Square was not
just a square, it was a stage where the state could project its
power at any moment.

It is May Day 1991 in Moscow, and it seems for a moment as
though the old conspiracy between the rulers and the ruled is
still in place. A year ago, counterdemonstrators joined the
official parade and shouted angry slogans at the gray men on
the mausoleum. Mikhail Gorbachev and his colleagues turned
away and filed back to the Kremlin under a chorus of jeers.
In November 1990, a Leningrad man fired a hunting rifle at
Gorbachev from a corner of the square. This year, nobody can
demonstrate on May Day without an invitation, and thousands of police and Interior Ministry troops have sealed off
the city center. Stray American tourists and strolling Russian
families alike are turned back. Only athletic young KGB men
in jeans and sneakers flash their red identity cards and are
allowed through, eyes peeled for protesters.

But despite the tight security, the mood has changed
irreversibly from 1981. Marx, Engels, and Lenin have disappeared from the streets and even from Red Square. Instead,
their portraits hang only from the Communist Party Central
Committee building on Staraya (Old) Square and from the
Lubyanka, headquarters of the KGB. On Red Square, instead
of triumphant red slogans about the victory of communism,
there are wishy-washy pastel shades of blue and yellow with
insipid messages: "Our strength is in unity" or "Success in
work." The parade is now organized not by the Communist
Party but by the reorganized "free" official trade union movement, which is no longer considered a mere "transmission
belt" for the interests of the Kremlin. Instead, it is floundering uneasily in a no man's land somewhere between the state
and the emerging civil society. Gorbachev listens impassively
to a series of speeches which combine complaints over falling
living standards with warnings that the state must not be
allowed to collapse. "People are tired not of politics, but of
the politics of slogans," says one speaker.

Behind the mausoleum, in the shadow of the Kremlin
wall, stands a stone statue of Josef Stalin. What would the
"Father of the Peoples" make of this sad occasion, where the
Party is clearly no longer the owner of the state but a tenant

whose lease may be ended at any minute? Perhaps, like Pushkin's Stone Guest, he will spring to life and leave his plinth to denounce his fainthearted successor for bringing chaos on the land?

Within an hour the parade is over. Gorbachev leaves the mausoleum and the police cordons dissolve. Young women hose down the granite steps in front of Stalin's statue, like stagehands clearing away the scenery for the next act. On Red Square it is like the moment in a Shakespeare play where the principal characters exit and the stage is invaded by a crowd of rude mechanicals, speaking prose instead of verse. One play is over, but another is just starting. A toothless old man wearing a war decoration shouts to anyone who will listen: "All Communists are bastards!" Tight, angry little knots of people form on the square in front of the mausoleum to argue about Lenin, Stalin, and Gorbachev.

"Lenin was a bandit," says one man. Another complains about the price of meat. A third declares with a wave of his arm toward the Kremlin that "they" (the Communists) have to be removed before anything will change. Socialism is bad, but then so is capitalism, counters one of his audience. "What do you mean? Capitalism is the highest form of human civilization. If you go on thinking like that you will go on eating just noodles for the rest of your life."

The mood on the square is relaxed rather than tense. Lenin, the object of much of the controversy, has been closed to pilgrims for months, and rumor has it that he will not reopen. Already there are proposals for him to be given a decent reburial.

In front of the closed mausoleum, a white line on the dark cobblestones marks the dividing line between the state, or what remains of it, and society. A young policeman stands on it and gossips about politics with a group of *babushki* (old women). Behind him, the KGB guards goose-step from the Spassky Gate to the mausoleum in an unchanged ritual. In front of him, the Russian people, for so long subservient to the state, have displaced it.

Two *babushki* march up the slope past the Historical Museum into the square. One carries a placard telling passersby: "Russians: Vote only for Yeltsin, B. N. Ryzhkov and others, we do not believe you."

"We still believe him so far. Yeltsin's the only one. We've lost faith in all the others. With Yeltsin, we will win," she tells me.

Walking around the Moscow streets, with their crumbling facades, I think of the favorite metaphor Gorbachev uses to explain the meaningless word *perestroika*—the rebuilding of a house. Each spring, for generations, old Moscow houses have undergone a *remont*. Vigorous peasant girls with spattered overalls and headscarves plaster over the cracks and splash on new layers of yellow and white paint. For a few months, the building's facade will look like new, only to crack and fall apart again.

Gorbachev's *perestroika* (literally "reconstruction") was aimed at breaking this cycle; he promised the tenants not an ordinary *remont* but a *kapitalny remont*—a "fundamental reconstruction." But it is six years since Gorbachev's building team moved in, and the house is in a sorry state. There are gaping holes in the walls; the cracks turned out to be not in the plasterwork, but in the foundations; some tenants have given notice that they want to move out altogether, while others are quarrelling over their living space. Some of them are asking, does the master architect in the Kremlin have a blueprint at all for their new home, or has he just been improvising since 1985, laying a few bricks here and there?

Rebuilding has barely started, but demolition is well under way. Underneath the plasterwork and red paint of seventy years of Soviet rule, older Russian structures are being laid bare—forgotten except by the very old. On the corner of Kachalova Street and Moscow's inner Boulevard Ring stands the large white church where Pushkin was married. Closed for many years, it reopened for worship in September 1990, with its decorated walls still covered in whitewashed layers of plaster. Worshippers pray and light candles in front of the blank walls, knowing that the holy pictures are still there, though invisible.

The windows of the house, previously tightly sealed like those of a Russian home in midwinter, are now wide open to the gusty winds of the outside world. Old beliefs, like a poster of Lenin hanging lopsided on the wall, seem about to be blown away for good. Portraits of White generals from the Civil War are now on sale a few steps from the Lenin Museum; private book stalls in every metro station are selling a new generation of anticommunist newspapers and magazines. What sells fastest is what was banned yesterday—a mixture of sex manuals, palmistry, extrasensory perception, religion, and detective stories. Alexander Solzhenitsyn rubs shoulders with Agatha Christie and James Hadley Chase. Lee Iacocca and Dale Carnegie share space with Friedrich Nietzsche and the lives of the Orthodox saints. At the October cinema, Muscovites line up to be shocked by Charlotte Rampling in *The Night Porter*. Theaters now mostly put on plays by the authors of the internal and external emigration—Bulgakov, Nabokov, Aksyonov, Pasternak. Communism is dead, but nobody can quite agree on how to organize the funeral, or what new values should replace it. The old icons coexist uncomfortably with the new.

In 1979, I interviewed Moscow's chief architect, Mikhail Posokhin, about a plan to turn the Arbat Street into the city's first pedestrian mall, an elegant walkway dotted with "literary cafés." The architect's drawings showed a kind of Russian *St.-Germain-des-Prés*, in which Russian intellectuals sipped coffee while discussing the finer points of Pushkin. I thought the whole idea so absurdly improbable that I never wrote about it. Like many Russians, I felt the Brezhnev era would last forever.

Long years went by and the Arbat confounded my predictions. In the mid-1980s it did become a pedestrian mall, but not quite in the way the architects had in mind. Like the flea market at Izmailovo and the market at the Riga railway station, it has become a new kind of zone, where the economic power of the state has finally withered away. From end to end the Arbat is now a tourist market where, for the first time since the 1920s, a new generation is enjoying not free speech but free enterprise. Street musicians perform, poets declaim, and artists paint portraits. Kiosks sell T-shirts with the arms of Tsarist Russia or of the KGB. Samovars, paintings of churches, cartoons about *perestroika*, and exquisite painted lacquer boxes and wooden carvings line the pavement for half a mile.

But the most popular souvenir is a Gorby doll, a traditional Russian *matryoshka*. On the outside, a painting of Gorbachev. Open it and there is his predecessor Brezhnev. Inside Brezhnev, in descending order of size, you find Khrushchev, Stalin, and Lenin. For a couple of hundred rubles extra, devotees of Russian history can find a set which goes back even further to include Nicholas II, Peter the Great, and Ivan the Terrible. Some enterprising artists with a feel for the political *konyunktura* (trends) now sell dolls with Yeltsin on the outside and a diminished Gorbachev inside. Under Brezhnev, free enterprise existed, but like free speech, it was restricted to life's private sphere, to the illegal world of black marketeers or *fartsovshchiki* (a Russian slang word coined from the English "For Sale").

"These young people are never going to go back to the old system," says a Russian friend. All over Moscow, newly legal private stalls and shops are shooting up amid the decay of the old state system. A minute's walk away from the color and life of Arbat Street is Kalinin Prospect, a gaunt and windswept throroughfare of 1960s shops and tower blocks, built in the years when Posokhin and his architects were encouraged by the Kremlin to demolish, rather than preserve, the city's nineteenth-century heritage.

In one of its leading department stores there are huge empty spaces where nothing is being sold. The gaps are being filled by small private retail outlets, selling scarce imported consumer goods at sky-high market prices.

Nextdoor to the department store, a huge *gastronom*, or food store, which used to be crowded with thousands of peasants from outside the capital, now has empty spaces and mostly bare shelves. But a private pizza outlet is doing a roaring trade. The same process is starting at GUM, the dreary state department store next to Red Square. Now it seems set to be reborn the way it was designed in the 1890s, as a giant covered trading bazaar of individual shops. There is an overwhelming sense of a return to an older type of trading culture, more Asiatic than European. The future will be a return to the past, to the merchant world of Nizhny Novgorod and its trading fairs, to a business culture which more resembles Istanbul or Bombay than Houston or Frankfurt.

But there is an alternative vision of the Russian future, an American dream that appeals to Westernizers rather than Slavophiles.

A short walk away, up what used to be Gorky Street but has now recovered its old prerevolutionary name of Tverskaya, stands the glossy temple of a new cult. McDonald's, with its name in latin script and its giant yellow M symbol, has all the incongruity of a Russian log cabin in the middle of Wall Street—with far more seductive power. In the 1970s, an earlier generation of invaders from outer space left red, white, and blue Pepsi-Cola stands dotted around Moscow. The new aliens have gone one better, building a huge steel and glass spaceship which can actually be entered. Worshippers line up patiently behind crush barriers, under police supervision, to board a time machine that will whisk them away into the capitalist future. For Russians, filling the belly with a hamburger is only incidental; what counts is entering a previously forbidden zone. Having to stay in line for up to an hour for fast food merely intensifies the cultural experience. The freedom to enter McDonald's is the freedom to cross the threshold of all those previously taboo zones which Moscow used to reserve for foreigners—embassies, diplomatic apartment blocks, hard currency stores. Like South Africans, Russians know that the real apartheid barriers are not the ones marked by noticeboards, but the invisible ones inside their heads. Now the barriers are crumbling.

Tarkovsky, the only poetic genius of Russian cinema, died in exile in 1987 and never saw McDonald's on Pushkin Square. But I am sure he imagined it in his dreams.

The heroes of the new Moscow business world manage without cellular phones and degrees from McDonald's Hamburger University. Instead they reincarnate the "Nepmen" of Russia's roaring 1920s, a decade of fast fortunes made on borrowed time while the Bolsheviks consolidated their power.

In the Kolkhida, a small private Georgian restaurant on Moscow's Sadovo ring road, one of the new stars of the shadow economy rises to his feet and climbs unsteadily onto his chair. Around the table, laden with bottles of champagne and bowls of fruit, his Russian friends join a toast to future prosperity. *"Davai, musykanty, davai!"*—"Play, musicians, play!"—calls the host in a thick Georgian accent. The musicians smile obsequiously, ready to play at his command.

Elsewhere, the temples of the old system are still standing, but possibly not for long. In the Aragvi, for years Moscow's best-known state-run Georgian restaurant, customers are scarce. Despite the fact that most of the tables are empty, the door onto the street is firmly locked and guarded and a lighted sign proclaims: *"svobodnikh mest net"* ("No Free Tables"). As if doing an unprecedented favor for special customers, a waiter leads two foreigners to an empty table and confesses, "A lot of things have changed since you were here last. The whole country's in a mess. But our food's still *normalno* [okay]."

It is a gloomy evening in the Aragvi. A bored black marketeer at the next table tries to sell us caviar. Up in the balcony, the band plays with all the enthusiasm of a team of civil servants. Perhaps this is quite logical; after all, they *are* civil servants. As the grim porter unbolts the door to let us out, the sign saying "No Free Tables" is still alight.

Whatever kind of market economy is around the corner—American, Asian, or European—the Aragvi is likely to sink in it without a trace. Like the Lenin mausoleum, it exists through inertia, because nobody can be bothered to close it down.

The new economy is leaving many Russians adrift in a world where prices bear no relation to reality.

"I am a Doctor of Sciences and I earn five hundred rubles a month," says Viktor, as he drives me through the muddy roads north of Moscow in his tiny Zaporozhets car.

He pauses. "That is twenty dollars."

A few quick calculations: Viktor would have to work for two months to buy a painted Gorby doll on Arbat Street (1,000 rubles). A day's work would earn him almost enough for a pack of Marlboros or a can of imported beer, both of which sell in private kiosks for 25 rubles.

"We are a spartan generation," says Viktor, as if to cheer himself up. He seems depressed by my forecast of an Asian bazaar economy.

Again and again, Russians seem bewildered by the state of their country. "How can all this have happened in a land with so much natural wealth and intelligent, educated people?" The question is on everyone's lips. Even Gorbachev asks it. People feel themselves the victims of a gigantic confidence trick in which the past has exploited the present. In the same way, each republic believes it has been exploited by the others, or by the "center." Originally a borrowing from English, the Russian word *tsentr* has acquired subtle layers of meaning which are lost when translated back. It is a scape-goat word, a pejorative shorthand for the once-monolithic imperial state. The "center" is a black hole in the Communist universe where wealth disappears, not a physical space inhabited by real people.

But is nobody guilty for having propped up the old system?

"The real loss is not fear but guilt. Everyone in Russia is suffering from a complex of innocence," says a middle-aged philosopher. "Nobody wants to take responsibility for what has happened."

"We are a generation awaking from an anesthetic," says Byelorussian writer Svetlana Alexievich in a television interview. Writers and journalists and filmmakers are obsessed with exorcising what happened to them while the anesthetic was still working. If George Orwell was right when he said that "he who controls the past controls the future," then Gorbachev clearly has lost control of both. There was a time when, like a Russian Orson Welles, Gorbachev not only wrote the script but directed and produced the play in which he starred. But now when he appears onstage, he seems to be improvising desperately. Perhaps he is reading lines written by someone else?

Walking across the Crimea Bridge, on the Moscow River near Gorky Park, I suddenly see what appears to be Gorbachev, standing still on the sidewalk while pedestrians scurry by. But it is not the real Gorbachev, only a life-size cardboard cut-out, set up by a street photographer. Nobody stops to have their picture taken with him, however. Popular scorn seems to have reduced him to the level of a caricature on sale in the metro at Pushkin Square. An "anti-Soviet calendar" for 1991 shows Gorbachev as the *goly korol* ("Emperor With No Clothes"), wearing nothing but a crown and a red sash marked "President."

The emperor without clothes is a haunting image, a symbol of powerlessness which seems to break all the taboos of Russian history. Even in the days when the Tsar was a helpless child, a retarded adolescent, or a prisoner of powerful boyars, the fiction of his omnipotence was maintained for the outside world. Now even the fiction has been abandoned.

But even in this new Time of Troubles, power must rest somewhere. If the man at the head of the Soviet state is no more than a cardboard cut-out, who is really in charge? If Gorbachev's grasp on the cap of Monomakh, the symbol of Russian legitimacy, is shaky, then who is the pretender to the throne?

The State and Revolution

There is a painful paradox which is central to any analysis of Mikhail Gorbachev's rule. How did a political system which survived and even flourished under a succession of weak and senile leaders collapse under a man who was vigorous, intelligent, and determined to tackle its problems?

In 1985, the year Gorbachev took office, the Soviet Union had enjoyed a decade of unprecedented political stability under three leaders who were all medically unfit for high office. Leonid Brezhnev by the time of his death in 1982 was barely capable of making political decisions at all. His successor Yuri Andropov, while mentally more vigorous, was physically incapacitated by kidney failure and vanished from August 1983 until his death early in 1984. He was followed for a year by Konstantin Chernenko, Brezhnev's old political crony and chief of staff, who was incapacitated by emphysema and could barely deliver a coherent speech.

But despite debility at the top, economic decline, and increasing social problems, the Soviet Union was still, in 1985, a military superpower whose ability to project itself abroad rested on stability at home—on a political system that worked. It was no longer the autocracy that Josef Stalin bequeathed on his death in 1953, but an oligarchy that appeared to prove the truth of the view that over a period of centuries the Russian political system "worked best when the nominal autocrat was politically weak."[1]

Open political dissent had been successfully crushed both

in Russia and in the other republics, and there was no challenge to the system on the horizon. It was, as Chingiz Aitmatov called it, "the kingdom of stagnation." While in Poland and Hungary alternative civil societies were already in the making, the Soviet Union was still a totalitarian system, maintaining itself by inertia (rather than by direct fear). The party and the state structure created by Lenin and Stalin were still intact, though a little rusty around the edges.

But after six and a half short years under the youngest, best educated, and most vigorous Soviet leader since Lenin, the Soviet Union had to all intents and purposes ceased to exist. Not only Communism and the system of one-party rule, but the state itself was shown, by the coup attempt of August 1991 and the events that followed, to be made of cardboard rather than concrete, like a gigantic stage set. When Gorbachev issued a decree effectively dissolving the Communist Party, which he headed, it was a belated recognition that the old "center" had evaporated into thin air.

The Soviet Union's slow stumble toward collapse forms the backdrop for the careers of both Gorbachev and Yeltsin. Some Western experts argue that Gorbachev's revolution was inevitable by 1985, that any Kremlin leader would have been forced into radical policies in order to catch up with the modernization of Soviet society under Brezhnev. If there were no Gorbachev, would he have been invented? The weight of evidence points in the other direction: to the crucial role of Gorbachev himself in launching a "revolution from above" to destroy the old political system. It is tempting to speculate where the Soviet Union might be had Gorbachev lost the battle for party leadership in 1985 to Viktor Grishin, the candidate of the Politburo's old guard. A few more years of do-nothing leadership might have averted the crisis or merely postponed the day of reckoning.[2]

It is also tempting to speculate what might have happened to Kremlin politics had Boris Yeltsin been sent into exile as an ambassador to some African country when he was disgraced at the end of 1987, rather than transferred to a junior government job in Moscow. The man from Sverdlovsk, sent to languish in Cameroon or Togo, could have become just a footnote in the history books.

There are other might-have-beens: Suppose Yeltsin had lost the election for president of the Russian parliament in 1990 instead of winning by a narrow margin because of Gorbachev's clumsy efforts to keep him out of the job. Suppose Gorbachev had taken the risk of standing in a popular race for the Soviet presidency, instead of engineering his election by the Soviet parliament.

For those who see the decisions, mistakes, and flaws of individuals as the key to historical change, there is much to analyze in the period since 1985. There are countless questions that can be asked about the relationship between Gorbachev and Yeltsin, the two leading political actors of this period. Were they allies kept apart by personal jealousy, or political opponents forced together by expediency? Was their rivalry genuine or just a show, as Russian nationalists would argue? And when they promised to cooperate, was either of them being sincere, or was each man playing a double game and trying to use the other for his own ends?

Answering these questions is complicated by the sheer scale of change in Soviet politics since Gorbachev's accession. In the first years it was the clashes of powerful personalities in private that determined events: initially, the rivalries between Gorbachev and members of the Brezhnevite old guard, such as Prime Minister Nikolai Tikhonov, in 1985; then, the tussle between Yeltsin and Yegor Ligachev, ending in apparent victory for the latter in 1987; then, the fight between Gorbachev and Ligachev, ending in the latter's step-by-step removal from the center of power in 1988–1989.[3]

But by the late 1980s broader processes were at work in Soviet society. Gorbachev's decision to turn the Soviet people from spectators to actors in the drama was to set free forces that made the old-style politics irrelevant. By 1990, the Politburo and the Secretariat, once the nerve-centers of power in the Kremlin, had almost ceased to matter, because the Communist Party itself was no longer in full command.

Did Gorbachev quite understand the depth of the Copernican revolution he was introducing by allowing democratic elections? On one level he clearly understood that the communist system could no longer expect to depend indefinitely for its legitimacy on its seventy-year-old inheritance from Lenin. But in seeking a new, more rational source of legitimacy through the ballot box, so despised and ridiculed by Lenin, he seems to have made a miscalculation of historic proportions. A dose of democracy, far from making Communism stronger, dealt it a fatal blow. In their more lucid moments, any member of the Brezhnev Politburo would probably have predicted this outcome; but Gorbachev saw no logical contradiction in his ideal of democratic communism—what the Polish philosopher Leszek Kolakowski once described as "fried snowballs."

Once the principle of free democratic elections was accepted, politics became a game not for a few dozen old men in the Kremlin, but for millions of newly enfranchised citizens. After the appalling sufferings visited on the peoples of the Soviet Union under Stalin and his successors, it was no surprise—except perhaps to Gorbachev—that when finally offered a choice, they would vote against the Party and all its works.

Peter Reddaway traces Gorbachev's misreading of the Soviet man in the street to the political conditioning he received as a young *apparatchik* in the days of Nikita Khrushchev, who was eventually toppled by his colleagues in 1964.

This led him to believe, with Khrushchev, that if one trusted the people, loosened political controls, increased incentives, created opportunities for political participation, strove for social justice, and conducted a more peaceful foreign policy, the people would be grateful, would work harder, would overcome bureaucratic resistance to their newly released creativity, and would "make socialism work" rather than challenge it by supporting nationalism, regionalism, anti-Communism or multiparty democracy. Both leaders failed (or did not want) to see that within Soviet society lay the seeds of potential anti-Russian and anti-Communist revolutions.[4]

The new political arena that Gorbachev created was one where his own tactical skills, honed in countless closed-door party meetings, proved less effective than Yeltsin's more populist approach. For both of them, democratic politics and the rule of the ballot box were uncharted territory. It is fair to ask to what extent both of them were followers rather than leaders, swept along by political forces they could not control.

To understand the complexity of Soviet politics in this period, one can look for comparisons to the 1989 revolutions in Eastern Europe. In Czechoslovakia, Hungary, and Poland the struggle for power was a relatively simple one. Most of these countries witnessed the victory of non-Communists over Communists who had lost the main pillar of their rule—Soviet support. Only in East Germany did the battle quickly acquire a second dimension; there democracy led inevitably to demands for national self-determination and called into question the very existence of the East German state.

The Soviet experience since 1989 has followed the East German pattern in calling into question not just the ideology of the state, but its geographical and national foundations. Shorn of its ideological underpinning, the Soviet state has been found wanting in the eyes of many of its citizens. But while the absence of a genuine East German "nation" led quickly to the collapse of the state and union with West Germany, the outcome of the Soviet political crisis is less clearcut. The Soviet political battle has proved to be far slower and more complex, and it is fought by shifting alliances along a bewildering series of fronts. If the conflict is more than a fight over turf between Gorbachev and Yeltsin, where are the real dividing lines?

Are we witnessing a classic struggle between Communists and non-Communists? Between leftist radicals and rightist radicals, with moderate centrists caught in the middle? Between heirs of the Westernizers and Slavophiles, the two currents of classic Russian nineteenth-century thought? Between Communist reformers and dogmatic conservatives? Between supporters and opponents of democracy? Between central planners and free marketeers? Between capitalists and socialists? Between the exploited working class and the new bourgeoisie? Between the party *apparat* and the rest of Soviet society? Between those who want to isolate the Soviet Union and those who want to open it to the outside world? Between supporters of the all-powerful state and advocates of a civil society? Between the dominant Russians and the other nationalities? Between advocates of federation and confederation? Between supporters and opponents of national self-determination and sovereignty? Between the idea of a Russian nation-state and the idea of a Russian empire?

All of these explanations have been partially true at various times since 1985; they are far from mutually exclusive. But all these labels should be used with extreme caution because of the confusion of political language under Gorbachev. Even the terms "left" and "right" are confusing, as they carry meanings which differ from what they have meant in the West since the French Revolution. To the extent that the "right" favors the status quo and the "left" wants change, the usage corresponds to some extent to the Western pattern. But in the Soviet Union, the "left" wants private property and a free market while the "right" favors state controls and socialism. There are both pro-Communist and anti-Communist "conservatives"; there are "reactionaries" who are in favor of a Chilean-style free market economy but against democracy; there are "democrats" who are for national self-determination and "democrats" who want the Soviet Union to be a unitary state; there are supporters of the state who oppose the empire, and self-styled "Russian patriots" whose ideology is really imperialist.

When polemics and name-calling start, political terminology starts to part company completely with common Western usage and take on a life of its own. This was especially true, in 1990 and 1991, of the new-style Communist press, which threw overboard the hackneyed clichés of earlier years and hijacked the vocabulary of anti-Communism for its own purposes. Thus it is no surprise to see Communists denouncing Yeltsin, a non-Communist, as a "neo-Bolshevik" or a "Stalinist." Some words, such as "capitalism," are still too tainted to be used in polite company, though "contemporary civilization" or "the market" are acceptable alternatives. The old state-run economy is now known as the "administrative-command system."

Those who would analyze post-1985 Soviet politics have to cut through this fog of jargon and concentrate on Lenin's question: "*Kto kovo?*" In other words, where is power at any given moment?

During World War II some Western emissaries to Stalin saw him as a man whose power to act was seriously limited by the Politburo—a myth that Stalin no doubt found useful and did his best to encourage. Unwilling to be caught making similar errors, most analysts since Stalin's death have tended to overestimate the power of individual Kremlin leaders.

By 1990, when his power had ebbed considerably, Gorbachev had a standard reply to those who suggested he wanted to set up a personal dictatorship using new presidential powers: if he had wanted that, all he would have had to do was remain as Communist Party general secretary, with the powers he inherited from Chernenko, and forget about democratization. "Nobody ever had such powers," he argued. But as recent insider accounts by participants in a British television series have demonstrated, Gorbachev's power in his early years was severely limited by his Politburo colleagues.[5]

There were times since 1989 when Gorbachev's power seemed to have shrunk so far that it extended little further than the Kremlin walls. Writing in 1990, Reddaway diagnosed "a crippling and irreversible decline in his authority."[6] Sometimes power seemed to have slipped once and for all out of his hands and into those of the people, surging in their hundreds of thousands through the center of Moscow in mass demonstrations led by supporters of Yeltsin. But the strength of these self-styled democrats often proved illusory, as Yeltsin himself has often testified. While the democrats succeeded in mobilizing their strength in popular demonstrations and elections, they found that real executive authority eluded them. They found popular legitimacy to be no substitute for real power, just as the ruling party found the reverse. As Moscow's mayor Gavriil Popov told the *Washington Post,* in November 1990, "I essentially have no real power. I don't command anything. I cannot provide a building, I can't ensure protection for privately run shops. I can't do a lot of things."[7]

From mid-1990, when Yeltsin won election as president (or speaker) of the Russian parliament, until the coup of August 1990, there were in effect two rival governments in Moscow. While Gorbachev presided over the Soviet government in the Kremlin, Yeltsin moved into what was known as the "White House" on the embankment of the Moscow river, the headquarters of the Russian Federation. Power ebbed and flowed between the two political camps, though frequently it seemed to rest neither with Gorbachev nor with Yeltsin, but with shadowy figures elsewhere. These were the faceless men whose desperate and ill-planned attempt to preserve the old system through a seizure of power only hastened the system's collapse.

Russia has known similar times before: During the *Smutnoe Vremya* (Time of Troubles) of the early seventeenth century, the Muscovite state effectively collapsed for several years because there was no agreement on who should be Tsar. There are more recent parallels with the *dvoevlastie* (dual power) that existed in 1917 between the February revolution that ended the monarchy, and the Bolshevik coup in October. These months saw power ebb and flow between the Bolshevik-dominated Petrograd Soviet and the Provisional Government. But this time around, the struggle is harder to understand: Can there really be *dvoevlastie* between Russia and the Soviet Union?

A fight for power over Russia between two political leaders who are ethnic Russians would appear at first sight to have not much to do with nationality problems. In the popular Western mind, Russia and the Soviet Union have been interchangeable concepts, a view which embodies a certain historical truth. But serious Western analysts have for years pointed out that the non-Russian peoples of the Soviet Union make up half its population. National feelings and grievances among Ukrainians, Lithuanians, Tatars, and countless other nationalities undoubtedly grew during the 1970s and 1980s, leading political scientists to wonder how long the Russians could stay in control of their periphery—especially its Moslem areas. "Will the non-Russians rebel?" asked one American author in the title of a book.[8]

What nobody predicted was that the most serious challenge to Gorbachev's political authority would come not from the non-Russians on the periphery of the Soviet Union, but from his fellow Russians. It was, in a strange sense, the Russians who rebelled against the Soviet state, not the (remarkably quiescent) Moslems. It was also the Russians—Yeltsin and his supporters defending the Russian White House—whose defiance put a stop to the August coup, while other republics waited anxiously for news from Moscow. How these things happened, and the role Boris Yeltsin played in them, are the subjects of this book.

Among all the possible scenarios for developments in the Soviet Union, this was one that both Westerners and Soviet citizens have found the most unforeseeable and the most baffling. As a liberal Russian Jewish intellectual told me in May 1990, "If you had told me two years ago I would be out on the street at demonstrations shouting '*Ross-i-ya, Ross-i-ya,*' I would have thought you were crazy."[9]

Some acute observers had for years identified Russian nationalism as a potentially powerful alternative state ideology to Marxism-Leninism. Alexander Yanov, a Russian émigré scholar in the United States, warned of "The Russian Challenge"—a resurgence of right-wing, even fascist Russian nationalism by the year 2000. Some Westerners, unlike Yanov, argued that the West should encourage this trend.[10]

While correct in some respects, these predictions did not come true. There was indeed a conflict between Russian and Soviet values, and when civil society began to emerge in Russia under Gorbachev, there were overtly fascist and anti-Semitic groups as well. The black-shirted enthusiasts of Pamyat and their more respectable sympathizers existed, but were marginalized as a political force. The elections of 1989, 1990, and 1991 showed that Russian nationalists were trounced at the ballot box. The emerging challenge from inside Russia to the Soviet system borrowed some ideas from Russian nationalist thought but proved to be fundamentally democratic. In Soviet political jargon, it came from the "left" rather than the "right."

The conflict between totalitarianism and democracy reached its climax in August 1991. It was a long battle in which Gorbachev doomed himself by trying to keep a foot in both camps. It can be plausibly argued that this was the real dividing line in Soviet politics. Yeltsin emerged stronger than Gorbachev after the defeat of the coup because his commitment to the democratic cause was clear and unambiguous, unlike Gorbachev's. In this view, the battle over Russian sovereignty between Yeltsin and Gorbachev was merely a reflection of the struggle for power between the new forces and the old for control of the Soviet state.

If this explanation were true, then the end of the August coup would have cleared the way for a new, democratic Soviet Union. The overthrow of Communism, as in Eastern Europe, would have happened without destroying the state.

It will be argued here that the rise of Yeltsin and the decline of Gorbachev reflected another conflict, less easy for the Western mind to grasp than the simple one between dictatorship and democracy. What was at stake was the future of the Russian state.

At the risk of oversimplification, the argument can be summarized as follows: the conflict divided those who believed in the maintenance of the Soviet Union as a viable single state with a central government and those who saw it as an empire, doomed to give way to a loose grouping of nation states.

The concept of "empire" has not been much favored by modern political science, and has fallen even further from favor since Ronald Reagan's description of the Soviet Union as an "evil empire" gave the word a polemical and pejorative tone. There is, however, a good case to be made for describing the Soviet Union as an empire rather than using the blander and more general term "multinational state." In the nineteenth century, when empires had yet to surrender their role as the basic building blocks of the international order to nation-states, the word "empire" carried no pejorative ring. In the nineteenth century, an empire was treated as a self-evident political unit, a particular kind of multinational state created by the expansion and conquests of a single nation. Even as far back as the eighteenth century, Montesquieu had written of the contradiction between empire and democracy. It is arguable that a century ago, when the Russian empire could be compared with the Austro-Hungarian, Ottoman, British, and French empires, political writers had a better opportunity to understand its problems than we do today.

It will be argued here that the root of the conflict of which Gorbachev and Yeltsin have become the symbols lies in the Russian imperial legacy. It is this factor—absent in Eastern Europe—that has so complicated the Soviet political transformation and the end of Communism. Russian nationhood, statehood, citizenship, and identity are being redefined in a process that even the direct participants find difficult to articulate and describe.

Writers who have chronicled the end of empires have usually concentrated on the birth of new states and the rise of nationalism. The other side of the coin, the trauma of identity suffered by the imperial nation as it loses its empire, has attracted less attention. Despite the wide differences in time and space, there are common strands in the experience of nations that have undergone this unsettling process, one which may take a whole generation to complete.

Kemal Ataturk forged a new Turkish national identity out of the ruins of the Ottoman empire; other postimperial nations were less fortunate. Austria, as the successor to the Habsburg empire, failed to become a viable nation-state between the two world wars and was swallowed up by Hitler. After 1945, cured of pan-Germanic temptations, Austria succeeded at its second attempt.

France's loss of empire was in many ways the most traumatic, leading to the collapse of the Fourth Republic in 1958. It took the authoritarian intervention of de Gaulle to wipe out the national shame of the loss of Algeria and restore French pride in their state. The internal wounds and domestic divisions have still not fully healed.

Britain's divestment of its empire was concluded without any equivalent, in terms of bloodshed, to France's Algerian war, but the trauma of the failed Suez intervention of 1956 was just as painful. "Britain has lost an empire and not yet found a role," as Dean Acheson remarked. While the British at home groped for a new identity as Europeans, the British abroad were also left floundering. Colonial residents of what was once Southern Rhodesia, a British possession, had to define themselves in quick succession as Rhodesians and then as Zimbabweans. No wonder their identity is confused.

For someone who has spent time in all these countries, the parallels with Russia's postimperial identity problem are striking. Many would argue—like Gorbachev—that it is too early to write off the Soviet Union and that the comparison with other empires is at best half-true. But the evidence to the contrary is compelling. What is far from clear is whether the Soviet Union can break up neatly into fifteen new nation-states, still linked in a loose partnership and defended by a single army. The viability of such an unlikely structure has yet to be tested.

This book covers only the first steps in what is likely to be a long and painful process of constructing a new Russian identity. Boris Yeltsin's election as Russia's first President, in June 1991, and his triumphant role in the events of August were not the end of the story—just the end of the beginning.

3

It's Hard to Be a God

For a man who has been at the leading edge of political change in the Soviet Union, there is something rather old-fashioned about Boris Yeltsin. It is not just a question of age.

Standing next to Mikhail Gorbachev, who is only one month younger, Yeltsin looks like an old-school party *apparatchik*, accustomed to getting his way by thumping the table and using brute force. He exudes an overwhelming impression of brawn rather than brain. This is what Gorbachev meant when, in a speech in Minsk in March 1991, he called Yeltsin a "neo-Bolshevik"—a calculated insult.

Vladimir Bukovsky, one of the most unyielding critics of the Soviet system that jailed him repeatedly for his dissident views, is now a Yeltsin supporter. But his first glimpse of Yeltsin on television astonished him:

> I could not believe my eyes. It cannot be true, I thought; this type of person does not exist any longer. For looking straight into the camera was a typical Bolshevik, a Bolshevik straight out of central casting. Stubborn, overbearing, self-assured, honest, irresistible, a human engine without brakes—he must have jumped from an armored car just a few minutes ago. We have all seen such faces in the old photographs, except that they were usually dressed in leather jackets, they usually dangled a huge Mauser from their belts, and they were usually executed by Stalin. Where did they find this man?[1]

Bukovsky's description catches perfectly the impression Yeltsin sometimes gives of having been preserved like a coelacanth, a fossil from an earlier, more heroic age of Soviet history around the time of his birth. This was the time of the first Five Year Plan, when Stalin proclaimed, "There are no fortresses the Bolsheviks cannot storm," and his Stakhanovite shock workers built dams and factories with their bare hands.

The first visual impression is not entirely false. Yeltsin was indeed a party *apparatchik*. For nine years until 1985, he was one of a breed of Soviet politicians now all but extinct— a provincial party baron with the title of *Obkom* [Provincial Committee] First Secretary. He was a prominent member of the second echelon of the Soviet Communist Party. Virtually all those who were his contemporaries are now in obscurity, swept away by the post-1985 winds of change.

But Yeltsin, like the coelacanth, survived. Not by following the traditional rules of Kremlin politics, but by breaking them. Not by sitting tight and following a safety-first line that echoed the leadership, but by taking risks and defying it. In the process—painfully, slowly—he became a different sort of politician.

If Yeltsin is a Stakhanovite, he is a reformed one. Before his election as Russian President in 1991 I watched him chair the Russian parliament, in ultrademocratic style. Shunning the hectoring and schoolmasterly tone which Gorbachev used to adopt in chairing the all-Union parliament, Yeltsin was at pains to appear at his most tolerant: "I propose that we restrict speakers to five minutes on this subject. But of course, the final decision is yours. Please raise your hands in favor of a five-minute limit."

On one occasion, fumbling with the unfamiliar rules of parliamentary procedure, Yeltsin managed to get badly lost in the intricate order of voting on amendments and clauses of a bill. A man known for his autocratic temper, he was determined not to let it show—democracy was a new script which had to be learned by heart.

This ambivalence between old and new has made some Russians, mostly intellectuals, distrust Yeltsin. They suspect that he is an old-style party hack with an opportunistic streak, one who lacks the intellectual equipment to make the shift to democratic politics. Others have been instinctively suspicious of his popularity among the working class. Nationalistic Russians have dismissed him as a "Russophobe" prepared to sell out his fellow Russians in other republics for his own political ambitions.

For supporters, it was the same awkward duality in Yeltsin which proved that his conversion to democratic politics was

sincere. Yeltsin was for them a man who wielded power close
to the summit of the old regime, then turned his back on it in
disgust. He often seemed to be deeply ambivalent about
power, both seeking it avidly and mistrusting its corrupting
effects. He has built a second political career partly on the
basis of the spectacular failure of his first. From being a party
insider until 1987, he became an outsider; but unlike most
outsiders, he knew what it is like inside the charmed circle of
power. All this gave him the irresistible appeal of a bankrupt
former millionaire chasing a second fortune in order to give
it away to the deserving poor. Yeltsin's credibility was largely
based on where he had come from. As an entire country
renounced Communism with the fervor of former drinkers
forswearing vodka, Yeltsin was in the front rank of what often
appeared to be a nationwide meeting of Communists Anonymous. Among reformed drinkers, the man who once knocked
back two bottles a day has greater credibility than the man
who put away only half a bottle. So it was with Yeltsin's ex-
Communism—all the more persuasive because of his Politburo past.

Among those who are true believers in power and the
state, such a man arouses intense suspicion.

Sergei Shakhrai, one of Yeltsin's closest associates in the
Russian parliament, is little more than half Yeltsin's age and
comes from a different generation, but says he is easy to work
with:

> He has one good quality in that he is open to criticism and
> argument. And he stands by people, irrespective of whether
> they are party members or not. To go from being an *obkom*
> first secretary to where he is now is a big achievement. There
> are some things about him which are still the same—the
> expressions he uses and a certain reserve with people. One of
> his old habits is that he makes decisions too quickly without
> hearing all the arguments. He is consistent on the general
> strategy of democratization and the market, but he makes
> mistakes in details.[2]

Millions of ordinary Russians are less critical. Yeltsin
seems to them to represent their only hope for a better future
in a time of political confusion. Like Ronald Reagan, he has
an ability to make Russians feel good about themselves and
an instinct for the reactions of people in the street. But unlike
Reagan, his skill as a communicator owes nothing to television and everything to his own instinct for the feelings of the
crowd. Yeltsin is never happier than when he is in the thick of

the melee, pressing the flesh with reckless abandon and showmanship, amid a chorus of "Yeltsin, Yeltsin," from the Russian crowd. In his internal struggle between the old ways and the new, they see their own. He inspires feelings of idolatry in middle-aged Russian women, his most fanatical supporters. "Yeltsin is not a politician, he is a leader," one admiring Russian woman confided to me. "That's what Russia needs."

Others have judged him more harshly. The Marxist historian Roy Medvedev, outcast to the fringes of the dissident movement under Brezhnev but now a prominent Gorbachev supporter in the Soviet parliament, has compared Yeltsin to Trotsky and Mussolini. "In my view, Yeltsin is not a radical, he is just a political adventurer. He has changed his viewpoint several times and he is not a man who is capable of stabilizing the situation and finding new paths for the country."[3] And *Glasnost*, a weekly newspaper published by Gorbachev's Communist Party Central Committee, compared Yeltsin to Hitler, Pol Pot, and Mao Tse-tung, all of whom it described as "typical adherents of radicalism."[4]

Yeltsin's political foe Nikolai Ryzhkov, his main rival in the June 1990 election for the Russian presidency, is a fellow native of Sverdlovsk but has no time for Yeltsin, describing him as a man who should not be allowed to have political power. "Boris Yeltsin is an awesome man. If, God forbid, he ever succeeds in gaining supreme power, he will stop at nothing. There will be gallows in the streets," Ryzhkov told the London *Sunday Telegraph* in April 1991.

Inside the Soviet Union, most people have seen enough of Yeltsin, at least as an opposition leader, to decide whether they would like to see him exercise power.

Outside the Soviet Union, however, the world has had great problems coming to grips with the Yeltsin phenomenon. One leading American political scientist, Professor Jerry Hough, of Duke University, believes Yeltsin is merely an irrelevance alongside Gorbachev, who is a "modernizing, Westernizing Tsar with enormous power." In March 1991, Hough told a congressional committee hearing in Washington that Yeltsin was of no more importance than Abbie Hoffman, the radical leader of U.S. antiwar protests in the late 1960s.[5]

Until August 1991, many politicians, including President George Bush, President François Mitterrand, and Prime Minister John Major, treated Yeltsin gingerly, out of an exaggerated fear of offending or undermining Gorbachev. Yeltsin, for his part, has often appeared ultrasensitive to any real or imagined slights to his position.

When Yeltsin visited Strasbourg, headquarters of the European Parliament, in April 1990, he was treated to an astonishing insult. In what was supposed to be a speech of welcome, Jean-Pierre Cot, a minor French Socialist politician, assured himself of a footnote in the history books by accusing Yeltsin to his face not only of irresponsibly opposing Gorbachev, but of being a "demagogic personality who surrounds himself with a few social democrats and liberals, and above all with many right-wing extremists." When Yeltsin tried to interrupt him, Cot cast doubt on his democratic credentials and suggested that he head for the door: "We are in a democratically elected parliament here: if you do not want to listen to me, you may leave."[6] Yeltsin was not amused, and canceled a scheduled trip to Grenoble. It was small consolation that *Le Monde* rebuked Cot for his lack of manners the next day, in a front page editorial.

When Yeltsin journeyed to the United States, in June 1991, as President-elect of the Russian Federation, nobody insulted him anymore. But he was still dogged by his reputation as the Kremlin bad boy who made life difficult for Gorbachev. George Bush, who had declined to shake his hand before the cameras in September 1989, welcomed him in the White House Rose Garden. But in his speech, Bush concentrated on praising Gorbachev: "Let's not forget that it was President Gorbachev's courageous policies of *glasnost* and *perestroika* that were the pivotal factors enabling us to end the Cold War and make Europe whole and free." Yeltsin took the hint. "I shall seek to develop this achievement together with President Gorbachev," he told Bush.

So eager was Bush to reassure Gorbachev of his loyalty that, while meeting Yeltsin in the Oval Office, he placed a call to the Soviet President in Moscow. Perhaps fortunately for Bush, his attempt to play the peacemaker in internal Soviet politics misfired when the call did not go through. Nonetheless, he spoke to Gorbachev for forty minutes the following day to brief him on his meeting with Yeltsin.[7]

Before returning home, Yeltsin also met the editors of the pro-Gorbachev *New York Times*, who gave him their blessing with a somewhat patronizing editorial which praised the "Yeltsin touch" as a revelation to Americans who thought he was capable of nothing more than sloganeering. What the *New York Times* noticed was an increasingly savvy, American-style politician who "talked easily with professional politicians, journalists and others, warmly complimenting the American system. He demonstrated wit, tenacity, and a comfortable willingness to defer to his advisers on detail. He showed that he knows how to deal deftly with symbols, when he donned a cowboy hat and posed for photographers."⁸

The image of Yeltsin as the Soviet Union's first consummate Western-style politician has some foundation: His 1991 election campaign was the third he had fought in three years, and it showed him skillfully adjusting his appeal to different audiences. Just like a candidate for political office in New York City making the rounds of the Irish bars, Jewish delis, and Italian pizza parlors, he deftly made his pitch for votes from Communist Party supporters and from devout Orthodox Christians.

Interviewed by *Izvestia*, he reminded the first group that he had spent twenty years as a Communist Party worker. "I will tell you frankly: taking the decision to leave the Party was not easy."

Then he was asked about his attitude to the church, the interviewer noting that he had been shown holding a candle at the Easter service in Moscow's Orthodox cathedral. Yeltsin reminded Christian voters that he had been baptized.

My name and date of birth are in the church registry book, as required. My grandfather and grandmother were believers. My father and mother were believers until we left the village for the town. Then at school and at college, undergoing our excessively ideologized education, I always heard, read and—why should I conceal it—absorbed and shared the most distorted views about the church and religion. Of course, this was a big mistake and unfair, just like the division of people into believers and nonbelievers. Even today this division has only been weakened.

Nonetheless I have the greatest respect for the Orthodox church, for its history, for its contribution to Russian spirituality, morality, in the tradition of charity and good works—now the church's role in this is being restored. Our duty in turn is to restore the church's rights. I often meet with the Patriarch of Moscow and all Russia and with other church leaders. In church I light a candle and the four-hour service doesn't bother me. Neither me, nor my wife. And in general, when I come out of the church, I feel something new, something light has entered me.

But all the same I cannot cross myself in front of people. Something doesn't permit me. It's probably because you cannot half-believe in something. But in general this process, this work of the soul—it is continuous and it is just as difficult [for me] as changing my views on totalitarianism was earlier.⁹

Any Western politician with a cynical mind would recognize this as pure electoral hot air, a pitch for the votes of
millions of Christian believers. But it also shows the changing
rules of Moscow politics. Until at least 1990, a public declaration of sympathy or connections with the church would
have spelled ruin for any Soviet politician hoping for high
office.

It also shows Yeltsin wrestling publicly with his own
spiritual and intellectual development, his heart permanently on his sleeve. The battle between old and new beliefs
going on in Russia is also going on inside its elected leader.
Asked by *Izvestia* if he felt guilt for what the party had done
to the people in the past, he replied, "Undoubtedly."

Yeltsin has often seemed to lack the intellectual sparkle of
Gorbachev in impromptu speeches, though he is more direct
and less verbose. When he speaks without notes, he sometimes lapses into a crude, almost Stalinist vocabulary. When
he reads a set text to the television cameras, he often sounds
wooden. Though he lacks Gorbachev's political agility and
sometimes his short-term tactical sense, Yeltsin seems to
display a greater consistency over the long term. One interviewer, Barbara Amiel, in the *Times* of London, compared
him to the slow-moving General Kutuzov in Tolstoy's *War and
Peace*, whose solid Russian qualities in the end overcome the
wily Napoleon. "Of course, Napoleon is the more brilliant
general. Kutuzov seems to be the worse for wear and drink
and with no great strategic muscle. But he is so much at one
with the land and the people and their pain that it does not
matter so long as he does not give up. If only he plays his life
in accord with the dictates of the land and the mystery of the
people's despair, he will win. It may be that Boris Yeltsin has
this kind of oneness that Tolstoy ascribes to Kutuzov. Mikhail
Gorbachev would underestimate it at his peril."[10]

But the argument for Yeltsin's long-term political consistency can be challenged: why did he call for Gorbachev's
resignation in February 1991 and then, in April, sign an all-
embracing pact with him, which many of his strongest supporters saw as a terrible mistake?

The alternative view is that Yeltsin's strategy toward Gorbachev has been geared to the long term, hoping not to
remove his rival but to whittle away his power gradually by
tying him into a coalition or round-table agreement. This is
the strategy that Poland's Solidarity opposition successfully
used against General Wojciech Jaruzelski, reducing him from
the effective ruler to a figurehead. In this interpretation, the

inconsistency has been on the side of Gorbachev, as he has twisted and turned to avoid becoming the hostage of Yeltsin and his supporters. This view is supported by the evidence of the August coup and its aftermath, which ended with Gorbachev returning to Moscow to be humiliated by Yeltsin in a piece of stage-managed political theater in the Russian parliament. As Yeltsin pushed home his advantage, it became clear that the unsuccessful coup had allowed him to complete a long-standing political strategy, detaching Gorbachev from his power base and leaving him to reign in name only.

Yeltsin's intellectual convictions, as expressed in his speeches, place him squarely among the Westernizers, rather than the Slavophiles, in the Russian political tradition. In a speech to the European Parliament on April 16, 1991, which was forgotten in the fuss over Cot's insulting remarks, he stressed Russia's place in Europe and its Western intellectual heritage. Russia's return to Europe after decades, even centuries, of separation, was a return to normal existence, Yeltsin said. "I am convinced that Russia must return to Europe not as a totalitarian monolith but as a renewed democratic state with its diverse way of life, its renewed traditions and spirituality. The Iron Curtain erected between Europe and Russia in the twentieth century has not only divided our peoples. It has mercilessly distorted the development of Russian culture and, I think, harmed European culture too."[11]

Such a wholehearted embrace of Western values is controversial in a Russian political context, because it rejects the cherished ideal of a "special path" for Russia outside the European mainstream. For nineteenth-century Slavophiles, as for their spiritual descendants among twentieth-century Russian nationalists, such sentiments are anathema. For the Slavophiles, the villain of Russian history was Peter the Great, whose determination to make Russia part of Europe they saw as a fatal blow to Russian culture and the spiritual traditions of Orthodoxy. Their twentieth-century heirs among Russian nationalists have generally shared this suspicion of Europe and the West.

Much of Yeltsin's Strasbourg speech, with its stress on human rights and common human values, could have been spoken by Gorbachev, though he would have objected to Yeltsin's stress on the fight for Russian sovereignty against the "center." The same ideas were evident in Yeltsin's second visit to the United States, in June 1991, though this time they were tailored for an American audience: Russia was heading for American-style human rights, free enterprise, democracy—a message made more plausible by his own election as the first-ever freely chosen Russian leader. As he told an audience at the National Press Club:

> Something has happened in Russia that seemed incredible to many people. A totally unprecedented event: a direct election of a president by secret ballot in a popular vote. This has happened for the first time in Russia's one thousand years of history. And what is important is not so much the man that the people elected, but the fact that, in the past, there were many people who wanted us to believe that the Russians were not ready for democracy, that they would not accept market reforms, that they would not accept private property, that they did not understand what a public company was—this is what they wanted us to believe.
>
> But then the people elected their president out of six contenders and they elected him on a platform which did not include any promises of a "shining bright future" but which instead called on the people to follow the civilized path of development, the path of development that has been covered by many other modern, civilized nations of the world, including the United States of America.
>
> I believe that Russia will be reborn. I believe that we shall see a rebirth of Russia, an economic rebirth, a spiritual rebirth of Russia, a human rebirth of Russia, that Russia will rediscover its ancient traditions which were once suppressed and trampled by the totalitarian empire built in our country since 1917.[12]

4

How the Steel Was Tempered

Who is Boris Yeltsin and how did he pass from ortho-doxy to heresy?

No Soviet politician, with the possible exception of Nikita Khrushchev, has given us quite so vivid an account of his childhood and early years as Yeltsin, in his autobiography, *Against the Grain.*[1] The book is by turns bombastic, funny, self-serving, and highly informative. The old Yeltsin and the new Yeltsin battle each other on every page.

When he wrote it in 1989, Yeltsin, at the age of 58, had successfully negotiated the first stage of a political comeback after his dismissal in disgrace from the Communist Party Politburo two years earlier. Much to the dismay of the Party apparatus, he had won a stunning vote of confidence from the Moscow voters in elections to the new USSR Congress of People's Deputies in March 1989, becoming a leader of the reformers in the new parliament. His final breach with the Communist Party was to come only in July 1990. While writing his autobiography he was therefore still a member of the party Central Committee and subject, at least in theory, to party discipline. While the book's judgments on leading party figures, including Gorbachev himself, are frank and outspoken, they should be treated as part of a continuing political polemic rather than as an unbiased historical rec-ord. Not surprisingly, Yeltsin emerges as the hero of the tale, always triumphing over impossible odds.

Yeltsin tells a vivid story of his boyhood and youth in the grim poverty of the Urals in the 1930s and 1940s. It is a Horatio Alger story of self-improvement Soviet-style, of a rise that began—literally—in a log cabin. In the process the man is revealed, consciously and unconsciously. The picture Yeltsin paints rings true: a maverick rebel with a compulsion to succeed, an overachiever with an un-Russian love of taking risks, a thin-skinned and vulnerable man with a streak of self-discipline, a born leader who hates to be second in command but who is sometimes his own fiercest critic. In short, a real Bolshevik, just as Bukovsky saw him on television.

"I was born on 1 February 1931, in the village of Butko in the Talitsky district of Sverdlovsk province, where all my forebears had lived." Many a Soviet autobiography of impeccable orthodoxy has begun along lines like these, depicting the young hero's humble origins and peasant or worker descent. Yeltsin's story, by contrast, begins with a Gogolesque tale of how he was nearly drowned in the baptismal tub by a drunken Orthodox priest, only to be rescued by his screaming mother. "They then shook the water out of me. The priest was not particularly worried. He said, 'Well, if he can survive such an ordeal it means he's a good tough lad . . . and I name him Boris.' "

Despite more than a decade of repression against the church since the Bolshevik revolution, there would have been nothing unusual in the decision of Yeltsin's peasant parents Nikolai Ignatievich and Klavdia Vasilievna to have their child baptized. In the depths of the Urals, militant atheism would have been the exception, not the rule, in the early 1930s.

When Yeltsin describes his childhood as hard and says there were "very bad harvests and no food" he is referring to something far worse than just the usual rough existence of the Russian countryside. Stalin's collectivization, completed in the Urals by 1931, was accompanied by ruthless requisition of grain from the peasantry, who were often literally left to starve in their huts. While the Ukraine suffered most, areas of Russia such as the Urals also witnessed great suffering and, as a consequence, violent peasant resistance. Yeltsin refers to "gangs of outlaws" and adds, "Almost every day there were shootouts, murders and robberies."

He continues: "We lived in poverty, in a small house with one cow. We had a horse, but it died, so there was nothing to plough with." For four more years the Yeltsin family survived on the collective farm thanks to their single cow, but in 1935, "the situation became unbearable; even our cow died." First

Yeltsin's grandfather left home to seek work as a traveling odd-job man, building the traditional Russian brick stoves; then his father joined millions of other peasants who left the collective farms for good to become industrial laborers. Because the rush to the towns threatened to depopulate the farms completely, strict controls bound the peasants to the land in a new form of serfdom. No peasant could leave without a contract from his future employers, ratified by the collective farm authorities.

The Yeltsin family abandoned their native village, harnessing themselves to the cart for the twenty-mile journey to the nearest station. Nikolai Ignatievich signed on as a laborer at the site of a new potash plant at Berezniki in neighboring Perm province, joining the expanding proletariat of Stalin's first Five Year Plan right at the bottom of the heap.

Home for ten years was a single room in a draughty wooden barracks block housing twenty families with no plumbing. The Yeltsins—grandfather, parents, and three small children—slept on the floor, huddling together with the family goat to keep warm. "From the age of six, the household was in my charge," he recalls.

"Perhaps it is because to this day I can remember how hard our life was that I so hate those communal huts. Worst of all was winter, when there was nowhere to hide from the cold. As we had no warm clothes, it was the nanny-goat that saved us. I remember huddling up to the animal, warm as a stove. She was also our salvation throughout the war; although she gave less than a liter a day, her rich milk was enough to enable the children to survive."

Yeltsin describes his mother as kind and gentle but his father as rough and quick-tempered. He was frequently violently beaten with a strap despite his mother's efforts to defend him. "I always clenched my teeth and did not make a sound, which infuriated him."

Later Yeltsin ascribed his hatred of Stalin to a childhood experience: "I remember only too well when my father was taken away in the middle of the night, even though I was just 6 years old at the time." It is not clear why or for how long his father was arrested, but the date of 1937 marked the high point of Stalin's purges.

At school Yeltsin "was always the ringleader, always devising some prank." His grades were excellent, always five on the Soviet five-point scale, but his conduct was atrocious. It is not hard to see a parallel between the Yeltsin of 1987, scandalizing the Communist Party Central Committee with his resignation speech, and the young teenage rebel who stood up at his primary school graduation to denounce his teacher for mental and physical cruelty to her pupils. The result of the *skandal* was the same in both cases—expulsion followed by a triumphant comeback. As Yeltsin tells the story, he emerged victorious, getting the teacher investigated and dismissed and winning back his right to an secondary education after a solo offensive against the bureaucracy.

Young Boris seems to have caused his mother a few sleepless nights; he lost two fingers of one hand trying to take apart an army grenade which he had stolen from the local armory, crawling through barbed wire and dodging an armed sentry. His nose was broken by the shaft of a cart in a mass fight involving dozens of village boys.

Possibly he was born three hundred years too late. He would have made an ideal playmate for another towering young giant: Peter the Great, who as a teenager showed a similar taste for battles, scandals, rude pranks, and deafening explosions.

While his family stayed in Berezniki, Yeltsin completed his secondary education at the Pushkin school in Sverdlovsk, "of which I have the fondest memories." His final triumph as a schoolboy was to pass his exams and enter the Urals Polytechnical Institute despite missing most of his final year because of typhoid, caught on a disastrous summer expedition into the taiga with friends. In this story, like all the others, young Boris triumphs, truly a heroic figure in a heroic age, turning defeat into victory like the protagonist of a Socialist Realist novel.

Despite an early interest in shipbuilding (another link with Peter the Great?) he decided to study civil engineering. First he had to obtain the approval of his grandfather, who insisted he must prove his talents by building a wooden *banya* (bath house) single-handed. Young Boris passed the test, as always, with flying colors.

At this point it may be useful to draw some parallels with the career of another ambitious young provincial, Mikhail Gorbachev, born precisely four weeks later than Yeltsin in Privolnoye, a small village of Stavropol province in the fertile plains north of the Caucasus.

Like Yeltsin, Gorbachev came from humble peasant beginnings, though in the rich North Caucasus it is doubtful whether he ever suffered the same level of privation as his future rival. But there was a crucial difference in background: Gorbachev was a third-generation Communist from a family whose commitment to the Bolsheviks dated back to the early 1920s; his maternal grandfather, Pantelei Gopkolo, was a party member and a pioneer of the collective farm system. Both his parents were also Party members.[2]

Gorbachev's father, Sergei, was not a member of the collective farm's peasant rank and file but a *mekhanisator* employed by the state Machine Tractor Station. These units were not only responsible for operating tractors and harvesters on the collective farms but were also the political strongholds through which the Party tightened its hold on a recalcitrant peasantry. The strength of the "red" family tradition emerged later as a crucial element in Gorbachev's value system, buttressing his deep personal loyalty to communist ideals. As he told a group of writers and cultural figures in November 1990, he would never accept the idea of private land ownership or abandon the ideal of socialism because it would mean betraying the memory of his grandfather. Yeltsin's family appears to have had no such links to the Party, so perhaps his identification with it was never as deep as that of Gorbachev.

The real divergence in their careers began with their student years. Gorbachev won a Red Banner of Labor award, thanks to his prowess, as a teenager, helping his father on the combine harvester. This helped him secure entry into Moscow State University, the country's elite educational institution. He chose, or was directed into, the highly political subject of law and seems to have spent most of his leisure time as an activist in the Komsomol, the Party's Communist Youth League, becoming a member of the Party in 1951, at the very early age of 20.

While Gorbachev was running the Komsomol in Moscow, Yeltsin's energy and drive were finding an outlet elsewhere: on the volleyball court. Not only did he sleep with a volleyball on his pillow while still at school, he spent almost all of his spare time on sports. Yeltsin tells us that as a student he spent at least six hours a day playing volleyball, not just at student level but for Sverdlovsk city in the Soviet senior league, traveling all round the country. He also coached student teams and ran the college sports association. "I could only study (no concessions were made to me on that account) late in the evening or at night. I had schooled myself to do without much sleep and I have somehow kept to that regimen ever since, sleeping for no more than three and a half or four hours a night."

He also describes a summer holiday spent traveling penniless around the Soviet Union, hitching rides like a hobo on the roof of passing trains. It is hard to imagine Gorbachev risking his Komsomol career by doing likewise.

What emerges from Yeltsin's account of his student years? First, the formative experience of top-level sports, with the relentless self-discipline required to combine work, travel, and training. Second, the total absence of any sign of interest in politics. Where was Yeltsin at the momentous hour, in March 1953, when Moscow Radio announced that the ". . . heart of Lenin's comrade-in-arms . . . has ceased to beat"? Almost certainly, on the volleyball court.

If he gave any thought at all to Stalin's death and the subsequent thaw, he does not mention it in his autobiography. The aftermath is mentioned only in the most roundabout way, when Yeltsin describes losing his prized watch in a card game with some criminals freed in the mass amnesties declared by Stalin's successors.

Both Yeltsin and Gorbachev graduated successfully in the same year, 1955. But while the bookish Gorbachev returned to Stavropol with his wife Raisa to be a full-time Komsomol propagandist, the first step on the career ladder of a party *apparatchik*, Yeltsin switched from jock to hard hat. He was laying bricks on a construction site, learning the basic skills of his chosen profession. He tells us that he turned down the standard first job for a graduate engineer, that of building site foreman, to spend a year mixing concrete, driving cranes and learning carpentry and other trades. "I considered it a great mistake to go straight into a job that put me in charge of men and construction work without ever having acquired direct experience of such work myself."

It was then the Khrushchev era, when the Soviet leadership tried to remedy the acute housing shortage Stalin had left behind. There were plenty of opportunities for a young, hard-driving engineer to rise to the top. Yeltsin advanced from site foreman to chief engineer and, despite conflicts with his bosses, acquired a reputation as a man who got things done. It was a rough environment—Yeltsin recounts how he faced down the axe-wielding leader of a gang of convict workers, using only his booming voice. "My style of work was generally described as tough."

It was at this point, in the early 1960s, that he was admitted to party membership, a full decade behind Gorbachev. It was probably less a sign of a consuming interest in politics than of professional ambition to succeed in his career. Joining the Party would have been the automatic step for anyone in his position at the time—rather like his baptism in 1931. As a rising young manager, to refuse to join would have been a black mark serious enough to block his chances of promotion. Was this just the reflex of a careerist, a conformist? Yeltsin denies it. "I believed sincerely in the ideals of justice which the Party espoused," he wrote later. This was the high water mark of Nikita Khrushchev's campaign against Stalin, when the dead dictator was removed from his place next to Lenin in the mausoleum on Red Square. By the age of 32, Yeltsin was manager of a *domostroitelny kombinat*, a large state enterprise manufacturing and erecting prefabricated housing for the city of Sverdlovsk and employing twenty thousand people.

Yeltsin worked around the clock, driving his subordinates hard and himself even harder. He built up a fearsome reputation as a tough manager who met his deadlines. In 1969, he was offered and accepted, "without great enthusiasm," a job as a senior full-time Communist Party official, responsible for all construction in the Sverdlovsk *oblast* (province), moving up another notch in 1975 to be a secretary of the *obkom* (provincial party). When, in 1976, Sverdlovsk's Party First Secretary Yakov Ryabov moved to Moscow, to a job in the Central Committee apparatus, Yeltsin was ushered into Leonid Brezhnev's office in Moscow and told, to his surprise, that he was being promoted to take over Ryabov's job. It was an exceptionally fast promotion for someone with only fifteen years in the Party.

Gorbachev's smooth political rise, meanwhile, was continuing through the ranks of Stavropol's Komsomol and party *apparat*. In 1961, the year Yeltsin joined the Party, Gorbachev was already a member of the Stavropol delegation to the Twenty-second Party Congress in Moscow, where he heard Khrushchev's attacks on Stalin. In 1970, six years ahead of Yeltsin, he moved up to be First Secretary in Stavropol province. By 1976, the two men held jobs of equal rank, although Gorbachev's mainly agricultural Stavropol *krav* (region) was less vital economically than Sverdlovsk, the Soviet Union's third most important province for industrial output and a vital center for defense industries.

Yeltsin held the key job of Sverdlovsk First Secretary for nine years and all the indications are that he was regarded in Moscow as a success. What is more surprising is that after leaving his home city he remained popular, a fact he was able to count on in his subsequent political career. According to Western diplomats in Moscow, at least two of his close aides in 1991 were former officials of the Sverdlovsk Komsomol.

How could such an obvious rebel have succeeded in being popular, with both the rulers and the ruled, amid the toadying conformity of the Brezhnev era? The question seems to puzzle Yeltsin himself. "I sometimes wonder how I managed to land up among all these people," he wrote in his autobiography. The answer probably lies in two factors. First, as Yeltsin makes clear in the book, Moscow left him largely in peace, supervising from a safe distance. Under Brezhnev's policy of "stability of cadres," provincial party first secretaries could be virtually sure of keeping their jobs for life, unless their level of incompetence or corruption became outrageous. Yeltsin describes how his immediate supervisor in the Central Committee apparatus left him to get on with it, quietly ensuring that any overfrank Yeltsin speeches were consigned to the archives in Moscow where they would not be noticed.

Second, provincial party bosses were judged by Moscow principally on their records as economic managers. Under Brezhnev, "politics," in the Western sense of the word, had effectively ceased to exist outside a small inner circle inside the Kremlin. Yeltsin fitted the Brezhnev-era model of a vigorous *delovoy rukovoditel* ("businesslike leader"), firmly in command of his province's economic performance. In a system without real economic incentives it was only the drive and initiative of the party first secretary that determined whether milk appeared in the shops, housing was built on schedule, and factories fulfilled their plans. If they did, the first secretary was left in peace. Yeltsin's style of leadership was to get out and about to towns and districts. He also held conferences with different social groups, from factory managers to students to academics.

In view of later accusations against Yeltsin of political immaturity once he reached Moscow, it is fair to ask how much strictly political experience he acquired during his time in Sverdlovsk. The comparison with Gorbachev, who had twenty-three years of full-time party work under his belt by the time he moved to Moscow, shows that Yeltsin was a relative novice, even under the fairly limited Soviet definition of what constituted politics. After an apolitical student career devoted to sports, Yeltsin spent his formative years tramping the mud of Urals construction sites before switching, in his late thirties, to the life of a party official, where his work still involved supervision of the economy. Like Gorbachev's Prime Minister Nikolai Ryzhkov, another man from Sverdlovsk and a fellow graduate of the Urals Polytechnic, Yeltsin was more a technocrat than a professional party *apparatchik*. Interviewed in 1990 about his party background, Yeltsin said, "I am neither an official nor an *apparatchik*. I started as a worker and worked my way up step by step. . . . I am primarily a man from the production sector. I understand the people and the common man. I know how to work with the people. I developed this ability during that time, not during the time when I worked in the Party."³ Gorbachev, by contrast, never managed a farm, a factory, or a construction site, specializing instead in party organization, agitation, and propaganda. Unlike Yeltsin, he was a persuasive talker with considerable charm.

Of course, Yeltsin learned how to lobby the leadership in Moscow and protect his position; he describes how he dictated to the enfeebled Brezhnev the draft of a Politburo decision ordering the construction of a metro in Sverdlovsk. But most of this lobbying concerned economic issues and was addressed to government ministers rather than party officials. Although he was elected to the party Central Committee in 1981, its meetings had by then become brief, formal affairs, without real debate, held twice a year for two or three hours.

There were occasional unwelcome brushes with authority in Moscow, however. One day Yeltsin found himself forced to comply with what he later described as a "senseless" secret decision by the Politburo to demolish the Ipatiev House in Sverdlovsk, where Tsar Nicholas II and his family had been murdered in 1918. "We were given three days to tear the house down. I asked the people who had sent the paper to Sverdlovsk—how am I to explain this to the people? 'However you want to.' They told me to take responsibility for everything. At that time I was the youngest province first secretary, and though I had teeth, they had not yet been sharpened."⁴ Yeltsin's role in demolishing the Ipatiev House was to be held against him by Russian nationalists, years later.

During the heyday of Brezhnev's absurd personality cult in the early 1980s, Yeltsin was pressured to install a museum at a house in Sverdlovsk where the bemedaled General Secretary had briefly worked as a land surveyor in 1928 and 1929. "I asked: and the baptismal font in the town where he was born—did you line that with gold? The trough in which I, for example, was baptized you cannot even find now. . . . That was perhaps the first time I showed my disobedience—I did not submit to the decision of the Central Committee. They called me to Moscow and put me through the wringer."⁵

Back home in his own province, his political power was unlimited and the "leading role of the Party" ensured that his every command was obeyed. "The First Secretary was a god, a tsar," he recalled. Persuasion and political skills were hardly needed, only the ability to give orders and ensure they were followed. "I was brought up in the system; everything was steeped in the methods of the 'command' system, and I too acted accordingly. Whether I was chairing a meeting, running my office, or delivering a report to a plenum— everything that one did was expressed in terms of pressure, threats, and coercion." Gradually, however, a certain disillusion seems to have set in. "The system was beginning to fail," he wrote in 1989. This description of his mood after several years as Sverdlovsk first secretary may have been written with hindsight, but Yeltsin would have had to be blind to overlook the economic stagnation of the late Brezhnev period.

It was in this period that Yeltsin first met Gorbachev, who had moved to Moscow as the Party's farming expert in 1978. "We had a good relationship. And I think that when he first came to work at the Central Committee he was different from his present self; more open, sincere, and frank." Nonetheless, Yeltsin recalls the first sign of tension, when Gorbachev backed up party inspectors who had written a negative report on Sverdlovsk province's agricultural performance.

The record of Yeltsin's Sverdlovsk period and his historical popularity there serve as evidence against the charge that he was no more than a typical Brezhnev-era *apparatchik*. L. Pikhoya, a Yeltsin staffer in his 1990 election campaign in Sverdlovsk for a Russian parliament seat, recalled:

> Back in the 1970s, he was one of the few leaders unafraid of meeting the people and, indeed, actively sought out various encounters. He met with us sociologists at the beginning of each school year, presenting the Party's plans and listening to our suggestions and grievances in a get-together which would last five or six hours. At that time, no one had thought of *glasnost*, yet he appeared on television to answer letters and to take phone calls. During these appearances, real questions about everyday life were discussed. Ought we to end rationing coupons for meat? Where ought we to build the new theater? Yeltsin's openness made a positive impression, and people responded enthusiastically when, for example, he said help was required to bring in the harvest.[6]

Yeltsin tells us he made a "fighting speech" against stagnation at the Twenty-sixth Party Congress, in 1981. This can be checked against the published record, which—unless the printed version was doctored—reveals his claim to be exaggerated. Apart from a routine swipe at the central economic ministries in Moscow for failing to pool their resources at provincial level, there was nothing in the text of Yeltsin's speech to distinguish it from dozens of others scripted in the uniquely flatulent, self-congratulatory style of the late Brezhnev period. He included an obligatory fulsome tribute to the "wise collective reason, titanic labor, unbending will, and unsurpassed organizational talent of the Communist Party and its combat headquarters—the Central Committee and the Politburo headed by Comrade Leonid Ilyich Brezhnev." Yeltsin mentioned Brezhnev five times in his speech—about average—and it would be unfair to single him out more than others for the sin of flattery. Gorbachev did not speak at the congress so no comparisons are possible, but the man Yeltsin was eventually to replace as chief of the Moscow party organization, Viktor Grishin, mentioned Brezhnev nine times.[7]

Not long after the Congress Yeltsin wrote a rousing 60 kopecks worth of party propaganda to publicize its "historic" decisions in Sverdlovsk. "The Central Urals—Frontiers of Creation" was 154 pages of pure jargon, which displayed no trace of its author's personality or views. The chapter headings, written by a specialist in uplifting late-Brezhnev prose, included "Inspiring Perspectives," "Union of Work and Knowledge," "To Educate in Work and Deed," and "For a Leninist Style of Party Work." Pages of meaningless statistics alternated with quotes from Brezhnev, such as "The Economy Must Be Economical," and descriptions of outstanding labor victories in the fields and factories of Sverdlovsk province. It was not an auspicious debut as an author, but it would be most charitable to assume that most of it was written not by Yeltsin but by his staff.[8]

In November 1982, Brezhnev was dead. In fact the stagnant waters had started to move a little in January, with the death of the Politburo's kingmaker and ideological watchdog, Mikhail Suslov. Yeltsin was still in Sverdlovsk in relative obscurity, while Gorbachev had been in Moscow for four years, undertaking the thankless task of supervising Soviet agriculture as a secretary of the Central Committee. Gorbachev became a full member of the Politburo in 1980, rose in stature and influence under Brezhnev's ailing successor, Yuri Andropov, and became the heir apparent when Andropov was replaced by another invalid, Konstantin Chernenko. When Chernenko succumbed to emphysema in 1985, Gorbachev moved quickly to rule out any challenge by the Brezhnevite old guard and became General Secretary. It was a decision made by the Politburo and only ratified by the

Central Committee, though Yeltsin wrote in his autobiography that he and other provincial party bosses supported Gorbachev.

In April 1985, a few weeks after the appointment of Gorbachev at a Central Committee meeting, Yeltsin was busy as usual exercising the Party's right to be infallible. He was deciding on behalf of the farmers of Sverdlovsk province whether it was time for them to sow their crops—one of the routine duties of a provincial chieftain in a system that never trusted farmers to make such decisions themselves. He had already turned down several offers to move to Moscow as a minister; this time he was asked by Central Committee Secretary Vladimir Dolgikh to be head of a section in the Central Committee construction department. Again Yeltsin turned it down, saying he wanted to stay in Sverdlovsk. After a second phone call from Moscow, this time from Gorbachev's deputy Yegor Ligachev, he was obliged to follow party discipline and reluctantly packed his bags.

In view of the later friction and enmity between Ligachev and Yeltsin, there is some irony in Ligachev's role in bringing him to Moscow. Ligachev was a few years older than Yeltsin and had served for many years as First Secretary in the west Siberian province of Tomsk, not so far from Sverdlovsk. Neither he nor Yeltsin were tainted by the sleazy corruption of the Brezhnev era. Each was, in his own way, a puritan, though subsequent events were to reveal an enormous gulf between their political views and methods of work. Ligachev had been to Sverdlovsk, in September 1984, and found its residents enthusiastic about Yeltsin, his aide Valery Legostayev recalled. He came back to Moscow ecstatic about the 53-year-old local party chief. "Ligachev is the kind of person who gets enthusiasms for people. He called the department together and told us about this great person he'd found, the First Secretary in Sverdlovsk."[9]

"I had never had any ambition or even wish to work in Moscow," Yeltsin wrote later, an interesting admission from a man who was frequently to be charged with Napoleonic ambition. His reluctance to move was also prompted by a feeling that the job of a section chief was hardly a promotion from being in charge of one of the largest provincial party organizations in the country, with a quarter of a million members. His two predecessors as Sverdlovsk First Secretary, Andrei Kirilenko and Yakov Ryabov, had both moved to Moscow—like Gorbachev—at the higher rung of Central Committee Secretary. Yeltsin, a man with a keen sense of his own worth, felt he should get equal treatment.

The new job he had accepted without enthusiasm was in no way political: "I was, as it were, a manager in disguise." His new job of supervising construction work duplicated what he had done in Sverdlovsk, but this time the responsibilities covered the whole Soviet Union. Two months later, in June 1985, he moved up to become a Central Committee secretary, still responsible for construction, but with a wider brief and frequent travel to meet the leadership of the Soviet republics. From a trip to Uzbekistan he returned with evidence of bribe-taking by the local party leaders, but Gorbachev did not want to know and lost his temper.

As a Central Committee secretary Yeltsin was now in the inner circle of the leadership, gaining his first glimpse of the spoils of high office and the way of life which he later described ironically as "full Communism." Yeltsin was offered the luxurious *dacha* (country house) which Gorbachev had vacated on his promotion to be party chief. Only six months later, in December 1985, Yeltsin was summoned by Gorbachev and the other Politburo members and told he was to replace Viktor Grishin as head of the Moscow city party organization. According to his own account, he accepted the job only with great reluctance, after a discussion he describes as difficult and embarrassing.

Yeltsin realized he was being used as a weapon to remove and discredit Grishin, the man who had been Gorbachev's main rival for the General Secretary's job when Chernenko died. Grishin, accurately described by Yeltsin as "a mixture of bombast and servility," had engineered a series of macabre televised appearances with the invalid Chernenko before he died, designed to show Grishin as the heir apparent. He was therefore a marked man and was to be one of the early casualties in Gorbachev's first wave of personnel changes, masterminded by Ligachev.

Grishin's removal was "a very painful process," according to an aide. Gorbachev summoned the 70-year-old Grishin to his office to break the news. "He told me there was a lot of criticism and discontent among the people, and said maybe I should think about giving someone else a chance to try working in Moscow." Grishin wanted to stay on for a month until a scheduled conference of the Moscow party, but Gorbachev was firm.[10]

Yeltsin, one of the few officials at the top with a reputation for vigor and drive and a successful record running one of the most important provinces in the country, was seen as the best available candidate to replace Grishin. "We needed an experienced and energetic man, with a critical attitude to certain things. Comrade Yeltsin had these qualities," Gorbachev was to tell the Nineteenth Party Conference in 1988, when the "Yeltsin affair" was finally laundered in public. Reluctantly, Yeltsin agreed to take the job. Looking back, he wondered why Gorbachev picked him. "He [Gorbachev] knew my character and no doubt felt certain I would be able to clear away the old debris, to fight the mafia, and that I was tough enough to carry out a wholesale cleanup of the personnel."

5

Dead Souls

According to Yeltsin's account, Grishin's removal went smoothly. The Moscow City Party Committee (Gorkom) met on December 24, 1985, to hear an address by Gorbachev, retire Grishin on pension, and install Yeltsin as its new leader. Gorbachev's presence was seen by some Western analysts as a sign of resistance by Grishin to his removal, but there was no hint of this in public.

In 1985, there were still fixed rules and customs in the Soviet political system: Once Yeltsin's appointment had been decided by the Politburo, the Party's inner council, the meeting of the Moscow party committee to elect him was a mere formality. It would have been unthinkable for Grishin or his supporters to have resisted openly. The signal sent by Gorbachev's presence was that a wholesale cleanup of the Moscow party structure was on the agenda. The Grishin system, a major unit in the network of mutually supporting clans which had flourished under Brezhnev, was under threat. Yeltsin's mission was to reform the biggest and most influential party organization in the country. It was a tall order.

At this point Gorbachev had been CPSU (Communist Party of the Soviet Union) General Secretary for less than a year, and the scope of his reform policies was still uncertain. Many hoped that behind the fog of new words and the bustle of new academic advisers *perestroika* would turn out to be just another Brezhnev-style campaign which would last a few months, then fade away. Later, one of Gorbachev's conservative critics, the writer Yuri Bondarev, was to compare him to a pilot who takes off without knowing where he is going to land. Bondarev's jibe was close to the mark, but Gorbachev's initial vagueness was also due to tactical caution. His room to maneuver was severely limited by the lack of a decisive majority in the Party's leading organs for anything more than cosmetic change. Under Brezhnev, even the word "reform" had been banned from the official vocabulary because of its echoes of the 1968 Prague Spring in Czechoslovakia, suppressed by Warsaw Pact intervention.

Gorbachev was therefore forced to move ahead step by step, leading his conservative colleagues down a road they would probably have refused to travel, had they been able to imagine the likely destination. In the Politburo, the presence of Ligachev was a mixed blessing for Gorbachev. While he was certainly an ally in cleaning up the corruption and cronyism of the Brezhnev period, he was a conservative ideologue with no real interest in reform.

A more experienced politician than Yeltsin would have been better attuned to the ambiguities of Gorbachev's position and aware of his patron's relative weakness in the Politburo, which was still largely staffed by holdovers from the Brezhnev period. Yeltsin, from Gorbachev's point of view, could be counted on as a counterweight to the veterans and a source of support for his limited reform agenda: to reverse the slowdown of the Soviet economy, to promote a new generation to replace the Brezhnev men, to curb corruption, and to restore vigorous party leadership. In this early stage of Gorbachev's rule, democratization and *glasnost* were not yet fully on the agenda, and reform was envisaged as a process moving in the traditional Soviet direction—from the top down.

Yeltsin's axe fell first on the elderly Vladimir Promyslov, the globe-trotting Chairman of the Moscow Soviet, or mayor of the capital. Out he went, to be replaced by Valery Saikin, manager of the ZIL truck factory. Yeltsin picked Saikin because he wanted a man from outside the ranks of full-time party officials. Out went Grishin's personal staff and his assistants, the other Moscow party secretaries left over from the old regime. Within days of his appointment, Yeltsin was touring suburban shops and factories, waiting in line for buses, and catching the metro. Sometimes he took the television cameras with him, as when he signed on at his local polyclinic, rather than the Kremlin hospital. This was the style he had adopted in Sverdlovsk. For a Western politician, it might be thought routine image-making, but for Moscow it was a radical innovation.

A month after his appointment, Yeltsin summoned the party elite to a city conference at which he denounced the Grishin era for "ostentation, overemphasizing successes, and covering up shortcomings." Under Grishin, Moscow was supposed to turn into a "model communist city" but its economy was in decline and its municipal services were creaking. Muscovites, he told them, "are no longer simply complaining. They are indignant." Some 35 percent of the capital's buses were off the road each day, 65,000 people were waiting for kindergarten places, and 16 percent of people still lived in a communal apartments. The retail network was riddled with "money-grubbing, thievery, and bribe-taking." What was needed, he said, was criticism, as vital as fresh air.[1] It was a traditional tough speech in the language of an *apparatchik* with no doubts about the Party's mission to control society from the top.

On February 18, 1986, the eve of the Twenty-seventh Party Congress, Grishin lost his seat on the Politburo, and the Central Committee promoted Yeltsin to be a candidate member. At the congress Yeltsin headed the second-largest delegation. With 321 delegates, the Moscow party group represented 1.1 million Communists, more than in many of the 15 union republics. Only the Ukraine, with 889 delegates, sent more.

Yeltsin's speech was one of the most vigorous pleas for reform yet heard, going further than Gorbachev in denouncing what he called "an inert layer of time-servers with party cards." At this stage Yeltsin, far from arguing that society should be free from party control or democratized, was arguing that the power of the center was too ineffective; he complained about "a weakening of party influence over literature and art." The Party's central apparatus had become so closely involved with economic management that it was unable to give any political leadership. What is important to note is that Yeltsin's speech attacked the very people in the Central Committee apparatus whom he needed as allies if he was to have any hope of succeeding in Moscow. Then came a personal confession, which for older listeners would have instantly recalled the moment when Nikita Khrushchev, in his "secret speech" denouncing Stalin at the Twentieth Party Congress in 1956, confessed his failure to resist Stalin. Khrushchev had declared: "Some comrades may ask us: where were the members of the Politburo of the Central Committee? Why did they not assert themselves against the cult of personality in time, and why is this being done only now?"

Echoing Khrushchev, Yeltsin asked: "Why did I not say this in my speech at the Twenty-sixth Party Congress [in 1981]? So be it. I can answer, and answer frankly, that I clearly did not have sufficient boldness or political experience at the time."[2] One Muscovite, recalling the moment five years later, commented, "At the time I thought it was rather cheap. He was trying to win credit for having kept his mouth shut. But I now realize he was the only one who was even prepared to raise the issue of responsibility for the past."

His next remarks on the issue of social justice broke a party taboo. "It is particularly painful when people talk bluntly about special benefits for leaders." Citing Lenin to back up his argument, he said such privileges should be abolished at all levels, though he qualified this radical demand by adding "wherever they are unjustified." Yeltsin's call won no support from other Politburo members and it was clear he was going out on a limb. The origin of the split between Gorbachev and Yeltsin can be seen in the populist tone of this speech and in Yeltsin's abrasive attitude to the party *apparat*, led by Ligachev.

It is hard for outsiders to imagine just how sensitive a subject Yeltsin was raising. The privileges of the party elite were not just a fringe benefit but a vital part of the structure of political control at all levels. Yeltsin describes the system in his autobiography: "The higher one climbs up the professional ladder, the more there are comforts that surround one, and the harder and more painful it is to lose them. One becomes therefore all the more obedient and dependable." As a new Politburo candidate member, Yeltsin found to his horror that he and his wife Naya were allotted three cooks, three waitresses, a housemaid, a gardener, and a whole team of under-gardeners. His new *dacha*, previously occupied by Gorbachev, had marble walls, countless outsize rooms, and its own cinema.

In a shortage economy, where most goods and benefits, such as decent medical care and housing, were in short supply, the right to allocate these benefits was an all-powerful political weapon. Privilege was minutely graded with rank: At the bottom, there was a monthly food *zakaz* (order) with some scarce sausage or a couple of tins of crab. As the ambitious party official climbed up the ladder, he would first gain access to the car pool, then his own chauffeur-driven Volga, then a Chaika limousine and a *dacha*. As he began to enjoy more and more benefits, not only for himself but for his family, the idea of losing them became unbearable. For a man at the top, all the material things of life—housing, transport, vacations, leisure, "Kremlyovka" food parcels from the Central Committee shop on Granovsky Street—were linked to status in the Party. In such circumstances, political rebellion or resignation, and the resultant loss of privilege, become unthinkable.

To the Western eye the grant of a government *dacha* or a Volga car with chauffeur might seem a modest perquisite of office, easily replaceable from private funds. But in the Brezhnev period it became apparent that shortages performed a political function, giving even modest privileges a high relative value. If *dachas*, cars, tins of caviar, and Black Sea holidays were freely available to all, the party privileges would have had no meaning. As a system of allocating resources, it made good political sense. The system proved its worth by preventing any large-scale movement of support for the isolated Soviet dissidents of the 1960s and 1970s among those who had something to lose.

Yeltsin cut back the privileges of the full-time Moscow party workers who reported to him, but he was unable to do anything more to change the system. Yeltsin's attitude did little to endear him either to his subordinates or to his Politburo colleagues, who looked with great suspicion on his populist streak. Even Gorbachev was clearly reluctant to support him, something which Yeltsin later attributed to his wife Raisa's love of luxury. Interviewed by the Italian Communist newspaper *l'Unita* in May 1987, Gorbachev said he was opposed to *uravnilovka* ("leveling") and defended the privileges of party leaders as no worse than the existence of a works canteen in a factory.

After the congress, Yeltsin resumed his unscheduled tours of Moscow streets and shops, joining lines himself to find out when scarce goods were being sold under the counter or through the back door. On one famous occasion he went to a butcher counter to ask for some veal which he knew had been delivered, but which was being kept instead for sale on the black market. "There was an almighty fuss and the management was sacked," he recounted. Such stories spread quickly around Moscow and made the new party leader something of a folk hero; a kind of Haroun al-Rashid stalking the streets incognito.

Meanwhile party officials were squirming under the lash of Yeltsin's tongue. Every time he made a speech, their faults and shortcomings were listed in *Moskovskaya Pravda* the next day. Those on the line were the secretaries of the city's district party committees, most of whom were to lose their jobs. *Perestroika* was for Yeltsin not a diplomatic campaign or even a military flanking movement, but a head-on cavalry charge. As Gorbachev told it to the Party Conference, in July 1988, "At first we thought it was right, that we had appointed the wrong people. But then he began changing personnel for the second and third time. It began to worry us." Gorbachev gave Yeltsin a public rebuke at a Politburo meeting, and told him too that *perestroika* did not mean turning things upside down.

In April 1986, Yeltsin addressed party propagandists; an unofficial transcript which circulated in Moscow gives the flavor of his earthy style. Many Moscow apartments had kitchens that were too small, Yeltsin complained. "But we have many stout women in our country. Once one of them gets into the kitchen, there's no room for the husband!" Yeltsin said the Moscow metro, one of the symbols of the capital, was in a sorry state, with two thousand accidents a year, wornout rolling stock, and a financial deficit. Up came an anonymous note from the floor: "We're told that Yeltsin travels by metro himself. But we've never seen him there."

"What answer can I give? I didn't see you either," Yeltsin retorted, adding that, because of his recent arrival in the capital, many people did not recognize him on his visits to shops. When they did, they quickly took out the goods from under the counter and put them on sale. He also attacked party privileges, revealing that many Moscow officials had had their black Volgas taken away and that their special shop had been closed down. Eight hundred shop directors had already been arrested, but he complained that the bottom of the well had not been reached. Some of the notes handed up to the platform were hostile and contemptuous. "Khrushchev tried to make us all dress like peasants, but he didn't succeed and neither will you. We've always stolen, and we'll go on stealing," said one. Another gave him some frank advice: "Go back to Sverdlovsk while there is still time." One propagandist asked where Yeltsin bought his shoes. He replied that he paid 23 rubles for them in Sverdlovsk, where they were made by the Uralobuv factory.[3]

His style of leadership had worked well in Sverdlovsk, where few officials would ever dare defy him or have the influence in Moscow to complain about him behind his back. The godlike authority of the party First Secretary was strong enough to enforce obedience at any factory or institute, through the local party committee. However, the Yeltsin method proved ineffective in Moscow for several reasons. One

was the sheer size of the city and the party organization, with
1.1 million members, more than four times as many as in
Sverdlovsk. This alone would have been enough to blunt
Yeltsin's solo offensive.

Also, Sverdlovsk was Yeltsin's home city, where he could
rely on his personal acquaintance with thousands of key
figures, many of them his friends, to get things done. In
Moscow, he was a lonely provincial outsider with no friends
or allies. In a world where politics was based on clans and
alliances between groups, he did nothing to win himself
friends and seems to have made enemies quite quickly of
those he promoted. "I did not know the personnel," he admitted afterwards. "I had just arrived in Moscow and had to pick
new people."[4]

Moreover, the Moscow institutions he was trying to reform
were all powerful in their own right and had their own
channels through which they could lobby the government
and the Central Committee against him. One example was
his unsuccessful crusade to shut down some of Moscow's
thousands of redundant scientific research institutes. As he
angrily told the City Party Committee, on July 19, 1986, many
of the institutes merely reopened under a new nameplate.
One of his most controversial decisions was to forbid enterprises to hire any more *limitchiki*—workers without permanent residence in the capital. Yeltsin's view was that this step
was essential to stop the expansion of the city's population
and the growing pressure on its services. But there were howls
of protest from industrial managers and for applications of
exemption—Yeltsin was trying to use the ban as a blunt
instrument to force managers to make better use of existing
labor resources. In economic terms, it was a classic measure
of the command economy, interfering with one of the few
market forces at work in the Soviet economy, the free or
semifree movement of labor. In 1987, the Central Committee
overruled Yeltsin and granted an exemption to allow the
hiring of more *limitchiki* for the building of the Moscow
metro.

Another of Yeltsin's targets was Moscow's special foreign-
language schools, supposedly for talented children, but in
fact monopolized by the sons and daughters of the elite. This
initiative provoked bitter opposition from the beneficiaries of
the existing system. As the dissident historian Roy Medvedev
pointed out, Yeltsin's motives were laudable, but he would
have had more success if he had tried to get the Ministry of
Education on his side. He also needlessly antagonized the

military with outspoken comments about their incompetence, after the young West German flyer, Matthias Rust,
landed his light plane in Red Square.

The Moscow public liked Yeltsin's introduction of street
fairs in the summer and an open-air exhibit for artists at
Izmailovo park. Hundreds of new state-run wooden booths
sprang up to sell fruit and vegetables. In order to bypass the
creaking and corrupt retail network, state and collective
farms were invited to drive straight into Moscow and sell
their produce from trucks directly on the street. Meanwhile
the well-entrenched mafia in the food retail trade were finding life more difficult. In September 1986, after ten months
of investigation, the head of Moscow's retail trade network
and two dozen others were tried for corruption and sentenced
to up to fifteen years in jail. This was a case launched by Yuri
Andropov, before Gorbachev and Yeltsin. But by Yeltsin's own
admission the real chiefs of the Moscow mafia and their
political protectors in the Party got away. The system was
impossible to dismantle without dismantling the Party itself.
"Of course, we do not use this word and we do not want to
admit it, but we have a mafia. Struggling against it is one of
the most difficult things I have ever been confronted with,"
he told an interviewer in September 1988.[5]

By this time there was active resistance to Yeltsin. One
district party first secretary after another was fired until the
final scorecard was twenty-three removed out of thirty-three.
Typical was the fate of B. A. Gryaznov, chief of the Party in
the Frunzensky district, "who was accustomed to stagnation,
encouraged ostentation, ignored collective opinion, lost the
feeling of party comradeship and only pretended to be carrying out restructuring," according to *Moskovskaya Pravda*.[6]
There was open grumbling about too much criticism, but
Yeltsin had no intention of relaxing the pressure. "No, we will
maintain it," Yeltsin told a plenum of the city party committee on October 4. "If you are capable, work and prove it by
action. If you are not, make way." It was not the system which
was to blame, just the incompetent and corrupt people running it, he seemed to believe. If they could be smoked out into
the open, *perestroika* would succeed.

Meanwhile Gorbachev, far more sophisticated at inner-
party politicking, was still trying to avoid any kind of showdown with his opponents, and for many months he would go
on denying for tactical reasons that any opposition to *perestroika* even existed. Toward the end of his time in Moscow,
Yeltsin began to realize that it was not just the people, but

the system. The Party, far from being the main vehicle of change, was in fact the main obstacle to any meaningful reform of Soviet society. But he could not say so publicly. Gorbachev was eventually to come to similar conclusions, but much later.

In October 1986, Yeltsin told the Yugoslav magazine *NIN* that "an economic reform does not yield benefits if it stops halfway, if it comes down to a compromise, to an attempt to paint the car instead of replacing the worn-out engine." With an eye to his Yugoslav audience, Yeltsin explained that the goal of *perestroika* was "communist social self-management" and called on the public to fight against bureaucracy. In December, he was shown on Moscow television visiting the ZIL factory and confronting the issue of boredom, apathy, and misbehavior among young workers. He blamed the Party for contributing to the Komsomol's inability to solve such problems, by issuing too many formal instructions. Instead, he welcomed the idea of young people setting up their own informal clubs and associations, "but of course, not on the basis of a lack of ideological outlook."

After a year in the job, Yeltsin's frustration was growing and so was that of the Muscovites, who had seen little real change in their lives. Two years into the Gorbachev era, one of the few noticeable results was a shortage of vodka and other hard liquor, as a result of an anti-alcohol campaign launched by the Party. This campaign, though blamed on Gorbachev, was largely the initiative of the puritanical Yegor Ligachev. Yeltsin had no time for this campaign and took the pragmatic view that if people could not buy vodka they would brew their own—when sugar disappeared from the shops, it was clear that moonshine was being brewed everywhere. The collapse in state revenues from alcohol also contributed to the state budget deficit, and the lack of alcohol damaged Gorbachev's popularity. Jokers called him the *"mineralny sekretar,"* a pun on his title of *generalny sekretar.*

The friction between Ligachev and Yeltsin was evident from the start. "Yeltsin immediately reacted negatively to Ligachev's style and the way he worked in the Central Committee," Vladimir Dolgikh recalled. Yeltsin described his relations with Ligachev at Politburo meetings as confrontational: "He was on one side and I was on the other." Ligachev's version is that "Mr. [not Comrade] Yeltsin talked a lot. But he never did anything."[7]

Yeltsin came under fire not just for failing to take the anti-alcohol campaign seriously enough: Ligachev and others objected to the way he began to tolerate political street demonstrations in Moscow and the first glimmers of a cultural free-for-all in the Arbat Street pedestrian zone. Yeltsin was instructed to restore order on the streets; he wanted the Moscow equivalent of London's Speaker's Corner in Hyde Park.[8] His approach was a risky one. Later his critics were to use as ammunition against him his decision to receive a noisy protesting crowd from the right-wing Russian nationalist group Pamyat (*pamyat* means "memory"). Given the group's reputation at the time—a mixture of nostalgia for restoring old churches and outright fascism and anti-Semitism—a more cautious politician would have sent someone else to deputize for him. Yeltsin met the Pamyat leaders himself.

By mid-1987, Yeltsin's assault on the Moscow party machine was targeting even party officials whom he had initially praised when he took over in Moscow. Such was the fate of Fedor Kozyrev-Dal, singled out by Yeltsin, early in 1986, as a model district party committee leader and promoted to be first deputy mayor under Saikin. Now he was singled out by Yeltsin for his inefficiency. Yeltsin, despairing of the party apparatus, tried to activate the moribund city Soviet, or council, by reminding its deputies of their responsibilities to the voters who had elected them. This was an open heresy, because deputies were supposed to act as faithful guardians of the Party's interests, not those of the voters.

The party and city bureaucracy in Moscow was beginning to fight back by this time. His original allies had turned against him. Even Valery Saikin, Yeltsin's hand-picked choice for mayor, was trying to undermine him. One of the few real Yeltsin supporters, Mikhail Poltoranin, whom Yeltsin had picked to edit the Moscow party newspaper *Moskovskaya Pravda*, described what happened: "We had hardly started to denounce the Moscow mafia when Valery Saikin, chairman of the Moscow Soviet, the city council, telephoned me and, in an irritated tone, said: 'What are you trying to do? Yeltsin is here today, but tomorrow he'll be gone. And you'll still have to work with us.' That was the climate we had to work in."[9] In the summer of 1987, while Yeltsin was away on holiday, Poltoranin was summoned by Yuri Belyakov, Yeltsin's right-hand man and second secretary of the Moscow party organization. "He told me clearly that I had to choose which side I was on." Poltoranin said the sabotage of Yeltsin's initiatives by Saikin and other officials extended to keeping fresh fruit and vegetables to rot in warehouses, instead of putting them on sale, and sending trains loaded with fresh produce back to the Caucasus without being unloaded.

Interviewed by *Moskovskaya Pravda*, in April 1987, Yeltsin acknowledged that "I haven't totally grasped the specific character of Moscow" and complained that there was too much unanimity in the party bureau. As if admitting that his authoritarian style might not always be effective, he added, "I sometimes see how hard a comrade finds it to raise his hand when he wants to object."[10]

It was evident that the Russian tradition of the Potemkin village, of *pokazukha*, was too ingrained to be swept away. Yeltsin said the Party's window-dressing had deep roots and compared it to coal dust eating into the pores of the skin. "Many leaders have outdone even the clergy in ritualism. They know at what point to clap, when to say what, how to greet the authorities, and what decor to put up for an event."

It was no longer a matter of individuals: Yeltsin was in conflict with a whole political culture, whose rules and rituals he had come to detest. Yet he was himself a product of this system and its prisoner. The result was an inner tension.

Instinctively, he felt he was on the side of the people against the party *apparat*, of which he was a leading member. But Yeltsin lacked the political ability to conceptualize his dilemma satisfactorily. The further *perestroika* advanced, the stronger the resistance would be, he told an interviewer, in what may have been an unconscious echo of Stalin's theory of the permanent sharpening of the class struggle. Either way, there was no room for compromise. "The choice is simple. Either throw open the windows so the wind can blow away the cobwebs, or again sweep the dust into the corners and close the heavy bolts."[11]

According to Poltoranin, Yeltsin's inevitable conflict with the other leader had its roots in his human moral qualities, which made him an outsider:

> He was the same Yeltsin as today, with the same natural intuition and ability to keep his feet firmly on the ground.
> It was as if, when they became members of the Politburo, they passed through some kind of radioactive zone where everything human was squeezed out of them, and their personality got left behind at the gates of the Kremlin. Yeltsin should have been the same but the rays in the zone failed to demagnetize him. He came here from Sverdlovsk, where he had imagined people in Moscow were handling high affairs of state, and he discovered this *shaika* [criminal gang]—that's what they were in the Politburo, and he was really shocked by where he had ended up.[12]

From their first meeting, a talk of several hours, Yeltsin and Poltoranin discovered a common desire to demolish the system: "Our views were completely identical. This was a man at the top level of the leadership who seemed to me a real dissident. This dissident had to come to the surface sooner or later."

Yeltsin took his Politburo differences with Ligachev into the open at a Central Committee plenum in June 1987. According to Poltoranin's account, Yeltsin also criticized Ligachev in the summer of 1987, at a meeting of the Moscow party *aktiv*. This would have been a clear violation of the Party's unwritten rules. By this time, Yeltsin began to realize he had entered a battle he could not win. Ligachev, as the man who helped bring Yeltsin to Moscow, should by rights have been entitled to Yeltsin's fealty. But Yeltsin was not prepared to play by the patronage rules.

Ligachev managed to wield an effective veto over Yeltsin's ability to carry out further personnel changes in the Moscow party districts. Poltoranin cites two occasions where Yeltsin tried to remove district first secretaries linked to the mafia but found they were untouchable. In the Central Committee headquarters, moves were under way to build up a dossier against Yeltsin, as a prelude to his removal. Poltoranin was summoned to the Central Committee and asked to sign a statement saying that Yeltsin had forced him to publish critical articles in his paper. "I refused. I spoke about this to Yeltsin himself. He replied: 'I know that they are digging my grave.' "

While Yeltsin's problems with his party superiors in the Politburo and the Secretariat were mounting, he had little in the way of concrete results to show the capital's residents how he had improved their lives. In August 1987, when he visited a Moscow suburb, he was shouted at by angry residents. "Go down to our basements and you'll be kneedeep in stinking slush! The sewage pipes burst ages ago. The roofs leak everywhere and nobody cares about us."[13]

Yeltsin's exit had become inevitable by this stage. "Somehow everything had accumulated gradually and imperceptibly," he recalled in his autobiography. The only question was how the final breach would occur. In Poltoranin's view, he might conceivably have recovered his position, if he had appealed to Gorbachev directly to back him against Ligachev. But his increasingly outspoken speeches led to worsening relations with Gorbachev, who was not prepared to tackle the party *apparat* head-on. In January 1987, the Central Committee had blocked his ideas for introducing inner-Party democracy, with several candidates for each post. "You can't ride two horses at once," Yeltsin commented, when he summarized his objections to Gorbachev's style in his autobiography. For Gorbachev, riding two horses at once was the essence of his political style. Given Yeltsin's total contempt for most of the other members of the Politburo, it is hard to see what concessions Gorbachev might have been able to offer him, to avoid the final breach. The two men met for two hours and twenty minutes to discuss their grievances, but without reaching a conclusion.

Before Yeltsin decided to resign, there was one final dispute, when the Politburo met to discuss an early draft of Gorbachev's November speech. Yeltsin volunteered a string of caustic comments. According to Yeltsin's account, Gorbachev exploded and stalked out of the room, reappearing half an hour later to deliver a diatribe that was "almost hysterical." Gorbachev was also under great strain at this time, though Yeltsin was not prepared to take this as an excuse. "There can be no doubt that at that moment Gorbachev simply hated me." After that, their relations cooled rapidly. "I was too obviously a misfit in his otherwise obedient team," Yeltsin wrote.

Yeltsin was pushed over the brink by another big run-in with Ligachev, at a Politburo meeting on September 10, at which Ligachev objected to Yeltsin's tolerance of demonstrations and set up a commission of inquiry into how he was running Moscow.[14] Gorbachev had gone away for six weeks, to work by the shores of the Black Sea on his speech for the seventieth anniversary of the Bolshevik Revolution, leaving Ligachev in charge at the Kremlin.

Yeltsin wrote to Gorbachev, still on his Black Sea vacation, on September 12, to tell him of his decision to resign from the Politburo. "My style, my frankness, and my past history reveal me as being untrained for work as a member of the Politburo," he confessed. He appealed to Gorbachev to do something about Ligachev's way of running the party apparatus; *perestroika* had been reduced to a crawl by the party bureaucrats, half of whom should be fired. There were too many members of the Politburo whose apparent support for reform was insincere, he told Gorbachev.

I am an awkward person and I know it. I realize, too, that it is difficult for you to decide what to do about me. But it is better to admit one's mistakes now. Later, given my present relations with my colleagues, the number of problems I am likely to cause you will increase and will start to hamper you in your work.

I wish you to release me from the duties of First Secretary of the Moscow City Committee of the CPSU and from my responsibilities as a candidate member of the Politburo of the Central Committee of the CPSU.

"Please regard this as an official statement," his letter concluded.

Yeltsin's letter was almost certainly an unpleasant surprise for Gorbachev when it reached him at Pitsunda; he seems to have hoped that the Yeltsin problem could be postponed, at least until after the anniversary celebrations in early November. But the showdown came in October, on the day when the big November speech on which Gorbachev had been working for months would be unveiled before the Central Committee. Yeltsin was convinced, afterward, that the attacks on him at the October plenum "had been prepared in advance" and described his resignation speech as a preemptive strike because he knew he was going to be fired. There is no evidence, however, that Gorbachev had been planning to get rid of him at the Central Committee meeting.

It is virtually certain that Gorbachev, knowing since early September that Yeltsin wanted to resign, wanted to preserve the facade of party unity and postpone the whole issue of Yeltsin's future until after the November 7 anniversary. This was not just the usual annual Red Square parade, but a big international jamboree to celebrate seven decades of Soviet power and to show that the Kremlin was under new and united management. The sudden ouster of a candidate member of the Politburo, just before the ceremonies, would hardly have served Gorbachev's interests.

Besides, Yeltsin's presence in the leadership enabled Gorbachev to hold the center ground between radicalism and conservatism, a tactical advantage which he would lose if Yeltsin were removed. Gorbachev was later to accuse Yeltsin of breaking an agreement with him to postpone the issue of his future until after November 7. Yeltsin's version is that Gorbachev, on his return from vacation, said ambiguously, "Let's meet later." When no invitation to discuss his resignation arrived before the plenum, Yeltsin concluded Gorbachev had changed his mind about a meeting and decided to make his own plans. Later he was to admit: "The mistake was not in the content of what I said but in the timing."[15]

Yeltsin's resignation speech to the Central Committee was

planned in advance, rather than being a spontaneous outburst. But it was what Poltoranin later called the "gesture of despair" of a man under severe mental and physical strain. He had been working eighteen-hour days almost nonstop. Some nights when his chauffeur drove him home, he was too tired to climb out of the car.

Although it was not until November 9, nearly three weeks later, that Yeltsin collapsed and was taken to the hospital with a heart attack, it is likely that he was already psychologically and physically near the end of his tether, by the time of the showdown, on October 21.

6

The Insulted and Injured

GORBACHEV: Comrade Yeltsin has some kind of statement to
  make.
LIGACHEV (CHAIR): I give the floor to Comrade Yeltsin, Boris
  Nikolayevich—candidate member of the Politburo of the
  CC of the CPSU, First Secretary of the Moscow City Com-
  mittee of the CPSU. Please, Boris Nikolayevich.
*(Minutes of the CPSU Central Committee plenum, October 21,
  1987)*

If Gorbachev's *perestroika* had a script, this was the moment
when one of the leading actors threw it away and began to
improvise, to the horror of the author and the other members
of the cast. It was the moment when the sacred rules and
rituals of the Soviet political elite were suddenly called into
question. The old Kremlin culture was beginning to crack.
For the first time in decades, the monolith began to tremble,
and the tremor was felt far and wide. It was the start of what
became known as the "Yeltsin affair."

Gorbachev had ended his lengthy report to the Central
Committee setting out the speech he would deliver to mark
the seventieth anniversary of the "Great October Socialist
Revolution." To mark the occasion, he had undertaken a
major reexamination of the period stretching back to Lenin,
even viewing old newsreels of Soviet history to help him
define his views. Ever since Khrushchev's denunciation of

Stalin in 1956, Soviet leaders have found such historical anniversaries a tricky exercise. How can the Party reach back to 1917 for historical legitimacy, when, for a large part of the intervening period, it was headed by one of history's greatest mass murderers? Under Brezhnev, the answer was to mention Stalin as little as possible, but to give the Stalin period an increasingly positive gloss. Gorbachev wanted to shift the balance against Stalin, without going too far and provoking alarm among party conservatives. He had spent several weeks by the Black Sea, drafting and redrafting his speech, in search of an acceptable formula, and was apparently pleased with the result. When he had finished speaking, Ligachev, who was chairing the meeting, asked for comments from the floor, but to Gorbachev's relief, there were none. The plenum was about to end at that point, without any debate, when Yeltsin asked for the floor.

Yeltsin tells us he broke with his usual habit and spoke without a text, relying only on a note of the seven points he planned to raise. After giving support to Gorbachev's report, he began criticizing the way the party leadership was operating. This was a subject he had raised at the previous plenum in June, when he had complained about Ligachev in particular. "Although five months have passed, nothing has changed in the style of work of secretariat of the Central Committee of the Party and of Comrade Ligachev," Yeltsin said. He went on to protest against the continuing use of "bullying reprimands and dressings down [*raznosi; nakachki*]" at all levels. It was a somewhat clumsy accusation, considering Yeltsin's own often brutal treatment of his subordinates in Moscow. But the thrust of his criticism of Ligachev would have been clear to his audience, who had heard him raise the same points in more detail, four months earlier.

The main point of Yeltsin's speech was far more dangerous to Gorbachev. It amounted to an accusation that his *perestroika* had so far produced little for the Soviet people except words. People were starting to lose their enthusiasm and to doubt whether the Party could deliver on its promises, he told the meeting. Central Committee decrees, such as the one ordering a cut in the number of research institutes in Moscow, were being widely ignored.

Next, he directly criticized his fellow-members of the Politburo for creating, around Gorbachev, an atmosphere of adulation (*slavoslovie*), which, he said, should be quickly nipped in the bud, before a "cult of personality" took hold. Finally, he announced his resignation, saying he was "clearly

out of place as a member of the Politburo." Yeltsin cited
several reasons, including his own lack of experience and also
a lack of high-level support, notably from Ligachev. "As far
as my position as first secretary of the Moscow city committee
of the Party is concerned, that will, of course, be decided by a
plenum of the city committee of the Party," he concluded.

"Having said all that, I sat down. My heart was pounding,
and seemed ready to burst out of my ribcage. I knew what
would happen next. I would be slaughtered, in an organized,
methodical manner, and the job would be done almost with
pleasure and enjoyment."

Writing some two years later, Yeltsin said he still felt "a
rusty nail in my heart" when he recalled the attacks on him.
Yet as he himself admitted, he could not have expected anything else. The prosecuting speeches were made off the cuff,
but every speaker knew his part instinctively. The unanimous
chorus followed a ritual which dated back to Stalin's purges,
in which the deviationist who dared to think he might be
right against the Party would be shown the error of his ways
and invited to confess publicly. The atmosphere of a public
witchhunt was emblematic of Russian political culture, with
its inability to tolerate dissent. He who disagreed with the
prevailing orthodoxy instantly became a schismatic, a heretic. Yeltsin certainly knew the script, because he had spent
two years handing out public humiliations to party officials
in Moscow. One is tempted to conclude that he was good at
dishing out criticism, but not quite so good at taking it.

In Western culture, the resignation of a politician over a
point of principle, or even a personal difference, is a routine
occurrence which carries with it no disgrace or opprobrium.
In the Soviet tradition, however, it is a deeply subversive act,
because it reveals that the monolithic unity of the Party is
only a facade. For this reason, resignations and dismissals of
the losers in Kremlin power battles have nearly always been
camouflaged as retirements for health reasons—however hale
and hearty the appearance of the actors. By resigning, Yeltsin
broke this unwritten rule, and it was only natural, in the
military language of Soviet politics, that he was accused of
acting like a deserter. Some accounts attribute the shock
impact of Yeltsin's speech to a "vitriolic" attack by him on
Ligachev, but the record does not bear this out.[1]

The subversive nature of his intervention lay not in his
language, but in the way he broke the rules of the inner-Party
game, by voluntarily renouncing membership in the highest
level of the *nomenklatura* and its accompanying privileges. By

resigning, he was saying goodbye to the *dacha* with its marble floors, the cooks, the gardeners, and the big black limousine—breaking the golden chains which were supposed to keep him in line.

Gorbachev launched the debate by summarizing Yeltsin's speech and accusing him of wanting to split off the Moscow city party organization from the rest of the Party. Yeltsin tried to object that this was a distortion of the last part of his remarks, but Gorbachev told him sharply to sit down. Formally, Yeltsin was correct in saying his future as head of the Moscow party would be decided at city level and not by the central committee. Both he and Gorbachev knew it would be quite impossible for him to keep his Moscow job after resigning from the Politburo, so Gorbachev's accusation was merely a way of setting the accusatory tone for the speeches that followed.

The speeches, not published until February 1989, give a fascinating insight into the persistence of Stalinist norms in the political culture of the Kremlin, more than three decades after the dictator's death. The long list of those who attacked Yeltsin included not only his conservative opponents, but men he thought were old friends, such as his predecessor as Sverdlovsk province party chief, Yakov Ryabov, and prime minister Nikolai Ryzhkov. Liberals, such as Alexander Yakovlev and Eduard Shevardnadze, who privately shared some of Yeltsin's ideas, also joined in. The only speaker to even partially defend his right to speak his mind was Georgy Arbatov, head of the US and Canada Institute.[2]

Ligachev began by defending himself vigorously, an easy task in view of the vague nature of Yeltsin's personal charges against him. He denied that the two had ever clashed and said he personally had helped promote Yeltsin to his present posts. He accused Yeltsin of remaining silent at Politburo meetings, in order to voice his complaints in the wider forum of the Central Committee. He denied there was any adulation of Gorbachev and described Yeltsin's main accusation, that *perestroika* was not working, as politically incorrect. "This casts doubt on our whole policy," he exclaimed, rounding off with a fervent expression of confidence in the Party's complete victory.

Next came Sergei Manyakin, a veteran provincial party baron elected to the Central Committee in 1961, now chairman of the People's Control Committee. He attacked Yeltsin's record in Moscow, saying he was clearly not up to the job. "Things in Moscow have deteriorated sharply," Manyakin declared, pointing a finger at the capital's poor supplies of fruit and vegetables. "I have been in the Central Committee for twenty-six years. Never have I heard such a speech, such a statement," Manyakin continued. "This has happened because of the political immaturity of Comrade Yeltsin." He accused Yeltsin of being a latecomer to the party ranks, who had risen too far, too fast, and lacked the necessary *zakalka*, or "steeling," a word synonymous with the iron discipline of the Stalin period. He said Yeltsin's personal faults of character had led him to what he described as "the inevitable finale" of his resignation. In Manyakin's view, Ligachev had been far too tolerant of Yeltsin, when he should have "thumped the table." He poured scorn on Moscow's "stupid little kiosks [*pavilionchiki duratskie*]" for fruit and vegetables. "They're standing empty, nobody wants them, they just annoy people. It's window-dressing [*pokazukha*]!" Yeltsin's views about *perestroika* showed he was in disagreement with the Politburo and the "general line of the Party"—another Stalinist phrase.

Another member of the old guard, Astrakhan province First Secretary Leonid Borodin, highlighted the way in which resignation was regarded as an unacceptable betrayal. He compared Yeltsin to a deserter who chose to run away instead of fighting till the end of the battle. "You should fight to the end, not run away into the bushes making noisy statements." Fedor Morgun, first secretary of Poltava province party organization, said Yeltsin had made the speech of "a weakling, of whom there will be one less in the leading organs of the Party."

Valentin Mesyats, party boss in the Moscow province and formerly Brezhnev's agriculture minister, voiced the unease of conservative bureaucrats at Yeltsin's breezy, populist style. Yeltsin's main mistake was trying to be original and mark himself off as different, he said. Why, at a meeting of the Moscow city council, had Yeltsin chosen to sit in the hall rather than on the platform, if not in order to create an effect? And why had he revealed to foreign diplomats that Moscow had eleven hundred prostitutes and two thousand drug addicts? Gorbachev, who had personally pushed hard for greater frankness in discussing social problems in the press, must have wondered whether some of these criticisms of Yeltsin were not also aimed at him.

Arbatov defended Yeltsin's right to speak out as a sign of *perestroika* and took issue with those who were now hurrying to condemn him. "You cannot deny his courage," he added. But, he said, Yeltsin had damaged party unity just before the anniversary of the revolution, when the eyes of the world would be on Moscow.

Ryabov, who was Yeltsin's party superior for seven years in Sverdlovsk, recalled how he had personally picked Yeltsin out to become a party official in 1968. "But even then we noticed . . . the negative aspects of his character." He had hoped that, with further promotion, Yeltsin would overcome his faults, but now he had relapsed. "Yes, he is ambitious, sometimes unpleasant to his friends and comrades, and his megalomania has never left him."

Ryzhkov, like Ryabov, had to fulfill another unwritten law dating from the Stalin purges: those with the closest personal ties to the object of the party's wrath—then a Trotskyite, now Yeltsin—were expected to give the sharpest denunciations. He came close to calling Yeltsin a dissident. "Comrade Yeltsin and I are from the same city. I have known him for many years, even before he was first secretary of the province party committee." Yeltsin's outburst was no accident but the gradual culmination of his "political nihilism," Ryzhkov charged, accusing him of getting a taste for hearing his name mentioned on foreign radio stations, of distancing himself from the rest of the leadership and showing personal ambitions.

After the stab in the back came the blow from beneath, delivered by Moscow's mayor, Valery Saikin, the man Yeltsin had plucked from the ZIL truck factory less than two years before. After spelling out that he had not been warned in advance that Yeltsin was going to speak, he gave Yeltsin his due for achieving certain improvements in Moscow; he then went on to make clear the Moscow party organization would now wash its hands of its first secretary and take the side of the leadership against Yeltsin.

Next came the Politburo members. Vitaly Vorotnikov, prime minister of the Russian Federation, said Yeltsin had begun well in Moscow but had begun to show "excessive self-assurance, excessive ambition, leftist phrases." The Politburo had pointed out Yeltsin's mistakes, but he had taken no notice. "You even have some sort of mask on your face all the time. One gets the impression of some kind of permanent dissatisfaction, some kind of alienation."

Viktor Chebrikov, head of the KGB, condemned Yeltsin for daring to oppose the party line and described him as a man who had "failed the exam of *perestroika*." Yeltsin's remarks about the Politburo were slanderous and demagogic and made just at the time when imperialism was trying to ensure that *perestroika* failed, he said.

Alexander Yakovlev, Gorbachev's reforming ideological adviser, said Yeltsin had put his personal ambitions above the party's interests; he had made himself a mouthpiece for "petty bourgeois moods" in the capital. Yeltsin's revolutionary style was in fact deep conservatism, and by resigning, he was showing "capitulationism in the face of difficulties."

A similarly tough verdict on Yeltsin came from Foreign Minister Eduard Shevardnadze, who accused Yeltsin of betrayal of the Party, slander, and irresponsibility. His predecessor, Andrei Gromyko, now head of state, avoided any personal attacks on Yeltsin, but implied that party unity—or at least the appearance of it—had to come first.

Mikhail Solomentsev, another veteran of the Brezhnev era, accused Yeltsin of trying to provoke a split in the Party and of hoping to find others to support his views. If the West was finding Yeltsin interesting, it was clearly time to get suspicious of him. Why were Yeltsin's speeches always being quoted by foreign radio stations? Because they contradicted the Party's policy, and this was what the ideological foe needed. Yeltsin had even broken the secret of how many people were imprisoned in the Soviet Union, thus giving meat and drink to foreign correspondents, who would reveal it to the whole world. "Who needs this? Do our people and our party need this? No, those who wish us evil, our opponents need this." Solomentsev said that the story of Yeltsin's speech was bound to leak out all over Moscow. Yeltsin's conduct was motivated by a buildup of personal grudges, which had now broken like an avalanche. "I tell you, Boris Nikolayevich, the Muscovites do not approve of such behavior."

One of the more nuanced and sympathetic speeches came from Gennady Kolbin, who had worked alongside Yeltsin from 1970 to 1975 as a secretary of the Sverdlovsk province Party. After working in Georgia, he had been sent by Gorbachev to clean the Augean stables as first secretary in Kazakhstan, a mission almost as difficult as Yeltsin's in Moscow. Because he was a Russian and not a Kazakh, Kolbin's appointment to replace the Brezhnevite Dinmukhamed Kunayev had provoked riots in Alma-Ata. "Finding myself in this situation, I can easily imagine, in the conditions of *perestroika*, how complicated the processes are in the Moscow party organization," he said. As if trying to plead mitigating circumstances, he ascribed Yeltsin's speech to emotion in the heat of the moment. Of all the speakers, Kolbin came closest to an accurate diagnosis of why Yeltsin's head-on assault on the Moscow *apparat* had failed. Nowadays, problems could no longer be solved by administrative orders, but only by dialogue and consensus, Kolbin said. He praised Yeltsin as a close colleague, from whom he had learned a lot, but concluded, "Today you have made a mistake."

After the political heavyweights came one of the handful of token proletarians in the Central Committee, Vladimir Zatvornitsky, a Moscow construction worker, who was later to play a key part in attempts to destroy Yeltsin's image in the press. "I have been in the Central Committee for several five-year terms, and this is what now comes to mind . . . Boris Nikolayevich, what respect we are showing you! We dealt with Khrushchev in only half the time! You can count yourself proud."[3]

Finally Gorbachev gave Yeltsin the right to reply. This speech, which Yeltsin does not reproduce in his autobiography, was a rather feeble attempt to justify himself by rephrasing some of his remarks—not a defense that had any chance of succeeding. The meeting had been a "harsh lesson [*surovaya shkola*]," Yeltsin said. He repeated his claim that public enthusiasm for *perestroika* had fallen sharply since the start of the year and argued that the Party should recognize that, between waves of public support, there would also be troughs. He denied wanting to split the Central Committee or the Politburo. He watered down his remark about "adulation" of Gorbachev by saying this only applied to two or three comrades and not to the whole Politburo.

Gorbachev, sensing a weakness, went on the attack. "You know what the cult of personality is . . . Are you so politically illiterate that we have to organize a class here to teach you how to read and write?" How could he even make such an accusation, when the country was heading for democratization? Yeltsin tried to reply and Gorbachev cut him short. An unidentified voice cried out, "You have been worrying about yourself, about your unsatisfied ambitions." Gorbachev added, "I think so too. Isn't it enough for you that all Moscow revolves around your person? Do you need the Central Committee to bother itself about you as well?" He accused Yeltsin of wasting the Central Committee's time on a personal question and of being so preoccupied with his own vanity that he put his personal ambitions above the Party and the cause. Irritated, Gorbachev pressed home his advantage and asked Yeltsin for his response.

It was the moment when Yeltsin had to either defy the Party or submit. He submitted: "Apart from some expressions, I am as a whole in agreement. By letting down the

Central Committee and the Moscow city organization in my speech today, I made a mistake."

"Do you have the strength to go on?" Gorbachev asked. From the floor came cries of "He can't. You can't leave him in such a post."

Yeltsin repeated his confession: He had let down the Party and wished to resign from his Politburo and Moscow positions. Finally, after ascertaining that nobody wished to comment further on his anniversary speech, Gorbachev went on to the trickiest issue of all: what should the meeting do about Yeltsin?

In normal circumstances, his resignation from the Politburo would have been accepted immediately. Gorbachev's problem was that the last thing he needed on the eve of the anniversary was a public signal of high-level bickering in the Kremlin. At this point, Gorbachev revealed to the Central Committee and the Politburo that he had already received a resignation letter from Yeltsin some weeks before. He accused Yeltsin of bad faith in breaking an oral agreement to postpone the whole question until after the holiday. As a result, the world was being distracted from the seventieth anniversary of 1917 by Comrade Yeltsin, with his egotistical questions. "He can't wait, he always wants something! He's in a flap all the time."

Gorbachev's anger was understandable. All his careful preparation for the seventieth anniversary had been ruined, and the party conservatives were baying for blood. Yeltsin had to be sacrificed, but Gorbachev had at all costs to limit the potential damage to his own policies from the backlash. He argued that *perestroika* was on course and would have to continue. Anyone who had doubts should show "revolutionary restraint" (in other words, keep quiet) for the good of the cause, so as not to demoralize the Party at a difficult time. "We are on the right path, comrades!" How could Yeltsin say that the people had received nothing from *perestroika* in two years? That, Gorbachev said, was Yeltsin's style. It was not the first time he had tried to force his "negative and leftist views" on others. Gorbachev compared Yeltsin's style to that of Khrushchev, who had also tried to turn society upside down—an interesting piece of political shorthand, designed to reassure the Party that change would remain within acceptable limits.

Yeltsin, he said, had tried to seek allies for his views in the Central Committee, but now he was isolated and had gotten what he deserved. "I am struck by the theoretical and political helplessness of Comrade Yeltsin," Gorbachev thundered. Then came a concession to the conservatives which betrayed his own vulnerability. He promised that the party *apparat*, the real target of Yeltsin's rebellion, would be left untouched. "Now, when the whole economic and democratic mechanism is being reworked, if Comrade Yeltsin wants to shake up the whole Party as well, the whole party *apparat*, that is something we are not going to do," he pledged. Gorbachev was at pains to reassure the Central Committee, most of whom were probably not fully familiar with the balance of forces in the Politburo, that none of Yeltsin's revelations about internal tensions were true. Yegor Ligachev was at times an emotional man, but he was fully committed to the cause of *perestroika*, he declared. Reports of differences at the top were just "chattering by foreign radio stations." Less than a year later, Gorbachev was to sideline Ligachev and do exactly what he said he would not contemplate—undertake a major reorganization of the Central Committee bureaucracy.

Gorbachev proposed a two-stage solution which would effectively end Yeltsin's political career but avoid a scandal on the eve of the anniversary: the Central Committee would vote to condemn his speech as mistaken but would not remove him from the Politburo immediately. Meanwhile, the Moscow party would be asked to replace him as its first secretary, as soon as the holiday period was over. Gorbachev no doubt hoped that the news could be kept secret for a few days. In the longer term, his tactical sense told him that Yeltsin's humiliation should be kept within bounds. He deliberately left the door to a political comeback slightly ajar, by saying he could not rule out Yeltsin's returning one day to a senior position.

As Yeltsin himself wrote, in his autobiography:

> If Gorbachev didn't have a Yeltsin, he would have had to invent one. Despite the dislike of me that he has shown recently, he realizes that he needs someone like me—prickly, sharp-tongued, the scourge of the overbureaucratized party *apparat*—and for this reason he keeps me close at hand. In this real-life production, the parts have been well cast, as in a well-directed play. There is the conservative Ligachev, who plays the villain; there is Yeltsin, the bully boy, the madcap radical; and the wise, omniscient hero is Gorbachev himself. That, evidently, is how he sees it.

What Gorbachev probably had in mind were three factors: his possible need to use Yeltsin again, one day, as a counterbalance to the conservatives; the immediate risk that Yeltsin, in his unpredictable way, might start to wash the Party's dirty linen in public, by giving interviews to the foreign press; and the effect on public opinion, which was strongly on Yeltsin's side. After the plenum was over, this manipulative scenario was only a partial success. After ten days, the story of Yeltsin's offer to resign leaked out, in reports by foreign correspondents. Initially denied, it was confirmed by Anatoly Lukyanov, a Central Committee secretary, at a news conference on October 31. Yes, Yeltsin had asked to be relieved from his work. No, there were no divergences in the Central Committee or the Politburo, he said. Yeltsin himself said nothing and behaved as if nothing had happened, presiding over a meeting in Moscow to mark the anniversary and joining the rest of the leadership on the Lenin Mausoleum in Red Square on November 7. Two days later, he was taken to the hospital with severe headaches and chest pains, the results of a breakdown under the strain of the previous three weeks. His condition was serious enough for the doctors to refuse to allow his wife to visit him.

But on November 11, the telephone rang by his hospital bed. It was Gorbachev, telling Yeltsin to get dressed and attend a meeting of the Moscow city party committee. He was required to attend his own execution. "However much Gorbachev may have disliked me, to act like that was inhuman and immoral," Yeltsin commented in his autobiography. Pumped full of drugs and barely conscious, he attended a Politburo meeting and then the Moscow plenum, at which Gorbachev made the main speech. This was Yeltsin's second political trial, this time carried out from a script, rather than impromptu, and designed for immediate public consumption.

Gorbachev described Yeltsin's October 21 speech as "politically immature, extremely confused, and contradictory." He had displayed demagoguery and personal ambition. Turning to Yeltsin's Moscow record, he accused him of trying to use "pressure, hectoring, and blatant administration by decree" to get results. "These, as is well known, are methods from the old arsenal and could not provide stable long-term successes." He had shown "immoderate vanity and desire to be always in the public eye" and had ignored Politburo instructions by proceeding with wholesale personnel changes in the Moscow party *apparat*. "Comrade Yeltsin's style and methods, which are characterized by pseudorevolutionary phrases and pseudodetermination, proved inadequate. As life has shown, all he was capable of was mouthing appeals and slogans, but when the time came to reinforce the words by concrete deeds, what was shown was impotence, fuss, and panic," Gorbachev declared.

Then came a prepared series of speeches, in which many of Yeltsin's recent victims took their revenge. Yeltsin's autobiography compares the speakers to a pack of hounds tearing him to pieces. Revenge was particularly sweet for the district party first secretaries whom Yeltsin had humiliated. First in line was Fedor Kozyrev-Dal, who accused Yeltsin of political adventurism and "elements of Bonapartism." Yeltsin liked to be in a state of permanent struggle, so as to look good before the public; but he had shown political incompetence by agreeing to meet the "Black Hundreds" of the Pamyat organization.

Another speaker, anticipating public reaction, poured scorn on attempts to turn Yeltsin into a Jesus Christ figure, who had suffered for his commitment to democracy; others accused Yeltsin of faults of character and inability to handle people; Yeltsin's much-touted walkabouts among the people were nothing but excursions. "In general, what began to be welcomed in our organization was a style whereby criticism had to border on abuse and self-criticism had to amount to self-annihilation." One subordinate accused him of brutality and suspicion and said working with him was sheer torture.

It went on for more than four hours. Yeltsin listened with his head in his hands. According to Mikhail Poltoranin, seated in the fourth row, "His lips were purple—he was all blue, and he had difficulty holding his head up." Sitting beside him, Ligachev enjoyed his triumph.[4]

When Yeltsin finally got the chance to speak, he stumbled to the rostrum, and his words were barely coherent. Rather like the victim of a Stalinist purge trial, he admitted his guilt, attributing it to overwork and ambition and denying his resignation was political. "I have lost the political face of a leader. I bear a great burden of guilt . . . personally, before Mikhail Sergeyevich Gorbachev, whose prestige is so high in our organization, in our country, and throughout the world."

Yuri Prokofiev, a senior Moscow party official, saw that Gorbachev was upset. "He was shaking his head, his face was flushed." After Yeltsin's abject apology Gorbachev softened his tone, saying he was personally upset by what had happened. When the meeting broke up, there was a moment of humanity, which Poltoranin watched: "Yeltsin was slumped over the table, his head in his hands. They were all walking

out. Gorbachev looked back from the doorway and saw Yeltsin. He went back, took his arm, and helped him out of the
hall." Gorbachev and Yeltsin went back to Yeltsin's old office,
where they sat together for a while, before an ambulance
came to fetch Yeltsin back to hospital.[5]

A few days later, Gorbachev offered Yeltsin the consolation
job of First Deputy Chairman of the State Committee for
Construction (Gosstroi). Yeltsin, still in the hospital, accepted.
His membership in the Politburo was effectively over, though
formally, he would not lose his seat until February 1988, at
the next Central Committee meeting.

Until the Yeltsin affair, Soviet citizens were massively
indifferent to changes in the Politburo line-up. While Western
diplomats and journalists would count the names in obituary
notices in *Pravda* and check the giant street portraits erected
each holiday, to make sure nobody had been left out, the
great Soviet public took the view that the faceless members
of the Politburo were all interchangeable. But for the first
time, there were signs that things were changing. In November, there were protests in Yeltsin's home town of Sverdlovsk
against his disgrace. The post office in Sverdlovsk even
hoisted a notice saying that no mail addressed to "B. N.
Yeltsin, Moscow" would be accepted. In Moscow, too, people
were concerned, and those who liked to follow the way the
political winds blew wondered if *perestroika* would run out of
steam.

The Party's answer to the public unease about Yeltsin
came in a newspaper article, by Vladimir Zatvornitsky—a
fellow hard-hatted construction worker had been chosen to
deliver the *coup de grace*. Some people were engaging in "idle
talk and absurd suggestions and questions" about what had
happened at the Central Committee meeting, he wrote. People were saying that the newspapers had failed to print what
Yeltsin had really said at the Moscow city party plenum, but
this was untrue. Without mentioning that Yeltsin had been
dragged from the hospital to attend the Moscow meeting,
Zatvornitsky described his speech as painful and vague. As
for his criticism of other Politburo members, this was something quite normal. "Did it cause perplexity? Of course not."
Yeltsin had been wrong, not to criticize, but to present his
resignation, "a highly meaningful slamming of the door."
Responsible people did not act like that. "A feeling arises that
the commander has abandoned his troops in the battlefield."
Yeltsin had now acknowledged he was a misfit in the job of
Moscow first secretary and confessed the sin of personal

ambition. He was a "significant personality" who would no doubt do better in his new, more modest post.[6]

It was an epitaph for a player whose first-team days were clearly over. As Gorbachev himself told Yeltsin, he would not be allowed back into politics.

7

The Lower Depths

Altogether, it cannot be said that Yeltsin handled his resignation well. Not only did he misread Gorbachev's intentions and pick the wrong moment, but his inability to present a coherent political case and his humiliating climbdown gave plenty of ammunition to his enemies. It was a setback for reform in the short term, though in the long term, Kremlin politics would never be quite the same again.

According to Poltoranin, the version of Yeltsin's resignation speech published in 1989 omitted three key passages, including personal criticism of Gorbachev and the Party and an attack on high-level privileges. "The speech was an attempt to bring the top leadership to its senses. . . . Why did he apologize? He had not finally managed to rid himself of the fear that sits in all of us, in every Homo Sovieticus. We all have to get rid of this fear, and for him that speech was the first step. Today he is a different man, but then he was not the 100 percent fighter he is today."

Yeltsin confessed to Poltoranin that if he opened up and disclosed his real views he might be taken away to a mental hospital, as many dissidents were, under Brezhnev. "They can get rid of me and just leave a damp spot," he confided. At that stage his resignation was "a gesture of despair, a cry from the soul" and certainly not part of any long-term plan for a political comeback. Poltoranin compares Yeltsin's break with the Politburo to a butterfly shedding its cocoon. "It was a painful process of rebirth. He did not know where he might land with his new wings, but he felt he could take off."[1]

Politically, Yeltsin became a nonperson, expelled into the outer darkness. Even though he remained in the Central Committee, he was in a kind of quarantine, isolated by the taboo, imposed by Lenin, against forming inner-Party factions. Yeltsin was punished under the old rules, but his action helped to destroy them for the benefit of those who would follow. Three years later, when Foreign Minister Eduard Shevardnadze resigned, the rules of Soviet politics had become more fluid, thanks in part to Yeltsin's willingness to be a pioneer. In December 1990, Shevardnadze, like a Western politician, delivered a coherent statement of his political motives for resigning and skillfully positioned himself as a democratic opponent of dictatorship. As French political analysts say, when a socialist minister resigns on a left-wing issue of principle, "He fell to the left."

Yeltsin's second major error was to personalize his dispute with Ligachev and thus strengthen his opponent's position. Gorbachev was forced to rally publicly to the defense of Ligachev, making his conservative number two untouchable for the next few months. Throughout the winter of 1987–1988, the reformers were on the defensive. In March 1988 came the most serious attempt yet to reverse Gorbachev's reforms, through what became known as the Nina Andreyeva affair.

The publication, in the conservative newspaper *Sovietskaya Rossiya*, of an anti-*perestroika* manifesto written by Andreyeva, a Stalinist teacher from Leningrad, took place while Gorbachev was abroad in Yugoslavia. The article, which had the approval of Ligachev, in his role as the Party's ideological chief, was entitled, "I Cannot Compromise My Principles." Although Ligachev subsequently denied responsibility, recent interviews with those involved in the publication of the article leave no doubt about his role.[2]

Andreyeva's message was splashed over an entire page of the newspaper, a sure sign that it was important. She defended Stalin's achievements and the idea of the class struggle at home and abroad. She attacked liberal intellectuals and said the Party should return to its role as a bulwark of the workers. She condemned political pluralism and "cosmopolitanism"—a code word for Jews dating from the darkest days of Stalinism. Ligachev summoned newspaper editors to the Kremlin. According to one of them, Ivan Laptev of *Izvestia*, he said: "I read an excellent article yesterday in *Sovietskaya Rossiya*, a wonderful example of party political writing. I hope you have all read it. I would ask you, comrade editors, to be guided by the ideas of this article in your work."

For three weeks, the fate of Gorbachev's policies seemed to hang in the balance; the rest of the Moscow newspapers waited to see if the new conservative line would be upheld. According to Roy Medvedev, Gorbachev had to threaten to resign to persuade the rest of the Politburo to denounce Andreyeva's pro-Stalin manifesto.

With hindsight, it is possible to say that Ligachev, though his career was to continue, had overreached himself. From that point onward, it seems unlikely that Gorbachev ever trusted him again.

While Yeltsin's career within the party leadership was clearly over, the Soviet public was troubled. In previous times, promotions and demotions from the Politburo had created not a flicker of public interest, but Yeltsin's case was different. Why had his resignation speech not been published? Did his demotion mark the high water mark of *perestroika*? Apocryphal texts purporting to reproduce the missing speech began to circulate, as if to satisfy the public curiosity over Yeltsin's political testament. Gorbachev admitted later he would have done better to have published everything Yeltsin said immediately, to forestall public curiosity.

In the absence of an authorized text, the apocryphal versions reflected the fantasies of the man in the street about the bold things Yeltsin had dared to say on his behalf. One such text quoted him as calling for a troop withdrawal from Afghanistan and complaining of "petty supervision from Raisa Maximovna" (Gorbachev's increasingly unpopular wife). Yeltsin was also quoted as blaming Ligachev for the lavishness of the party festivities to mark the November anniversary, a sign that his denunciation of privilege had touched a popular nerve: "Yes, comrades, it is difficult for me to explain to a factory worker why, on the seventieth anniversary of his gaining political power, he is forced to stand in line to buy sausages in which there is more starch than meat, whereas our tables are loaded with sturgeon, caviar, and all kinds of delicacies, easily acquired from a place that he cannot even approach."[3]

Yeltsin's departure was, however, not greatly mourned by the intelligentsia, the strongest supporters of *perestroika*. Yeltsin wrote that the intelligentsia believed wrongly that he was a Stalinist. Vitaly Korotich, editor of *Ogonek*, told a Dutch newspaper, "He was far from the intellectuals and sought no contact with us. He was a man who did not shirk his work, but in the long run, he was unable to give the Muscovites everything." Korotich pointed out that the manner of Yeltsin's removal indicated progress toward democracy, because under Stalin, he would have been executed and under Khrushchev, he would have been punished. "Perhaps Yeltsin really was an adventurer?" he asked.[4]

A more sophisticated attempt to analyze the strengths and weaknesses of Yeltsin's role appeared in the liberal weekly *Moscow News*, from the pen of Gavriil Popov, a Moscow University economics professor, who was later to become the capital's first reform mayor in 1990. Yeltsin's problem, Popov wrote, was his "vanguardism." His authoritarian concept of *perestroika* involved no real economic reform nor democracy from below, merely orders given from the top and endless personnel changes.

While supporting *perestroika*, Yeltsin tried to achieve its goals by leaps and bounds; because he was unsuccessful, the final result was to help the conservatives. Popov pointed out that some conservative criticism of Yeltsin was really criticism of Gorbachev. When Yeltsin was accused of preferring spontaneous encounters with ordinary people to taking part in party meetings, this was an attack on "the entire new style of leadership approved by the people and the Party." Yeltsin's approach was characteristic of those who saw the solution to *perestroika*'s problems in a change of personnel. "When people like that . . . discover that the problem lies not so much in replacing the crew as in rebuilding the ship, . . . they tend to panic." Popov shrewdly pointed out another problem with Yeltsin's charismatic leadership style: It encouraged passivity among people who wanted *perestroika* to be accomplished by somebody else and presented to them "on a silver platter," while they remained aloof. "The situation in Moscow presupposed only one hero of *perestroika*. The rest of us were to admire and applaud the solo performance in this one-man theater."[5]

It certainly looked as though Yeltsin's political career was finished. As one Western commentator wrote, "Yeltsin will probably be remembered as a transitional figure."[6] In this view, Yeltsin's authoritarian style was suited only to the first phase of the post-Brezhnev reform, and he would be out of his depth in the second phase. This judgment was to prove incorrect—Yeltsin was to bounce back, still recognizably himself, but in many ways a changed character. His earthy, populist style was unchanged, but the new Yeltsin would owe his loyalty more to the people than to the Party. He was also to develop a sense of political guile and timing that he had not shown before.

After his resignation Yeltsin had to fight not only heart problems but deep depression. Stories circulated that he tried to take his own life, and most of his colleagues and friends shunned him. "It was as though a circle had been traced round me, which no one could enter for fear of contamination." Unable to seek relief either in God or in the bottle, according to his autobiography, Yeltsin began an obsessive analysis of himself, his career, and his beliefs. "All that was left where my heart had been was a burnt-out cinder." Tormented by headaches and insomnia, he finally survived thanks only to his family and to old close friends from his student days in Sverdlovsk.

On January 14, 1988, the Soviet government spokesman, Gennady Gerasimov, announced that Yeltsin had left the hospital and begun his new job at Gosstroi, the State Construction Committee. A month later, on February 18, at the next Central Committee session, Yeltsin was, as expected, dropped from the Politburo. In his autobiography, he tells us that he rejected an offer from Gorbachev to retire on pension, something which would probably have been fatal to such a natural workaholic as himself. The autobiography describes his period at Gosstroi as "something of a nightmare." The job was mostly paperwork and did not allow him enough contact with ordinary people. By now, he had the itch to be a real politician, not a supermanager.

But on a wider front, the atmosphere was changing. *Perestroika* and *glasnost* were starting to move Soviet society in new directions, provoking increasing unease among party conservatives but offering Yeltsin hope that his eclipse might be only temporary. "New times were on the way, unpredictable and unfamiliar, in which I had to find a place for myself," he wrote. Not everything was being guided from above.

In February, Gorbachev, now convinced that some kind of deeper political reform of the system was needed, had persuaded the Central Committee to summon a special party conference for June 1988. Without confronting the conservative dead weight of the Party head-on, as Yeltsin had wanted, he was looking for a way to outflank it, by creating stronger state institutions. The primacy of the Party in the Soviet system made the General Secretary the prisoner of his colleagues. But a strong state presidency, on the French or even the American pattern, would give greater freedom of maneuver to the man who held it. Gorbachev, possibly without understanding fully where he was going, was seeking a new basis for legitimizing the Soviet leadership. The mandate of history, transmitted down the decades from Lenin, was no longer sufficient, but a new kind of legitimation, based on a genuinely popular mandate, would demand some kind of democratization of the electoral system.

Yeltsin seems to have realized only belatedly, in his political isolation, that he risked not being elected a delegate to the Nineteenth Party Conference, despite his position as a minister and his membership in the Central Committee. Grass-roots party groups in Sverdlovsk, Moscow, and elsewhere tried to nominate him, but each time, the party *apparat* intervened to prevent his name going forward. Finally, Yeltsin squeaked home just in time, managing to get elected as a delegate from the small autonomous republic of Karelia, between Leningrad and the Finnish border. Other reformers and Gorbachev supporters had similar problems getting elected as delegates, a sure sign that the conservatives were beginning to organize.

During this period Yeltsin was still a "nonperson" for the Soviet press, although Western journalists sought him out for interviews. In one interview with BBC television, broadcast during President Reagan's May 1988 visit to Moscow, Yeltsin raised again the issue of Ligachev's opposition to *perestroika.* "It would be possible to develop the process more actively with someone else in his post," Yeltsin said, confirming with an emphatic "da" that, yes, he did think Ligachev should quit.[7] Gorbachev, who no doubt privately shared Yeltsin's opinion, was forced to defend Ligachev at a summit news conference and call for a transcript of Yeltsin's remarks. Yeltsin was summoned to party headquarters by Mikhail Solomentsev to be questioned about what he had said. But this time, the final result of his outspokenness was to weaken Ligachev's position rather than his own. Subtly, the rules of the game were changing to his advantage.

The Nineteenth Party Conference was the first gathering since the 1920s to break the pattern of well-scripted unanimity at the top of Soviet politics. For the first time, there would be spontaneity and disagreements; not everything would be pre-ordained from above. And the political balance had shifted from the moment, eight months earlier, when Yeltsin had been shot down in flames. Unlike a closed-door Central Committee meeting, the conference was a public and televised occasion.

When Yeltsin heard Gorbachev address the conference, he must have felt a certain satisfaction at hearing his former patron repeat some of his own ideas. Calling for a cardinal reform of the Soviet political system, Gorbachev acknowledged that *perestroika* had essentially failed to get society moving. "We underestimated the whole depth and weight of the deformations," he admitted. Now, he argued, was the time to introduce new political freedoms, freedom of conscience, a separation of party and state, legal reform, and a degree of pluralism. Lenin, he told the delegates, was resolutely opposed to persecuting those of his colleagues who thought differently. The new political system was to comprise a new Congress of People's Deputies, which would elect a full-time parliament.

Yeltsin, seated right at the back of the balcony of the Palace of Congresses, in the Kremlin, was as far away as he could be from the center of events. When he had arrived, everybody had avoided him, except for the liberal film director Elem Klimov, who grabbed him by the arm and walked inside with him, amid nervous stares. Some curious delegates came up to Yeltsin just to gawk at the party's *enfant terrible*. "I felt almost like an elephant in a zoo," he recalled.

He asked for permission to speak but was not called to the rostrum. However the "Yeltsin affair" found its way on to the agenda all the same. German Zagainov, a delegate from an aviation research institute, wanted to know what Yeltsin had said in his interview to foreign television networks. Why had he not given an interview to the Soviet press? Yeltsin wanted to reply, but his requests to the platform were ignored. By the fifth and final day, Yeltsin realized that nobody planned to rock the boat by inviting him to speak. So he left the balcony for the main hall and strode to the front, challenging Gorbachev to allow him to the rostrum. "All eyes were on Yeltsin and no one was listening to the speaker," Klimov recalled.[8] This characteristically bold maneuver succeeded and Yeltsin was finally allowed to have his say.

After setting the record straight about his television interview and repeating his call for Ligachev to resign, Yeltsin made his speech. It was a far more coherent performance than his resignation speech. Yeltsin said the idea of applying *perestroika* to the Communist Party itself had come far too late. All elections, inside and outside the Party, should be universal, direct, and secret, with office-holders limited to two terms and an age limit of sixty-five. This alone would provide guarantees against a return to "leaders and leaderism" [*vozhdi i vozhdism*]—in other words, to Stalinism. Yeltsin's call went further than anything Gorbachev was proposing, though not as far as Gorbachev himself was to go later on. At this stage only those outside the Party were posing the daring demand for a multiparty system, and Yeltsin was not prepared to go this far. He demanded that Politburo members who shared responsibility for the sins of the Brezhnev era should be dismissed and the system changed to enable a new leader to assemble his own team. Returning to a theme he had raised at the time of his resignation, he said the party leadership was still effectively beyond criticism. Yeltsin urged the creation of a Central Committee commission to set long-term policy guidelines and oversee policy implementation, a proposal which would balance the power of the secretariat and the Party's permanent executive organ.

Next Yeltsin renewed his criticism of *perestroika*'s failure to solve any real problems and the Party's failure to confront its past mistakes. He followed this up with a powerful plea for greater inner-Party openness and democratization and an attack on the privileges of the *apparat*. "In my opinion, the principle should be as follows: If there is a lack of anything in our socialist society, then that shortage should be felt in equal degree by everyone, without exception," he declared to applause. The *apparat* should be drastically trimmed, he said.

So much for politics. Yeltsin next raised a personal issue— his own rehabilitation. Noise erupted in the hall, and Yeltsin offered to leave the rostrum, but Gorbachev intervened to tell him to continue. "I think we should stop treating the Yeltsin affair as a secret," he said.

"Comrade delegates! Rehabilitation fifty years after a person's death has now become the rule, and this has had a healthy effect on society. But I am asking for my personal political rehabilitation, while I am still alive." Yeltsin pointed out that, while his speech at the October 1987 plenum had been condemned as politically erroneous, many of the issues he had raised had since been voiced by others, including Gorbachev himself. "I consider that the only error in my speech was that I delivered it at the wrong time." Yeltsin asked the conference to withdraw its condemnation of his views, which he said would help the cause of *perestroika* by boosting popular confidence in the Party.

Yeltsin's demand posed a dilemma for Gorbachev. Although he probably agreed with most of what Yeltsin had said, it was politically impossible for him to reopen the question of Yeltsin's rehabilitation. But neither could the whole subject be left hanging in the air. Because the whole conference was being watched on television by the masses,

Yeltsin's speech had to be given an organized reply after the lunch break.

First up to bat was Gumer Usmanov, party leader in Tataria, who opposed Yeltsin's rehabilitation on the grounds that he was "giving interviews right, left, and center to various foreign agencies." Then came Ligachev, who came to the podium "leering like a hungry wolf, ready for the kill."[9] Ligachev's emotional and rambling address proved to be the beginning of the end of his political fortunes.

He accused Yeltsin of not just tactical but strategic political mistakes and again, implausibly, denied rumors of Politburo differences over *perestroika*. As for himself, nobody should question his anti-Stalinist credentials. After all, he had lost family members in the purges. But nonetheless, the Stalin period was not all bad: "We know how heroic our people were, despite the cult of personality and the phenomena of stagnation." Here Ligachev signaled his true views by saying he agreed with Yuri Bondarev, the conservative writer who had earlier in the conference compared *perestroika* to a plane that takes off without the pilot's knowing where it is going to land. Using a different metaphor, he made clear he shared the view that Gorbachev did not know where he was going. "Wisdom tells you that, before going *in* somewhere, you should think about how to get *out*." Ligachev declared that, in his view, the Soviet press was going too far in criticizing both the Stalin and Brezhnev periods and the opponents of *perestroika*.

"During the years of stagnation, I lived and worked in Siberia, a harsh land, but a truly wonderful one. I am often asked what I was doing at that time, and I reply with pride: I was building socialism. And there were millions like me." Then came a personal jibe at Yeltsin; while Ligachev's province (Tomsk) had been self-sufficient in food, Yeltsin's province (Sverdlovsk) had been forced to introduce food rationing. He also defended the privileges of party workers, arguing that their ruble salaries (not the issue Yeltsin had raised) were already too low. Finally he attacked Yeltsin for breaching party discipline by talking to the "bourgeois press." "Do you like having all the foreigners running round you, Boris?"

The speech was a self-inflicted defeat. Ligachev had abandoned normal rules of politeness by addressing Yeltsin not as "Boris Nikolayevich" but as plain "Boris," like a teacher speaking to a schoolboy. "*Ty, Boris, ne prav* [Boris, you are wrong]" became a catchphrase for liberals, rewritten as "*Ty Yegor, ne prav.*" The virulence of his attack came over badly on television. "Under different circumstances, even a few months earlier, Ligachev's defense against Yeltsin . . . might have worked. But [it] did not."[10]

The chorus against Yeltsin was not as unanimous as it had been in October. *Pravda* chief editor Viktor Afanasyev, a man with a keen ear for the political winds of the moment, neatly came down on both sides of the fence, by saying he agreed with part of Yeltsin's speech, which he compared favorably to the muddled address he had delivered in October.

Next came a departure from the scenario. V. A. Volkov, a delegate from Sverdlovsk, came to the rostrum to praise Yeltsin and his record. "Yes, Yeltsin is a very difficult man, with a difficult character. He is a tough man, perhaps even cruel," he conceded. But why had the Central Committee not published the full record of Yeltsin's resignation?

Two sharp attacks on Yeltsin followed from Moscow speakers, one of whom accused Yeltsin of driving a district party secretary to suicide, by criticizing him, a charge Yeltsin was subsequently to deny. I. S. Lukin, party leader in Moscow's Proletarsky district, said he and his colleagues were still clearing up the mess left by Yeltsin, whom he accused of driving a wedge between the Party and the workers.

Gorbachev summed up, like a judge balancing arguments of the prosecution and the defense. While he disagreed with Yeltsin, he pointedly failed to defend Ligachev. First, he dealt point-by-point with Yeltsin's arguments and defended his own policies. Next, he went back to Yeltsin's record in Moscow and the circumstances of his resignation, accusing him of using "command methods" in the capital. Gorbachev was deliberately repeating much of what he had said behind closed doors to the Central Committee the previous October, but this time there was a crucial difference. Not only was there was an audience of five thousand delegates, but later tens of millions of curious Soviet citizens would watch the whole dispute on television. Acknowledging that the information should have been published earlier, Gorbachev read out the text of Yeltsin's "confession" of his errors to the Central Committee. By implication, a rehabilitation of Yeltsin was not possible, but the blame for what had happened was to be shared more equally: "This is a lesson not just for Comrade Yeltsin, it is a lesson for the Politburo, for the General Secretary, for the party Central Committee, for all of us."

Shortly after the conference, Yeltsin gave his first interview to the Soviet press—to the Latvian youth newspaper

Sovietskaya Molodezh—while resting at a sanatorium in the Baltic resort of Jurmala, near Riga. The interview was not published for several weeks because of high-level resistance in Moscow. It was reprinted by 140 other Soviet newspapers, thus reaching a much wider audience.[11]

Yeltsin gave a positive view of the party conference, glossing over his own failure to achieve rehabilitation. "It had a fundamental impact on the minds of people, their attitudes, and even on the entire situation in the country," he said. Spelling out his critique of Gorbachev's reform course in more detail, he singled out its failure to do anything to improve the dismal Soviet standard of living. Without a swift improvement in food and consumer goods, the Party's prestige would take a nosedive, he implied. Clearly on his best behavior, Yeltsin referred sanctimoniously to the precedent set by Lenin, when asked about his taste for "going to the masses." It was not just a matter of gathering economic data, he insisted. "No, in party life, and it is particularly important to realize this, there must be a driving emotion, if you like, passion. Sometimes they urged me to be calmer, more restrained, as this would give greater stature. I personally did not understand this. Lenin was a very emotional, passionate man, and at the same time, this did not prevent him from solving major problems. Certainly we are his followers. It is absurd to call oneself a Leninist and carry an icy heart in your chest."

In the interview, he angrily denied the suggestion that he was trying to advertise the fact that his wife used normal shops and stood in line. "But the principles of Soviet justice are measured not only by the ruble, a *dacha*, or a fancy trip," he went on. It was clear that Yeltsin's views were evolving toward a more radical critique of the lack of democracy in the Soviet system.

"We have stifled man spiritually. He has been under the pressure of exaggerated authorities, orders, unceasing instructions, an infinite number of decrees, and so forth. We have accustomed others not to unanimity but rather to unanimous stifling. Is this socially just? If we are voting, then inevitably it is almost all one hundred percent; if we are raising our hands, everyone to a man is 'for.' It is a shame that the word pluralism has reached us from our ideological enemies."

Thanks to his televised duel with Ligachev, he had become more than ever a national figure, a symbol of resistance to the party *apparat*. As he told an Austrian interviewer, in

September 1988, "Unfortunately, I am popular in Chekhov's sense! Chekhov tells about a man who lay down in front of a train to become popular. When he was run over, he was popular. This is probably also true for me, because I was axed."

Sometimes, the adulation was embarrassing. When he went privately to the Bolshoi theater in Moscow, the audience applauded spontaneously. "This is not pleasant; I will not go to the theater anymore."[12]

The Austrian interviewer described Yeltsin as humorous, but also as unbroken and militant. Yeltsin's changed mood reflected not only his recovery from depression but a new atmosphere in the country at large. Soon the balance of Soviet politics was to shift even further toward reform, as the country lurched through a worsening economic crisis and the disaster of the Armenian earthquake.

Less than a year after Yeltsin's disgrace, his criticism of the conservatives in the Politburo was to be spectacularly vindicated. In September 1988, Gorbachev mounted a sudden coup against his conservative opponents and did exactly what he had promised the Central Committee he would never do— he reorganized the central party apparatus from top to bottom. Former foreign minister Andrei Gromyko retired as Chairman of the Presidium of the Supreme Soviet, effectively head of state, and Gorbachev took his place. Solomentsev and other conservatives were dropped from the Politburo, and Ligachev lost his key job in charge of ideology. The way was clear for the Supreme Soviet to approve Gorbachev's constitutional plans for a new Congress of People's Deputies, to be elected in multicandidate elections on March 26, 1989.

Gorbachev was creating an opportunity for Yeltsin's political resurrection. The Party clearly had no intention of rehabilitating him, but the people might.

8

Resurrection

With his spectacular televised duel with Ligachev at the Nineteenth Party Conference, Yeltsin had forced himself part of the way back from disgrace. Public curiosity about him and his views was mounting. The political quarantine to which he had been confined was starting to break down. Gorbachev's revolution from above was starting to be replaced by a grass-roots revolution, as hundreds of informal discussion groups and clubs sprang up. It was the first stirring of a civil society, the first breach in the Communist Party's right to control all social and intellectual activity.

In November 1988, the students of the Higher Komsomol School in Moscow defied their superiors and invited Yeltsin to address them. He treated them to a four-hour question-and-answer session, in which he did not duck the difficult questions about what he called the "*skandalchik*" of his dismissal. Describing himself as dissatisfied with his current job at Gosstroi, which was 80 percent paperwork, he said he wanted "a dynamic, interesting job, with people."

What were his duties as a member of the Central Committee, one questioner asked. "Voting—that's the prerogative of a Central Committee member. The *apparat* decides everything," he replied. His criticism of Gorbachev's *perestroika* was becoming sharper. How could socialism be "renewed" when it had not yet been built? he asked. As for communism, it remained out of sight. He expressed concern that Gorbachev's new two-tier parliamentary system had been rushed through without adequate discussion and had been designed to filter out political dissent. Classic democracy required direct elections for the post of Soviet President, and major political issues should be settled by referendum, he argued.

The Party should stop trying to make *perestroika* succeed on all fronts at once, and focus instead on an immediate improvement in food supplies and consumer goods and services. This would give people a sense of achievement and restore faith in the reform process. Spending on the space program and the military should be cut. Yeltsin coupled this with his familiar call for an end to special party privileges. "My wife goes to the [ordinary] shops . . . we eat sausage, though to tell the truth, it's better not to inspect it too closely beforehand."

"One must get rid of the inborn dread of waging political struggle. . . . This dread comes from the fact that the monopoly of political power in the country belongs to the party-bureaucratic apparatus, to which we have long learned to sacrifice our own well-being and dignity," he told his young communist audience.[1] But he was careful not to criticize Gorbachev himself. At this point, Yeltsin clearly saw the decline of Ligachev as a political opening for himself, a further sign that the old system was cracking.

Accounts of his talk with the Komsomol spread around the country, first in *samizdat*, and more widely, when a youth newspaper in the Urals city of Perm printed a transcript. Yeltsin gave a more circumspect interview, to a wider public, in the pages of the national daily *Komsomolskaya Pravda*, at the end of 1988. But after this the press ignored him totally—a move which only increased public curiosity about his views. According to Radio Vladivostok, which broke the taboo on Yeltsin by broadcasting an edited recording of his Komsomol School meeting, in February 1989, one listener letter in three sought information about his views.

Interviewed by an Italian journalist, in January 1989, Yeltsin forecast that he and Gorbachev would soon reach a rapprochement. "I know he regretted condemning me, and even then, he was my most loyal comrade. The time has come to say that this split between us was caused entirely by Yegor Ligachev."[2]

Gorbachev, and Soviet politics as a whole, were catching up with Yeltsin. The second half of 1988 was a turbulent period in which the pace of reform quickened. In September, Ligachev paid the price for his defiance of Gorbachev and his sponsorship of the Nina Andreyeva letter, when Gorbachev destroyed his power base, at a surprise session of the Central

Committee. Ligachev was transferred to taking charge of agriculture, while the Party's permanent apparatus, in its old form, was effectively scrapped. Several senior figures, including head of state Andrei Gromyko, were retired. The swiftness of the operation made it look like a successful coup. Yeltsin's name was not mentioned, but to some extent, Gorbachev was following his advice.

By the end of 1988, Yeltsin had already been contacted by hundreds of districts and workers' collectives to stand as a candidate in the March 26 elections, but the road to a political comeback was full of obstacles.

Gorbachev's plan for democratic elections was a flawed compromise. Nonetheless, it stood every principle of Soviet politics since Lenin on its head. Though he had won the assent of the Nineteenth Party Conference for his ideas, the precise timetable for the election of the new parliament was bulldozed through in the last few minutes of the meeting, before delegates quite realized what they were voting for. By the time the old Supreme Soviet, the outgoing rubber-stamp parliament, approved the new electoral system, late in 1988, it was clear that the voting would be, at best, half-democratic. The central principle was that of a two-level parliament, composed of a Congress of People's Deputies—a fine Leninist-sounding title—which would, in turn, elect a smaller, full-time parliament from among its ranks.

To get into the full-time Supreme Soviet, the first task was to win a seat as a deputy to the Congress. There were 2,250 seats, but only two-thirds of them were to be filled by a popular vote. The remainder were to be filled by the representatives of "public organizations," led by the Communist Party. This was a throwback to the old electoral system, where the Party decided who was to be elected. It insulated Gorbachev and his top party colleagues from the need to face a public vote—something which, in hindsight, may have been a fatal mistake. Not all of these 750 deputies owed their election to party patronage, but many did. The remaining fifteen hundred seats were divided between two chambers; one elected according to population, from roughly equal electoral districts; and the other, like the US Senate, reflecting existing territorial and national divisions, irrespective of population size.

Would-be candidates had to face a complicated set of hurdles in order to get their names on the ballot. First, they had to be nominated at a public meeting, and then be registered, at a second meeting controlled by local officials. Only the most determined and crafty outsiders managed to get to the starting line. Once they did, they sometimes found the election race itself the easiest part of the contest.

Yeltsin and his campaign team, headed by his chief of staff at Gosstroi, Lev Sukhanov, were determined to outsmart the *apparat* and make sure the candidate's name was registered on the ballot. That would be the difficult part—persuading the electorate to cast what amounted to a protest vote against the party hierarchy would not be such a problem. As a fallback, in case he failed to secure nomination in a major city, Yeltsin managed to ensure, in early January, that he would be on the ballot in Berezniki, the Urals town where he had grown up.

"Like a fox, I covered my tracks," he recalled. After sending a telegram saying he would be unable to attend, he sprang a surprise on the party apparatus by turning up unexpectedly in Berezniki, arriving in a rattling AN-26 military transport plane via Leningrad, after the last scheduled flight had left Moscow. In two hours of hard talking, Yeltsin met everyone who mattered, before senior party officials even got wind of his presence. He was adopted as a candidate.

The real campaign battlefield, however, would be Moscow. Yeltsin and all the other candidates learned, as they went from one constituency nomination meeting to the next, how far the party apparatus was prepared to go to keep control of the process. Like the rest of the country, Moscow had been divided into several equal-sized national constituencies, each to elect one of 750 deputies to the new Congress. But the whole city of Moscow was also zoned as a single constituency, as part of the election of a further 750 deputies on a "national-territorial" basis. With more than six million voters, this constituency carried the number "1" and a victory for Yeltsin there would clearly carry more weight nationally than a triumph in little-known Berezniki.

The nomination meeting took place on February 22, in the Hall of Columns in central Moscow, a neoclassical building as rich in historical memories as any place outside the walls of the Kremlin. Once the Club of the Nobility, it was where the bodies of Lenin, Stalin, Andropov, and Chernenko had lain in state. It was also the setting for the purge trials of the 1930s, where Nikolai Bukharin and dozens of other old Bolsheviks abjectly confessed their guilt before Stalin and the Party, before being taken to their deaths.

Of the ten potential candidates, two were clearly on the Party's short list for nomination—Yuri Brakov, manager of the ZIL truck factory, which also made limousines for the Politburo, and the popular crewcut cosmonaut Georgy Grechko. Yeltsin persuaded the other candidates to appeal to the meeting to let all their names go on the ballot. "From the mood of the hall, I sensed that, on this occasion, this tactic wouldn't work. Only two names—Grechko and Brakov—had been firmly hammered into their heads."

At Soviet public meetings, questions are normally written down and passed up to the platform. This custom is convenient both for the questioner, who can avoid public identification, and for the speaker, who can pick and choose which questions to answer. Oral questions, if any, come later. Yeltsin turned this to his advantage, by deliberately picking out the most hostile questions first. But the ace he was keeping up his sleeve was a secret promise from Grechko to withdraw in his favor. Grechko had approached Yeltsin privately, before the start, and told him that he did not want to stand in his way; his decision was irrevocable. Yeltsin craftily persuaded Grechko not to announce his withdrawal until just before the voting. "Grechko played his part to perfection," he recalled. The final result of the thirteen-hour meeting was that, while Brakov topped the ballot, with 577 votes out of 875, Yeltsin came close behind, with 532, enough to secure registration as a candidate.

"Because I had cleared this particular hurdle and my chances of winning had therefore increased, the resistance of those who saw my election as a catastrophe also increased a hundredfold. I represented to them a collapse of faith in the unshakability of the established order of things. The fact that the established order had long since turned rotten through and through did not worry them. The main thing for the *apparat* was to keep Yeltsin out."

Yeltsin's decision to stand in Moscow, rather than in Sverdlovsk or Berezniki or one of the two hundred or so other places where he had been invited to be a candidate, was a characteristic gamble for high stakes. Instead of a safe seat, he faced a big battle, in a place where the Party could easily concentrate all its efforts against him. Immediately after his Moscow nomination, he flew to Sverdlovsk, to explain, in person, to his many supporters why he was standing in the capital instead.

In fact, Yeltsin's election campaign in Moscow turned into a gentle cakewalk, thanks not only to his own campaigning skills and his extrovert personality and booming voice but also to the ineptitude of his opponents. By giving him no publicity, they only turned him into a martyr. The mighty Communist Party was flabby and complacent, like a boxer who goes too long without sparring practice. Its handling of the "Stop Yeltsin" campaign proved that, in seventy years without opposition, it had become a bureaucratic administrative structure, rather than a political party. It had totally forgotten the basic skills of politics. Yeltsin began to joke about Moscow city party leader Lev Zaikov being one of his secret supporters. As he swept from rally to rally, through crowds chanting his name, it was clear to both camps that a landslide victory was in the cards.

A televised phone-in debate between Brakov and Yeltsin, on March 12, two weeks before the voting, was marked by a crude attempt to rig the questions. Yeltsin's aide Mikhail Poltoranin revealed that some of the Moscow voters named as the authors of hostile questions addressed to his candidate either did not exist or denied any connection with the questions. There were other allegations from the Yeltsin camp that Brakov's supporters had made threatening phone calls and carried out attacks on his car.

Ten days before the poll, the Party played its last card—an attempt to use internal disciplinary methods against Yeltsin, for going against party policy. At a Central Committee plenum, on March 16, a number of members, all carefully picked for their blue-collar profiles, urged an investigation of Yeltsin, for his campaign speeches. One urged his expulsion from the Central Committee.

The list, which included Yeltsin's old hard-hat critic Vladimir Zatvornitsky, was headed by another proletarian thoroughbred, Moscow lathe operator Vladimir Tikhomirov, a twenty-seven-year veteran of the Vladimir Ilyich factory, where Lenin was shot and wounded by an assassin in 1918. Yeltsin defended himself against charges that he advocated a multiparty system by saying he had only called for the subject to be thrown open to a national discussion.

The result was a vote to establish a commission to investigate Yeltsin's alleged heresies against the party line, a move which only served to reinforce public support for Yeltsin. When permission for a Yeltsin rally, on March 19, in Gorky Park, was withdrawn, thousands of Muscovites marched to the capital's city hall in protest and held the rally on its doorstep. Public anger was fueled by an article, in *Moskovskaya Pravda*, in which Tikhomirov assailed Yeltsin as a hypocrite and accused him of disloyalty to the Party. Several days went by before the paper printed Yeltsin's reply, reportedly after intervention at Politburo level.

The more intelligent and liberal members of the Gorbachev team, such as Alexander Yakovlev, distanced themselves from the clumsy attempt to investigate Yeltsin, realizing that the old way of labeling him a heretic would only
backfire. "Who said that he has done anything wrong?"
Yakolev asked in an Italian newspaper interview.[3] But the
damage had been done. Yeltsin won cheers from the workers
at the ZIL truck plant, at a three-hour rally during which he
carefully refrained from any criticism of his opponent. "I
consider it immoral for a candidate to attack his opponent.
Brakov is a comrade," Yeltsin declared.[4]

The explosion of popular feeling on the streets of Moscow
began to worry Yeltsin, but the demonstrations remained
peaceful. Something unprecedented was taking place. "Some
people within the bureaucratic apparatus still believe they
can direct the people with a baton, like an orchestral conduc-
tor," Yeltsin commented.

Throughout his campaign Yeltsin stuck to familiar
themes. On the privilege issue, he spelled out that he was not
in favor of *uravnilovka*, or the "leveling" of wages. All he
insisted on was that the rubles earned by everyone, from
cleaners to ministers, should have equal purchasing power.
In other words, Yeltsin did not want to reduce everyone's
wages to the same level, just to end the secret system of
subsidies, under which top officials received goods and services either free or at nominal cost. While Gorbachev was still
opposed to a multiparty system and to private property,
Yeltsin made clear he was prepared to reopen the debate on
both these taboos. But his radicalism had its limits. He went
on record as opposing both a return to a capitalist economy
and the secession of the Baltic republics from the Soviet
Union.

His strongest campaign argument was a call for genuine
democracy—free, secret, and direct elections at all levels and
a decentralization of effective power. He was particularly
critical of the way one third of the 2,250 Congress deputies
would be picked directly by "social organizations," including
the Communist Party.

But he was quick to smother any speculation that he
might challenge Gorbachev for the job of head of state.
"Someone or other is trying to speculate and set me up as an
alternative figure to Gorbachev," he complained. "I fully
support Gorbachev in strategic questions, in foreign and
domestic policy questions, and I do not intend to oppose
myself to him under any circumstances."[5]

The day before the poll, a crowd, estimated by Western reporters at around twenty thousand or more, rallied in Yeltsin's support at the Luzhniki sports grounds. As an independent political meeting, Moscow had seen nothing like it since 1917. On March 26, Yeltsin and his family voted at the Palace of Pioneers, in Frunzensky district, surrounded by a human wave of hundreds of foreign journalists and television crews. When the votes were counted, he had won a staggering 89.6 percent. Of the 6.8 million registered voters, 5.1 million voted for him and only 400,000 for his opponent.

In a country holding its first democratic election since 1917, Yeltsin's was the most striking upset for the party old guard. For Gorbachev, still fighting his own war against conservatives, it was a double-edged result. Like an earthquake, the voters' anger helped to demolish the bastions of his conservative opponents, but it also showed the cracks in his own concept of reform and gave a new political forum to his radical critics.

Like other successful candidates, notably the prosecutors of the "Uzbek mafia," Telman Gdlyan and Nikolai Ivanov, Yeltsin had ridden the wave of popular protest against the *apparat*. "There has been a deficit of truth, which has resulted in a situation where people are now reaching out for it," he told a Japanese interviewer.[6]

But, as *Moscow News* analyst Vitaly Tretyakov pointed out, Yeltsin's popularity was more than just a protest vote or a flash in the pan. It could be traced back more than three years to the day at the Twenty-sixth Party Congress when he, alone among the leadership, accepted a share of responsibility for the sins of the Brezhnev era. This gave him a store of public credibility, which was only reinforced by his concern for bread-and-butter consumer issues, during his spell in Moscow. "Yeltsin was the first to tear from himself the shroud of secrecy which usually veils personal acts by representatives of the 'upper crust.' The image of a destroyer of secrets always has a great appeal to people."[7]

Tretyakov said that Yeltsin had won popular trust by his campaign against privilege and compared him to the legendary character from the *1001 Nights*, Caliph Haroun al-Rashid, who "is remembered because he studied the real life of rank and file people of Baghdad, without any suite and in ordinary dress."

Tretyakov identified other sources of Yeltsin's appeal: He asked people for their support instead of lecturing them and telling them what to think; he had resigned from high office, so he was no careerist; and his past as a political insider in disgrace gave him a special aura. Tretyakov pointed out that Yeltsin had been in the advantageous position of a shadow opposition leader, able to campaign without responsibility. If *perestroika* was going to fail, he forecast, Yeltsin's popularity would continue to soar, but if it succeeded, others would share the credit.

After the voting was over, Yeltsin vanished with his wife to Kislovodsk, a spa in the northern Caucasus, for a rest, but the rumor mill kept turning. On April 7, *Pravda* quoted his assistant, Lev Sukhanov, as denying that the people's hero had been hurt in a car crash. "The phone at Gosstroi has been ringing off the hook. Boris Nikolayevich has not been in any car crash."

A month after the election, Gorbachev assembled the bruised and battered party Central Committee and used the election upsets to force the resignation of 110 "dead souls"— mostly holdovers from the Brezhnev period, such as Mikhail Solomentsev. Gorbachev faced furious criticism from senior party leaders, who had been humiliated by the voters. All criticism of Yeltsin was forgotten.

"I believe the great election victory had some impact on everyone. It caused them to reflect," Yeltsin commented. Gorbachev had undermined the conservatives but had not removed them completely. He had weakened the Party's grip on all aspects of Soviet life in favor of a new parallel body, which he would find more difficult to control. A new page had been turned in Soviet history thanks to Gorbachev's tactical skill, but his victory set in motion processes that would ultimately whittle away his power. Democracy was a game where someone else might turn out the winner.

Less than eighteen months earlier, Gorbachev had telephoned Yeltsin: "He told me to bear in mind that he wasn't going to let me back into politics. At the time, he evidently believed in what he was saying with all sincerity; it did not occur to him that he had created and put in motion a set of democratic processes under which the word of the general secretary ceased to be the word of a dictator."

As Gorbachev's adviser, Georgy Shakhnazarov, described it: "This was the real revolution. Everything up to that point was just the overture."[8]

When the Congress of People's Deputies assembled in the Kremlin, it soon became clear that Yeltsin and other reformers, despite their victories, would be in a minority. Of the two and a quarter thousand deputies, only between three and four hundred could be counted as reformers, enough to form a vocal opposition but not enough to form a serious impediment to Gorbachev. Though 88 percent of the deputies were there for the first time, only 13 percent were from outside the Party—less than in the old rubber-stamp Supreme Soviet, where the Party had always included obligatory quotas of milkmaids and non-Party tractor drivers among its candidates.

The outnumbered reformers, mostly from Moscow, began meeting in April, several weeks before the Congress was due to open. Yeltsin missed these initial meetings but joined others in May, after his holiday was over. The "Moscow group" of liberal deputies were alarmed by the plans of the outgoing Supreme Soviet leadership to restrict the Congress to a formal session of three days, with no live television broadcast. After many days of debate the deputies agreed on a list of demands, with direct television broadcasts and a full political debate on the situation in the country. "We had to make sure that the Congress did not become formalized, did not turn into just another ceremonial occasion, the gathering of an electoral college."[9] It was Yeltsin who helped ensure the live television broadcast, insisting that without it there would be an explosion of popular anger.

What the reformers wanted was to delay Gorbachev's inevitable election until there had been a full debate on his record and his program. They also wanted to turn the Congress into a kind of Constituent Assembly, which would take upon itself the power to rewrite all the rules of Soviet politics and begin the subordination of the Party to elected popular organs at all levels. This kind of forum would mark a return to the principles of the 1917 Constituent Assembly, Russia's only previous freely elected parliament, which the Bolsheviks shut down on the day it met. This vision, articulated by Andrei Sakharov, went far beyond what Gorbachev intended. It was clear that the reformers were in a minority and, in Murashev's words, "The absolute majority was prepared to carry out everything that was required of it." But the way the minority's views were brushed aside inevitably sharpened the divisions.

Though many who rallied in support of Yeltsin at Luzhniki stadium, a few days before the opening of the Congress on May 25, wanted him to challenge Gorbachev for the presidency of the Supreme Soviet, this was out of the question. At a Central Committee plenum, on May 23, Gorbachev was formally nominated as the Party's candidate for the job.

Yeltsin abstained, on the grounds that the election for the post should be contested. But when challenged about his intentions, he promised to obey party discipline and vote for Gorbachev. So when he was nominated from the floor of the Congress to challenge Gorbachev, he quickly refused. Most reformist deputies probably shared the view of Alexander Kraiko, a reformist Moscow deputy, who said that he greatly respected Yeltsin's decisiveness, but the task of Supreme Soviet president required someone who was ready for "compromises, dialogue, perhaps concessions." Any challenge by Yeltsin would have violated not only party discipline but would also have contradicted his campaign speeches. Most important, it would have been doomed to fail. "Gorbachev was the idol of the deputies at that stage," the young radical deputy Arkady Murashev recalled. "When I asked my voters whom I should vote for, the result was seven to three in favor of Yeltsin, but I voted for Gorbachev anyway. In fact, Yeltsin's chances were zero and he knew it."[10]

About a week before the Congress opened, Gorbachev summoned Yeltsin for a talk. The conversation lasted an hour and was, according to Yeltsin, tense and nervous. Each man was trying to probe the other's intentions, while neither wanted to reveal his own hand. "His answers were harsh and brusque, and the longer we talked the thicker grew the wall of incomprehension between us," Yeltsin wrote. Gorbachev floated the idea of bringing Yeltsin back into government as a full minister—which would have forced him to resign his deputy's mandate, but Yeltsin refused to be tempted.

When the Congress opened, the radical deputies, though outnumbered, were strong enough to leave their mark on the proceedings right from the start, when one of them seized the initiative by condemning the killing of twenty peaceful demonstrators by troops in the Georgian capital, Tbilisi. Thanks to live television broadcasts—not prerecorded, as in the case of the Nineteenth Party Conference—the impact of every speech entered virtually every Soviet home. People stopped working and watched in fascination. As Yuri Chernichenko, a radical deputy described it, "On television the effect . . . was like a gigantic Shakespeare play, but without a script. We made up the script as we went along, and nobody knew what was going to happen next."[11]

One of the star debaters, a Leningrad University law lecturer named Anatoly Sobchak, singled out the television relay as the key factor. "The political awareness of people changed more in three weeks than in the preceding fifty years."[12] Yeltsin took the same view: "On the day the Congress opened, they were one sort of people; on the day that it closed they were different people."

The radicals dominated the rostrum, but they did not have the votes. Many of the deputies from rural areas had been elected unopposed, in the old style, and were used to being told how to vote. They were like performing seals, as Chernichenko put it.[13]

Tensions boiled over when Yeltsin failed to win election to the Supreme Soviet, the permanent parliament. Because his Moscow constituency was a "national-territorial" one, he had to win one of eleven places allotted to the Russian republic in the Soviet of Nationalities, one of the two Supreme Soviet chambers. Virtually all the other republic lists were chosen without a contest, the party chief in each republic having the final word. Yeltsin could probably have bargained behind closed doors for a place on the slate of eleven, but insisted in principle that the election should be contested. In the event, there were twelve candidates for the eleven RSFSR (Russian Soviet Federated Socialist Republic) seats, and Yeltsin trailed in bottom of the poll with 1,185 positive votes.

Reformer Yuri Afanasyev, a historian, angrily complained that the Congress had elected a "Stalinist-Brezhnevist Supreme Soviet." Gavriil Popov complained that a "mechanical majority" was steam-rolling through decisions and called on like-minded deputies to join him in forming an interregional group.

Gorbachev, seizing on this as a call for the formation of political factions, which Lenin had outlawed, appealed deftly to the conservative majority's sense of what was historically taboo. But as Kraiko reminded Gorbachev, there was a new actor on the political stage, Soviet public opinion. Yeltsin was the "first candidate of the RSFSR," with five million votes; he had been nominated as a potential candidate in two thousand factories; the opinion of the people could not be ignored. As one Ukrainian deputy said before the presidential vote, "We will vote for Gorbachev, but all the same, we will have Yeltsin on our minds."

Gorbachev also needed Yeltsin in the Supreme Soviet, or the voters would dismiss his new parliament as no more than a rubber stamp, like the old one. So when a solution was found, nobody was more pleased than Gorbachev himself. "His face showed a look of unconcealed relief," Yeltsin wrote. Alexei Kazannik, a bearded law professor from Omsk university, announced that he was willing to give up his place on the RSFSR slate—but only to Yeltsin. For form's sake, Yeltsin said he was not in favor of Kazannik's withdrawal, having himself proposed the Siberian lawyer for the Supreme Soviet. "I tried feebly to dissuade him," Yeltsin recalled.[14] But Kazannik insisted on withdrawing. "Tell me, Boris Nikolayevich, what will I tell my constituents? For they know the six million people of Moscow are behind you. If I remain, they will kill me." After a moment of procedural uncertainty, Gorbachev ruled that Yeltsin could hold the seat in Kazannik's place without a further election.

Outside the Kremlin, Yeltsin was mobbed by his supporters. "Mr. Yeltsin's walk from the Kremlin, up Gorky Street to his apartment, turned into a triumphal procession. Hundreds of Muscovites flocked around him, pumping his hand and handing up babies to be kissed."[15]

On the street, the feedback was immediate; fired by what they had seen on television, crowds rallied every day to meet their radical heroes. The people had been given the right to vote, but they effectively won the right to demonstrate as well.

Yeltsin's speech to the Congress was a mixture of old heresies and new warnings, skillfully avoiding outright rebellion against Gorbachev's policies, while marking his differences. He told the Congress he had proposed to the May 23 Central Committee plenum a wholesale transfer of power from the Party to the Soviets but had found no support. The Congress itself was a hostage of laws and decisions passed by the old rubber-stamp Supreme Soviet, and its powers were severely limited.

Meanwhile the country's problems—economic inequality, crime, corruption, food shortages—were rapidly getting worse. The press was still shackled, demonstrations were still banned, and nobody was prepared to take responsibility for the killing of unarmed protesters in the streets of Tbilisi. "Organized crime has penetrated all structures of society, including its highest echelons, the Party," Yeltsin said. *Perestroika* had failed to tackle the vested interests of the *apparat*, and this explained why so many decisions were hesitant and contradictory. "A degree of self-criticism in Comrade Gorbachev's report does not remove his responsibility for all this," he declared.

Yeltsin's solutions included land reform, a law freeing the press from party control, a law restricting the Party's powers, and internal party reform. The Congress, as a state body, was not the place to discuss inner-Party questions but Yeltsin was determined to use it as a platform, to appeal over the heads of the Central Committee and the *apparat* to the Communist rank and file, watching on television. He also urged quick action to stabilize the ruble and a cutback on capital construction. There was no mention of the space program or of military spending cuts, but he gave explicit backing to Baltic demands for greater republican sovereignty. Then came a familiar call for an end to *nomenklatura* privileges.

His parting shot was a warning which turned out to be prophetic. As the situation in the country deteriorated, Gorbachev was being granted wider and wider powers to tackle it, he said. "This 'scissors' may lead to the temptation of solving our complicated problems by means of force. We may again, without noticing it, find ourselves prisoners of a new authoritarian regime, a new dictatorship." Some mechanism must be found to control the powers of the head of state, such as an annual referendum, he argued.

The Congress showed that Yeltsin was no longer the only, or even the main, lightning rod for the party conservatives. That function was fulfilled by the frail figure of Andrei Sakharov, subjected to a hysterical torrent of abuse, for having allegedly insulted the Soviet army in remarks about Afghanistan. When Sakharov mounted the rostrum, on the final day of the Congress, his verdict on the failure of the Congress to take power was couched in terms much harsher than Yeltsin's. Angrily, Gorbachev ordered Sakharov's microphone to be disconnected, making clear his tolerance had been exceeded. "That's enough!"

The Congress, as Gorbachev told the deputies, was something new for all of them. Bill Keller, of the *New York Times*, described it as "part morality play, part parliamentary improvisation, part exorcism." Everybody had to learn the ropes as he went along. Some, like the eloquent Sobchak, were born legislators, who took to the new environment like ducks to water. Others had more difficulty swimming. This applied just as much to Yeltsin, who had to redefine his position. He was no longer a solo rebel, but a member of a group, most of them intellectuals, who were reluctant to accept him as their leader. Marju Lauristin, a deputy from Estonia, commented, "He can't imagine anything without himself in command." Yeltsin, in other words, would have to live down his authoritarian reputation and, against his instincts, become a team player.

There was no doubt that, in the short term Gorbachev was the real winner in the new game, having the advantage of being able to write most of the rules as he went along. As chairman, he could switch from scoring goals, as captain of the winning team, to blowing the whistle, as umpire or referee. Using a term familiar to a soccer-watching Soviet audience, he declared, "I'm showing you the red card!" as he cut short a deputy who tried to defend Sakharov.

For the reformers, there was no alternative but to take whatever crumbs of influence were offered. When the Congress ended and the new Supreme Soviet met in June, Yeltsin became a member of the Presidium, through his election as chairman of the Standing Committee on Construction. Gorbachev may have felt Yeltsin could be detached from the radical minority and co-opted, or at least kept busy. Yeltsin told Bill Keller, in early June, "I think Comrade Gorbachev is a little nervous about me. Yes, unfortunately I think he has the idea I want his job."[16]

But the real lesson of the first Congress was that individual deputies, no matter how popular they might be with the voters, were bound to be ineffective, unless they formed a permanent group. This was the origin of the Interregional Group, set up despite Gorbachev's stern warning against forming factions.

9

Virgin Soil Upturned

"**A**t school and later at the polytechnic, I had studied Marx's theory of the exploitation of man under capitalism. I now experienced that indisputable theory being applied to myself."

Yeltsin's first visit to the United States, in September 1989, only lasted a week, but it was a formative experience. It marked the moment when he threw overboard the last of his illusions about "building socialism" and communist ideology, so it is worth looking at in detail.

Yeltsin was, even by Soviet standards, an inexperienced foreign traveler when he boarded an Aeroflot plane for New York in September 1989. Although he was in his late fifties, his trips abroad could be counted on the fingers of one hand. Gorbachev, while still a provincial party official, had spent a month driving round France with his wife at the invitation of French communists; Alexander Yakovlev had studied at Columbia University; and many other Soviet politicians had traveled in the West, at least on business. Yeltsin had been a few times to Czechoslovakia, but had otherwise missed out. One reason may have been that his early career was spent in Sverdlovsk, a city closed to foreigners because of its defense industry, and therefore off the beaten track for visiting delegations. He seems to have been unaffected by the lure of foreign travel for its own sake, preferring to spend his vacations camping in the taiga.

In the mid-1980s, he twice led party delegations to West Germany, and visited the western hemisphere on a trip to

Cuba and Nicaragua, during which he established a good personal rapport with Fidel Castro. Conscious of his inexperience, Yeltsin rehearsed for his first US journey by getting Soviet academic experts on the United States to fire questions at him.

If he had been less of an innocent abroad, he would probably not have agreed to visit eleven cities in a single week at the invitation of his American hosts, the Esalen Institute, a California group promoting cultural exchange. "The Central Committee of the Party would only let me go for one week," Yeltsin wrote in his autobiography. It seems unlikely however that Yeltsin suffered any kind of personal discrimination, as he suggests. The trip was originally planned to be two weeks, but the announcement of a plenum of the party Central Committee meant that he was obliged to shorten his journey by five days. This measure would have applied to any member of the Central Committee, whatever his standing.

Yeltsin had not been invited by the US government, and he was not on official Soviet business. His trip was a private lecture tour, at the invitation of the Esalen Institute and other organizations. He was accompanied by Lev Sukhanov, his chief of staff, *Komsomolskaya Pravda* journalist Pavel Voshchanov, fellow deputy Viktor Yaroshchenko, and Gennady Alferenko, chairman of the USSR Social Inventions Foundation board.

Before the effects of jet-lag and his punishing schedule began to tell, Yeltsin showed every sign of enjoying himself, though Voshchanov later described the first day's schedule as "an absolute nightmare." After flying round the Statue of Liberty in a helicopter and applauding in what one journalist called "a spontaneous gesture of delight," he told a news conference in New York: "All of my impressions of capitalism, of the United States, of Americans, that have been pounded into me over the years, including by the [Stalinist] *Short History of the Communist Party*—all of them have changed one hundred eighty degrees in the day and a half I have been here." Yeltsin was whisked from the Museum of Modern Art to the Trump Tower, to the United Nations, and even to a Korean fruit and vegetable store, which so impressed him that he joked about Ligachev (now responsible for Soviet agriculture) holding seminars. "It appears that capitalism is not rotting away, as we were told, but it seems to be prospering. The Statue of Liberty is not some sort of a witch, but a very attractive lady."[1]

In Washington, the White House, anxious about offending Gorbachev by welcoming a rival too warmly, treated Yeltsin like an unexploded bomb. Spokesman Marlin Fitzwater told the *Washington Post*, "We don't want to do anything to foster internal conflict that might be associated with this trip. . . . We didn't want to indicate that we were trying to provide a platform for dissent."[2] So there was no invitation to the White House until the last minute, when he was summoned from Baltimore to meet President Bush's National Security adviser, Brent Scowcroft. For fifteen minutes of the two-hour session, Bush himself "dropped in," though photographers were not admitted. It allowed Yeltsin to say he had met the President, while permitting Bush to avoid the political symbolism of a formal call in the Oval Office.

Yeltsin was keen to make his meeting look as substantive as possible, telling reporters he had presented a ten-point program for American investment and help for the Soviet economy, a message which was listened to politely, but skeptically. A. M. Rosenthal of the *New York Times* said Yeltsin's proposals "went down like a lead pirogi" with Bush and his team and accused him of treating Americans the way American politicians do—"like a bunch of nincompoops."[3]

Others came away much more impressed with Yeltsin's directness, native wit, and political skills—what one reporter called his "mastery of the photo opportunity, the sound bite, and the nonresponsive answer."[4] After listening to him at the Council on Foreign Relations, in New York, David Rockefeller praised him as "a charming and impressive person, who is clearly a highly skilled politician."[5]

However some portraits were less flattering. Paul Hendrickson described, in the *Washington Post*, how Yeltsin had drunk a bottle and a half of Jack Daniel's bourbon on an overnight stop in Baltimore. "Boris's Boozy Bear Hug for the Capitalists," said the headline. Hendrickson wrote: "Boris N. Yeltsin, Soviet politician of the people, imbiber nonpareil, radical legislator, and member of the Supreme Soviet, nyetter within the system, came swaying and galumphing and bassooning and mugging and hugging and doom-warning through the greater Baltimore–Washington corridor yesterday." And he compared following Yeltsin to "watching a circus bear negotiate a skateboard. The bear never once fell off, though there were moments when it seemed perilous."[6]

Hendrickson's piece appeared not in the news section of the paper but in the Style section, where journalists who have trouble controlling their metaphors are normally deployed.

Whether by accident or design, this atmospheric story, describing Yeltsin's groggy appearance at a breakfast talk at Johns Hopkins University in Baltimore, was to have more consequences than the journalist imagined. "Yeltsin came in. He clasped his hands over his head like a boxing champion. He tilted, he rocked. He swerved. He careened." What happened, according to Voshchanov and Sukhanov, was that Yeltsin, after two sleepless nights, finally swallowed two sleeping tablets around four A.M., and they had difficulty waking him two hours later. Yaroshchenko went to greet the breakfast audience, while Yeltsin followed later.

Other members of the press described Yeltsin in equally unflattering terms. In the *Baltimore Sun*, Stephens Broening, a former Moscow correspondent for the Associated Press, described Yeltsin as "not at his freshest" for the breakfast rendezvous and said he even lost his balance at one point. "Mr. Yeltsin's gaze was sometimes vague, his grasp listless as the guest shook his hand." After some coffee, Yeltsin managed to deliver his main address of the day and "was able to speak without slurring his words."[7]

The *Washington Post* story posed an enormous problem for Yeltsin's aides, who were horrified when they saw it. What would their thin-skinned chief say if he saw himself described as a colorful buffoon, in terms that *Pravda* would never use about a Soviet legislator: "He has an elastic face that would have been perfect on a '40s burlesque stage. His silver hair has a wondrous upsweep. His nose is a proboscis. He wears his watch on the inside of his wrist. The voice volume is enough to shatter dishes."

Fearing an explosion, they decided not to show it to him. Voshchanov wrote later that this was a mistake: "Through our silence, we almost put him in an awkward situation. During the visit to a hog farm, in a suburb of Indianapolis, its owner, Jim Hardin, invited us into his home, and without a trace of irony, remarked, 'Unfortunately, I don't have any of your favorite, Jack Daniel's!' It was only later, back in the car, that Yeltsin was to ask his aide: 'Lev, I did not quite get it, which Jack was he talking about?' "[8]

Yeltsin zoomed from coast to coast, from one university rostrum to the next, telling audiences what was wrong with Gorbachev's *perestroika*. In anti-Communist Miami, his final stop, he deftly sidestepped questions about his chum Fidel Castro, but he charmed his audience, by declaring unambiguously that the Baltic republics should have a free choice whether or not to remain in the Soviet Union and by calling for bold constitutional changes to remove the Party's monopoly of power. His repeated calls for the removal of Ligachev and other conservatives from the Politburo and his disparaging jibes about Communism and the Soviet system were, word for word, the same as in Moscow. His praise for what he had seen of America went beyond routine pleasantries. "Although I am not a religious believer, I sometimes have a dream about heaven when I am asleep, and what I saw of Miami, by helicopter yesterday and today by car, was something that far exceeded any vision of paradise that I might ever have had in any dream," he told his audience.[9]

After he was back in the Soviet Union, Yeltsin continued to praise the United States and its two hundred years of democracy. "The people of this country are able to work excellently and relax with good taste. They are not obsessive, they are quite free, and they live without looking back. On the streets I met many polite, smiling people. Did I see any of the social problems in America? That is not what I went there for—I have seen enough social problems at home to make me sick. I was not looking for the speck of dust in someone's eye."[10]

According to Voshchanov, the real shock for Yeltsin was his ten-minute visit to a supermarket, in Houston. Yeltsin described it as a shattering experience. "When I saw those shelves crammed with hundreds, thousands of cans, cartons, and goods of every possible sort, for the first time I felt quite frankly sick with despair for the Soviet people," he wrote.

Voshchanov clearly suspected that the negative US press stories were inspired by a deliberate Soviet attempt to discredit Yeltsin. This probably gives too much credit to the KGB's disinformation skills, and too little to the tendency of journalists to borrow each other's stories. Whether or not the original Jack Daniel's material corresponded to the truth, it was tailor-made for Yeltsin's party opponents back in Moscow.

Just as the jet-lagged Yeltsin got back to Moscow, millions of readers of *Pravda* were being treated to a colorful description of his American tour as a drunken rampage during which he spent most of his thousands of dollars of lecture fees on consumer luxuries, such as videocassettes and clothes. The account was lent extra credibility by the fact that it was not written by a Soviet journalist but by Vittorio Zucconi, Washington correspondent and former Moscow correspondent of *La Repubblica*, a respected Italian daily. Yeltsin was furious, particularly because, instead of keeping his lecture fees, he had donated them to buy a million disposable syringes, for the Soviet anti-AIDS campaign. "The article . . . made me look like the usual drunken, lumbering, ill-mannered Russian bear at his first encounter with civilized society."

Yeltsin received thousands of telegrams of support, and an unprecedented apology from *Pravda*. Zucconi also apologized, acknowledging his story was a secondhand compilation, based partly on the *Washington Post* and partly on information from a source he had unwisely chosen to trust. Yeltsin told one interviewer that the article could have been written in Russian and translated into Italian, but his real anger was reserved for *Pravda*'s editor, Viktor Afanasyev, who lost his job shortly afterwards. "At the Central Committee plenum, I told Afanasyev approximately the following: 'If we were to settle this as men, we would have to . . . But I would knock you down, and lying there on the floor would be a piece of something, and the members of the Central Committee would have to look at that piece of something. . . . I despise you. . . .' I turned round and left. Sometimes I am sorry that the age of duels is over."[11]

Two weeks after his return, on October 1, Soviet television broadcast a prime-time seventy-minute film of Yeltsin in America, including his wobbly early morning appearance at Johns Hopkins. By Yeltsin's own account, the film had been deliberately tampered with, to make him look even slower, an allegation which state television officials denied, when he repeated it publicly, during the February 1990 election campaign.

However, worse was to come in the form of an even more colorful incident, which Yeltsin described as "a premeditated act of provocation." In early October, rumors suddenly swept Moscow that Yeltsin had been attacked or assassinated. Why was he no longer attending the Supreme Soviet sessions? In fact, he was in bed with pneumonia after a mysterious dunking in the Moscow river. Yeltsin told well-wishers he had caught a bad cold in America and was resting, but Moscow still buzzed with speculation.

The affair became public on October 16, when Yeltsin was well enough to resume his seat in the Supreme Soviet. Gorbachev announced that so many rumors were flying around about an attack on Yeltsin that the affair had to be cleared up. "We cannot evade it; an answer must be given." He then asked Interior Minister Vadim Bakatin to the rostrum to read a prepared statement. Bakatin said that, on September 28, shortly after 11 P.M., a soaked and bedraggled Yeltsin had appeared at the *militia* (police) post guarding a group of government *dachas* at Uspenskoye, on the Moscow River, just west of the capital. Yeltsin told the police he was on his way to visit friends in one of the *dachas*, after a constituency meeting with voters, in Moscow. (The area, dotted with *dachas* for the Soviet elite, is one of the mostly heavily guarded in the country, with police posts every few hundred yards.) According to Bakatin, Yeltsin told the police that, shortly after dismissing his car and driver, to walk the last part of the way on foot, he was pushed into a car by unknown persons and then flung into the river, emerging some three hundred yards downstream. The police helped Yeltsin dry out his clothes, and later his family collected him. Yeltsin asked the police not to report the incident, but next day Bakatin personally ordered that there should be an investigation. Some initial inquiries were made, which turned up discrepancies with Yeltsin's initial story. Bakatin ordered a halt to investigations, after Yeltsin told him by telephone, on September 30, that there had been no attack on him.

After Bakatin had finished, Yeltsin took the floor, but did not challenge the minister's account. "There was no attack on me. . . . That is all I have to say." Amid uproar, he added, "That is my private life." Two days later, Yeltsin accused Bakatin of trying to discredit him, to distract the voters. Bakatin denied this at a news conference on October 19, saying that Yeltsin had contradicted himself. Who was telling the truth? Why, if Yeltsin had been the target of some kind of assault, rather than just falling in the river, had he tried to cover the incident up?

Yeltsin, in his autobiography, gave only sparse details of what happened: "Suddenly another car appeared behind me and—I was in the river." He asked the police not to report the incident, because he was afraid it was a provocation, deliberately aimed at causing strikes and popular unrest, as an excuse for a crackdown. "Half of Moscow might have downed tools. And then, as a result of strikes in the defense industries, martial law would have been declared."

Whatever the real truth, the public "clarification" of the incident by Gorbachev—unprecedented in a country where private indiscretions normally remain private, and rumors are normally allowed to circulate unmolested—suggested, like *Pravda*'s reprint of the Italian article on his American tour, a desire to discredit him at all costs. Like the earlier attempts to hurt his reputation, in the long run, Yeltsin's soaking only helped his popularity at the grass-roots, though he admitted that, for a while, it damaged his standing with the public. For many Russians, it confirmed his larger-than-life image as a man who might occasionally have one glass too many and get into a scrape. Yeltsin's popularity was too strong to be permanently damaged by stories about him losing his balance or his trousers. Yeltsin treated the incident as part of the price of remaining in politics. "I always have had and always will have enemies—after all, this is no joking matter, politics."

For the rest of 1989, Yeltsin was uncharacteristically quiet. A Supreme Soviet committee, which was set up to look into *Pravda*'s treatment of his visit to the United States gave him partial satisfaction, by condemning the party newspaper. But it also rebuked Yeltsin, in mild terms, for not behaving abroad in a manner fitting to his position.

In December, Yeltsin visited Greece and told the newspaper *Kathemirini*, "Those who still believe in communism are moving in the sphere of fantasy. I regard myself as a social democrat." A few days later, Gorbachev replied to the Supreme Soviet: "I am a Communist, a convinced Communist. For some that may be a fantasy. But for me it is my main goal."[12]

The next month, Yeltsin was off to Japan, where he successfully negotiated the potential minefield of the Northern Territories, the four islands occupied by Moscow at the end of World War II, which Japan wants back but which the Soviet Union has refused to discuss. Yeltsin avoided the obvious diplomatic pitfalls by unveiling his own multistage plan for solving the islands problem, managing to sound statesmanlike but vague. If he had just stonewalled, he would have offended the Japanese; if he had offered to hand the islands back, he would have given ammunition to his foes at home. Like his American hosts, the Japanese listened politely to Yeltsin's ideas for large-scale economic cooperation, while realizing that he was not empowered to negotiate anything on Moscow's behalf. This time Yeltsin managed to avoid controversy on his return home.

10

Fellow Travelers

After four preparatory meetings, the first, on June 7, involving 150 deputies, the Interregional Group was formally established on June 29 and 30, 1989, during the first session of the new Supreme Soviet. Their request to use the facilities of the parliament was turned down, and the inaugural meeting was held at the Dom Kino, the Moscow "House of Cinema." Yeltsin, who had announced plans for the formation of the group to the Supreme Soviet, gave the keynote speech and was initially to be proposed as chairman. But finally the group made him only one of five cochairmen.

The others were Sakharov, the only non-Communist, the outspoken historian Yuri Afanasyev, economist Gavriil Popov, and Viktor Palm, an Estonian, representing deputies from the Baltics. "We wanted to maximize our support, and we did not want to set up a new idol or become identified as the followers of one individual," Murashev recalled.[1] The posts of cochairmen were to be rotated among the twenty-five-member coordinating council. Nearly four hundred deputies attended, though not all signed up as members immediately. Most deputies from the Baltics, pursuing their own agenda, in their own groups, cooperated but did not join. The group's program gave priority to further political reform, including direct election of the country's president, sovereignty for the republics, and human rights. During the succeeding Supreme Soviet sessions, it scored a number of legislative successes, though there were also many defeats.

For the first time in his political career, Yeltsin was moving among intellectuals, many of whom were initially suspicious of him. "The suspicion was natural. After all, Yeltsin was from the 'partocracy.' But it did not last for long," recalled Arkady Murashev, a leading member of the group.[2] According to Poltoranin, the intellectuals at first saw Yeltsin as being "like a big child, rather naive," but then were won over by his sincerity.[3] Most owed their primary loyalty to Gorbachev and were doubtful about someone identified as an opponent. Yeltsin and Sakharov first met during the election campaign, when Yeltsin promised Sakharov not to oppose him, if he were to stand in Moscow. "They drank tea together and liked each other," Poltoranin recalled.

It seems, however, that Yeltsin was more impressed by Sakharov than the other way round. Sakharov, in his last volume of autobiography, paid tribute to Yeltsin for his role at the Congress but described him as "not of the same caliber" as Gorbachev. Sakharov's widow, Yelena Bonner, remembered that the two men were never particularly close but added, "Andrei Dmitriyevich was always a lone wolf."[4]

"What Yeltsin learned from Sakharov was the ability to analyze. He had the natural instinct, but he had to learn to analyze. From Gavriil Popov he learned not to be so harsh and intolerant and coarse in his expressions," Poltoranin recalled. "It was a mutual learning process. What Yeltsin knew much better than the others was the inner-Party kitchen and what they were cooking up. I think he added some intellectual qualities to his natural wolflike intuition and became the fully formed personality he is today."[5]

"My relations with Yeltsin were difficult at the start: I felt his mistrust and caution and responded in the same way," Anatoly Sobchak wrote. "I did not like Yeltsin's speeches at the Congress and at the meetings in Moscow: Their populist tone at times got the better of common sense, and I thought that was not a good thing in politics."

Relations only became easier after Sobchak and Yeltsin spent three days together, on a parliamentary visit to Greece, late in 1989. "After a year, it appeared that we had no differences in principle at all."[6]

This unease between Sobchak, the urbane Leningrad law professor, and Yeltsin, the provincial ex–construction boss, reflected the historic gulf between the Russian intelligentsia and the people, which seven decades of Soviet power did little to bridge. It is something that Western Europeans and Americans find hard to grasp. The fact that Yeltsin was such a hero among the *narod* (the people)—who are seen by the intelligentsia as, at best, authoritarian and, at worst, Stalinist—awoke instant suspicion.

One Moscow intellectual tried to explain this to me: "A lot of older intellectuals, particularly assimilated Russian Jews, have an anti-Yeltsin complex. Yeltsin gives a feeling of crude popular force, which inspires deep mistrust, an intellectual demophobia, a fear of the dark Russian masses, and with Jews, the genetic memory of the pogroms. I don't want to idealize the people, but in practice, it has shown itself above all these passions and has voted for the democrats, not the so-called Russian patriots."[7]

Sobchak recalled: "For me, Boris Nikolayevich was, for a long time, a man from the party *apparat*. He might have been thrown out, he might have democratic tendencies, but all the same, he was a creation of the System. For him, I was a representative of the Soviet university professorate, a group which was, in many respects, conformists, obsequious, and weak." Sobchak found Yeltsin quick to take offense, like Gorbachev, and prone to making rash impromptu statements on the basis of unchecked information. "But we finally became intellectual allies [*edinomyshlenniki*]."

From the start, some leaders, including Yuri Afanasyev, saw the Interregional Group as an opposition to Gorbachev, at least in embryo: "The time has passed when he can successfully remain the leader of *perestroika* and the leader of the *nomenklatura*. He has to make a clear choice," Afanasyev told the inaugural meeting."[8]

Others, such as Sergei Stankevich, a young expert on the United States, who was later to become deputy mayor of Moscow, were less keen to stress their differences with Gorbachev and wanted to give him critical support against the conservative majority. He played down the "oppositional" element and described the formation of the group as part of the parliamentary machinery needed to reach sensible compromises.

Yeltsin clearly saw the danger of being maneuvered by the majority into the role of a powerless opposition and marginalized. "We do not aim, by any manner of means, to split the Supreme Soviet, struggle for power, create opposition, or block any bills sponsored by the people's deputies," he told *Moscow News*.

Gorbachev's conservative opponents, still reeling from their election defeats in March, had regrouped for a counteroffensive by July 1989, and for the rest of the year, tried hard to regain the initiative. In this atmosphere, the Interregional

Group became a target for their attacks. "In the newspapers, at constituency meetings, at local party meetings, on every possible and impossible occasion, people were told that they—that is, we—were greedy for power; that we wanted to subject the country to a dictatorship; that we were an opposition; that we were a clique of intellectuals and bureaucrats removed from the people; that most of us had an obscure and shady past," Yeltsin wrote in his autobiography.

The Interregional Group was refused official parliamentary status and the right to publish its own newspaper; on October 13, Gorbachev accused Yeltsin and the other leaders of forming "a clique striving for power." The sharpness of his attack was a reflection of his increasing difficulties within the Party, which looked likely to break up into reformist and conservative wings. In the Baltics, Lithuania's Communist Party was in the process of breaking away from Moscow, and in Eastern Europe, popular revolts were beginning to threaten the foundations of communist rule.

Yeltsin's view was that the unwieldy joint leadership was a mistake. "As soon as things come around to organizational questions, our wheels start spinning. One cochairman is afraid to show initiative, the third thinks that everything proceeds from the fourth, and the fourth . . . ." Most of his work on behalf of the group took place behind closed doors, in the Supreme Soviet Presidium, where he was the only radical representative. "Nobody else from the Interregional group is on it, and this means that I have to look out for our interests all by myself."[9] Yeltsin's repeated interventions led to heated clashes with Gorbachev. "It reached a point where Comrade Gorbachev tried to shut me up: 'You, Comrade Yeltsin, calm down . . .' I had to respond: 'No, you, Comrade Gorbachev, calm down. Or do you get to do whatever you want?' "

Meanwhile Yeltsin was kept occupied by his new post as chairman of the Supreme Soviet Committee on Construction, traveling to inspect a troubled dam project in Tadzhikistan and grilling government ministers on their plans. The give and take of parliamentary committee work and the begnnings of a separation of powers between executive and legislative organs were a new experience for all involved, Yeltsin included. Thumping the table, giving orders, and old-style *trebovatelnost* (making demands) would no longer work. A journalist, from *Literaturnaya Gazeta*, watched him chair his committee and noted: "Even Yeltsin was a pleasant surprise. Having heard about his hot temper at work, I expected to see severe pressure on the audience. No, everything was different: he had become less abrasive and more democratic in the Supreme Soviet."[10]

He was reluctant at first to accept the committee chairmanship, which Gorbachev had earmarked for him. He knew that, under the reorganization of Prime Minister Nikolai Ryzhkov's government the former State Construction Committee, Gosstroi, had been made redundant. All complaints about shortages of cement and cranes would therefore flow directly on to Yeltsin's parliamentary desk. "There was a simple calculation to 'drown' Yeltsin and his committee in a heap of papers and requests, to harry them with complaints, and so on. For the committee has neither staff nor funds. It is as naked as a newborn babe. . . . With one problem after another, when will Yeltsin have any time for politics?"[11]

The end of 1989 saw the collapse of communist rule in the Warsaw Pact states of Eastern Europe. The process was different in each country, though the final result was much the same. The old system bowed out through a mixture of negotiations (Poland), free elections (Hungary), street demonstrations (Czechoslovakia and East Germany), and violent revolution (Romania). Only in Bulgaria did the ruling party manage to make more than a token attempt to stay in power.

Not all of the effects of these events on Soviet politics were immediately apparent, though everyone began to draw parallels with Eastern Europe. For those who wanted radical reform and those who wanted to prevent it, the example of Romania, with its bloody street battles, was a warning of how things could go wrong. Radicals in Moscow could take heart from the successes of their counterparts in Prague, Berlin, and Warsaw, though only the naive imagined that the rulers of the Kremlin would surrender power in the same way. Gorbachev's readiness to withdraw from Eastern Europe gave a particular boost to those who were close by, such as the Moldavians, West Ukrainians, Latvians, Estonians, and Lithuanians. They too had been under communist rule since 1945, as part of what had always seemed to be an immutable postwar settlement. But if their neighbors to the west could now overthrow Communism, without Moscow intervening, why should they not do the same?

Gorbachev, however, did not share this perspective, as he was to make abundantly clear. What his spokesman, Gennady Gerasimov, dubbed the "Sinatra Doctrine" (referring to the singer's hit, "My Way") stopped at the Soviet frontier. However, it became increasingly difficult to fend off calls for the legalization of a multiparty system and the abolition of article six of the Soviet constitution, which guaranteed the Party's sole grip on power. The Eastern European lesson proved that the "socialist choice" was an ideological, political, and economic failure; when the people were given a free vote, they wanted not a Gorbachev-style reform socialism but Western-style capitalism. But if this was the inevitable destination, the road there was still far from clear.

For Yeltsin and his allies, it was the Polish solution through negotiations at a "round table" which provided the most attractive model to follow. Poland was the first Eastern European country to break the universal pattern of sole Communist Party power in the spring of 1989. Nearly eight years after the Solidarity trade union had been driven underground, it had re-emerged as a force in the land, and the country's politics were stalemated. Finally, after years of being snubbed and persecuted, Solidarity leaders were invited to round-table talks, which led to a formula for partially free parliamentary elections, under which the Communists would retain overall control. But the voters gave Solidarity such overwhelming support that the final outcome was a Solidarity-led government. President Wojciech Jaruzelski, the ramrod-backed general who had moved into power before the 1981 crackdown, was gradually transformed into a figurehead. Perhaps this formula could be adapted to Soviet conditions, as a route to power-sharing?

Meanwhile, Communist Party conservatives, the Soviet military, and the KGB security forces drew their own conclusions. Gorbachev's strongest card was that they had no real alternative policy to offer, except massive military intervention. But the fate of the Stasi secret police, in East Germany, and the Securitate, in Romania, left thousands of their Soviet counterparts worried about their future. For the first time, Gorbachev's conservative critics could argue that reform policies would lead not to renewal but to their own extinction. Rather than meekly accepting Gorbachev's hated medicine, many of them decided they would rather stand and fight.

This was the background to the first turbulent months of 1990, a period in which Gorbachev began to look increasingly like a man following events rather than leading them. Several separate but linked political battles were under way. The first was the fight, in the new Soviet parliament, over a new constitution, especially over article six and the power structure of the state. The second struggle was for internal reform of the Party itself, which was to culminate at the Twenty-eighth Party Congress, later in the year.

The third battle, the one in which Yeltsin was to play the biggest part, reflected stage two of Gorbachev's democratization; the 1989 elections for an all-Union Congress of People's Deputies were to be followed, a year later, by parliamentary elections in the fifteen Soviet republics. On March 4, voting was to be held for the new Congress of People's Deputies of the Russian Federation, largest of the republics.

In the republican elections, Yeltsin and the radicals found their task easier than a year earlier. Not only were they more experienced and more numerous, but the rules had been changed. As a result of widespread criticism of the nomination procedures for the 1989 elections, the system of candidate registration was streamlined for the 1990 poll, and so, Yeltsin and other radical candidates in the RSFSR were able to have their names placed on the ballot without hindrance.

This time it was agreed that there would be no reserved proportion of seats for the Communist Party and other "public organizations"; this also improved the radicals' chances of winning a large slice of the 1,068 seats in the RSFSR Congress of People's Deputies. Yeltsin, interviewed some months before the voting, forecast that the radical/conservative balance in the new Russian parliament would be about 50–50. His forecast proved surprisingly accurate.[12]

Yeltsin, after deserting his home base of Sverdlovsk for a Moscow constituency in 1989, kept his promise to his local supporters and was one of a dozen candidates for constituency 74, which included the city of Sverdlovsk and nearby Pervouralsk. Despite the large field, there was no doubt about his victory, and he was able to spend part of his time campaigning in support of other reformist candidates. When the votes were counted after the first round of voting on March 4, 1990, he had won more than 80 percent, easily avoiding a second-round runoff.

When the radicals finally counted their gains, after the second round of the March elections, they had reason for satisfaction. Not only had Yeltsin been elected by a large margin, but reformers would control the city soviets of Moscow and Leningrad. The Russian parliament would have a reasonably large bloc of reformers, if not a majority, while in other republics, notably the Baltics, popular fronts had swept aside the local Communists. The multiparty system had in effect arrived, and when the all-Union Congress of People's Deputies abolished the Communist Party's constitutional monopoly on power, in mid-March, it was no more than a belated recognition of reality.

Yeltsin was hoping that Gorbachev would be forced by the rapid pace of events in the republics into a coalition with the radical opposition at the center. The idea might have seemed wishful thinking, but so did the idea of Solidarity sharing power in Poland, before the round-table talks. Yeltsin told a Danish interviewer, in February, that if the opposition won the March elections, it was "extremely likely" Gorbachev would be forced into round-table talks on the Eastern European model.[13]

It was in order to give Gorbachev the strength to move in this direction and to help him detach himself from the Communist Party that the radicals supported the idea of an executive presidency. However, when the time came, in March, for the plan to be approved by the Third Congress of People's Deputies, Yeltsin and others had grave doubts. What the opposition wanted was a presidency, not on its own, but as part of a new constitution which would embody the Western principle of separation between legislative, executive, and judicial powers, and would simultaneously devolve authority to the republics.

Yeltsin said that to introduce a strong presidency on its own was "not only premature, but also dangerous."[14] But Gorbachev did not fully share this Westernized vision of a separation of powers. When the presidency was approved by the Congress of People's Deputies, on March 13, after a hurried debate, few of the radicals' objections were met. The reformers, heavily outnumbered as always and lacking the moral presence of Sakharov, who had died in December, were unable to seriously influence the outcome, as Gorbachev pushed through his plans. They were also seriously divided over whether the Congress should elect the new president or make Gorbachev face popular election, which he might lose. Sobchak argued that the Congress should carry out the election, but Yeltsin and many others disagreed.

Finally the vote went ahead at the Congress, and Gorbachev was elected; though he was unopposed, his margin of victory was unimpressive, with less than six out of every ten delegates voting for him. From March 15, he was no longer a mere parliamentary speaker, but a fully fledged head of state. However, the presidency was to fall well short of the new power base which Gorbachev needed to win back control of events. This was partly because real executive power had always belonged to the Communist Party, and no new structures existed to replace it. More damaging to his position in the long run was the lack of the kind of mandate that could only be won in a popular ballot.

The struggle for reform within the Communist Party proved to be the most difficult of the three for Yeltsin and the radicals. Within the Central Committee, still overwhelmingly conservative, despite the April 1989 retirement of the "dead souls," Gorbachev was trying to hang on to the political initiative, while Yeltsin was a lone figure on the fringes. Other communist radicals were talking about leaving the Party altogether and forming a new one, but Yeltsin was more cautious. He still felt there was a chance that Gorbachev could be persuaded to launch an all-out offensive against the conservatives, relying on popular support. In early January, he told Yegor Yakovlev, editor of *Moscow News*: "My positions and Gorbachev's do not vary on many points." Yeltsin said he saw no direct threat to Gorbachev from the right.[15]

Yeltsin and the reformers were pinning their hopes on the Twenty-eighth Party Congress, originally scheduled for 1991, but brought forward by Gorbachev to the summer of 1990. At the Nineteenth Party Conference, in mid-1988, Yeltsin had still been a pariah. But now, for the first time, radicals were confident that they would at least have a chance to canvas openly and defend their ideas against the leadership. It was a widening of the small breach which Yeltsin had himself created in the monolith, and the logical path was to make use of it.

On January 20 and 21, a conference of party clubs from 102 cities met to draw up what they called a "Democratic Platform," demanding radical reform within the Party. Their draft went beyond a demand for the abolition of article six: It would have transformed the CPSU into a parliamentary party and legalized the formation of factions and groups within its ranks. The power of the *apparat*—the permanent party officials—would have been abolished in favor of the rank and file members.

For the first time, the reformers were able to mobilize on the street in favor of their goals. On February 4, a crowd of two hundred thousand Muscovites poured into Manezh Square, opposite the Kremlin, to hear Yeltsin, Popov, Afanasyev, and other speakers demand inner-Party reform at the Central Committee plenum, to be held the next day. It was the biggest spontaneous demonstration in Moscow since 1917. "This is the last chance for the Party. This is also Gorbachev's last chance. Either he acts or he loses us," Yeltsin told the crowd. While some were demonstrating against Gorbachev, the majority were on his side, pushing him to go farther and faster toward reform. The big show of popular support for reform undoubtedly helped Gorbachev against his conservative party critics. Some radicals even believed the party leader had helped organize it, behind the scenes. At the Central Committee plenum, on February 5, Yeltsin repeated the message. He warned the Party that it had reached a crisis point through its dogmatism, sloth, and reluctance to reform itself. "The Party's long monopoly of power has turned it into a bureaucratic structure which has reduced the country to a desperate condition and the people, tens of millions of them, to poverty." The Party, he declared, now had one last chance to redeem itself at the forthcoming congress. Yeltsin did not need to spell out what each member of the Central Committee knew: that Eastern European communist parties had been swept away by popular revolts after refusing to reform. His demands included the abandonment of democratic centralism and a guarantee of freedom of opinion for individual members; the abolition of the full-time *apparat*; a multiparty system; the formal recognition of internal party factions; the abolition of article six of the Soviet constitution, guaranteeing one-party rule; a change in the party structure from vertical to horizontal; democratic party elections; an end to the *nomenklatura* system of party control over appointments; decentralization of the party finances; the transformation of the Party into a federal structure of parties from individual republics, including Russia; and the bringing forward of the Congress, from the autumn of 1991, to May or June.

Some of these demands, notably the abolition of article six, were also on Gorbachev's list of reforms, but the majority went far beyond what he was prepared to contemplate. Yeltsin spoke several times in a debate, which he described as "heated and animated." "I put forward twelve proposals, of which four were accepted, three accepted slightly, and five rejected."[16] Yeltsin finally cast a lone vote against the leadership's draft platform for the congress. Many others secretly sympathized, but lacked the courage to follow him. He told a Danish interviewer: "The fact that there were no others who followed my example does not mean that I was alone in being opposed to the platform. But it is not easy to raise your hand and vote against, when the whole Politburo is sitting there staring at you. Fear still sits deep in the stomach."[17]

Yeltsin still hoped that pressure from the party grass-roots might shift the balance at the forthcoming congress, especially if Gorbachev swung his weight firmly in favor of reform. After all, there was evidence that ordinary party members, still numbering in the millions, were losing their awe of the leadership. One miner, invited to attend the plenum, told a television interviewer: "My first impression when I came there was that I thought I had ended up in an old people's home—such age. And in my opinion, these people can decide absolutely nothing. No changes can be expected in the near future, until the whole apparatus is replaced completely."[18]

Yeltsin grudgingly admitted that the leadership platform "is, if not a step forward, then at least half a step forward . . . this is what I have been waiting for for so long—for Gorbachev personally to take at last half a step toward the left, toward the center." What was wrong was not Gorbachev, but the composition of the Central Committee. "He is capable and has not exhausted all of his possibilities. And if one is to speak about cooperation between us, then I say that I am ready to cooperate with him, providing we are not standing, with him on the right and me on the left."[19]

If reform failed, however, Yeltsin was ultimately prepared to draw the conclusion and form another party. Some radicals, such as Yuri Afanasyev, were not prepared to wait for the Party Congress, but handed in their membership cards beforehand. Yeltsin also saw a multiparty system as inevitable, but wanted to form factions within the Communist Party as a first step. If the Communists were to split, then the reformers might be able to lay a claim to some of their considerable assets.

"At present it is difficult to say what political parties will arise in a situation of full political pluralism. It is my view that in the first round what is needed is a renewal of the Party, so that it becomes possible to form different factions. If this happens, we could well wait for a time and see how the situation develops. But if far-reaching changes do not take place at the Twenty-eighth Party Congress, new parties will be formed immediately," Yeltsin said.[20]

By the time the Twenty-eighth Congress convened, in July 1990, however, it was clear that the party *apparat* had successfully kept control of the selection of delegates, and supporters of the Democratic Platform were just a tiny minority. The real battle would be between Gorbachev and the conservatives, who were determined to put his policies into reverse.

Buoyed by their success in establishing a conservative Russian Communist Party outside Gorbachev's control, the party *apparatchiks* went on the offensive at the Congress, but finally failed to achieve their objective. However, Gorbachev's victory, which appeared to many as decisive at the time, proved short-lived. By the end of 1990, the conservative resistance to reform forced him into a major correction of course. While the battle raged between Gorbachev and the conservatives, Yeltsin was reduced to a marginal role. It was clear that the time had come for a parting of the ways, and the only question was whether he would go quietly or would slam the door behind him.

Yeltsin, making what was essentially a farewell speech to the Congress, on July 6, obliquely criticized Gorbachev for allowing the conservatives to hide behind him for so long:

> It has not proved possible to neutralize the activity of the Party's conservative forces. On the contrary. We have spoken too much about us all being in the same boat, on the same side of the barricades, that we are fighting shoulder to shoulder, with identical thinking. This position has discredited those Communists who are sincere and consistent supporters of change. This position has created a regime of security for the conservative forces in the CPSU and has strengthened their conviction that it is possible to gain revenge.

Yeltsin told the conservatives that their debates were increasingly irrelevant to the course of events and the fate of *perestroika* in the country at large:

> This question is being tackled by the people outside this building and it is being tackled in the Soviets of People's Deputies. The question facing this Congress is primarily that of the fate of the CPSU itself. To be more precise, the only question being tackled here is the fate of the apparatus of the party upper echelons.

If the *apparat* failed to change, it would inevitably doom the Party to lose not only its traditional vanguard role but also its chance to maintain itself as an elected political force, he warned. An unreformed CPSU would share the fate of the ousted Communists of Eastern Europe—facing a nationwide struggle to nationalize its property and put its leaders on trial for the damage they had inflicted on the country and the people.

> I can mention just one of these cases—the damage inflicted as a result of the anti-alcohol campaign. The people will hold them responsible for everything else, too—for the failure in foreign trade, agriculture, for the nationalities policy, and so on, and so on. The country should know what inheritance the CPSU has left it.

The only way out was for the Party to undergo a radical renewal and turn itself into a democratic, parliamentary party, capable of leading a broad coalition, to ensure that *perestroika* would be irreversible. Yeltsin's speech was also a signal to Gorbachev that the time was fast approaching when he would have to make this choice.

On July 12, as the outcome of the Congress became clear, Yeltsin mounted the rostrum for the last time to announce his withdrawal from party membership. He picked the moment when his name had been put on the list of nominations to the new Central Committee.

But he chose to leave without slamming the door. Rather than denounce the Congress once again for its conservatism, Yeltsin justified his decision by a technicality. Now that he had been elected chairman of the Supreme Soviet of the RSFSR, he had to maintain political impartiality and could no longer commit himself to be bound only by Communist Party discipline. "As head of the republic's highest legislative authority, I must submit to the will of the people and to its plenipotentiaries. Therefore, in accordance with the commitments that I gave during the pre-election period, I announce my departure from the CPSU," he told the delegates.

Four months later, he recalled: "The atmosphere was extremely tense, and two thirds of the five thousand people in the hall were feeling negative, but I did not respond to the booing, because everything was very serious by now. I spoke after having thought everything over beforehand, but when I descended from the podium I felt that the eyes of the people in the hall were following me: would I go back to my seat or leave? I left, and I think that put an end to it."[21]

To cries of *"Pozor"* ("Shame"), he put his notes back in his pocket, left the rostrum, and walked slowly up the aisle of the Kremlin Palace of Congresses to the exit at the back of the hall, without looking back. Gorbachev showed no particular emotion but responded by calling for a vote to cancel Yeltsin's mandate as a Congress delegate. If Yeltsin wished to resign, he would not be allowed back into the hall. That evening, Yeltsin was at work and "in very low spirits," when he received a call, asking how he was, from Alexander Yakovlev, the only one of Gorbachev's team who did so. Yakovlev, an intellectual and the leading liberal in the Politburo, was pilloried by the conservatives at the party conference and not reelected to the Central Committee.

Yeltsin's departure was not as spectacular as some might have expected; he left the impression that his decision was taken reluctantly and with genuine anguish.

Back in June, before the Congress opened, he confessed that the prospect of leaving the Party was causing him distress. Logic required that he should at least suspend his CPSU membership in his new parliamentary job, he told *Pravda*. "But on the other hand I have been in the Party for thirty years. And it is very, very difficult to make this decision." Despite the Party's faults, not all Communists were to blame, he added. "All this time I have had a great doubt when making this decision. I have constantly put it off."[22]

Relaxing by the seaside, in Latvia, a few days after the Congress, Yeltsin told an interviewer he did not sleep for three nights before his resignation: "I could not stop thinking. I had colossal doubts, but I could do nothing else. After all, I have always said that a one-party monopoly is harmful to society, that it should be placed under the control of the legislative powers."[23]

There were, however, sound tactical reasons for Yeltsin to tone down his anti-Communist rhetoric and make his breach with the CPSU as smooth as possible. He did not want to antagonize the powerful Communist bloc in the Russian parliament, whose cooperation was essential to elect a functioning government.

He told his Latvian interviewer that by resigning from the Party, he had taken a fairly big political risk. "I was indeed concerned mostly about whether or not I would lose the confidence of the deputies of the (Russian) Supreme Soviet and the Congress. For my majority in the parliament hung in an easily destroyed balance, and therefore, I really did not know how the deputies would feel about my statement at the Twenty-eighth Party Congress." Yeltsin said that, on the day following his resignation, he felt a "terrible strain on my nerves" at the prospect of a hostile reception when he mounted the rostrum to chair the RSFSR Supreme Soviet. "But then I entered the hall and there was . . . applause! I was even confused. I did not expect such a greeting."

Yeltsin said he had realized long ago, as far back as the crisis of October 1987, that the Party was incapable of reform, that its show of leading *perestroika* was only deception. "In essence the Party was incapable of changing structurally and organizationally, and consequently nothing truly innovative . . . could be generated there."

Asked if leaving the Party was a "personal tragedy," he replied: "I had been in it for about thirty years and had entered it out of conviction, at a time when, with Stalin's death, a certain thaw had begun. The mood was romantically high." Now he realized that the Party had led people astray. "No, it was not a tragedy but rather a liberation from a false religion."

Yeltsin had followed a well-beaten path in turning his back on Communism. But for tactical reasons, rather than becoming an outspoken anti-Communist, like many other radicals, he chose to keep his lines of communication open to those who were still in its ranks. He explained in September: "Yes, I broke with the communist ideal. But people have begun to say I do not support it in principle. No, as an ideal it has the right to live, but as a goal it is too vague. Therefore I no longer support it."[24]

The Russian Forest

The Supreme Soviet of the Russian Federation, the arena where Yeltsin and his allies were planning to establish themselves, was a cobwebbed backroom in the country's political structure. To some extent, this reflected the purely decorative function of all the Soviets, or parliamentary bodies, before Gorbachev. Real power lay with the Party, not the state, and with the all-Union structures, not the fifteen union republics. This was true everywhere, but above all in Russia, which Yeltsin was later to describe as a "ghost state [*gosudarstvo-prizrak*]" within the Soviet Union.

The historical and geographical place of Russia within the Soviet Union is much harder to define than that of, say, Georgia. Both before and after 1917, Georgia was part of a larger whole, first of Russia, then of the Soviet Union. Russia was, for many centuries, the larger whole to which the smaller parts belonged, but in 1922, it became technically one of the parts, an equal subject of a larger federated structure, known as the USSR. Behind the formal shift in status, however, the reality was one of continuity between the old empire and the new. To some extent, this ambiguity between the part and the whole had its parallel in the outer circle of the Soviet empire, where the Soviet Union was formally just one member of the Warsaw Pact alongside six others. What this amounted to in practice was that the armies of the other six nations were, to all intents and purposes, part of the Soviet armed forces.

The dual nature of the Russian/Soviet state was a direct

result of the unique pattern of Russian imperial history. In 1815, the year Russian troops marched into Paris, the historian Nikolai Karamzin surveyed what was already the largest state in the world:

> If we take a look at the expanse of this unique state, our minds are stunned—Rome in its greatness, ruling from the Tiber to the Caucasus, from the Elbe to the sands of Africa, never equaled this state. Is it not astonishing that lands separated by the eternal barriers of nature, immeasurable deserts and impenetrable forests, cold and hot climates—that [lands like] Astrakhan and Lapland, Siberia and Bessarabia, could make up one state with Muscovy? And is her population, a congeries of different races, different in appearance and far apart in level of civilization—any less astonishing? Like America, Russia has her savages; like other countries of Europe, she displays the fruits of age-long political life. One need not be a Russian, one need only be a thinking individual, in order to read with interest tales from the history of a nation which, by dint of its courage and fortitude, won domination over one-ninth of the world, opened up countries until then unknown to anyone, brought them into the universal system of geography and history, and enlightened then in the Divine Faith, merely by setting a better example, without recourse to the violence and villainy to which other devotees of Christianity resorted in Europe and in America.[1]

As historian Richard Pipes has pointed out, the classic colonial empires of Europe came into being after the construction of national states had been completed, and were distinct not only in time but in territory: "Because of the peculiar geographic location of Europe as an appendage of the Eurasian continent, European imperial expansion directed itself across the seas and into other continents; hence, there was never doubt about the spatial separation between colony and metropolis. In sum, Western empire-building—that is, the acquisition of masses of other ethnic groups—was always chronologically and territorially distinct from the process involved in building the nation state."[2]

The growth of the small medieval principality of Muscovy into the mighty Russian empire involved almost continuous expansion. Pipes cites an estimate that, between the end of the fifteenth century and the end of the nineteenth, the empire grew at the rate of 130 square kilometers (or 50 square miles) a day.[3]

Already in the sixteenth century, when Ivan the Terrible conquered the neighboring khanates of Kazan and Astrakhan, Muscovite rule included many Turkic and other non-Russian peoples. "Russian" was, at this stage, not a national concept in the modern sense. In the centuries that followed, the expansion of what was to become not Muscovy but Russia proceeded inexorably but followed no single pattern. While British and French admirals were planting their respective national flags on farflung territories such as Australia or Tahiti, the armies of Peter the Great and his successors were busy subduing the Swedes and the Turks, fighting their way to establish ports on the Baltic and the Black Sea. While, in North America, bold hunters and freebooting trappers pushed back the line of the frontier, in Siberia, Russian Cossack adventurers and fur traders were advancing in the same way into areas which were either empty or scantily populated by indigenous tribes.

Russia emerged as a European military and diplomatic power in the eighteenth century, winning the largest slice of dismembered Poland at the negotiating table, while Austria and Prussia took the remainder. Finland came under imperial rule early in the nineteenth century, as a byproduct of the Napoleonic wars, while Georgia, a Christian kingdom threatened by the Turks and Persians, sought Russian protection and was annexed. Later, in the mid-nineteenth century, the Moslem tribes of the Caucasus and their leader Shamyl were conquered by force, after decades of resistance. While France, Great Britain, and Germany were engaged in the scramble for Africa in the late nineteenth century, the heyday of colonialism, the Tsar's armies were marching into Moslem Central Asia and sending settlers into the nomad steppes of what is now Kazakhstan. Russian imperial ambitions finally collided in Central Asia with those of Britain, determined to keep the Russian bear at a safe distance from its Indian possessions.

By 1914, after some four hundred years of expansion, it was almost impossible to disentangle what was really "Russia" in the Russian empire and what was not. As Pipes described the process, "The French in North Africa, the Germans in the Cameroons, or the Japanese in Korea had no doubt about their own identity. They crossed bodies of water, put down local resistance by force, and incorporated the conquered peoples. But the Russians were never fully conscious of being strangers in their vast and amorphous land."

With no real land barriers to stop them, the Russians moved onward and outwards, lacking any sense—except perhaps in Turkestan, toward the very end of the process—that their venture was a colonial one.[4]

Gorbachev was a classic example of the Russian imperial mind, considering everything from Riga to Baku to Tashkent to be Russian soil. When he criticized Alexander Solzhenitsyn, in September 1990, for advocating the end of the Soviet empire, he put it this way: "Each of us Russians has a genetically determined perception of our country in all its scale, vastness, and diversity of language, culture, people, and aspects. We are all like this, and we feel fine in this country. This is how we grew up. We don't have any negative complexes."

"The historical fusion of nationalism and imperialism, as well as the geographical contiguity of national state and empire, helps explain why the Russians never developed either an imperial mentality or an imperial constitution. They created and ruled an empire as if they were creating and ruling a national state."[5]

For the Tsars, the imperial principle meant that loyalty to the dynasty, and to the Orthodox faith, took priority over Russian nationalism in the hierarchy of values. "It was perhaps to be expected that Russians would be more enthusiastically loyal than others, but from the Tsar's point of view, a Baltic German, a Pole, or a Tatar who served him loyally was not less acceptable or praiseworthy than a Russian."[6]

Gradually, as the nineteenth century progressed, the stress on the Russianness of the empire increased, culminating in overt Russification policies. At no point was the structure of the unitary state modified to keep up with the pace of social change. "The Tsarist Empire ultimately did not succeed in establishing a modus vivendi with the Russian nation, as it was represented by the emerging civil society, and failed to gain acceptance as a Russian national state."[7]

This historical confusion over the nature of the state was to emerge as a central question, from 1989 onward, when Russians first began to address the prospect that the Soviet Union might no longer exist.

In September 1990, from his exile in Vermont, Alexander Solzhenitsyn, in his essay "How Do We Rebuild Russia?" asked: "What exactly is Russia? Today and tomorrow (even more importantly). Who sees himself as a part of the future Russia? Where do the Russians themselves envisage the borders of Russia?" In other words, what kind of Russian state would take the place of the Soviet Union—imperial or national? If the second, then what was the Russian nation? Did it include only ethnic Russians (*russkie*) or anybody who lived in the borders of Russia (*rossiyane*)? If the second, then what was to happen to millions of members of the Russian speech community outside the Russian Federation? Would they fall into a new category of Russian-speakers (*russkoyazychnye*)?

The debate over Russian nationality and statehood was, of course, not a new one, though it had been largely dormant at the political level since the Soviet Union was created in the early 1920s. In the years before World War I, it was a debate with an international flavor. For revolutionaries, such as Lenin, the nationalities question involved not only the fate of Russia but those of the other two great Eastern European empires, based in Vienna and in Istanbul.

The Austro-Hungarian and Ottoman empires, already weakened by the emerging nationalisms of their subject peoples in the late nineteenth century, finally disintegrated in military defeat at the end of World War I. There was to be no resurrection. But for the Russian empire, the collapse proved to be only temporary. During the Civil War, the Soviet successor-state recovered most of its territory, reconquering a variety of independent or semi-independent states which had emerged after the 1917 revolution. The errors of the Whites and the determination of the Bolsheviks to use military force no doubt contributed to this outcome. Another factor which helped the empire to win a new lease on life was the underlying numerical strength of the Russians as the dominant nationality. Ethnic Russians (Great Russians) accounted for under half the population of the Empire in 1897 (44.3 percent), but this was a far stronger position than that of the dominant German-speakers in Austria-Hungary. With the heavily Russified Ukrainians and Byelorussians added in, the Slavs accounted for almost three out of four of the Tsar's subjects. In most of the Empire, the backwardness of the minority nationalities and their lack of an educated middle class and an urban elite lowered the level of national consciousness. Only in Poland and in the Grand Duchy of Finland were modern nations able to emerge and seize their independence. Russia's temporary weakness also helped to bring statehood to Lithuania, Estonia, and Latvia. But in the Ukraine, Siberia, Central Asia, and the Caucasus, Bolshevik military strength prevailed.

By 1922, a new multinational state was in existence, on a new ideological foundation. At Lenin's insistence, it was no longer named Russia but the Union of Soviet Socialist Republics, a nominally federal state, where de facto power was tightly centralized and wielded through a single party. The Russian (*rossiiskaya*, not *russkaya*) Soviet Federated Socialist

Republic was linked by treaty with three other nominally sovereign states, the Ukraine, Byelorussia, and Transcaucasia. Stalin, the Bolsheviks' nationalities expert, had drafted a blueprint under which the other republics would be part of the RSFSR. Lenin overruled him, however, insisting on a facade of equality between Russia and the other republics, so recently subjugated by force of arms. As many scholars have noted, the difference was largely one of semantics, but it was to prove highly significant when the central monopoly on power of the Party was eroded.

In the Bolshevik view, the new Soviet state was initially not just a new Russia but the beginning of a new revolutionary system, which would sooner or later encompass the whole world. Loyalty to the proletarian revolution, rather than loyalty to the Tsar, was to be the ideological glue for the new structure.

"It was a unitary, centralized, totalitarian state, such as the Tsarist state had never been. On the other hand, by granting the minorities extensive linguistic autonomy and by placing the national-territorial principle at the base of the state's political administration, the Communists gave constitutional recognition to the multinational structure of the Soviet Union."[8]

Before his death in 1924, Lenin warned, from his sickbed, about the danger of "Great Russian chauvinism," but his words had little influence on Stalin, who saw the state he headed not as the headquarters of a denationalized world proletariat but as the successor to Imperial Russia. The 1937 Constitution kept the essentially decorative federal structure of 1924 intact while Stalin simultaneously restored the Russian character of the state. History was rewritten to rehabilitate the legacy of Tsarist Imperial conquest, first as a "lesser evil," then as a positive good. Russian rule was now historically "progressive," even when imposed by the bayonets of the Tsar's armies. Tsarist generals who had fought Napoleon, such as Kutuzov, were praised, while those who had fought against Russian conquest, such as the Caucasian mountain warrior Shamyl, were condemned as reactionaries. Policies of broad cultural autonomy in the 1920s gave way to Russification, terror, and centralization in the 1930s. World War II saw Stalin go further still in rehabilitating the Tsarist Russian past for his own ends, leading to an ever closer identification between Russia and the Soviet state. The trend was epitomized by Stalin's famous victory toast in 1945 to ". . . the health of the Russian people, because they are the most important nation of all nations forming the Soviet Union."

If the Soviet Union had become just another name for the Russian empire, then logically, there could be no question of a separate Russian identity. Such separate Russian institutions as did exist, notably the Supreme Soviet and Council of Ministers of the RSFSR, led an unremarkable existence in the backwaters of the Soviet bureaucracy. In a geographical sense, the RSFSR was what was left over once the boundaries of the other union republics had been drawn. Areas such as Kaliningrad province, formerly the Baltic German enclave of Königsberg, became part of Russia by default, and were then Russified, de facto, by settlement. Russia lacked many government institutions common to the other republics, both the decorative ones, such as the membership in the United Nations given to the Ukraine and Byelorussia in 1945, and the functional ones, such as its own security organs. It had no Academy of Sciences or broadcasting committee. Most of all, it lacked its own republican communist party. Few residents of Russia would have been able, until 1990, to name the leading political figures in what was theoretically their state. Internally, the RSFSR itself was a federal state, in which minority nationalities were given the status of autonomous republics or semi-autonomous national provinces or zones. After 1945, Russia was more and more allotted the role of "elder brother" in the Soviet family of nations, an ambiguous position in which overall dominance was combined with a lack of distinct identity. It is worth remembering that one of the charges against a group of senior party figures executed in the late 1940s was that they had plotted to separate the RSFSR from the Soviet Union and set up its capital in Leningrad.

After Stalin's death, his successors set up a party bureau for the RSFSR and founded a specifically Russian newspaper, *Sovietskaya Rossiya*. Other institutions, such as an RSFSR Writers' Union and various publishing houses, followed in the late 1950s. But these minor and halfhearted changes did not alter the basic pattern, and in 1966, the CPSU's bureau for the RSFSR disappeared, after ten years of existence. At the Twenty-third Congress of the CPSU, Brezhnev described the bureau as "purposeless," and it was abolished along with other Khrushchevian innovations or "harebrained schemes."

Under Brezhnev, the institutional position of Russia within the USSR remained essentially unaltered, although the total number of union republics had risen from four to fifteen since 1924. Official policy declared that the nationalities problem had been "solved" although, like so many other issues, it had merely been swept under the carpet, so as not to disturb the somnolent calm of the "era of stagnation." The Russians' ambiguous status as "elder brothers" made them more equal than the other nationalities. Official ideology now proclaimed the ideal of a single "Soviet people," formed by a gradual process of *sblizhenie* ("drawing together") and *sliyanie* ("merger") of the individual nations. These concepts, never much more than gleams in the eyes of Kremlin ideologists, were widely viewed as a way of justifying increased pressure for Russification to compensate for the Russians' declining share of the overall population.

In the West, there was a consensus that, as Marxist-Leninist ideology faded, Russian nationalist values might serve the regime as a useful substitute. The losers in the nationalities game would, in this case, be the other nationalities, principally the Ukrainians and Byelorussians, pressed into service as "younger brothers" of the Russians, to maintain the Slavic demographic superiority. But though other nationalities could be forgiven for seeing the Soviet system as government of, by, and for the Russians, not all Russians saw things this way. Alexander Solzhenitsyn's anguished view of Russians as the principal victims of the Soviet system was only one voice in a lively intellectual debate, which had been going on for twenty years by the time Gorbachev took power in 1985.

The story of Russian nationalism from the 1960s to the 1980s is a complex one, too long to be analyzed in detail here. Before Gorbachev, it was essentially a cultural debate fought out partly in official publications and partly underground, in the pages of *samizdat* and in publications of the émigré Russian intelligentsia. Officially, the Kremlin disapproved of Russian nationalism but manipulated its symbols when it chose, just as Stalin had done. It was not until the late 1980s that the ideas, which had circulated for years, became the stuff of practical politics.

Objectively, the Russians dominated the political structure, particularly the Party's leading organs; subjectively, their discontent was growing. This malaise was articulated not only by Solzhenitsyn but by many other intellectuals, whose attitudes to the Soviet system spanned a wide spectrum from close support to extreme hostility. The gradual decay of the official ideology of Marxism-Leninism led to a search for alternative values and beliefs; for many, a rediscovery of religion brought awareness of the wholesale destruction of the Russian Orthodox church, previously so central to

Russian identity. Rightly or wrongly, many felt that the Russians' religious tradition had been treated more harshly than that of the other nations. Declining economic performance under Brezhnev made Russians feel that it was the other nationalities who had profited most from the Soviet system. What kind of empire was it where the dominant people lived worse than those on the periphery? It was after all Russia which contributed most to the Soviet national budget, and which provided all the cheap energy and raw materials for the ungrateful republics.

Not all Russians saw wider use of their language as a blessing, either. Intellectuals felt that the language of Pushkin and Tolstoy had been hijacked to serve as a lingua franca between Tadzhiks and Estonians, a kind of Soviet Esperanto, comparable to the homogenized English in use at the United Nations. Russian cultural identity had been sacrificed in favor of a bogus Soviet identity, according to this perception. The Russian nationalist painter Ilya Glazunov complained that, on a poster showing children from all fifteen republics, all of them wore national dress except the Russian boy, who was clad in the red hat and scarf of the Soviet Pioneers.

Another fertile source of grievance was the ruined environment of Russia, needlessly laid waste for the needs of Soviet industry. This theme was particularly strong in the writings of what became known as the "village prose" movement. Writers, such as Valentin Rasputin, wrote eloquently about the moral emptiness of Soviet life and the destruction of Siberia through the building of gigantic hydroelectric dams. Other writers highlighted the neglected heartland of central Russia, the "non–Black Earth zone." The depopulated village became a symbol of how Russia and the Russians had lost their national memory, the link between past, present, and future. For some, looking at Russia's declining birth rates, rising alcoholism and infant mortality, and the declining life expectancy among males, the national gene pool was at risk. The attractions of belonging to a dominant imperial nation began to pall rapidly in the 1980s, as Russian soldiers died in the unpopular war in Afghanistan. For Russians who had migrated outside the RSFSR, life was also more difficult under Brezhnev, whose policy of "stability of cadres" meant more power for local non-Russian elites, who constructed their own sophisticated systems of patronage, influence, and corruption, from which Russians were excluded.

It is irrelevant to look too closely at how many of these feelings were based on fact. What mattered was not the reality but the perception of Russian disadvantage, which offered fertile soil for this type of cultural nationalism. There were many schools of Russian nationalist thought, though the historian Roman Szporluk has drawn a useful distinction between "nation-builders" and "empire-savers." Solzhenitsyn became the best-known spokesman for the nation-builders, describing 1917 as a "mortal fracture of the spine" in Russian history.[9]

This school of Russian nationalists argued that Russia's imperial expansion into a great power had been a great mistake. Solzhenitsyn argued that Russia could only save its future by letting twelve of the fifteen republics secede, retaining the Slavic nucleus of Russia, the Ukraine, and Byelorussia, as well as a slice of northern Kazakhstan populated by Russians. Although Solzhenitsyn left the door open for Ukrainian self-determination, he annoyed the Ukrainians by his assumption, common among Russians, that they were essentially one nation. Similarly, his remarks about Kazakhstan annoyed the Kazakhs.

Solzhenitsyn's advocacy of a Russia which would turn its back on imperial ambitions had something in common with the approach of Yeltsin and his allies, but there were also important differences. From 1990 onward, the debate over Russia's future became not just a cultural controversy but the subject matter of everyday politics. Not surprisingly, the terms of the debate tended to shift to a more prosaic level. Yeltsin, unlike Solzhenitsyn, specifically acknowledged the right of the Ukraine and Byelorussia to sovereignty and separation from Russia. As a practical politician, he did not advocate redrawing the existing borders of the Russian Federation to include Russian-speakers in other republics, as Solzhenitsyn did. Yeltsin's basic political ideology was that of a pro-Western democrat, while Solzhenitsyn remained a Slavophile at heart, suspicious of the West and all its works.

There was, however, the other tendency in Russian nationalism, less cultural and more statist. These were the empire-savers who "regard the Soviet Union, in its current boundaries, as the proper and legitimate national 'space' of the Russian nation."[10] They saw Russian history largely as the story of the Russian imperial state, a story in which 1917 was a relatively minor episode. They tended to be more hostile to the West than the nation-builders but placed the state at the center of their ideology. Some were explicitly Stalinist, others were anti-Communist, but grudgingly accepted the legacy of the Bolsheviks because they had preserved the integrity of the Tsarist empire. This strain in Russian thought in fact dates back to the "National Bolshevism" of the 1920s, a term used to describe those who fought against the Communists in the Civil War but later supported them, as the only force capable of preserving the empire. As Szporluk has pointed out, some empire-savers are liberals who believe the Soviet Union should be reformed as a single unit and turned into something resembling the United States. Their vision implies severing the link between nationality and territory and guaranteeing not national but individual rights. Other empire-savers tend more toward the fascism, anti-Semitism, and paranoia that Alexander Yanov has argued is the inevitable conclusion of the Russian nationalists' ideological journey.[11]

In the late 1980s, the extremist wing of the Russian nationalists was symbolized by the black-shirted, overtly fascist Pamyat movement. Also on the right were influential conservative Russian writers, led by such men as Yuri Bondarev, Stanislav Kunyayev, and Alexander Prokhanov, pleading for a return to conservative values and promoting the role of the Russian army as historic guardian of national patriotic values. In championing law and order against "democratic anarchy," they opposed both Gorbachev and Yeltsin. They supported the idea of building up the Russian Federation as a Russian national counterweight to the Soviet Union, but shied away from this, after Yeltsin's 1990 election victory, and reverted to a pro-empire position. "We have come to the conclusion that the 'Russian Idea' was always imperial," Prokhanov argued, when I interviewed him in May 1991.

Despite the contempt with which this conservative nationalist group regarded Gorbachev, they agreed with him that the Soviet Union should be held together. Gorbachev's speeches showed him to be unambiguously an empire-saver, a believer in preserving a strong central state. Any compromises he reached with the republics were the result of pragmatism, not of any change in his conviction that "separatism" was wrong. Gorbachev's commitment to preserving the state he heads was never in question; Anatoly Sobchak described him as a *gosudarstvenny muzh* (literally, "a man wedded to the state").[12]

But he was distrusted by the majority of empire-savers, who saw, more clearly than he did, that his westernizing policies of liberalism and democratization would undermine the Soviet state rather than preserve it.

It was this "imperial" ideology that was to inspire the coup plot against Gorbachev, when it became clear, in the summer of 1991, that his new Union Treaty would transfer most powers from the center to the republics. It was not Marxism-Leninism that the plotters most wanted to preserve, but the unity of the Russian and Soviet imperial state.

12

The Gambler

It is now hard to imagine that, when Gorbachev took power in 1985, nationalities policy was right at the bottom of his priorities. It was not until 1988 that he recognized it as a major problem, and not until late 1989 that the Communist Party Central Committee got around to discussing it. The Party's response was too little too late. After 1989, what seemed at first to be just one headache among many came to dominate everything, posing a threat to the very existence of the Soviet Union as a state. It is the consensus view of most Western experts that this is the field of policy where Gorbachev made the most mistakes, many of them attributable to an inability to grasp the imperial factor in Russian history and an extraordinary blind spot toward the national feelings of non-Russians.

Professor Gail Lapidus, writing in the watershed year 1989, identified six distinct types of national problem facing Gorbachev: outright demands for autonomy and independence from the Baltics and other republics; deep-rooted territorial and ethnic disputes between different nationalities, such as the conflict between Armenia and Azerbaijan over the Armenian enclave of Nagorno-Karabakh; spontaneous communal violence arising from economic grievances, as in Central Asia; the demand of smaller nationalities for upgrading of their territories' political status; the demand for full rehabilitation by the "punished peoples" persecuted and exiled by Stalin; and the rise of Russian nationalism.[1]

Of this complex of problems, it was the desire of the

smaller republics for greater autonomy which finally made Gorbachev realize that the old policy was bankrupt and some kind of new deal was necessary. After four postponements, the Communist Party Central Committee met on September 19 and 20, 1989, to design a new nationalities policy. The goal was to find a new kind of federalism to replace the old bogus federalism, under which everything important was decided in Moscow. Gorbachev's problem was that the republics were asking for something they already had, at least on paper—sovereignty. His other major handicap was that, by late 1989, any concessions he could offer were too small. The Baltic republics wanted a new Union Treaty to replace the 1922 settlement, but in 1989 Gorbachev and his Central Committee could not or would not agree. By the time he offered negotiations on a new Treaty, in 1990, the Baltic republics were no longer interested and had committed themselves to independence.

The introduction of partially free elections for the USSR Congress of People's Deputies, in March 1989, led to big wins for Popular Front movements in the Baltic republics, at the expense of the Communists. Suddenly, popular sovereignty through the ballot replaced the "democratic centralism" of the Communist Party as the legitimizing factor in Soviet politics. For the republics, this meant, in effect, there was the possibility of self-determination. In 1990, elections for republican parliaments made the process irreversible.

What happened in Lithuania and the other republics was that the ornamental trappings of statehood, which Lenin and Stalin had designed to mask the unitary nature of the state—parliaments, governments, and so on—suddenly became real. Elections, which used to be bogus, became real contests; parliamentary structures, which had previously been purely decorative, were suddenly functional, responsible not to Moscow but to their voters. Nations which had once been independent, such as Lithuania, Estonia, and Latvia, suddenly saw their lost statehood once again within their grasp.

The drive for "sovereignty"—a word with many shades of meaning—spread not only on the fringes of the empire, but also in the Ukraine, which many Russians saw as part of Russia itself. Millions of Russians lived outside the Russian Federation, some in areas of traditional industrial settlement, such as the Ukranian Donbass coal mining region, others in pockets of new industry established after World War II. These Russian communities, accustomed to seeing the entire Soviet Union as their homeland, were suddenly threatened with an identity crisis by the prospect of the republics where they lived gaining independence. For example, what would happen to a Russian engineer and family, living in the Latvian capital, Riga? Would they be treated as colonial settlers, as aliens from a foreign power, or as something new—Russian-speaking Latvians?

For Russians, such questions brought a special feeling of insecurity. In most other European nations, it is axiomatic that not every person who speaks the same language is a member of the same nation or carries the same passport. The English have, since the eighteenth century, been accustomed to the fact that Americans, while speaking the same language, form a different nation and are citizens of a different state. Australians of English descent speak English but would be insulted to be called English. Similarly, it is accepted on all sides that not every Francophone is French. One may be a French-speaking Swiss, or Belgian and still have a secure sense of national identity.

But the Russian historical experience is different. Unlike Ukrainians and Byelorussians, Russians have never had to live as part of an ethnic or linguistic minority in another state. Wherever they ended up, in their national history of expansion, the Russian state went with them, to protect them. Within the Soviet Union, Russians were protected by their numerical strength and never had to deeply ponder their identity. Previously, the Russian communities in other union republics, such as Lithuania, were secure in the knowledge that they were still part of the dominant nation in a larger entity, the Soviet Union.

Independence would change all that: Russians might find themselves compelled, for the first time, to learn a language other than their own, in order to qualify for citizenship. The alternative might be between repatriation to the RSFSR as *rossiyane* and a new postcolonial identity as Russian-speaking Lithuanian citizens—not *russkie* but merely *russkoyazych-nye*.

These insecurities led to widespread predictions of a Russian nationalist backlash. But despite the formation of various anti-independence Russian movements in the Baltic republics and in Moldavia, their cause failed to mobilize opinion outside their own areas. Under Yeltsin, Russian public opinion was eventually to mobilize for—not against—the right of the Baltic states to independence.

Gorbachev's dilemma, as he tried to restructure the Soviet state and make the federation a reality, was that he had to give the same sovereignty to the Russian federation as to the other republics. If the new federation was to be formed on a voluntary basis, then Russia's anomalous status at the center had to be resolved. The risk was that the enormous weight of Russia, with half the Soviet population and the bulk of its territory and resources, would end up on the other side of the negotiating table, allied with the other fourteen republics, against the central authorities. When Yeltsin was elected to head the Russian parliament in May 1990, this is essentially what happened.

In one of his last interviews, before his death in December 1989, Andrei Sakharov saw clearly that the real dividing line in Soviet politics was between those who were trying to preserve the Soviet empire and those who wanted to abandon it. The empire-savers included everybody from orthodox Communists, such as Vadim Medvedev, Gorbachev's chief ideologist, to anti-Communist nationalists, such as Igor Shafarevich. "All of them find a common language rooted in the shared concept of a Russian empire. . . . What is in fact at stake here is the preservation of power," Sakharov said.[2]

On the other side, there were those who saw Russia as in the same position as the other republics, as a nation seeking statehood and trying to shake off the "dictates of the center." Sakharov articulated these views: "It is in fact in the interest of the Russian people to enjoy the same rights as all the other peoples. Its privileged status carried with it the need to make greater sacrifices and more extensive self-denials, which in the long run meant that no other nation suffered such severe losses."

In Russia itself, public opinion surveys showed that the Russian will to preserve the empire was declining. Sociologist Yuri Levada said his polling data showed that "all strata, except for administrative-command groups, believe that no resistance (to Baltic secession) is possible." Levada said the popular mood was far ahead of the political decision-makers and even of the intelligentsia's debates in the press.[3]

It is important to stress that the "Russian question" was on Gorbachev's desk long before Yeltsin came to personify the problem. Long before the 1990 elections, the idea that the status of the RSFSR had to be upgraded had become a commonplace; so had the idea of the Russians as losers rather than winners in the Soviet nationalities game. Liberal and conservative Communists, democratic anti-Communists, and right-wing nationalists all called for a restoration of "sovereignty" for the Russian republic. Even non-Russians who wanted to draw the attention of the Russians to the problems of their own republics began to preface their remarks with a reference to the sufferings of Russia. By late 1989, the theme was already a standard element in speeches by the Kremlin leadership, although Gorbachev saw more clearly than some of his colleagues the dangers of allowing the establishment of a rival power center in Moscow.

Vitaly Vorotnikov, chairman of the presidium of the old RSFSR Supreme Soviet, told Russians as early as July 1989 that Russia would be granted greater sovereignty. Work was already under way to "create a whole series of political, administrative, economic, and other structures which we lack."[4]

In anticipation of the long-delayed September 1989 Central Committee meeting, the Communist Party daily, *Pravda*, acknowledged some specific Russian grievances: "All the country's peoples, including the Russian people, have sustained damage as a result of violations of the Leninist principles of nationalities policy. Today, in Russia itself, . . . there are also acute socioeconomic problems and problems of ecology, the restoration of historical monuments, and the preservation of national cultural assets."[5]

A few days later, Politburo member Viktor Chebrikov, who was drafting the main policy document for the Central Committee, told *Pravda:*

> It is no secret that often the term "center" is taken to mean the largest republic and the Russian people, and on the political plane this often leads to the fanning of anti-Russian sentiments. At the same time it is the Russian people who suffer most of all from central departments, since the latter operate with a noticeable lack of monitoring over Russia's vast expanses. Following lengthy debate and having thoroughly weighed all the pros and cons, the Politburo has arrived at the conclusion that radical changes are needed in the running of the Russian federation.[6]

Alexander Vlasov, a Siberian who was the RSFSR's prime minister, told *Izvestia*, "No other republic is in a situation where 72 percent of the enterprises in its territory are under all-union jurisdiction and only 27 percent under republican jurisdiction." Russia would have to have its own Komsomol, its own trade union structure, its own Internal Affairs ministry and Academy of Sciences, he argued. He also argued for a shift to real world prices, which would balance out the republic's unfavorable terms of trade with the rest of the Soviet Union.[7]

When the plenum met, Gorbachev acknowledged that "deformations" in nationality policy had also hurt Russia. He was, however, reluctant to accept the creation of a separate Russian Communist Party, fearing that this would mean an irrevocable departure from the unitary structure of the CPSU. As a halfway stage, the party bureau for the RSFSR, abolished in 1966, would be resurrected and chaired by himself. The first steps toward strengthening the government structure followed in October, with the creation of an RSFSR Ministry of Internal Affairs.

By the time the March 1990 elections came round, all candidates for seats in the Russian Federation Congress of People's Deputies were to some extent running on a "Russia first" ticket. Even more than in the other republics, the election was to breathe new life into dead structures which had had only a shadowy existence. The election was a moment of truth for conservative Russian nationalists, who had formed an electoral bloc with party hard-liners. Their manifesto proved to be an awkward marriage of ideas. It combined attacks on "separatism" with calls for increased sovereignty for the republics, and it defended the centralized planning system against the market but simultaneously attacked "interference" in the Russian economy by the center. The nationalists turned out to have little appeal to the voters, winning only a tiny handful of the 1,068 seats, and were so stung by their defeat that they called for the election results to be annulled.

The result of the March 4 voting was that the Congress of People's Deputies of the RSFSR would be evenly poised between orthodox pro-Gorbachev Communists and radical reformers under the "Democratic Russia" (demokraticheskaya Rossiya) banner, with Yeltsin as their probable leader. Like the all-Union Congress a year earlier, the Russian Congress had to elect a standing parliament, or Supreme Soviet, and choose a chairman who would become, in effect, Russia's head of state. With the nationalist right relegated to the sidelines, the contest, between the outgoing Vorotnikov-Vlasov leadership and Democratic Russia, for the post of chairman of the Supreme Soviet, drew both sides into a bidding war in which they promised a Russia-for-the-Russians agenda. Aleksandr Vlasov was frank about the lack of power he had enjoyed, as RSFSR head of government. "From the very first days, I have been constantly aware of my own impotence," he confessed.[8] Until recently, the government he had headed had controlled only 4 percent of the republic's industrial production. "Our cadres had developed their own standard way of resolving every question—writing hundreds of memorandums to the Union government, containing requests. It was frankly a petition factory, not a Council of Ministers!" Vlasov was, however, careful to rule out any direct legislative challenge to the all-Union authorities. Legislative acts passed by the new parliament would have to follow the USSR constitution, he said.[9]

Yeltsin went much further than Vlasov in demanding categorically that Russian sovereignty and Russian laws should take precedence over those of the USSR. "Russia, as a union republic, is also entitled to leave the Union, and this is not only a formal right," he declared.[10] The implication of a collision course with the central government was clear to all, and it worried some deputies.

Yeltsin said bluntly that Russia had to recover its independence from the "center"—in other words, from Gorbachev: "The issue of primary importance is the spiritual, national, and economic rebirth of Russia, which has been for long decades an appendage of the center and which, in many respects, has lost its independence."[11]

Was Yeltsin really concerned about the fate of Russia or just using it as a convenient arena in which to challenge for power at the all-Union level? What were his own deep-rooted feelings about his Russian identity? Yeltsin was asked this very question, in September 1990, some months after his election as head of the Russian parliament. *Soyuz* magazine reporter Alexandra Lukovskaya wondered if his feelings about Russia were the same as hers: "I do not yet have a national self-awareness, I have no sense of Russia—not only its statehood and history but also the feeling of territorial space."

His reply was revealing:

I used to have the same feelings as you have. I used to see myself as a citizen of the country and not Russia, and also as a patriot of Sverdlovsk *oblast*, since that is where I worked. And the concept of "Russia" was so conventional for me that, in my daily work as first secretary of the Sverdlovsky party *obkom*, most of the time I did not even go through the Russian authorities. I would go directly to the CPSU Central Committee, the Union government, and sometimes to the country's leaders. . . . It turned out that a decision adopted in the Politburo automatically became "law" for Russia. It [Russia] lacked the main thing—state institutions through which it could manifest its power and authority. Russia never had its own voice and it did not argue or disagree with the center.[12]

Stalin, Yeltsin explained, had been afraid of Russia.

> God forbid it should rise up and be a counterweight. Under-
> standably, a small republic could not affect the entire Union.
> But with the giant Russia, if it were to assume its real position,
> it would be difficult to fight it, or rather, impossible. Politi-
> cally, this was a precise calculation. This is why Russia was
> not represented at the United Nations—just the USSR, the
> Ukraine, and Byelorussia. Stalin was afraid to have its power-
> ful voice there.

He went on to say, "I have always been pained about
Russia, its history, traditions, and culture."

Yeltsin explained that his real motivation for picking Russia as his political arena came from his negative experience
in the all-Union Supreme Soviet.

> I was quick to understand that radical changes would not
> come from there. . . . I was convinced that the role of the center
> must be sharply reduced. It is still responsible for the strategic
> line, but the basic load had to be "shifted" to the local areas.
> It was clear to me that the vertical bureaucratic pivot on
> which the country rests had to be destroyed, and we had to
> begin a transition to horizontal ties with greater independence
> of the republic-states. The mood of the people, the democrati-
> zation of society, and the growth of people's national self-
> awareness led directly to this.

In other words, it was not Russian nationalism or national
feeling—to which he paid only lip-service—but a belief in a
broad devolution and decentralization of power, which motivated his challenge.

Yeltsin said his other goal was to see if it was possible to
carry out real reforms in Russia, as a way of prodding Gorbachev into moving faster and more decisively toward
change. In other words, Russia might be able to tip the
balance at the all-Union level and force Gorbachev's hand.

As part of his commitment to decentralization, Yeltsin
promised full autonomy to all the national republics and
areas within the Russian Federation, including the right to
secede. Yeltsin's idea was to invert the traditional Soviet
pyramid in which all power flowed down from the top. Instead, sovereignty would be vested in the lowest level of
government, the district, which would then delegate powers
upwards to provincial and national level. Although the general commitment to a broad devolution of power was clear,
this ultraradical theory was to create serious problems of

authority for the Russian state in the months after Yeltsin and his team assumed power.

Yeltsin also promised a market economy and eventually the creation of a directly elected Russian presidency. He knew that he would be unlikely to find the two-thirds majority needed for a constitutional change at first, so he proposed waiting a year. Even getting himself elected to the chairmanship of the new Supreme Soviet by a simple majority vote would be difficult. "My changes are below fifty percent," Yeltsin told Moscow Radio two weeks before the session opened.

The Russian radicals, determined to organize themselves more effectively than they had at the opening of the all-Union parliament the previous year, assembled in Moscow at the end of March, to begin drafting an agenda for the Congress, in mid-May. They formally named Yelstin as their candidate for chairman of the Russian Supreme Soviet. This time, as Yeltsin promised his supporters during the campaign, there would be no question of him withdrawing from the race.

The new grouping, an umbrella organization of movements and political tendencies, called itself "Democratic Russia." It was not a political party, but it was something more than just a parliamentary caucus, such as the Interregional Group in the Soviet parliament.

Yeltsin and his allies knew that, as in the all-Union Congress in 1989, the initial procedural battle over the agenda would be vital. Gorbachev's election as chairman of the Union Supreme Soviet had been pushed through, right at the start, without any real debate on his record. This time, the radicals insisted that Aleksandr Vlasov, as outgoing RSFSR prime minister, should deliver a report. Vlasov's lackluster performance weakened support for him among uncommitted deputies.

Yeltsin had no doubt that Gorbachev was opposed to his becoming Russia's Supreme Soviet chairman and would try to get his own candidate elected instead. But what he did not realize was just how blatantly Gorbachev would intervene in the election. Speaking to the Congress, as a guest, on May 23, Gorbachev denounced what he described as "an attempt to seize power." Without mentioning Yeltsin by name, he attacked "political swindlers" who were pretending that they had the answers to the country's problems but were really only interested in opposition for its own sake.

Gorbachev supported the idea of increased sovereignty for the RSFSR—he could hardly do otherwise. He also reversed his previous opposition to the formation of a Russian Communist party, realizing that its formation would be hard to prevent. But he warned the deputies that while other republics might eventually secede, without Russia there could be no Soviet Union at all. "There you have the special feature of Russia. We have to grasp all this and feel not that history starts with us but that there are thousands of years behind us, and that the Russian people have given a great deal to ensure that so many peoples should be united in this family of this federation on these vast expanses, and who have entered the arena in the form of a mighty state." Then Gorbachev, consciously or unconsciously echoing the Russian nationalists, proclaimed that "for all us Russians, this is in our genes, it is preprogramed."

Speaking off the cuff, as usual, Gorbachev could not resist the temptation to respond to many questions posed about his reaction to Yeltsin's program. Why had Yeltsin not mentioned socialism even once? His speech was "an attempt to separate Russia from socialism." He described Yeltsin's remarks as politicized and confrontational: "This is a call for the disintegration of the Union." Yeltsin's call for sovereignty at the grass roots would bring only anarchy and the disintegration of the Russian Federation. His ideas were "corrosive acid," Gorbachev warned, telling the delgates that he was confident they would come to what he called the "right decision" when they voted.

Yeltsin's nomination speech to the Congress, on May 25, set out a bold agenda: "Without destroying the system straightaway, we should build a new building alongside it, abandon in practice the Party's monopoly on power, and hand over power to the people and the soviets." The transition to the market would allow the old system to die a natural death, he promised. He argued for a constitutional reform and a law on Russian sovereignty, the centerpiece of a series of economic and legal reforms. The new Russian constitution should be put to the people in a referendum and followed by a direct election for a Russian president. He served notice on the central government that Russia would no longer be taken for granted, insisting that its share of the total Soviet military budget would have to be trimmed by 10 to 15 percent. Capital investment would be slashed and economic power decentralized, with a shift to world prices and a convertible ruble. Yeltsin sidestepped the issue of how this agenda could be carried out without a clash with the central government. Finally he promised the deputies to seek a deal with Gorbachev and put personal quarrels aside: "The complexities of the process of *perestroika* have forced me to appreciate the importance of political compromise, the ability to take account of various points of view, the significance of dialogue with various political forces. . . . I am for businesslike relations, for dialogue, for talks with the president, with the government, but on a principled basis, not to the detriment of the sovereignty or interests of the republic."

There was nothing inevitable about Yeltsin's victory in the ballot for the chairmanship of the Supreme Soviet; he might very well have lost, had it not been for Gorbachev's clumsy intervention against him. If Gorbachev had found a more convincing candidate to oppose him, Yeltsin might have had to continue his career in opposition. In any event, it was not until the third ballot that he finally squeaked home with the minimum 531 votes, or 50 percent of the total number of deputies. Vlasov had withdrawn before the first round, leaving the conservative Communist Ivan Polozkov to carry the Party's banner against Yeltsin. The first two times, Yeltsin fell about 30 votes short of what he needed, winning the support of 497 and then of 503 deputies. Before the third round, uproar broke out, when the acting chairman tried to bar Yeltsin from standing again. In the third round, Vlasov reentered the contest, and predictably lost. He did not help his chances by admitting he had helped Prime Minister Nikolai Ryzhkov draw up an inept plan, for a massive round of price increases, which had just been announced by the central government.

Gorbachev again intervened on the eve of the vote, appealing in private to the Communist deputies not to vote for Yeltsin. "At this turning point, I would never take the risk" of voting for Yeltsin, he told them.[13] His heavyhanded intervention, in an election which was constitutionally none of his business, was counterproductive. As Yevgeny Ambartsumov, a Yeltsin supporter, described it, "His move had the opposite effect [from what he intended]. The deputies do not want to be subjected to pressures, and there was an increase in the number of votes for Yeltsin."[14] What may have been the deciding factor for many deputies was the flood of telegrams they received from their own voters, telling them to support Yeltsin and ignore the official party line. "We all feel the hot breath of the voters," General Dmitry Volkogonov said.[15] The final voting gave Vlasov 467 votes to 535 for Yeltsin and 11 for a third candidate.

To win the votes of the uncommitted, Yeltsin had to promise to avoid confrontation with the central government and to tone down his rhetoric. "I have never advocated Russia's secession. I am in favor of the Union's sovereignty, equal rights of all republics, the autonomy of the republics, so that the republics are strong and so that, with this strength, they reinforce our strong Union," he declared. He also reassured the deputies, many of them in uniform, that he did not favor splitting up the Soviet army into republican armies, but merely favored military reform and a professional army. He also promised to establish a coalition government representing a broad spectrum of deputies' groups, and to seek reelection after two years, rather than the allotted five. As chairman of the parliament, he pledged to discontinue his membership in any political or public organization, in order to serve as a defender of "all the people." This meant that unlike Gorbachev, who retained his post as Communist Party general secretary, when he became Supreme Soviet chairman, Yeltsin would turn in his Communist Party card, at least temporarily. His promise also barred him from becoming a member of any rival party.

Even with the rough edges removed, his program involved the risk of a major constitutional upheaval. It is fair to assume that most uncommitted deputies supported Yeltsin because they wanted him and Gorbachev to put aside their differences and work together. Most thought the two men would be able to compromise over the introduction of a market economy, now recognized as essential by most experts. Such an alliance between Gorbachev's "center" and Yeltsin's "left" wing would finally finish off the Communist Party conservatives and open the way to radical reform.

Conscious that his support from the deputies was shaky and conditional, Yeltsin opted for compromise, setting up a conciliation commission, to plan parliamentary business and share out the remaining posts.

News of Yeltsin's election, on May 29, reached Gorbachev in Ottawa, and his graceless response betrayed considerable irritation at a political defeat which would cast a shadow over his visit to North America. Without a word of congratulations, Gorbachev said he was concerned by the situation at the RSFSR congress. "A kind of confrontation has arisen," he commented. If Yeltsin's promise to be conciliatory was merely a political ploy, there would be "difficult times," he predicted. "Then things will not be easy. We will wait and see."

Yeltsin's election not only capped a remarkable personal

comeback; it gave the reformers a political base close to the center of the Soviet power structure. Physically, it meant that radicals now controlled not only the Moscow City Council but the *bely dom* ("White House"), the big, white marble-clad RSFSR government headquarters by the Moscow River, built under Brezhnev. Inside the Kremlin, power remained, at least in theory, with Gorbachev, who had introduced the idea of popular sovereignty through the ballot box but proved reluctant to accept the consequences.

It is clear, in retrospect, that Gorbachev would have faced serious problems handling the RSFSR in 1990, with or without Yeltsin's personal role. As it happened, the parliamentary challenge came from the left, who narrowly succeeded in getting Yeltsin elected. If a few votes had gone the other way, the winning candidate might have been Ivan Polozkov, a party conservative whose capacity to undermine Gorbachev became clear, when he and his allies seized control of the founding congress of the new Russian Communist party in June. Even if the old RSFSR leadership of Vorotnikov and Vlasov had been reappointed, their campaign promises to increase republican sovereignty would have led to increased friction with the central government.

To some extent, Yeltsin skillfully jumped aboard a train that was ready to leave the station. There is more than enough evidence to suggest that he was late to adopt the cause of the RSFSR. However, once he did so, he went further in his demands for sovereignty than either the orthodox Communists or the new alliance of party conservatives and right-wing nationalists would have done.

Yeltsin's record in office was to reinforce the mistrust of hardcore Russian nationalists. For those who believed in the integrity of the empire, he was far too sympathetic toward the breakaway Baltic states. For those who idealized the Russian past and the Russian countryside, Yeltsin, with his hard-hat construction background, represented the detested onward march of cranes, concrete, and bulldozers through the unspoiled forest. For those who believed in the strong state and its authority, he was far too keen on shifting power to the grass roots.

The new chairman of the Russian Supreme Soviet provoked strong emotions, as he himself admitted. Many considered him no more than an old-school *apparatchik*, with an authoritarian streak. Intellectuals were still suspicious of him and of the shrill enthusiasm of some of his supporters. Many, like Sakharov before his death, thought he was not of the same caliber as Gorbachev. Friends of Sakharov told David Remnick, of the *Washington Post*, that the Soviet Union's leading human rights campaigner had been too suspicious of Yeltsin to vote for him in his Moscow constituency in March 1989.[16]

But those who watched him more closely saw that he had matured between his disgrace in 1987 and his election in 1990. He was much more crafty, more self-controlled, and less dictatorial than the Yeltsin of the early years of *perestroika*.

Bill Keller, writing in the *New York Times*, described Yeltsin as consistently underrated, both in Moscow and in Washington. "Many Soviet intellectuals disdain Yeltsin as a lowbrow and a demagogue. The Bush administration belittles him as a lightweight, possibly unstable, and certainly an inconvenient disruption to the plans of Mikhail Gorbachev. Much of the outside world seems to view him as a cartoon Russian, subject to pratfalls and outrageous statements, important mainly as a foil for Mr. Gorbachev."[17]

Keller pinned down Yeltsin as "an instinctual politician, with a nose for the political mood," who had begun to adopt a more presidential, tactful style. Yeltsin "may be the one man who can cheat the hardliners out of the Russian vote and deploy it in a more benign direction."

"Yeltsin has been accused of being a populist—and partly, he is—and of being a reactionary, which is entirely untrue," the deputy Yevgeny Ambartsumov told the Italian magazine *Avanti*. "The time has passed when we used to criticize him for his political *faux pas*, his misstatements, which he has eliminated from his program; he has spoken as a shrewd and responsible politician."

Yeltsin, questioned by the deputies about his good and bad points, admitted that there was some truth in the description of him as *zhestky* ("hard"), especially in his past career. "However, in this period of the democratization of society and *perestroika*, I have broken with what linked me in this respect . . . there is some kind of progress toward democratization."

He also told the deputies that he did not consider populism to be a term of abuse. "In my opinion, the greater part of this word consists of links with the people . . . links with the masses."

Pavel Voshchanov, of *Komsomolskaya Pravda*, said Yeltsin proved his newfound flexibility as a politician by the way he got himself elected, despite the fact that his hardcore support only amounted to one deputy in three. He singled out the way Yeltsin had made a deal with deputies from the smaller national autonomous formations in the RSFSR by promising them a number of key posts.

But if his political skills had improved since his Moscow days, had his ideas changed as well? He was still a member of the Party, but was he still a Communist?

Yeltsin made no real attempt to deny Gorbachev's charge that his plans for Russia did not include any more socialist experiments.

> I consider that, in our world, there is neither the capitalism spoken of in the classic works, nor is there the socialism of which they speak, although socialism has existed in various forms. There has been developed socialism, national socialism, Pol Pot socialism. There have been various interpretations of socialism. I do not believe in socialism for its own sake. I believe that the people of this country should live well, that the people should respect the leadership and supreme authorities of their country, their republic, and that, vice versa, the supreme authorities of the republic should respect their people.

This distrust of ideology placed him at odds with Gorbachev, who despite his willingness to embrace the market, proved unable to part company with his belief in the "socialist choice" of 1917 or to accept the idea of private property.

Yeltsin was now a firm convert to a market economy, with none of the qualifications that Gorbachev and Ryzhkov attached to the idea. But he also managed to leave the impression that the switchover would be relatively painless, without the "shock therapy" of Ryzhkov's price rises. Some analysts in the West forecast he would hit trouble when the inevitable conflict emerged between his supporters' desire for economic equality and the reality of the market. "A huge segment of Yeltsin's populist constituency consists of social Luddites who are afraid of the havoc, the uncertainty, the need for initiative and self-reliance that radical economic reform will bring," wrote Leon Aron in the *Washington Post.* "The contradiction between democracy and the growth of economic inequality is bound, sooner or later, to split the Yeltsin constituency." Aron concluded that Yeltsin's commitment to democracy still had to be tested: "Only time will tell whether Boris Yeltsin is a democrat among the populists or an authoritarian populist among the democrats."[18]

Yeltsin's critics, including Gorbachev, saw him as a windbag, whose grandiose promises, in opposition, would dissolve as soon as he took responsibility. His supporters argued that the masses trusted him, not because of any pie-in-the-sky promises but because he met them on equal terms and gave them straight answers, instead of lecturing them like Gorbachev.

One of his Sverdlovsk election teams, sociologist L. Pikhoya, after observing Yeltsin at close quarters, said there was more to him than the popular image of a brave and determined leader, with limited intellectual powers—"big, open, strong, a little coarse, and a bit dumb," like the Russian folk hero Ilya Muromets. "My experience with him indicates that he is actually a thoughtful and calculating politician. He is a Westernizer rather than a Slavophile and does not support primitive redistribution ideas. Intellectuals . . . understand Yeltsin's position and view him as a proponent not only of political freedom but also of economic reform."[19]

Valentin Yumashev, the journalist who helped Yeltsin write his autobiography, described his subject as "a classic *apparatchik* of the Brezhnev and *perestroika* eras, and he comes complete with all the flaws appropriate to such an individual. Yet he is also a man who is learning new ways quickly."

Yumashev noted Yeltsin's pragmatic streak and his concentration on immediate matters to the exclusion of all else. "This exclusive emphasis on the present would seem insufficient at a moment when Russia also needs an intuitive politics. Yet pragmatism is working well for Yeltsin. His outstanding personal quality is that he can learn and is not afraid to do so—an important quality in a man who is nearly sixty years old. And he is also a surprisingly hearty worker, who usually puts in from sixteen to eighteen hours a day."[20]

Giulietto Chiesa, Moscow correspondent for *l'Unita*, also pointed to the distance Yeltsin had traveled since 1987, when he was still a "crude provincial *apparatchik*." His experience in parliament had brought him into contact with intellectuals such as Afanasyev, Sakharov, and Popov. He was now surrounded with more experienced associates and had "enriched his political platform with democratic-liberal content that has been totally lacking before; and he had a detailed plan for economic reform." Most important of all, as Chiesa noted, he had a priceless advantage over most of the intellectuals, in his inside knowledge of how the Party and government machine operated at the highest level. "Unlike the intellectuals, with whom he had made common cause, and who continued in part to mistrust him, he remained a professional politician, a profound student of the Party's apparatus, tactics, and weaknesses."[21]

Many of those who tried to analyze the source of his appeal noticed he had the classic politician's knack of letting everyone, from Bolshevik old-timers to young free-marketeers, from believers to atheists, from anarchists to discontented low-level bureaucrats, believe he identified with their views.

Sergey Kredov, writing in the newspaper *Rabochaya Tribuna*, compared Yeltsin's appeal, after his 1987 fall, to that of a rowdy Greek god who had been expelled from Olympus and sent to live among ordinary mortals. He was the first politician to voluntarily jump off the *nomenklatura* ladder. "Boris Nikolayevich's role was not that he offered a sick society ready-made wise prescriptions which, unfortunately, were rejected. Yeltsin was reminiscent more of a selfless physician who has injected himself with viruses of an unstudied disease to observe its course from within. People suffered with him, they liked him, and they put their faith in his experiment."[22]

Kredov, only half in jest, compared him to the famous "pretenders" in Russian history, leading the common people in an uprising against the evil Kremlin boyars who have removed the divinely anointed Tsar. "He was both against and for. He was both the enemy of the Kremlin nobility and flesh of its flesh. Everyone considered him his man."

If Yeltsin had been as interested in the Russian past as in the present, he might have reflected ruefully that the success rate of such pretenders in gaining and keeping power over Russia was not too high.

13

The Young Guard

Back at the end of April 1990, Mikhail Gorbachev had made clear he neither wanted nor expected to have to negotiate with Boris Yeltsin again. On a tour of Sverdlovsk, Yeltsin's home turf, he launched into a bitter attack on his rival, accusing him of setting off on a course of confrontation. "What are we getting from him? Nothing except a full dose of criticism." Yeltsin's speeches were like a worn-out old record, he complained.

Once Yeltsin was elected head of the Russian parliament, however, Gorbachev knew he could no longer dismiss him as irrelevant. From the end of May onward, their relationship entered a new phase, in which it was to swing from cooperation to confrontation and back again. In the long term, it was unlikely that there would be room for two parliaments and governments in Russia, both claiming the right to supreme authority.

During June and July, Yeltsin marshaled his forces, worked out his strategy, and appointed his chief lieutenants. This was of necessity a compromise process. Not all those elected to fill the seats of Supreme Soviet deputy chairman were Yeltsin supporters, and some were later to turn against him. However, his first deputy, Ruslan Khazbulatov, a pipe-smoking academic, was to prove invaluable to Yeltsin, as his understudy in handling relations with Gorbachev and with the other republics. Khazbulatov's ethnic origins made him particularly conscious of the injustices of Soviet nationalities policy. He was a Chechen, a member of a small nationality in the Northern Caucasus, deported to Central Asia in 1944 by Stalin, as a collective punishment for allegedly aiding the German invaders. Khazbulatov grew up in a remote collective farm in northern Kazakhstan, where his mother was a milkmaid. In 1990, he was a professor of economics at the Plekhanov Institute in Moscow.[1]

Assembling a new Russian government proved a laborious process, and some of the jobs were not filled until October. Following the principle that all posts should be contested, candidates for the post of prime minister had to make nomination speeches before the Supreme Soviet and submit to a popular vote. Mikhail Bocharov, the candidate whose radical views came closest to Yeltsin's own, trailed behind Ivan Silayev, a deputy prime minister in Ryzhkov's government. In a second ballot, Silayev won the required majority and promised to secure Russia's genuine economic independence. Silayev was a figure whose career profile made him an unlikely reformer: He had headed a big aircraft factory in the closed city of Gorky, where, as he acknowledged in a newspaper interview, he had been nicknamed Ivan the Terrible. He then moved to Moscow to supervise the entire aviation industry as a deputy prime minister in Ryzhkov's government. However, he told the Supreme Soviet he was no conservative and appealed to the deputies for new radical ideas. "I will not dare say I was a born radical. We are all children of our times," he told an interviewer from *Moscow News*.[2] Silayev's main strength was his intimate knowledge of the central government bureaucracy. Like Yeltsin, he was a grandfather, an engineer, and a tennis player, but their personalities were different.

Yeltsin and Silayev agreed that the new government would be streamlined, with the number of ministries drastically pruned. There was no point in duplicating the dozens of sectoral ministries in the central government, which were supposed to become superfluous under economic reform. Silayev announced that the total number of ministries would be cut from fifty-one to twenty-one and the government apparatus from 22,500 employees to 11,300. Standing the traditions of the *nomenklatura* on its head, Silayev appealed on television for candidates to fill ministerial jobs, giving a telephone number for applicants to call.

The final line-up, with an average age of 47, included some ministers who were extraordinarily young by Soviet standards: Boris Fedorov, the finance minister, was a 32-year-old banker who had been in charge of Soviet monetary policy and had also worked as a policy expert at the Communist Party Central Committee. Minister of justice Nikolai Fedorov, (no relation) was the same age. Silayev's government also included an Economic Reform Commission and a brain trust of part-time economic and scientific advisers, some of them from outside the Soviet Union.

Yeltsin began with a piece of parliamentary muscle-flexing designed to rally the new Russian parliament behind him. A television interview he had given which was not broadcast on the day he had agreed to with Mikhail Nenashev, head of Soviet TV, provoked him to an angry outburst: "I regard this incident as a planned political provocation," Yeltsin thundered, making clear that he felt the "political leadership" (i.e., Gorbachev) was to blame. "It is an affront not only to the chairman of the RSFSR Supreme Soviet, but to the entire Congress, all deputies of Russia, and their voters."

Gorbachev replied by sending his adviser, Yevgeny Primakov, to deny any role in holding up the broadcast and demand an apology for his name being taken in vain. The dispute was not a good beginning to the new relationship with Gorbachev. When Russian viewers got to watch Yeltsin's interview a day later, they saw him appeal to them for a grace period of two or three years, to manage the transition to a market economy. "Trust us as the new leaders of Russia," he pleaded, promising that the reform would not lead to any decline in living standards. "That is the fundamental difference between our program and the government—the Union— program. Therein lies the difference. In their program, everything is heaped on the shoulders of the people, while in ours that is not the case."

On June 12 Yeltsin secured approval from the Congress of the Declaration on State Sovereignty of the RSFSR, the document which would give him a mandate for challenging Gorbachev. The vote was 544 to 271 in favor of the declaration. Its key clause proclaimed the primacy of Russian over Soviet laws and said the republic would itself resolve all questions, except for those which it would voluntarily hand over to USSR jurisdiction. It also declared sovereignty over Russian natural resources and the right to leave the USSR. The declaration, enshrining the classic principle of the separation of powers, was to serve as the basis for a new RSFSR constitution and for the negotiation of a new Union Treaty with the other republics.[3]

That same day Yeltsin and Gorbachev met, for the first

time in the Council of the Federation, comprising leaders of the Union republics. Yeltsin told the RSFSR Supreme Soviet: "We walked toward each other, held out our hands to each other, and said that we would work only on a mutual businesslike basis, cooperating together, because Russia cannot exist without the country [the Soviet Union], nor the country without Russia."

Yeltsin said the idea that, in the future, each republic would decide for itself what powers to hand over to the USSR "was accepted by absolutely everyone" at the meeting. The formula would not have to be identical in each case, he argued. "Each state will determine its place along a path, ranging all the way from a federation to a confederation." The Yeltsin formula for the new USSR would allow each republic to pick and choose from an à la carte menu for membership. As far as Russia was concerned, only a short list of functions would be delegated to central USSR ministries. The message was spelled out by a Congress resolution which listed them as follows: Defense, KGB, Civil Aviation, Railways, Maritime Fleet, Communications, Power and Electrification, Nuclear Power, and the defense sector industries. The RSFSR Interior Ministry, controlling the police, would be subordinate only to the RSFSR government and would "collaborate" with its USSR counterpart. Russia would organize its own banking system and negotiate with the central government a share of control over currency emission and other monetary powers.

Yeltsin's ambitious vision of the new decentralized Soviet Union was bound to provoke great suspicion from the central government. With its deliberate insistence that RSFSR laws should take precedence over USSR laws, it set the stage for a full-scale constitutional conflict. Despite Yeltsin's assurances that he did not want to break up the Soviet Union, his disagreement with Gorbachev over the structure of the state was to prove fundamental. Yeltsin's vision of the Soviet Union would strip the center of almost all its powers. Real power would rest with Russia and the fourteen other republics, who would rebuild the state on their own, negotiating a new Union treaty and bypassing the center. Such a state would leave no role for a USSR president as anything more than a figurehead.

Pavel Voshchanov, of *Komsomolskaya Pravda*, foresaw this clearly in June 1990. "If the idea of Russian sovereignty becomes a reality, how will the center react? Will M. S. Gorbachev reconcile himself to the role of 'president without territory?' . . . It is not a matter of the personal relationship between the union and republic leaders. It is a question of their different approaches to the structure of a union state. Whereas Gorbachev is a supporter of the idea 'strong center, strong republics,' Yeltsin sees it, so to speak, the other way round." Voshchanov also foresaw correctly that Yeltsin's weak point, when dealing with Gorbachev, would be the shallow coalition supporting him in his own parliament.[4]

Yeltsin's position at the head of the Russian parliament was not that of an executive president. As he was quickly to discover, the job carried little real authority. Without the cooperation of the central authorities, both he and Silayev's government would be able to achieve little. If Yeltsin took too many risks in challenging Gorbachev, it might become painfully evident that he was the emperor without clothes. But if he did nothing and waited politely for agreement from the Kremlin before every step, Russia would remain a ghost state. Yeltsin knew he could expect no favors from Gorbachev and even fewer from Ryzhkov, whose government he had repeatedly dismissed as incompetent. But real change in Russia would be difficult, if not impossible to implement, unless Gorbachev could be persuaded to support it.

Yeltsin did however have some cards to play: Gorbachev was on record as promising greater sovereignty and a new deal for Russia, so he could ill afford to block all of Yeltsin's initiatives. Nor could he immediately reject the Russian declaration of sovereignty, without offending all the deputies who had voted for it.

In mid-1990, Gorbachev was finding, for the first time, that his customary position at the center of Soviet politics was no longer so comfortable. Instead of deftly holding the balance between left and right, he was losing the political initiative and being squeezed between the new independent power centers which his own policies had created. He was being challenged on all fronts: by the drive for independence of the Baltics and other smaller republics, by a conservative backlash in the Communist Party, by Yeltsin in the Russian parliament, and by the formation of a new Russian Communist Party outside his control.

With the Soviet economy deteriorating rapidly, Gorbachev had an obvious fear of leaving Yeltsin deprived of power and free as before to capitalize on popular discontent. If Yeltsin could be persuaded to share responsibility for the economy, this would help spread the odium that would be generated by painful reforms. Gorbachev was painfully aware that Ryzhkov's government did not have all the answers. In fact, its prestige was at its nadir in the summer of 1990, after popular resistance forced it to abandon its unpopular and poorly planned package of price increases.

If Gorbachev had picked an immediate quarrel with Yeltsin over Russian sovereignty at this time, it would have forced him to fight on two fronts, at a time when he was trying to cope with a counteroffensive by party conservatives.

The conservative threat to Gorbachev came from an influential group of the party *apparat,* who had effectively hijacked preparations for the formation of a Russian Communist Party. Gorbachev, who realized the dangers of a break-up of the CPSU and fought hard to prevent the Lithuanian Party's breaking away at the end of 1989, had resisted the idea of a separate Russian Party as long as he could. The Central Committee Bureau for the RSFSR, approved at the September 1989 plenum as a compromise, was not in fact created until December. Gorbachev, addressing the Central Committee, on December 9, 1989, stated: "Unfortunately, not everyone in the Party is fully aware of the possible destructive consequences of federalizing the CPSU. There are also those who sense the danger that threatens, but who do not know how to combat it, how to withstand the political storm, and who are thus moving in the direction this elemental force is carrying them."

The sixteen-member Russian Bureau failed to satisfy demands for the creation of a full-scale Russian party, which intensified after the abolition of article six of the Soviet constitution, in March, opened the door to a multiparty system. If non-Communist parties were now able to organize themselves on a republican basis, the CPSU could hardly make a plausible case for defending Russian national interests unless it did the same. But as late as mid-May, Gorbachev still resisted the idea.

Speaking to Moscow factory workers who were to elect him as a delegate to the Twenty-eighth CPSU Congress in July, Gorbachev said that the Russian party was "a most difficult issue." The demand for its establishment had "captured Russian minds." But such a party would represent 58 percent of all CPSU members. The danger was that the Russian party would be able by force of numbers to dominate the others. "The Russians will vote on any issue and that will be it." The result would play into the hands of those who wanted to break up the Soviet Union into a confederation and the CPSU into a union of independent parties. Gorbachev reminded his audience that Lenin, while favoring a federal state, was totally opposed to any similar federal structure for the Party.

Two weeks later, Gorbachev acknowledged the inevitable. In his speech to the RSFSR Congress of People's Deputies, he referred to the mushrooming of rival Russian political parties: "It is impossible to understand how this political spectrum of Russia will be without a registered Russian Communist Party. For me, this is already perfectly clear now."

It was a classic case of Gorbachev reacting too late to events. Preoccupied with foreign affairs, economic reform, and the establishment of his new executive presidency, he had allowed control of what was happening in the Party to slip from his grasp. Yuri Manayenkov, a Central Committee secretary and member of the Party's Russian bureau, did not have the necessary authority to keep control of preparations for formation of the new party.

Hardliners met in Leningrad, in early June, for an "initiative congress," followed almost immediately by a founding congress of the new Party, which elected Ivan Polozkov, the man Yeltsin had defeated for the chairmanship of the Russian parliament in late May, as its leader. Polozkov, first secretary of the Party in Krasnodar province, was a hidebound conservative who was best known for his attacks on cooperatives and the free market. His election, even more than that of Yeltsin, was a defeat for Gorbachev. As Pavel Voshchanov commented, in *Komsomolskaya Pravda*, "The party apparatus was literally caught unaware."

On June 19, Gorbachev reminded the Russian Party Congress that there was no way Russia could separate itself from the Union. "I resolutely disagree with those who seek the salvation of Russia in isolation, seclusion, and even withdrawal from the USSR. . . . Those who are prepared to partition the Union, to cut on the raw, so to speak, and to disrupt economic ties that have existed for years fail to realize that all this would inevitably lead to the weakening of the Russian Federation itself. Such attempts are a crime against Russia and its people," he declared.

One of the implications of Yeltsin's drive for Russian sovereignty was that the agenda for reforming the Soviet Union as a whole inevitably took a back seat. From this point on, the Interregional Group in the USSR parliament was to lose much of its significance. If real political decisions were to be made at the level of the republics, it was less and less logical to try to reform the center. By contrast, those who

wanted to keep the Soviet Union together as a unitary state—
the empire-savers—were to use the all-Union parliament as
their power base.

Some influential reformers close to Gorbachev argued
that the stress on republican rights was a mistake. Fedor
Burlatsky, editor of *Literaturnaya Gazeta*, commented: "I have
the impression that many of the movements in the country
have followed the wrong track. They went after the wolf—the
administrative-command system—lost their way and went
after the fox—national sovereignty. But let us get the wolf;
we will have the fox as well. In doing away with the administrative-command system, we will secure the sovereignty of
the republics. But where is the guarantee that an authoritarian regime will not be carried over to the republics, with the
appearance there of their own Pinochets and Khomeinis?"[5]

In other words, giving sovereignty to the republics, before
the process of political democratization and economic reform
at the center was complete, would open the way for authoritarian nationalism, Islamic fundamentalism, or even fascism
in the republics.

The philosopher Alexander Tsipko argued that the whole
idea of Russian sovereignty was an illusion, fostered by those
who had failed to oppose Gorbachev effectively at the all-
Union level and were simply seeking their revenge in another
forum. It was an illusion to think that Russian history could
be separated from Soviet history, he argued. "What will
remain of the USSR if the Ukrainians and Byelorussians, then
the Kazakhs, Uzbeks, and the others begin to think and act
in the way that many Russian deputies now do?" Tsipko
wrote that separating Russia from the Soviet Union would
not solve a single Russian problem. "And moreover, Russia is
not Lithuania: Vilnius can separate itself from Moscow, that
is its right. But Moscow cannot separate itself from Moscow.
It is unnatural, it is crazy."[6]

Some writers, such as political scientists Adranik Migranyan and Igor Klyamkin, argued that the real transition to the
market could only take place under the direction of a firm
central authority and that democracy would have to take
second place. This controversial theory, based on the example
of such countries as Spain and South Korea, became known
as the "Iron Fist."[7]

The counterargument of Yeltsin and his supporters was
that power had to be devolved to the republics first in order
to solve the other political and economic problems, for creating a true multiparty democracy and a free market.

14

What Is to Be Done?

When Latvian journalist Alexander Olbiks interviewed
Yeltsin in late July 1990, at the seaside resort of
Jurmala, he asked him if it was true he had little grasp of
economics.

"Tell me, was Reagan an economist?" Yeltsin asked in
return. "And where did they get the concept 'Reaganomics'?
It is not a matter of my education, but rather of how I
accumulate everything new and different and how I arm
myself with this. To be honest, I have delved fairly deeply into
economics."[1]

By 1990, Yeltsin could no longer get by with crowd-pleasing attacks on the privileges of the *nomenklatura* or criticism
of the Ryzhkov government for printing too much money,
however justified such charges might be. He had to articulate
his own alternative plan for the economy. His speeches and
televised appeals to the people of the Russian Federation
asked for two years of grace to carry out a radical market
reform and promised that living standards would recover
after that point. But some economists felt that, while this
made political sense, it was an illusion to pretend that reform
was possible without an actual reduction in living standards.

"Yeltsin is today repeating, as if by rote, Gorbachev's
mistake of three years ago," wrote *Izvestia*'s economic commentator, Mikhail Berger. "But there is no such thing as a
'free' reform."[2]

Yeltsin could plausibly say that his strong point was not
how much economics he understood himself but how open he

was to using the brains and new ideas of others. One of his criticisms of the Ryzhkov government was that it relied essentially on the ideas of one man—Leonid Abalkin—rather than seeking a broad range of views. This was the motivation behind the unusual new structures which he and Silayev were setting up, including a Supreme Economic Council of the RSFSR, which would be separate from the government and headed by Mikhail Bocharov. This body, a council of economic advisers modeled on similar institutions in Western countries, would bring in advice from academics, business-people, and other groups. Yeltsin's approach included an openness to new, radical ideas about the economy, which had been rejected by the central government.

Radical economic reform also made political sense for Yeltsin as a way of reaching his goal of a Polish-style round-table partnership with Gorbachev. His political strategy was to detach Gorbachev from Ryzhkov and the central planners, whose blueprint for reform had been rejected by the USSR Supreme Soviet at the end of May. Ryzhkov and Leonid Abalkin, the deputy prime minister in charge of reform, had been told to come back with a better plan by September 1. In view of the general lack of confidence in the government, Gorbachev might be prepared to take the risk of choosing a more radical scheme for creating a market economy. If this were to spell the end of the Ryzhkov government, then so much the better, from Yeltsin's point of view.

The Russian reform plan had originally been drafted under the title "Four Hundred Days of Trust," early in 1990, by Grigory Yavlinsky, an economist working for Abalkin and the central government. But the plan found no favor with Abalkin. It was circulated abroad and then reworked by Mikhail Bocharov, who used what was now dubbed the five-hundred-day program as his platform, when he stood against Silayev for the post of head of the Russian government. Yeltsin and Silayev adopted the plan as their own and brought Yavlinsky into the government, as a deputy prime minister. It was an attempt to set a timetable for a rapid changeover to a market economy, combining bold measures to simultaneously stabilize and privatize the economy. The plan was one which had been drawn up not for the RSFSR, but for the Soviet Union as a whole, and it depended on preserving a single market and a single currency.

Once Silayev had put together his government team, Yeltsin took the initiative and wrote to Gorbachev, proposing that they should set up an expert group to draft a plan for the entire Soviet economy, based on the Russian five-hundred-days program. Gorbachev, increasingly convinced there was no alternative to a market economy but not sure how to get there, accepted with alacrity. As his adviser Nikolai Petrakov recalled: "He showed me the letter [from Yeltsin]. He told us to drop everything and find this man [Yavlinsky]."³ Within half an hour, Yavlinsky, a tousle-haired economist in his late thirties, was ushered into Gorbachev's presence. He advised Gorbachev to call Yeltsin immediately. Final details were worked out in late July through several telephone conversations between Gorbachev, in Moscow, and Yeltsin, vacationing by the shores of the Baltic, in Latvia.

"I can already say that the center will adopt this program," Yeltsin told Soviet television triumphantly on August 2, at Riga Airport, as he prepared to return to Moscow. "It will not be the central government's program, which is now being criticized and which of course will not be adopted, I think. This will lead to the resignation of the central government." Yeltsin said he had told Gorbachev that if the Russian reform plan was not adopted, the RSFSR would go ahead on its own and introduce its own currency.⁴

The reform group of thirteen economists, set up by Gorbachev, Yeltsin, Ryzhkov, and Silayev, was given less than a month in which to draw up a plan for a transition to a market economy. The obvious conclusion of this approach was that the final version would have the approval of both the Soviet and Russian governments and would be implemented jointly. Gorbachev issued formal instructions to all central ministries, to make available to the group all the information it might require.

The chairman was to be Academician Stanislav Shatalin, a member of Gorbachev's presidential council, and included another Gorbachev adviser, Nikolai Petrakov, as well as the architect of the Ryzhkov government's ill-fated reform efforts, Leonid Abalkin. From the RSFSR side came Grigory Yavlinsky, a deputy prime minister, and Boris Fedorov, the finance minister. Also in the group was Nikolai Shmelev, a leading reform economist. The group was to work under the "direct supervision" of Gorbachev and Yeltsin, at a secluded government holiday resort at Arkhangelskoe, not far from Moscow.

The creation of this group was a serious blow to the Ryzhkov government, in particular to Deputy Prime Minister Yuri Maslyukov, the head of the State Planning Committee and the man regarded as the strongest opponent of a free market. Maslyukov, though less in the public view than

Abalkin for the past eighteen months, had been the main architect of the government's economic strategy.[5] For the first time, the central planners saw control over far-reaching policy reforms being wrenched from their grasp, by a group of outsiders determined to abolish their jobs.

"I told Gorbachev I didn't believe in this plan or in this compromise with Yeltsin," Ryzhkov recalled.[6]

Shortly after the group began work in early August, Yeltsin set off for a three-week tour of Russia, taking in the Volga, the Urals, Siberia, the Far North, and the Far East. By agreement with Gorbachev, he reluctantly broke off his journey, to return for a meeting with the economists on August 16. By this point it was clear that not everything was going according to plan. As Gorbachev told the Supreme Soviet, on September 11, "The process went badly . . . a split emerged. . . . I sensed that events were acquiring a very acute and dramatic character."

Ryzhkov and his team were doing their best to torpedo the work of the Shatalin group. Abalkin pulled out after the initial meetings, and the government, ignoring Gorbachev, set up its own group to work on a rival reform blueprint. Moreover, it did its best to sabotage the work of the Shatalin team, by refusing its demands for economic data, despite Gorbachev's direct instructions. Behind this power play lay the vested interests of a huge government bureaucracy, composed of dozens of central ministries and the vast network of defense industries.

When the Shatalin plan was finally published, its authors included an appendix which spoke volumes about the real nature of the bureaucratic battle they had been fighting. They pointed the finger at Maslyukov, accusing the State Planning Committee (Gosplan), which he headed, of "completely ignoring the working group's request for information." Second on the list of the accused was Finance Minister Valentin Pavlov, whose ministry, "to all intents and purposes, ignored the request of the working group" and furnished only data of secondary importance. The Foreign Trade Bank Vneshekonombank also ignored Shatalin's requests for data, leaving the group without the basic facts on the Soviet Union's foreign debt. The government's Foreign Economic Commission and the Defense Ministry also failed to cooperate.[7] Gorbachev's inability to assert his authority over the government bureaucracy explains his frantic efforts, throughout August, to stay in constant touch with both groups by telephone from his vacation residence. "He called me about five times a day: How are things going? How are things going?" Shatalin recalled.[8]

Finally Gorbachev decided to cut short his leave and return to Moscow. "I saw that a process of disintegration was simply taking place among the people from whom we counted on receiving this document." He tried to persuade Yeltsin to interrupt his tour of the Soviet Far East a second time and fly back to Moscow, but Yeltsin refused. The problems with the Shatalin group were coming not from his side, but from that of the all-Union government, and Yeltsin probably took the view that it was up to Gorbachev to sort them out.

On August 23, after a seven-hour meeting with the Shatalin group and the leading members of the Ryzhkov government, Gorbachev was still optimistic about the chances of arriving at a single agreed-upon plan. When the Shatalin group completed its report, at the beginning of September, it endorsed the Russian five-hundred-days program, with only minor amendments.

In a country with a long record of unsuccessful and still-born economic reforms, Shatalin's program stood out for its bold vision and readiness to make a complete break with the past. What it offered was not just a new system of economic management but a new kind of society. In the process, it envisaged a deliberate break with the centuries-old tradition of the Russian centralized state.

Its opening section, "Man, Freedom, and the Market" set the tone, declaring that the program would rely on a fundamentally new economic concept: "It plans to move toward a market-oriented economy at the expense of the state but not at the expense of the people." And at the core was a Western-style vision of individual economic liberties, based unambiguously on private property, which it described as "a guarantee of stability in society." While the words capitalism and socialism were avoided, both supporters and opponents of the program saw that it went far beyond the fuzzy concept of "market socialism."

Politically, it would give the Soviet Union a new structure, based on the primacy of the individual republics as sovereign states. "All-Union and interrepublican bodies act on the authority delegated to them by republics, under the terms of the new Union treaty." Local bodies would in turn have powers delegated to them by the republics. This was an improvement on Yeltsin's idea of the "inverted pyramid," based on sovereignty at the district level.

The new Economic Union would resemble the European Economic Community, limiting the role of the state, and requiring all members to accept in full the obligations of membership. Any state which did not accept these obligations would be allowed associate or observer status or the freedom to leave. The republics would have complete sovereignty over their natural wealth and resources and would share the existing Soviet diamond, currency, and gold reserves. Their laws would take precedence, but they would delegate to the Union authority to organize defense, fight organized crime, undertake long-term forecasting and planning, and implement common credit, financial, and monetary policies. There would also be common customs policies and price controls, a common foreign trade strategy, a common ecological program, a common social welfare program, and other services, such as standards and statistics. The only activities that would still be managed from the center would be fundamental research, defense, a common power supply, trunk rail routes and pipelines, nuclear power, space research, communications, and preparations for emergencies. Taxation would be under the authority of the republics, although a fixed contribution, set according to GNP or GNP per capita, would be transferred to the Union budget. Together, the republics would manage an all-Union hard currency fund.

This revolutionary political vision corresponded to that of Yeltsin and his advisers. Not surprisingly, it was anathema to the central government and other powerful interests—the defense industry and the state collective farming sector. The link between the future vision and the reality of the state of the economy in 1990, the concept of transition, was also highly political in its emphasis on high-speed privatization and stabilization of the ruble, as a way of restoring public confidence. The five hundred days were to begin on October 1, 1990, and would involve granting Gorbachev and the leaders of the fifteen republics emergency powers. The period was broken down into a four-stage timetable, with a precise list of deadlines and measures.

Ed Hewett, a leading American expert on the Soviet economy, wrote: "The unique strength of the Shatalin plan, among all the plans under discussion, lies in its serious attempt to come to grips with current political and economic realities; it assumes the union is breaking apart and seeks to construct a viable economic logic to reconstruct it." While noting the plan's internal inconsistencies and lack of quantitative analysis, Hewett described it as "an exciting document, infused with a spirit of liberation from the dogmas of the past and from the bureaucracy that has used those dogmas to retain its oppressive hold over the lives of Soviet citizens."9

Meanwhile, the rival government team produced a revised version of the program which the Supreme Soviet had rejected in May.

Instead of one plan by the beginning of September, as Yeltsin and Gorbachev had intended, there were now two. Each set of authors insisted not only that their plan was better but that it was impossible to combine the two plans. "I left him in no doubt that I was defending the interests of the government," Ryzhkov said.[10] This posed an agonizing problem for Gorbachev, whose political instinct was always to look for the center ground and find a compromise by splitting the difference. At a news conference on August 31, not long after a five-hour meeting with Yeltsin, he made a virtue of necessity by welcoming the existence of the two plans, as a sign of pluralism: "I think it's a good thing we have something to choose from." At this stage Gorbachev seemed to acknowledge that a choice was inevitable. "We must emerge with one of these drafts," he declared.

While indicating a preference for the Shatalin plan, he declared that he was not prepared to take the risk of changing the Ryzhkov government. "We cannot today allow ourselves the luxury of getting involved in a shake-up of political structures, whether at Union or at republican level." By acknowledging publicly that Ryzhkov could not be removed or allowed to resign, Gorbachev made himself, in the short term, the government's prisoner.

In the longer term, however, Ryzhkov's ultimatum to Gorbachev was a mistake. He had overplayed his hand, as Ligachev had done two years earlier. Gorbachev's interior minister, Vadim Bakatin, described it as "political suicide."[11] Gorbachev's whole political existence depended on retaining the initiative, on not falling captive to any other political group, whether it was led by Ryzhkov or Yeltsin. In mid-November, Gorbachev was to give Ryzhkov only a few minutes notice that his government, in fact his job of Chairman of the Council of Ministers, was to be abolished and replaced by a new Cabinet directly responsible to the president.[12]

The refusal of Ryzhkov's government to have anything to do with the Shatalin plan, coupled with Gorbachev's refusal to replace his prime minister, effectively meant that the reform was doomed, and with it the Gorbachev-Yeltsin deal announced on August 2. But his did not become apparent immediately. The final death agony stretched through September, and it was not until mid-October that the outcome became clear.

On September 3, the RSFSR Supreme Soviet met to hear Silayev spell out the politics of the Shatalin reform package. Such a far-reaching economic devolution of power would, if approved, determine in advance the outcome of negotiations on a Union treaty, by turning the Soviet Union into a confederation.

Silayev said there were "deep and fundamental differences" between the conceptions of the Shatalin group and those of the government. The government program would continue to leave most of the power at the center and failed to deal successfully with the increasing budget deficit and the collapse of the ruble.

By the time the all-Union Supreme Soviet met, on September 10, it was clear that Gorbachev would have to sacrifice Ryzhkov and his government, if the Shatalin program was to be adopted. As Abalkin told an *Interfax* journalist, on September 5, the two plans contained "fundamental differences where I think agreement is impossible." If Gorbachev chose the Shatalin plan and stayed in step with Yeltsin, then he would "take full responsibility for the consequences"—in other words, he would be on his own.

Meanwhile pressure was mounting in the Russian Supreme Soviet to demand Ryzhkov's resignation. Yeltsin urged the deputies to wait, seeing no point in further raising the temperature.

For Gorbachev, the Shatalin plan had some good points: unlike the Ryzhkov plan, it had the backing of fourteen of the fifteen republics. It might be the only thing that would keep some of them from seceding completely. Shatalin's recipe for controlling the money supply and stabilizing the economy also won Gorbachev's preference. What he could not swallow was the idea of a wholesale transfer of power to the republics.

While Gorbachev, clearly out of his depth in the world of higher economics, seemed genuinely torn between the two alternatives, Ryzhkov's speech to the Supreme Soviet, on September 11, was unambiguous. Adopting the Shatalin program's devolution of rights to the republics "means the USSR's elimination as an integrated state. The government will not accept such a path." He defended the government reform plan, called for strict adherence by the republics to all-Union laws, and took issue with the Shatalin program's favorable attitude to private farming.

In a television interview the same day, Ryzhkov confirmed he would resign rather than implement the Shatalin program. He said he saw a danger of the disintegration of the

Soviet state. "Some people these days only speak of an economic union. This really worries me. I support a political union, a federal state." Any other outcome would put in danger international stability and have "terrible consequences for all."

"If I were a foreign politician, I would also be worried. It is something different having to deal with just a single state which speaks on behalf of everybody, and suddenly being faced with a great number of republics, for heaven's sake, that all have perhaps their own armies and maybe even nuclear arms. All this is totally absurd."[13]

At a news conference the following day, Ryzhkov said the powers of central government were the fundamental issue of disagreement between the two programs. "This issue is therefore the main one—namely, whether or not there is to be a unified state." It was vital to maintain the existence of all-Union property rights over vital sectors of the economy, such as military plants, and to maintain a direct share of taxation revenues for the central government. Similarly, a unified state had to maintain a single central bank and not fifteen separate reserve banks.

Ryzhkov said his plan favored "destatization" rather than privatization of the economy, a halfway house, where property rights would be transferred out of the hands of the state and into companies in which the state would be the main or only shareholder.[14]

Shatalin himself began to give outspoken interviews vigorously defending his ideas. He rejected charges that his reform would leave the Soviet President as no more than a puppet, attacking the Ryzhkov plan for raising prices without stabilizing the money supply first and for failing to address the issue of private enterprise and land ownership.

Replying to Ryzhkov, he said warnings about the disintegration of the Soviet Union were being used just to fan unnecessary passions. "Let us consider what is really happening in our lives now. The Baltic states, Russia, the Ukraine, and Byelorussia have adopted declarations of sovereignty . . . in some places they are preparing to coin their own money and raise customs barriers. And will this lead to a strengthening of the 'unity of the family of fraternal peoples' as we were saying so recently? So what happens now? Do we send troops into all the territories from the Baltic to the Pacific? First, there are not enough troops, and second I think that the soldiers will not fire on the people. . . . So there is disintegration, and the central authorities are rapidly losing control of the levers of power. And this is obvious to anyone who does not watch life just through an office window. This is why we believe that the only way to save the state is to strengthen the economic union of the sovereign republics. This, I repeat, is the only chance."[15]

Meanwhile the Russian parliament went ahead and approved the Shatalin program, with only one dissenting vote. Yeltsin told Soviet television he hoped other republican parliaments would do the same, so that Russia would not be forced to go it alone and introduce its own currency. Introducing the five-hundred-day program, with its built-in deadlines, would be a major task, but "there is nowhere to retreat," Yeltsin said. "I traveled round Russia and saw so many heartrending things, although I thought I knew it all."

He repeated his call for the resignation of Ryzhkov and his government. "There must be a general change in the functions and running of the state. It should not be so unwieldly. We in Russia will not be providing the upkeep for sixty ministries, and that is all there is to it. We have dispensed with their services."[16]

Outside, in the streets, there was a demonstration, on September 16, in support of the Shatalin program. A crowd estimated at up to seventy thousand marched through the capital, shouting support for Yeltsin and calling for the resignation of the Ryzhkov government.

Gorbachev's next speech to the Supreme Soviet, on September 17, betrayed his increasing doubts about the transition to the market, which he said was not a panacea. Nor did it mean that retail prices would be totally handed over to the free play of spontaneous forces. He stressed that private ownership of land would have to be put to a referendum; the future role of private property should, on the whole, be rather limited; nor should life in the West be idealized.

It was clear that his earlier enthusiasm for the Shatalin program was cooling. Calls for the resignation of the government from the street and from "various podiums"—a reference to the Russian parliament—were "completely unacceptable," he said.

Meanwhile the search for a face-saving way to bridge the gap between the two plans continued. Academician Abel Aganbegyan was asked to find a synthesis, but his preference was clearly for keeping the Shatalin plan intact, with only minor modifications. Despite what Hewett described as "a healthy dose of blue smoke and mirrors," the compromise was unacceptable to Ryzhkov and his team. Abalkin, who like

Shatalin was becoming increasingly outspoken, said he and Ryzhkov would resign immediately if the Supreme Soviet adopted Aganbegyan's version. He compared popular enthusiasm for the Shatalin plan to a craze for flying saucers.[17]

Ryzhkov said the changeover to a market could last a full ten years. "The old cannot be done away with until the new has been created."[18]

Gorbachev came back to the rostrum on September 21, after an eleven-hour meeting of the Communist Party Politburo the previous day. For the first time, he said clearly that the Shatalin program could not be implemented: "It is as if it has lost touch and is hovering above the ground." The Shatalin plan ignored some of the realities of Soviet society. How could the defense industry be expected to switch to a market economy? Privatization in Soviet terms should not mean private ownership, but a change from state to collective ownership—cooperative or leaseholding, but not private property. Anyway, Gorbachev said, even such countries as Great Britain, France, and Germany still had "huge" state sectors.

Gradually, Gorbachev passed from economics to politics, to what was really on his mind—keeping the Soviet Union together. In a long, disjointed, and rambling discourse, he referred to the centuries-long pattern of mixed settlement and blood ties between Soviet peoples; by implication, the Shatalin program would set different peoples against each other. "I am convinced . . . that this would be a fatal choice and those who are pushing for this are playing for absolute sovereignty. . . . It is flirtation and populism, for which there is no place in politics." The idea of a vague commonwealth of states was unacceptable; the Soviet Union would have to remain a federation.

Gorbachev raised the specter of fifteen states, all armed with nuclear weapons, arising on the territory of the Soviet Union. Only "adventurists" could propose such a thing. Political stability had to come first and the system of authority had to stay in place. "If we all start shaking everything up throughout the whole country and the whole system, then it would be a gift for people with all kinds of aspirations."

What Gorbachev was unable to say clearly was that, essentially, Ryzhkov and Abalkin had won. The Shatalin plan, which was now to be combined with the government plan under Gorbachev's supervision, had been killed off.

Shatalin thought this was a sham, and said so. "Even the Supreme Soviet cannot combine Maxwell's Equation and

Ohm's Law. Do not get me wrong, comrades. I do not want to put any pressure on you. The situation is a reality, and economics is a science too. There can be no compromise between the government program and the program of the president and the Shatalin group. I do not want to take part in a show. I want absolute precision and clarity."

He told *Izvestia* that trying to combine the two programs was a waste of time: "They simply have different blood groups."[19]

The Shatalin plan had tried to blur the ideological aspects, by leaving out the words "capitalism" and "socialism." Gorbachev's view was that markets could exist under either system. Shatalin, asked by Soviet television if a state-planned market economy was possible, replied: "No. Well, of course, it's impossible." The state existed only to provide the basic conditions for business enterprise to flourish.[20]

Yeltsin and Silayev, who had carried out their half of the bargain they had struck with Gorbachev at the beginning of August, were left in an uncomfortable position. While the Supreme Soviet granted extra powers to Gorbachev and awaited his final compromise version of the two plans, the Russian authorities decided to delay their start of the five-hundred-days program from October 1 to November 1. It was clear that the reform ideas were in difficulty. On October 9, Silayev told the Russian Supreme Soviet: "To all intents and purposes, a retreat from the principles of radical reform is taking place, the sovereign rights of the union republics are being disregarded, and the entire system of economic relations in the Union, for the year 1991, is being shaped on the basis of the old administrative and unitary principles." This meant that the government was drafting plans and budgets for 1991 as if the existing system was certain to continue.

This created an awkward position for Yeltsin. Politically, he and Silayev could not abandon the five-hundred-days program without a humiliating climbdown that would demonstrate that Russian sovereignty and the decisions of the Russian parliament were mere soap bubbles. But a "go-it-alone" policy based on a separate Russian currency, the alternative Yeltsin had used to pressure Gorbachev, was not a realistic route. Silayev chose a middle path, telling the Supreme Soviet that Russia would push ahead with what it could. This meant privatization, land and housing reform, the indexation of incomes, and the creation of a labor market. But banking reform, budget cuts, a new foreign currency regime, and reductions in defense spending would have to be left on one side. The initial stabilization of the economy would also have to be looked at again: "One must bear in mind the fact that the program you have approved was worked out and submitted as a Union program, and that all the main levers of economic management continue for the time being to be concentrated on the Union level."

Meanwhile, Gorbachev was coming under more criticism at a meeting of the Communist Party Central Committee. His continued defense of "radical changes" and his invocation of the New Economic Policy (NEP) of the 1920s failed to convince many worried party and government officials. Moscow Party First Secretary Yuri Prokofyev, a centrist Gorbachev supporter, attacked both economic reform strategies. "Each of them, to a greater or lesser degree, absolutizes the market as a panacea for our ills, as something that can resolve all problems at a stroke, feed and clothe everyone, and make everyone happy."

A. S. Kamay, second secretary of the Byelorussian Party, attacked the idea of private enterprise: "We are in favor of establishing the priority of collective forms of ownership, of setting limits on private enterprise, and we want it to be monitored by the state and social organizations rather than take its course." Whatever a private market might do for the economy, it would clearly be bad news for the Party.

Stanislav Hurenko, Ukrainian party first secretary, thundered against the threat of anarchy in the country and warned that nationalist extremists were planning to annihilate Communists physically. The transition to the market "gives rise to great fears among the republic's working class and working people," he declared. Leaders of the Central Asian republics, traditionally supporters of Gorbachev, also made clear that a fast switch to the market was not on their agenda.

Minister of Metallurgy Serafim Kolpakov, the man in charge of the world's biggest steel industry, spoke for the powerful heavy industry lobby that Khrushchev had once dubbed "metal-eaters." His sector was being disrupted by "a desire for sovereignty that is degenerating into primitive economic separatism." Skilled Russian workers were leaving steel mills in Central Asia because of ethnic unrest, he complained. He spelled out in detail what others preferred to leave unsaid: Private control of industry was not acceptable. Instead, state industries should be transformed into huge "joint stock companies" that would still be entirely owned by the state. "Some comrades here have been saying that joint-

stock companies are almost the same thing as privatization,"
he complained. The sector should continue to be run from a
single center—instead of the ministry, it would be a metallur-
gical corporation. In other words, not much would change.
Those who wanted to ruin the country's economy were demanding the elimination of ministries and were engaging in
"glib talk" about name changes, he noted. But the status quo,
Kolpakov argued, would do just fine. He appealed to Gorbachev to use his new powers "to overcome the increasingly
evident desire of a number of republics, to break the rational
production ties prevailing in our sector and other sectors by
incorporating enterprises in artificial new formations at the
republic level."

Not surprisingly, Gorbachev's final version of the reform
package, published in mid-October, was a short and vague
statement of "basic guidelines," which set no dates or deadlines and postponed the real decisions. Gorbachev argued
that a more detailed program was an unrealistic goal. He
promised that public ownership would continue to be pre-
dominant and asserted that continued state ownership was
"vital," while private property would merely "have the right
to exist." The plan won swift approval in the Supreme Soviet,
and the Ryzhkov government took over the task of imple-
menting it.

Yeltsin's deputy, Ruslan Khazbulatov, placed the blame
for the final outcome firmly on the government, rather than
on Gorbachev or Aganbegyan. Speaking to the Russian Supreme Soviet, on October 16, he stated that, when Gorbachev
presented this plan to leaders of the republics, three days
earlier, many of them criticized it as a return to centralization. Gorbachev agreed, and tried to meet their objections,
restoring some of the balance by shifting some powers back
to the republics. "But this constructive proposal . . . came up
against a wall of incomprehension of government leaders,
who lined up in defense of their position that this will lead to
the disintegration of the Soviet Union." Pointing out the irony
of the government being more loyal to socialism and the
Soviet Union than the President was, Khazbulatov said the
outcome was that the reform program was now dead and
buried. "I must confirm the forecast and the predictions that
I made, starting from the end of August: the opposition to the
President evidently should be sought not among those on the
right, not among those on the left, not among the military,
but most likely in the government itself."

Yeltsin angrily accused Gorbachev of breaking his personal promise to support the Shatalin program "and no other." Making a late-night speech to the Russian parliament on October 16, his first appearance since being injured in a car accident on September 21, he also blamed Ryzhkov and accused the Prime Minister of telling lies about the size of the budget deficit.

Yeltsin told the parliament it had three choices: They could pursue a go-it-alone policy based on the creation of a new Russian currency, banking system, customs service, a division of the Soviet army, and a share-out of ownership. The second option, clearly the best, but for the time being, out of reach, was a "real coalition" with Gorbachev under which power would be shared. The third, which he recommended, was to go ahead with reform, as far as possible, and "defend the peoples of Russia from the Union program."

If the Gorbachev program was bound to fail in a few months, this made sense as a holding strategy. However the impression was bound to be created that Yeltsin's bluff about creating a Russian currency had been called.

The impression of disarray in the Yeltsin camp was increased when, on October 17, the architect of the original five-hundred-days plan, Grigory Yavlinsky, resigned his post as deputy prime minister, telling the Russian parliament that the program could not be implemented. He complained that politicians were interfering too much in professional economic decisions, though it was not clear if this was a reference to Yeltsin. He argued that the Russian government must face up honestly and frankly to its own lack of real power. Its real ability to get things done was in fact smaller than before the adoption of the declaration on sovereignty, because business could no longer be done on the basis of friendship and telephone calls.

In real terms, Russia's economic field of competence was very limited until it could wrest more power from the central government. Yavlinsky believed a go-it-alone policy was impossible. But he was clearly not willing to sit powerlessly by and take the blame, while the economy slid into a collapse. He rejected an appeal by Silayev to stay on, but hinted he would be prepared to rejoin the team if circumstances changed. "I think the deputies will understand that it will be better if, in about six months, my colleagues and I can propose a new plan to stabilize the economy, on the basis of new realities."[21]

Yeltsin, sidelined by the bruises he sustained in his car accident, was forced into the role of a spectator in the battle over the Shatalin program. There was little he could do to hold Gorbachev to their agreement, once Gorbachev began to side with Ryzhkov and the central government. Later he was to come to the conclusion that his mistake was to enter a purely bilateral deal with Gorbachev, rather than one which drew in the leaders of the other republics.

The collapse of the Gorbachev-Yeltsin pact had little or nothing to do with economics. The outcome reflected not the economic merits of the two programs but the realities of power. Finally brought face to face with the idea of private property and the market, Gorbachev might have swallowed his ideological objections, if the political framework had been more palatable. But behind the battle of two economic programs, the real argument was about the structure of the state and who should run it. Shatalin's plan would have involved too big a surrender of power by the central government, on which Gorbachev had to rely for executive authority.

15

War and Peace

While Gorbachev was sitting by the Black Sea, making his five telephone calls a day to Stanislav Shatalin, Yeltsin spent most of the month of August 1990 on a grueling voyage of discovery to places where no Soviet leader had ventured before.

Sterlitamak is not on the Intourist travel route, nor is it much favored by Kremlin leaders, on their rare excursions out of Moscow. It is a grimy industrial city, in the autonomous republic of Bashkiria, and the center of an ecological disaster zone. From the chimneys of its chemical plants 200,000 tons of toxic chemicals spew into the atmosphere each year and fall back on the 250,000 inhabitants.

As Yeltsin and his small team of aides and journalists approached the Kaustik chemicals plant, they felt queasy. "You're lucky, there's a slight breeze today, we can still breathe," one of the workers explained. Earlier that week, the wind had dropped so far that a bluish gray fog of chlorine gas had spread over the city. Columns of demonstrators, mostly women worried about their children's health, began marching on the city soviet and the city party committee.[1]

When Yeltsin arrived, thousands of workers and their families were packing the area outside the sweaty Palace of Culture, where he was due to speak. Abandoning the invited audience inside, he climbed through a window and addressed the crowd from a rooftop.

It was a vintage populist performance. The food situation in Sterlitamak, Yeltsin told the angry crowd, was appalling.

He promised action. Instead of building gas pipelines in faraway Romania, the Moscow ministries should be piping gas to rural areas at home. "In the end, charity begins at home, and Russia is not going to help other states." The audience cheered, and cheered again when he told them Russia was no longer going to waste its money on the Soviet space program. "Unless there is a sixteen to twenty percent cut in arms spending next year, Russia will refuse to finance these things." At the same time, Russia would insist that other states, to which the Soviet Union had "give away billions of rubles for nothing," should pay the money back in hard currency or in food and goods.[2]

So much for the sponging Cubans and Vietnamese. It was a crude populist message. Russia was poor and exploited but could win back control over its own destiny. But its inhabitants would have to stop waiting for people in faraway Moscow to solve their problems.

Out of the crowd came a voice: "Get rid of the Communist Party city committee!"

"You can get rid of it yourself," Yeltsin retorted.[3]

Sterlitamak, with its toxic fog and angry workers, symbolized the depth of the problems facing Yeltsin. Though it was part of the Russian republic, its industries were controlled not by the Russian government but by the central government. The city authorities and the republic of Bashkiria were still run by old-style Communist bureaucracies which owed Yeltsin no allegiance.

To solve any of Russia's economic or ecological problems, the political question of power and the related question of ownership had to be resolved first. Who was "sovereign" in a God-forsaken place like Sterlitamak, and what exactly did the word mean?

In Western countries, political sovereignty and ownership of land and resources have always been distinct. In Russian history, however, the Tsar became not only the ruler but the owner of his vast territories, in what Richard Pipes describes as the "patrimonial state."[4] Although, in late nineteenth-century Russia, private property rights became established with the rise of capitalism, Communist rule led to a return to confusion. It was a system where the Communist Party, like the Tsar, not only ruled the state but owned it.

To establish a market economy and political decentralization, property ownership and political sovereignty would have to emerge, or re-emerge, as separate concepts. But "on the ground," the two ideas of power were fused, like Siamese twins, into a single concept.

Part of Yeltsin's long-term strategy was to persuade managers and workers that their industries would be far better off under Russian, rather than Soviet, ownership. He promised oil workers, coal miners and factory managers that under Russian rule they would be free to set their own targets, sell their own products and run their own affairs. But no longer would the state be there to guarantee their supplies or bail out their losses.

In places like Bashkiria and Tataria, further upstream along the Volga, ownership was hopelessly entangled with political sovereignty.

As Sergei Shakhrai, chairman of the Russian Supreme Soviet's committee on Legislation, explained: "Russia is rather like a layer cake. At the top you have the Russian parliament. At that level, broadly speaking, the democrats have a fifty–fifty share of power. Then you have the autonomous republics and provinces. Here you still have the finest flower of the party old guard, the old version. The next layer down is the cities, and again the democrats are fifty–fifty. At the bottom you have the districts, and once again it's the local 'partocracy.' "[5]

The problem was one that went to the heart of Yeltsin's attempt to construct a Russian national state, as an alternative to the Soviet imperial state, in which Russians by 1989 made up only a bare 50 percent of the population. For Russia, as defined by the borders of the RSFSR, was itself an empire. Nearly a fifth of its population were non-Russians and 53 percent of its territory was split up into a patchwork of ethnic homelands of varying status, mostly in the Volga region, in Siberia, and in the Far North.

Bashkiria was the oldest of the Russian Federation's sixteen autonomous republics, dating from 1919. It had a population in the millions, and it could be argued that on grounds of size it had a better claim to full union republic status than, say, Estonia with its bare one million. In Tataria, the claim was even stronger. With their ancient capital, Kazan, the Tatars could argue a historic claim to statehood dating back to before their conquest by Ivan the Terrible. They were the heirs of the mighty Mongol empire, which had once ruled Russia. They had ample supplies of oil and gas and a powerful industrial base, with the giant Kamaz truckplant. But in both republics, between a third and a half of the population were Russians. Most of the Soviet Union's Tatars lived outside the frontiers of Tataria, in such cities as Moscow or in Ufa, the capital of Bashkiria.

Among the other fifteen autonomous republics, five autonomous provinces, and ten autonomous zones (*okrugi*) of the Russian Federation, the picture was even more complicated. At one extreme was the unsuccessful experiment of the Jewish Autonomous Province in the Far East, where less than 2 percent of Russian Jews lived and where less than 5 percent of the population was Jewish. There were Koreans and Greeks who were nationalities without territory; there were territories such as Daghestan in the North Caucasus which were home to several nationalities; there were Germans, who had once had their own territory but lost it, under Stalin. Among those nationalities which did have a national homeland, on average only 57 percent lived inside its borders while the other 43 percent lived elsewhere in Russia. Since the maps were drawn in the 1920s and 1930s, often based on arbitrary lines according to the numbers of Communist Party members, millions of non-Russians had gone to live in the "wrong" area while millions of Russians lived in the ethnic homelands designated for other nationalities. Out of 23.3 million people living in the autonomous territories, the 9.6 million people of the indigenous nationalities were outnumbered by 10.1 million Russians. Russians outnumbered the indigenous nationalities in thirteen out of the twenty-four autonomous territories.[6]

Politically, the existing scheme made little sense. The borders bore no relation to real ethnic boundaries. Some Russian radicals argued that the whole link between ethnicity and territory, while it might once have been a sign of progress, should now be scrapped. The state should be reconstructed, from the bottom, on a voluntary basis, and nationalities should be given cultural autonomy and political equality, regardless of size. This was broadly the approach Andrei Sakharov had put forward, just before his death, in a draft constitution for the "United States of Europe and Asia." Galina Starovoitova, a nationalities expert and a deputy in the all-Union and Russian parliaments, argued that the existing division into nationalities of greater and lesser importance had to disappear. She caused a storm in the Russian parliament, by arguing that existing borders would have to be revised to repair the injustices meted out by Stalin.[7] Economists argued that a vast state like Russia should be divided into economic regions which made sense, such as the Far East, East and West Siberia, the Urals, and European Russia.

The existing system did not make legal sense either. Russia was supposed to be a federation, but a look in the history books showed that there was no agreement on federation, to serve as a legal basis. Unlike the United States, not all of Russia's territories enjoyed equal status, for while the non-Russian areas were sovereign or semisovereign republics, the Russian areas were merely administrative provinces. But why should the mighty province of Tyumen, home to the West Siberian oil industry, have fewer rights than economically marginal Karelia, which was an autonomous republic? Even between the national territories, there was resentment that some traveled first-class, as republics, while others had to be content with second-class status, as mere provinces or zones. Some nations had been waiting half a century to have their lost territories restored—the Germans, the land along the Volga, for instance. But if their demands were granted, then a precedent would be set for a wholesale redrawing of internal frontiers. Perhaps it would be better, for the sake of stability, to accept the existing borders as a reality, however unjust they were, as newly independent African countries had done, when they founded the Organization of African Unity?

The task of sorting out this tangle made the task of reshaping the wider Soviet federation look simple by comparison. There was a consensus that there would have to be a new constitution for the Russian republic. But even here there was no agreement. Some democrats, such as Gavriil Popov, felt it would be quite natural for Russia to break up into several states. Others, like the influential Russian legislator Sergei Shakhrai, felt priority should be given to keeping Russia together as a single state. In the autonomous republics, there was strong pressure for more power and an improvement in their status. The local leaderships wanted to translate the "sovereignty" they had long ago been granted on paper into reality, and they formed a powerful lobby in the Russian parliament, in which ethnic minorities were overrepresented.

Yeltsin's problems in the Russian republic to a large extent duplicated those faced by Gorbachev in the Soviet Union as a whole. If anything, they were even more complicated. But he was determined not to repeat what he saw as Gorbachev's mistakes in using pressure tactics against those who wanted to secede.

Yeltsin's task was to keep a balance between all these different views and powerful lobbies. His own instinct was for a massive decentralization of power, with sovereignty coming from the bottom, through the "inverted pyramid."

The balance of power in the Russian parliament meant that he could not afford to offend the non-Russian lobby and their spokesman Ramazan Abdulatipov, a Daghestani expert on ethnic problems, who was chairman of the Soviet of Nationalities, one of the two chambers of the Russian parliament. But he also needed the support of the Russian provinces.

Working out a new constitutional division of powers was for the new Russian authorities a two-way process. While they negotiated with the Kremlin on how to redefine Russia's place in the Union, they had to face demands for a similar redistribution of power within their own Federation. It was a balancing act. Mistakes in handling relations with Russia's many nationalities would inevitably be exploited by Gorbachev, who was ready to deal directly with the autonomous republics in Russia, behind Yeltsin's back. Tataria and Bashkiria, the two largest, found Gorbachev ready to play along with their argument that they should join Russia at the top table and take part in negotiations on a new Union Treaty, alongside the other union republics. This would severely undermine Russian statehood. The other risk was that extreme decentralization and devolution of power might lead to Yeltsin becoming like Gorbachev—an emperor without clothes, or at least no territory. But in one way, Yeltsin's position was stronger than Gorbachev's. Within the RSFSR, none of the autonomous republics or other formations were of a critical size or economic weight comparable to that of the Russian Federation in the Soviet Union. They could embarrass the Russian government, but could not threaten to replace it, as Yeltsin could threaten Gorbachev.

When Yeltsin stood up before a crowd in Ufa, the capital of Bashkiria, he told them: "Take as much power as you yourselves can swallow!" This became a much quoted catchphrase.[8] His gamble was to tell all the Russian Federation's constituent parts to take as much sovereignty as they felt they could handle. Russia would defend their interests at the all-Union negotiating table. Unlike Gorbachev, he would not complain about "separatism" when the autonomous republics proclaimed their sovereignty, as most of them did in the months to follow. Tataria renamed itself Tatarstan and Bashkiria became Bashkortostan. Meanwhile, lesser territorial formations also decided to upgrade themselves; in the Urals, the Komi-Permyak *okrug* (zone) of Perm province voted to turn itself into an autonomous province in its own right.[9]

This approach reflected Yeltsin's instinctive feel for political realities and his determination not to repeat Gorbachev's mistakes. But it neglected the legal and constitutional complexities. It made political sense but carried the risk of administrative chaos. What if the autonomous republics called his bluff and tried to prevent Russian laws being applied on their territory? If Russia could demand sovereignty over its natural resources, then why should Tyumen province not claim ownership of its oil, and Yakutia, of its diamonds? There had to be a limit to self-determination, when not only the distant island of Sakhalin in the Far East but also the district of Kronstadt near Leningrad decided they would proclaim their sovereignty. In September, Yeltsin's deputy, Ruslan Khazbulatov, said such declarations showed "considerable confusion" and a failure to understand that the national republics in Russia were legally "indissoluble parts of a single state." The autonomous formations "are not states but administrative-state formations," he argued.[10]

For his gamble to succeed, and to keep the process from spinning out of control, Yeltsin had to appeal, over the heads of local Communist Party leaders, directly to the people. When he set off on his three-week grand tour of Russia in August 1990, he deliberately broke with precedent. In contrast to Gorbachev, he traveled with a very small entourage and on scheduled Aeroflot flights, an extraordinary step for a Soviet official of his rank.

It was intended as a fact-finding journey to the industrial heartland of Russia, particularly Siberia and the neglected Far East. It was also, as Bill Keller described it, in the *New York Times*, a "dispiriting crash course in the miseries of Russia."

Yeltsin started out in Tataria, on August 6, just as the local Communist Party leadership was drafting a declaration of the republic's sovereignty. "If you want to be in charge, please go ahead and be fully in charge," he declared on arrival, as he stood before touring oil rigs and natural gas fields. Oil workers asked him why their "black gold" was being sold at less than the cost of production. In Kazan, capital of Tataria, he escaped from an all-engulfing crowd by jumping on a streetcar. Addressing the demands for Tatar sovereignty, he declared: "This increase in national self-awareness is obvious. In my view, this is a normal and natural process. So-called machinations by the center have nothing to do with the situation here. I reckon that the Tatar people themselves are entitled to decide for themselves what kind of autonomy they need."[11]

In Bashkiria, he plunged into a bitter local dispute over

the building of a nuclear power station opposed by local residents. In Vorkuta, a former labor camp colony in the Arctic, where militant coal miners had gone on strike in 1989, Yeltsin criticized the Ryzhkov government for failing to fulfill promises to improve their conditions. He promised the conservative mine managers commercial autonomy. After a stop in his home city of Sverdlovsk, he traveled on to the Siberian Kuzbass coal basin, which was seething with discontent. Everywhere he proclaimed a new doctrine of independence and economic self-sufficiency. Miners were promised the right to control their own coal output and to set up free economic zones. "I understand your revolutionary explosion. I understand everything, including the strike movement which began here." After touring miners' slums, which he described as a disgrace to Soviet power, he predicted an outburst of discontent if nothing improved: "People's patience has reached its limit."

In the Far East, he toured food shops, oil rigs, shipyards, fishing ports, and became the first senior Soviet politician to make a trip to the Kurile Islands. "I imagined a fairly wild place, a sparse landscape, rocks, volcanoes, ill-suited for living. But in fact it is like a health resort. Tourism can easily be developed here." Yeltsin reaffirmed his opposition to any immediate handover of the disputed islands to Japan, but recalled his idea for a multistage compromise with the Japanese. In Sakhalin and Kamchatka, both neglected backwaters, he urged local communities to take control of their own fates and stop expecting decisions and subsidies from Moscow. It was a tour designed to avoid the "Potemkin villages" so often erected for important visitors. Journalists traveling with him reported that, in Kamchatka, he gave them the slip, jumping into a car with a local resident, to tour a highrise housing project. He also met KGB border troops and the Nivkhi, the indigenous people of Northern Sakhalin. Touring a nuclear submarine base on Kamchatka, he reaffirmed his opposition to splitting up the Soviet armed forces along republican lines. "There is no justification for dividing the army into national compartments. That is the path toward the collapse of the armed forces and the Soviet Union in general." Russia, he said, would continue to hand over its defense to the management of the Union, but wanted to see a transition to a professional army. Yeltsin added some significant comments distancing himself from widespread criticism of the Soviet military by local soviets. "I do not support those who are fuelling unhealthy feelings towards the military.

When I am told that military establishments are preventing the full economic development of regions, I reply that the military have their own serious arguments."[12]

On his return to Moscow, Yeltsin spoke bitterly of the poverty, backwardness and appalling ecological disasters he had seen. "I was able to feel the poverty and the low standard of living, the dissatisfaction that, in five years, the people's life has not improved anywhere, and the farther you go from Moscow the harder life is, with more and more problems." People had confidence in the Russian government, but they had none in Ryzhkov's government. He was not worried by declarations of sovereignty: "I consider this a historical inevitability, an objective reality that must be taken into consideration." But he said that for republics such as Tataria to take part in negotiations on a Union Treaty alongside Russia would be "somewhat problematic." Meanwhile, local government could be reorganized on a decentralized basis, without following the same pattern everywhere. "Russia is a big place. The differences in traditions, climatic conditions, dimensions, and so on are very great. Therefore, we may have to have different structures."[13]

While hoping to neutralize the pressures from below, by his promises to devolve power, Yeltsin was beginning to apply pressures of his own, to wrest more power, for Russia, from the center. The political momentum was to some extent on his side, but the struggle was to be long and arduous. As in the case of the argument over economic reform, Yeltsin had to use a large element of bluff and public rhetoric to get his way.

Ever since Lenin there had been a yawning gap between the formal constitutional arrangements and political reality. According to the letter of the Soviet constitution, all fifteen union republics were "sovereign." Two of them, the Ukraine and Byelorussia, even had their own seats at the United Nations; all of them had at least some of the panoply of statehood. But the reality was that the republican governments had very little authority or power over what happened on their territory. The central government could build a tank factory or a nuclear power station, dig for gold, pollute the local water supply, raise industrial prices, install an SS–20 missile battery, or move in a regiment of troops. "Sovereignty" was just another piece of window-dressing, and the reality was the power of the Party, which combined legislative, executive, and administrative authority.

But once Gorbachev enshrined the principle that power

should flow from below, through democratic elections, local politicans were responsible not to Moscow, but to their voters. They could no longer passively accept that their sovereignty was a sham and that real decisions were all made in the Kremlin. To avoid being displaced by more radical popular forces, they would have to give at least the appearance of fighting for sovereignty and power in reality, not just in words.

It was this dynamic which explained why orthodox Communists, who had previously followed Moscow obediently, suddenly began championing republican rights in 1990. This phenomenon was particularly noticeable in conservative republics, where the Party's rule was not seriously challenged. The Ukraine followed Russia's sovereignty declaration with one that went even further, declaring the theoretical right to establish its own armed forces. Byelorussia, even more firmly under party control, followed suit two weeks later, at the end of July.

By the summer of 1990, a new constitutional division of powers between the center and the republics was therefore long overdue. Events had outdated all the carefully crafted formulas of Gorbachev's nationalities policy, which had been drawn up in September 1989. As far back as 1988, the Baltic republics had proposed that a new deal could not just be imposed by the center or the all-Union parliament; they wanted to negotiate a new Union Treaty, to replace the one of 1922.

Gorbachev resisted this demand at the September 1989 Central Committee meeting on nationality problems, but finally caved in in 1990, when it became clear that the Baltic republics were serious about independence. It was a major concession, for it meant that the new document would have to be the product of consensus, with each republic having the right to veto. Although the existing constitution was to remain in force while the new Treaty was negotiated, it quickly acquired an air of complete obsolescence.

Gorbachev's big concession came too late, because by 1990, the Baltic republics were adamant that they did not want to sign a new treaty at all. In March, Lithuania led the way, by proclaiming the restoration of its prewar statehood. Estonia, Latvia, Moldavia, Georgia, and Armenia were to follow the same path, with differing degrees of firmness. Even the remaining nine republics were to insist on a deal that would probably leave the center with only a minimum, agreeable to all, of its former powers.

At a news conference after his August journey, Yeltsin summed up their aspirations: holding his hands a few inches away from each other as if measuring a small fish, he declared: "This is the sort of center we need."

Gorbachev wanted to keep the Soviet Union as a single state, but as a renewed federation. He argued that the idea was a good one but had not yet been tried properly in practice, for the old federation was not a real federation at all. By returning to original Leninist ideas, a true federation could be constructed under the slogan "strong center, strong republics." Economic separatism, he argued, would doom individual republics to isolation from the huge Soviet market, into which they were already integrated.

The flaw in this argument was that Lenin's federation ideas, while less Russocentric than Stalin's, were ultimately designed to pave the way for a unitary state. And the economic benefits of remaining in the Union were far from evident, given the inability of the Ryzhkov government to either stabilize the ruble or come up with a credible scheme for introducing a market economy.

Gorbachev's initial hope was for a quick agreement on a Union Treaty—within three or four months. He met with Yeltsin and the leaders of the other republics on June 12, at the Council of the Federation, and agreed to set up a working group to begin drafting a treaty. Anatoly Lukyanov, chairman of the USSR Supreme Soviet, said that he expected agreement by the fall on a draft to be approved by the republics and the all-Union Congress of People's Deputies. As things turned out, this was overoptimistic. Negotiations were to drag on for more than a year, until the second half of 1991. Not only was it a task of massive complexity to marry dozens of different drafts, but it turned out that only Gorbachev was really in a hurry. The other republics found that dragging out the negotiations would give them time to draw up their own new constitutions first and negotiate bilateral treaties with each other, thus strengthening their leverage.

The three Baltic republics took no part in the first session of the working group, on June 20, 1990, leaving only twelve republics to take part, a number that was later to fall to nine, when Moldavia, Georgia, and Armenia dropped out. The second problem for Gorbachev was that, led by the RSFSR, most of the republics wanted him to take a back seat in the negotiating process, arguing that it was up to them to agree among themselves what powers they would transfer to the center.

The RSFSR negotiating position was set out by Khazbulatov. He made clear that no return to an idealized Leninist formula would work. The 1922 treaty was "entirely confederative in form and strictly unitary in point of fact, depriving both the union republics and the autonomous organizations of any kind of independence." This system had disintegrated as a result of the "involvement of the broad masses of the people in the democratic process."

Under the existing system, irrespective of what was written in the constitution, power flowed from the top down. "The center, with its authority, indisputably determines the extent of both its own powers and the powers of the republics. The proclamation of sovereignty by the republics changes this procedure cardinally." The new deal should be negotiated between the republics, "without the participation of the currently empowered representation of the center"—in other words, bypassing Gorbachev. The treaty of Union would then replace the existing USSR constitution. Russia would insist on the primacy of its own laws over USSR laws and on delegating only limited authority to the center.[14]

By early September, it was already clear that the process would be a long one. Gorbachev's chief negotiator, Rafik Nishanov, said that there were seven draft texts from the republics, four drawn up by various public organizations, and another twelve independent versions. Altogether, he said, "We know of more than two hundred union treaties, and this is a cause for gladness."[15]

Nishanov disclosed, to nobody's great surprise, that there were "major differences of opinion" on the division of powers between the republics and the center. Yeltsin said the same on September 1, indicating he did not expect an agreement by the end of 1990. "I am not optimistic that it will be concluded, not just in the nearest future, but even this year. This is because one republic wishes to have an army of its own, another wishes to have its own customs, another wishes to have its own bank notes, and yet another republic only wishes to have its own currency."

By November, a preliminary draft of the treaty for a new "Union of Sovereign Soviet Republics" was published for discussion, but Gorbachev's hopes for a quick signing were not to be fulfilled. Speaking to the Communist Party Central Committee, on December 10, he said the republics' sovereignty and their right to secede had to be recognized, but he attacked "extremist national-chauvinist forces" for trying to tear the country apart. "There is no more serious danger in the country now than arrant extremist nationalism." He implied that republican leaders who did not want to sign a new treaty, such as those in the Baltics, were unrepresentative of their own peoples. Only a referendum could decide such questions, and secession was only possible if the law—highly restrictive—was followed.

"Is the Union to be a powerful sovereign state or a loose symbolic formation? I think the answer is clear," Gorbachev declared. Those who considered that the Soviet Union was a continuation of the Russian empire were out by seventy years. "The Russian empire ceased to exist in 1917 . . . and no one can reproach the Russian people with having effected imperial domination over other peoples."

The next day Yeltsin told the Russian Congress of People's Deputies that Russia favored a new treaty, but would not be rushed by ultimata from the center. His ideal was a treaty that would be signed by the maximum number of republics—a looser but wider union that would still include the wayward Baltics. "Our point of departure is the psychological disposition of the majority of inhabitants of Russia (*rossiyane*), in whose consciousness the idea of the Union has become deep-rooted." He suggested that membership in the new state should not be an all-or-nothing affair but should allow "varying conditions of entry," beginning with economic union.

Yeltsin went on to argue that it would be better for Russia to agree on its own internal constitutional reform before signing a Union Treaty. Natural links between republics, if allowed to develop, would help stabilize the situation and strengthen the basis for a new Union.

Instead, the center was failing to recognize the reality of Russian sovereignty and stalling on the question of dividing up Union and Russian property. "Decisive changes . . . are necessary. The center must finally come out to meet the republics and display understanding of the inevitability of this process. In one way, . . . we might all be brought closer to a new Union and the signing of a treaty." In other words, Russia would only sign after Gorbachev made major concessions. Yeltsin acknowledged that, since June, Russia had taken a tough line with the center. "This toughness was conditioned primarily by our aspiration finally to reach a constructive dialogue with the Union leadership."

The negotiations stalled, in early 1991, because of Gorbachev's bungled crackdown against the Baltic republics. It was not until April 1991 that they were to pick up again. By this time, the balance of political power had swung further toward the republics, and their leverage was greater.

While the negotiations between Gorbachev and the fifteen republics dragged on, a more concrete battle for power was being fought between Russia and the central government in the second half of 1990. Yeltsin's tactic was to be as cooperative as possible with the other republics and as tough as possible with the central government. One of the first skirmishes was fought in the summer, over control of banking on Russian territory.

On this issue, Yeltsin and the Russian parliament picked a fight with the central government, testing their reactions to the declaration of Russian sovereignty with a kind of reconnaissance in depth. Like many of the moves made by Yeltsin's team, this one contained a large element of bluff. The aim was to put some flesh on the bones of the Russian declaration of sovereignty and serve notice that Russia was no longer a "ghost state." The skirmishes foreshadowed a bigger battle, at the end of 1990, over Yeltsin's insistence that the Russian share of the Soviet budget for 1991 should be drastically cut.

The power struggle was to become known as the "war of laws," as the Russian and central authorities passed a series of rival decrees and laws, each claiming legal precedence.

On August 9, the RSFSR Presidium, headed by Yeltsin, fired a further warning shot at the Ryzhkov government, by issuing a resolution that barred the central government from exporting Russian natural resources without Russian consent.

Issued as a reaction to news of big gold sales by the central government, it declared that any sales of diamonds, gold, platinum, gemstones, silver, oil, coal, gas, uranium, minerals, ferrous and nonferrous metals, lumber, furs, grain, and other strategic resources and commodities concluded since the June 12 RSFSR decree on sovereignty would be considered invalid.

"Such actions frankly undermine the economic base of Russia's sovereignty," said Sergei Shakhrai, chairman of the RSFSR Supreme Soviet Legislative Committee, who charged that the center was selling Russian precious metals and gems at giveaway prices. Two weeks later, Gorbachev, as State President, issued his own decree declaring the Russian resolution invalid under the existing USSR constitution. The Russian Supreme Soviet replied with a statement saying Gorbachev's decree was null and void, because Russian laws took priority over Soviet laws until a Union Treaty was signed.

Although Yeltsin and Gorbachev agreed, in their five-hour

meeting at the end of August, to try to avoid such conflicts, Yeltsin told the Russian parliament, on September 11, that "an enormous struggle" was going on for every inch of sovereignty. The center did not want to renounce the power over Russia which was the basis for its power over the entire Soviet Union.

But as the summer of 1990, with its record harvest, gave way to fears of a starvation winter, the picture Yeltsin painted of an all-powerful center looked quite different from Gorbachev's Kremlin office. Far from controlling the entire Soviet Union, he could not even control his own government and army.

16

In the Trenches of Stalingrad

For Mikhail Gorbachev, November 13, 1990, was not a day to look back on with pride. At the moment when George Bush was confidently deploying America's imperial power, by sending hundreds of thousands of troops halfway round the world to liberate Kuwait, the leader of the other superpower was being heckled by his own troops. It was humiliating proof of how low his authority had sunk.

As the murmurs and jeers swelled up from the rows of khaki uniforms, Gorbachev glowered and snapped back: "Is this of no interest to you? I am not talking about this to you for nothing!"

The five-hour confrontation left Gorbachev shaken. Though it alone did not provoke his swing to the right at the end of 1990, the middle week of November, in which he collided head-on with the Soviet army and undertook a desperate reorganization of his administration, was a watershed.

Gorbachev's six-month flirtation with the conservatives was to last until April 1991. It was to weaken his prestige fatally among the democrats, his former allies, and lead directly to the coup against him in August. It was to provoke the resignation of his foreign minister, Eduard Shevardnadze, in December, and a clumsy military crackdown in Lithuania and Latvia, in January. Ultimately, the biggest victim was Gorbachev himself. The biggest long-term winner turned out to be Yeltsin.

To make sense of events in the last few months of 1990, one must appreciate the weakness of Gorbachev's position. He was losing power fast.

Despite hanging on to the job of Communist Party general secretary and occupying the new executive presidency since March, Gorbachev's isolation and loneliness were obvious to all. His apparent victories, such as his routing of the conservatives at the Twenty-eighth Party Congress in July, were Pyrrhic ones.

Since the election of Ivan Polozkov to head the Russian Communist party, the biggest contingent of his own party had been controlled by conservative forces hostile to him. In most of the other republics, the Communists had been either routed by the voters or were ending their subordination to Moscow, in order to survive by preaching the popular language of sovereignty. In any case, the Party no longer retained its old role as an all-purpose power structure, combining legislative, executive, and judicial functions.

Executive power rested with the government. But the battle over the Shatalin plan had shown that, on issues vital to its own survival, it would defy Gorbachev's orders when it felt like it. The President had no executive chain of command except that of the Council of Ministers, headed by Ryzhkov, who had his own priorities.

Intellectuals who met Gorbachev felt he was getting poor advice. Radical economist Larisa Piyashcheva, who met him, with other reformers, at the end of July, said she got the impression he had "poor information facilities and inadequate analytical services.[1]

Piyashcheva said Gorbachev's advisers did not have the courage to tell him that his idea of combining the radical five-hundred-days economic program with that of the government was a nonstarter.

The collapse of Gorbachev's power was partly the result of the increasing polarization and fragmentation of Soviet politics, which had slipped out of the control of the traditional oligarchy at the center. No longer could he keep the initiative by tacking deftly between the left and the right, relying on a solid core of centrist support for his policies. Caught between Polozkov and Yeltsin, he was isolated and unpopular. Soviet politics were becoming too polarized, and in any case, the initiative had largely passed to the republic level. It was now Russian politics, Ukrainian politics, and Georgian politics that mattered. "The political center of the USSR has outlived its usefulness," wrote political scientist Andranik Migranyan.[2]

Migranyan traced the root of Gorbachev's problems to the 1990 elections in the republics, which by legitimizing fifteen new governments, had dispersed a large measure of power outside the Kremlin. Gorbachev's scenario of an orderly economic reform at the center, to be followed by a political restructuring of the Union, was failing to materialize. Despite an economic blockade of Lithuania, Gorbachev had failed to bring enough authority to bear to end its defiant declaration of independence in March 1990.

If Gorbachev had at least retained undisputed authority in Russia, his position would have been much more solid. But Yeltsin's election had shifted the balance. As Migranyan wrote: "Russia's decision to gain independence is a simply epoch-making event, unparalleled in the state's thousand-year history. It means a complete reappraisal of all the supreme values which underpinned the existence, first of autocratic Russia, and then of Bolshevik Russia. This is essentially a repudiation of the idea of 'divine election,' 'exclusiveness,' and 'messianism.' "

With Russia, the Ukraine, and Byelorussia all declaring their sovereignty, "the ground has been cut from under the feet of the Union institutions of power," Migranyan wrote, adding that the only institution on which Gorbachev could now rely was the army.

More and more, Gorbachev's presidential orders were like scraps of paper carried away by the wind. On September 21, a Supreme Soviet deputy from Sakhalin asked him point blank: "Why are your decrees not being fulfilled? When will they start to be fulfilled? That's one thing. And what measures will be adopted by you in the future, to prevent your decrees from not being fulfilled? I should like to hear this from you."

Gorbachev did not deny that his authority was being flouted. But he seemed genuinely torn about what to do.

At the end of September, the Supreme Soviet granted Gorbachev a new set of powers, valid for eighteen months, to oversee economic reform. But the move drew a hostile reaction in the Russian parliament. And when Gorbachev at last unveiled his compromise economic reform package in mid-October, it was denounced by many of his own advisers, including Shatalin and Petrakov, as unworkable. As the newspaper *Izvestia* warned: "Today the moment of truth has arrived for Gorbachev and his team. Maneuvering between left and right is no longer possible. Any continuation of this line threatens to lead to a situation where the President will forever lag behind a departing train."[3]

The *Izvestia* article was an appeal to Gorbachev to make the choice he had been postponing for so long—to go into a coalition with the reformers and democrats, the "left." Despite the setback over the Shatalin plan, most reformers still trusted Gorbachev and wanted to shore up his authority. The weakness of executive power was something that the democratic city mayors of Moscow and Leningrad, Gavriil Popov and Anatoly Sobchak, knew from their own experience was a real problem. What the left wanted was a real coalition with Gorbachev, but they had little to offer him except their popularity, and even this was starting to look tarnished. Despite the legalization of a multiparty system, the democrats were weak and divided, having failed to build a convincing alternative to the Communist Party as a political movement. They were not in a position to help Gorbachev strengthen his executive powers.

Yeltsin's car accident effectively removed him from the political stage, from September 23 to November 3, except for a brief return to Moscow in mid-October. His injuries, initially thought to be only minor, turned out to require a longer convalescence. It was his second serious accident in less than six months, following a back injury sustained in Spain, in April, when an aircraft in which he was traveling made an emergency landing.

In his speech on October 16, Yeltsin pinned the blame for the demise of the Shatalin program on the Ryzhkov government, accusing it of obstructing the exercise of Russian sovereignty. "We cannot share power honestly and objectively. The center is doing everything to preserve the existing administrative-command system."

Yeltsin complained that 70 percent of industrial output in Russia still came from factories subordinated to the Union government. "We have come up against a powerful and undisguised sabotage, by the union government, Gosplan, Gosbank and the Union ministries, of Russia's efforts to demarcate union and republican property."

He also complained of blatant efforts by the press to discredit the democrats and blame democrat-controlled city soviets for economic problems. The fragile partnership between the center and the left was seriously under threat.

Turning to his relations with Gorbachev, Yeltsin sent him a clear signal that despite the setback over economic reform, he was still open to a political deal. On fundamental issues, he said, they were still moving in the same direction. "But we adhere to different paces, movements, and methods. We disagree primarily on tactical issues." Yeltsin stressed that he was ready for dialogue with Gorbachev, but any future understandings would have to be made public. This was a way of reminding Gorbachev that it was he, not Yeltsin, who had reneged on the Shatalin plan. "In our personal conversation, he said he would support only this program and no other. It was realistic for the program to commence on October 1. We were ready for this, but the union government pressed the President and he again changed his decision."

Yeltsin told the Russian Supreme Soviet that the real solution was not all-out defiance by Russia but a genuine coalition with Gorbachev, which would be based on the formation of a new central government stripped of much of its power.

> Perhaps there could be some other executive union structures, but they must be formed upon principles of parity and not just by the president alone. Some of the candidates for minister would be proposed by the president and some proposed by us, supporters of radical reforms. Let us say he proposes the chairman of the KGB and we propose the minister of defense.
>
> That is a real coalition. Otherwise we do not have power. Here we just sit and adopt resolutions and do not know whether these things will be carried out, because all the real power is in their hands. They have the apparatus—the administrative, state, and party apparatus—the army, KGB, and other structures. We have none of that.

Yeltsin's third option, the one which he recommended, was to pursue a holding strategy based on the assumption that Gorbachev would reject a coalition and stick with Ryzhkov's program. The result would be hyperinflation, and in six months time, when the program's failure was apparent, Russia would be able to come back with a revised economic reform plan, for the whole Union, as an alternative. This prediction was to prove remarkably accurate.

Three days later, Gorbachev replied with a sharp attack on Yeltsin for the "confrontational" tone of his address. He insinuated that Yeltsin was out of touch and had been led astray by his staff. "I fear that in this case Boris Nikolayevich has been let down by his consultants and advisers—let him sort them out himself."

The Russian leadership was giving up in the face of its difficulties and blaming the central authorities for all its problems, Gorbachev charged. Yeltsin's demand for a coalition was unacceptable. "It is an ultimatum; we are being given an ultimatum. A coalition engendered by an ultimatum is a strange coalition. What sort of coalition can there be? There is so much confrontational zeal and *diktat* in the way this has been raised that doubts arise as to the sincerity of these intentions."

Gorbachev then went on to accuse Yeltsin of having forgotten that besides Russia there were fourteen other republics. Stabilizing the economy was too important for anyone to play political games. As for coalitions, the most important thing was to consolidate all democratic forces that wanted to renew society "within the framework of the socialist choice." On this basis, he implied, the door for dialogue and cooperation was open. By implication, those who did not accept the "socialist choice" would not be welcome.

After these hostile public exchanges, Yeltsin resumed his convalescence. The two men were next brought together by the protocol demands of the Soviet calendar on November 7, the anniversary of the Bolshevik Revolution. Gorbachev had ordered that traditional military parades should go ahead everywhere, despite public opposition in many cities. In some republics his orders were disregarded, and in Moscow the ceremony was more like a funeral than a celebration.

For the first time, the Revolution was marked not as an occasion to glorify the Communist Party but as an important date in the history of the state—rather like Bastille Day in France, a date which the French agree is historically important, whether they approve of the events being celebrated or not. The Communist Politburo, for the first time ever, was banished from the top of the Lenin Mausoleum. Gorbachev made a valiant effort to please both supporters and opponents of 1917, paying tribute to the "imperishable values" of the 1917 Bolshevik Revolution, while denouncing the "totalitarian" system which it created. In a phrase remarkable even by Soviet standards of ideological contortion, he praised Lenin for having wanted to create a "normal, healthy, and prosperous society."

After joining Gorbachev on the mausoleum and walking through the square with him, Yeltsin and Popov then joined unofficial counterdemonstrations organized by Gorbachev's opponents.

Inch by inch, day by day, the people were reclaiming the city from the all-powerful state. Led by radical deputies, the alternative demonstrators shouted their demands for Gorbachev's resignation, amid shouts of *"Doloy!"* ("Down with them!"). "Who will defend *perestroika* from its architects?"

asked one slogan. In Staraya Square, outside the Central Committee headquarters, Yeltsin and Popov joined demonstrators carrying portraits of Andrei Sakharov and religious images. "Forgive us, crucified Russia!" said one placard. In Lubyanka Square, opposite the statue of Lenin's secret police chief Felix Dzerzhinsky, candle flames glimmered, as mourners laid flowers by a stone commemorating the countless victims of Stalin's repression. It was to be the last time "Iron Felix" would celebrate the anniversary of the revolution.

Four days later, on November 11, Gorbachev and Yeltsin met alone, for the first time since their long talk at the end of August. After two hours they were joined by Khazbulatov, Ryzhkov, and Silayev. The five-hour meeting was described by Gorbachev's spokesman Vitaly Ignatenko as "businesslike and constructive."

Yeltsin gave a full account of the talks, on November 13, to the Russian Supreme Soviet. After agreeing with Yeltsin that nobody was to blame for the failure of their previous agreement, Gorbachev opened the discussion by insisting that Russia sign a Union Treaty. Yeltsin replied that Russia had never opposed the Union and the Union Treaty, but would not sign it unless the center unequivocally recognized Russian sovereignty and stopped trying to impose its *diktat*. "I think these problems should be solved today, as soon as possible, while he [Gorbachev] believes these problems should be resolved after the Union Treaty: 'Let's sign the Union Treaty first, and then we'll determine what belongs to Russia.'"

Yeltsin stated that he and Gorbachev had agreed to set up a joint committee of the two governments, to establish a division of functions and property between the Union and Russia, aiming at a comprehensive settlement that would cover natural resources, taxes, debts, banking, foreign trade, and the budget for 1991. This work would proceed in parallel with negotiations on a new Union Treaty. Russia would continue to insist on handling all its own affairs except for the six areas of all-Union competence, the most important being defense.

Yeltsin then told the deputies that he had proposed to Gorbachev a coalition government of national unity. "In principle this proposal . . . was supported," Yeltsin declared. "I didn't claim many posts before consulting with you. But I expressed the wish for three—Prime Minister, Finance, and Defense," he said, amid laughter and applause. He then listed a number of other issues, some of which he and Gorbachev agreed on and others on which they failed to agree. The understanding would be drafted into a protocol. Whereas, after the August meeting, "I was very seriously disappointed because certain accords had been reached and then not fulfilled, . . . I think now that, with the signing of the protocol, . . . hopes are somewhat higher, from the point of view of fulfillment." In other words, this time Gorbachev could be made to stick to his word.

Yeltsin's account suggested that he badly misinterpreted Gorbachev's response to his offer of coalition terms. While by now, Gorbachev was quietly drafting plans for a more presidential system of authority, they did not coincide with Yeltsin's idea of "an extraordinary anticrisis committee, formed, on the basis of equal rights, from representatives of the union republics."[4]

Gorbachev may have supported the idea of a coalition government "in principle," but he was far too wily a politician to agree to it in the terms Yeltsin described. Speaking to the Supreme Soviet, on November 19, Gorbachev made clear that any such coalition would have to wait until the Union Treaty was signed. If a coalition of national unity was such a good idea, then why not apply it to all the governments of the republics as well, not just the Union government, he asked. "There cannot be double standards," Gorbachev insisted.

Yeltsin's offer of a deal with Gorbachev would have shored up the President's failing authority, but at a high price. It would have effectively handed over control of central executive power to the Russian democrats and their allies in the other republics. It is unlikely that Gorbachev was seriously tempted by Yeltsin's offer.

Even if he was, the temptation was short-lived. Two days later, Gorbachev was facing a challenge to his authority from a force far more formidable than Yeltsin and the democrats— the five-million-strong Soviet military.

The meeting, on November 13, between Gorbachev and more than a thousand military deputies was the moment when months of pent-up discontent boiled over.[5]

Coddled and privileged with the best of everything, under Brezhnev, the military had become the Cinderellas of *perestroika*. Gorbachev's "new thinking" abroad and radical arms reduction had significantly reduced their role. Morale had slumped in Afghanistan, a costly foreign adventure in which Soviet soldiers, like their American counterparts in Vietnam, felt they had become scapegoats for cynical politicians. Officers, once regarded as well paid, found their salaries eroded by inflation. The prospect of economic reform and the conversion of defense industries to civilian needs heightened their insecurities.

These were the grievances of Gorbachev's first four years, but from 1989 onward, things got rapidly worse. The rise of independence movements in the Baltic states and other republics in 1990 suddenly left the armed forces in the role of occupying troops, isolated amid a hostile civilian population. Local commanders found that their garrisons were meeting problems with housing, education, and supplies. Thousands of conscripts were failing to turn up for the draft and republican parliaments were showing increasing opposition to the use of conscripts for internal security duties outside their own republics.

Also, Afghanistan was not the only reason why the prestige of the Soviet armed forces was tarnished. The press had lifted the curtain on a flood of civilian complaints about the brutality of army life, the violent *dedovshchina* ("hazing") of new recruits and the thousands of noncombat deaths which occurred each year. The top military leadership was thrown on the defensive by the tragic, accusing faces of mothers who had lost their sons during military service.

Gorbachev's policy of military reform and the switch to a new defensive doctrine were accepted only grudgingly. Why, the generals grumbled, did conventional arms reduction agreements force the Soviet Union to make bigger cuts than anyone else?

Many in the military suspected that, despite Gorbachev's public commitment to preserving a united Soviet Union and a united army, it would be only a matter of time before he would compromise and agree to the establishment of republican armed forces. Despite their high level of Communist Party membership, many professional officers would have been quite happy to see the Party's power reduced. What mattered was the disintegration of the Soviet empire, which they blamed Gorbachev for setting in motion.

Some senior officers spoke as though the state and its politicians existed to maintain the army, rather than the other way round. General Boris Gromov, commander of the Kiev military district, was asked by the Yugoslav magazine *Danas*, in September 1990, what would happen if politicians were to take a decision of which the military establishment disapproved. "We are not interested in politicians," he replied. He warned that the formation of republican armies—which existed in a limited form until 1938—would have "disastrous consequences."

Marshal Dmitry Yazov, the defense minister, made clear he believed the republics should have no voice at all in defense matters. "If we were to separate now, each union republic would have to have its own army. Where do you put the troops? . . . It simply does not fit; it does not add up that each union republic, for example, should have its own army, or that each union republic should say: I do not want troops to be stationed here, or on the other hand, should ask for its troops to be stationed here." Yazov's television interview, on November 25, could not have been more scornful of the attempt by the Russian authorities to lay down rules barring the use of Russian conscripts in domestic conflicts. "Who gave the republic . . . the right to adopt such a decision? . . . it is an absurdity."

By the second half of 1990, the full cost of the planned Soviet withdrawal from Eastern Europe was starting to hit home. There was the acute psychological humiliation of having to abandon, without firing a shot, the huge defensive buffer zone which millions of Soviet soldiers had died to secure in World War II. There was also the painfully obvious fact that, with the collapse of Communist rule in all of the Warsaw Pact countries, the Soviet Union had no real allies. What had once been the pride of the Soviet army, the Group of Soviet Forces in Germany, was now to be left high and dry on NATO soil until housing was built at home, with German aid. What was left of the Soviet triumph of 1945?

At the founding congress of the Russian Communist Party, in June 1990, General Albert Makashov, commander of the Volga-Urals military district, complained that, "because of the victories, the so-called victories, of Soviet diplomacy, the Soviet Army is being driven without a fight from countries which our fathers liberated from fascism." Not all military commanders were so outspoken, but many felt that Eastern Europe had been "lost" by the politicians' mistakes.

There were more mundane grievances. In a country with a severe housing shortage, what was going to happen to hundreds of thousands of returning troops who had nowhere to live? It was not the rank and file conscripts who caused the problem—they could be put in barracks—but the tens of thousands of officers and their families, all of whom needed apartments and schools.

With the benefit of hindsight, it is not surprising that the military's discontent with Gorbachev should have bubbled over. The only real surprise is that it took so long to happen. On October 25, on the eve of Gorbachev's departure for a visit to Spain, the defense establishment showed what it thought of his peace-making trips abroad, by carrying out a nuclear test at Novaya Zemlya in the Soviet Arctic. An adviser lamely told the press that Gorbachev had not known about it in advance.

Since September, the press had been full of accusations and counteraccusations about a possible military coup, based on a flurry of unexplained troop movements in central Russia. While the military denied anything was afoot, many were convinced that more was involved than the potato harvest and rehearsals for the November parades.

The allegations about troop movements were serious because they came from within the military, increasingly divided between younger officers and the older generation. Colonel Sergei Kudinov, an Afghan war veteran and head of the political department of the Ryazan paratroop school, told deputies from Democratic Russia, on September 25, that troops of his unit had been suddenly put on the alert and issued with ammunition on September 9. Units of the Pskov airborne division and the Vitebsk airborne division of KGB troops—elite units who were to be involved in the Baltic events in January—were also reported to have made sudden unexplained flights in the Moscow region. Worried deputies asked questions in parliament but were told that nothing unusual was going on.

As the right-wing rumbling grew, there were attempts to turn Gorbachev, once and for all, against the left-wing democrats, by accusing them of attempting to seize power by force. A Tass commentary linked the democrats to a pamphlet calling for mass civil disobedience. Its author, a fringe right-winger named Valery Skurlatov, later turned up in a group of self-styled "centrists" who called for power to be transferred to a "Committee of National Salvation."

Discontent about Gorbachev was also rising in the powerful and secretive world of the defense industry, whose leaders signed an unprecedented letter to *Pravda*. Economic reform was destabilizing the defense industry and creating "a critical situation that is getting out of control," they complained.[6]

It is highly unlikely that an outright military coup against Gorbachev—the nightmare of some democrats—was on anyone's agenda at this time. But it was clear, by November, that the army was prepared to use its considerable leverage with the political leadership to defend its own interests. In return for propping up Gorbachev, the army would exact certain conditions. It was not an open rebellion, but a challenge to Gorbachev's authority.

The army's public lobbying was strongly enhanced by the presence of officers on active service as deputies in the parliaments of the Union and most of the republics. These outspoken uniformed deputies were, in effect, no longer subject to discipline from their superiors. It was these "lads in epaulettes" that Shevardnadze blamed for his resignation. Their most prominent spokesmen were army Colonel Nikolai Petrushenko, from Kazakhstan, and air force Colonel Viktor Alksnis, a Russified Latvian, whose grandfather had founded the Soviet air force.

In early November, a conference of military deputies in Moscow presented Defense Minister Marshal Dmitry Yazov with a long list of grievances and a request to meet Gorbachev in person, to voice their complaints. The meeting took place not on Gorbachev's home turf in the Kremlin but on what amounted to military territory, the Central House of the Soviet Army, in central Moscow.

Yazov opened by telling Gorbachev bluntly that the army was experiencing "negative moods, tension, and dissatisfaction." What followed was an angry and well-orchestrated series of complaints that Gorbachev was doing nothing to protect servicemen against hostile attacks from "ethnic extremists" in the republics. There was "anti-army hysteria" in Latvia and machine gun attacks on soldiers in Moldavia, Captain A. Dubinin complained. Turning to Gorbachev, he asked him point blank: "Do you, as president, the government, and the people need an army at all? If so, then it must not be left as it is."

Colonel V. Suvadevidze, from Georgia, complained that the army was being persecuted by newly emergent anti-Communist political groups. While the Communists sat in their offices, waiting to be elected as deputies, history taught them a lesson. "At first we called them informals, then we legalized them as sociopolitical parties, and now they will govern us," he declared.

The new Georgian authorities had halted the draft and declared a local cold war against the army, Colonel Suvadevidze complained. The army was isolated, deprived of its rights, and its officers turned into second-class citizens. Officers from the Baltic states and the strongly nationalist western Ukraine rose to tell similar stories of "moral terror."

"When is all this going to stop?" asked one. The litany of complaints included attacks on Soviet television and the press for undermining army morale. Virtually all the deputies insisted on the early signing of a new Union treaty, to

define the army's status in the republics, and on better pay
and conditions.

The atmosphere became charged with emotion. A Georgian officer, a deputy to the Estonian parliament, told Gorbachev that "I have many comrades whose destinies and
families are breaking up. Look at the auditorium. Before you
are people who imbibed the words 'Motherland, honor, and
loyalty to the Motherland' with their mother's milk."

When Gorbachev got up to reply in this highly charged
arena, his speech was repeatedly interrupted by shouts from
the floor. Soviet television edited out the worse moments, but
Izvestia's report left readers in no doubt about the heckling.

The next day, Colonel Alksnis told the Union Supreme
Soviet that "a terrible thing" had happened at the meeting
between Gorbachev and the military deputies. "Yesterday,
the USSR President was left without any armed forces." He
described it as a dialogue between a blind man and a deaf
man and said Gorbachev had failed to answer the army's
grievances. The army, Alksnis warned, had no intention of
staging a coup, but it was at the end of its tether and would
soon take up arms in self-defense. "And this will not be any
military coup, people will be protecting their human rights."

The emotional speech by Alksnis would not have mattered
if someone had sprung to Gorbachev's defense. But the debate, on the day the Supreme Soviet returned from recess,
turned into a general revolt in which the deputies overturned
their set agenda and demanded that Gorbachev appear in
person, to deliver a State of the Union address. *Izvestia* described it as a "legislative strike" by deputies, who were
reflecting the anger and fear in their home constituencies
over economic collapse and food shortages.

Gorbachev had his back to the wall. He could hardly go
back to the angry parliament and tell them he had decided
to go into coalition with Yeltsin. His aides Nikolai Petrakov
and Georgy Shakhnazarov urged him to resign as Communist
Party leader and stake everything on a direct presidential
election, but he ignored their appeals.[7]

When Gorbachev broke his silence, two days later, on
November 16, it was clear from his opening remarks about a
"struggle for power" that he was going to meet the hard-line
backlash halfway. He denounced the left-wing democrats and
the independence movements in the republics for "shameless
manipulation of public opinion" and "frenzied attempts to
discredit the army and other institutions of state power." He
proclaimed, "Enough of defending ourselves. We must go on
the offensive! We must rid ourselves of our inhibitions!"

Gorbachev's answer to the problem of the power vacuum was to sign the new Union Treaty as fast as possible. Until this was achieved, he proposed a new interim structure and a major reorganization of the central government. He promised the army their concerns would be met and told the deputies not to get excited about his talks with Yeltsin.

Yeltsin, speaking after Gorbachev, laid the blame for paralysis of power on the "crisis of the totalitarian regime" and renewed his calls for the departure of the Ryzhkov government. He called for its replacement by "a coalition body, perhaps an extraordinary anticrisis committee" formed by the fifteen union republics.

Replying, Ryzhkov accused Yeltsin of pursuing a destructive policy which would "lead to the collapse of a state which has taken centuries to create."

Gorbachev's speech had satisfied nobody. Overnight, according to Shatalin, he consulted old comrades from the party leadership, shunning advisers such as Yakovlev, who like Ryzhkov was totally taken unawares by his twenty-minute speech the following morning.[8]

In the short speech, Gorbachev announced the abolition of the Presidential Council, an increase in his own presidential powers, the upgrading of the Federation Council, which included the leaders of the republics, and the creation of a Security Council, to give the army and KGB a direct voice in policymaking, the creation of a new state vice-presidency, and the abolition of the old governmental structure. Instead of the Council of Ministers, there would be a new, streamlined Cabinet of Ministers headed by a *premyer-ministr*. But the hard-line deputies and the military wanted more. In particular they wanted the scalp of the liberal interior minister, Vadim Bakatin, who had negotiated the transfer of authority over the police to the governments of the republics. Colonel Alksnis, one of the new stars of the Soyuz ("Union") group of deputies, gave Gorbachev thirty days to restore order in the country or face demands for his resignation. In view of the rising strength of the Soyuz group, it was not a threat Gorbachev could take lightly. They also targeted Foreign Minister Eduard Shevardnadze, attacking him for siding with the West against Moscow's old ally Saddam Hussein and for allegedly offering to send Soviet troops to the Gulf.

Gorbachev also published his draft Union Treaty, appealing, over the heads of the "separatist" leaders of the rebel republics, for support. "I have come to the firm conclusion that we cannot separate," he declared.

Marshal Yazov appeared on television, on Gorbachev's explicit instructions, to denounce attacks on the army and announce that servicemen would be allowed to use their weapons in self-defense. Yazov also declared that the nuclear weapons would remain under central control and that the army would deploy itself anywhere on Soviet territory that it thought fit. If local authorities moved against the army by cutting its supplies of water or electricity, local commanders would have the right to seize these facilities and put them under military control.

More concessions to the military followed close behind: On December 2, Vadim Bakatin was dismissed and replaced as interior minister by Boris Pugo, a hard-liner who had once headed the KGB and the Communist Party in Latvia. Significantly, his first deputy was to be General Boris Gromov, one of the Soviet army's rising stars and the man who commanded the pullout from Afghanistan.

But the tide of right-wing complaints continued: In early December, Gorbachev faced another rowdy audience, this time of conservative industrial managers, who drowned out his speech with angry shouts and called for a state of emergency.

KGB chief Vladimir Kryuchkov was soon on television as well, painting a lurid picture of rising crime, foreign subversive intrigues, and economic sabotage. It was not just the army that was determined to remind Gorbachev of its vital importance. Kryuchkov promised that the KGB "has acted and will act as a barrier against those forces which seek to push the country toward chaos."

Pugo, Kryuchov, and Yazov were all to be leading conspirators in the August 1991 coup, as members of the self-styled "Committee on the State of Emergency." All of them were Gorbachev appointees. Gorbachev's reshuffle of the organs of power also involved the creation of a vice-president. Though the Moscow rumor mill had strongly tipped such names as Shevardnadze and Kazakhstan President Nazarbayev, Gorbachev's final choice rested on a colorless trade union chief and former party *apparatchik* named Gennady Yanayev. Gorbachev, in words he must have recalled with a stab of remorse a few months later, praised Yanayev as "a man I can trust." When Yananyev failed to win endorsement by parliament in the first round, Gorbachev laid what was left of his prestige on the line and insisted they should vote a second time. Yanayev provoked mirth among Soviet intellectuals when asked at a news conference about his health. "My wife is not complaining," he replied.

Gorbachev gave a dramatic speech to a group of writers at the end of November which betrayed his personal dilemma: either he could go on reforming the Soviet Union, or he could try to keep it together, but he could not do both. Stubbornly, he confessed his refusal to abandon his socialist beliefs. To do so would be to betray the memory of his grandfather, a collective farm pioneer, who had kept his faith in socialism, despite being arrested and tortured in 1937. "I cannot go against my grandfather, I cannot go against my father. . . . Did they live in vain?" In the same way, he would never give up his opposition to private ownership of land: "Do with me what you will, I do not accept it." As for the battle to keep the Soviet Union together, "One must fight to the last trench, as at Stalingrad." The state formed over a thousand years had to be kept together; splitting it up would mean a terrible civil war.[9]

What the hard-liners in the army and the security forces wanted from Gorbachev most of all was not the restoration of socialism or a return to the old monolithic unity of the Brezhnev era. It was vigorous use of force to reestablish central control in the republics. In order to keep the Soviet Union together, they wanted a combination of emergency powers and direct presidential rule. To win support for this goal, they used widespread popular concern over food shortages, crime, and economic breakdown to justify a crackdown. The strategy was to bracket the democrats with these problems and portray them as architects of the shadow economy. When Pugo addressed television viewers, he promised "decisive action against insolent criminals who are attempting to exploit the complexities and difficulties of the present time." For those who had not yet got the message, Kryuchkov rammed it home a few days later. Organized crime, leaders of the shadow economy, national chauvinists, and anti-Communists were pooling their forces to destroy the Soviet Union, he argued. Democrats and black marketeers were bracketed together under the catchall term "economic sabotage."[10]

It is hard to assess the extent to which Gorbachev was a willing participant or a reluctant dupe in this operation. He was probably a little of each. The new course showed all his characteristic ambivalence. When he addressed the Congress of People's Deputies, on December 18, he thundered against "dark forces" and promised "decisive measures" against separatists, but gave no specifics. Alksnis and Yuri Blokhin, another Soyuz leader, complained about the lack of concrete pledges. Vladimir Chernak, a Ukrainian deputy, provoked laughter by telling the Congress that Gorbachev was at the head of a silent, creeping, right-wing, reactionary *coup d'état*—and adding: "Possibly he himself does not know this."

Forced, by his own weakness, into seeking some kind of alliance, Gorbachev sought above all to avoid becoming a permanent hostage of any group. A full-scale coalition with Yeltsin and the left would tie his hands forever, but a partnership with the military could be just a temporary expedient. If the generals and colonels thought they could manipulate Gorbachev, then he could manipulate them, too.

On December 20, in a dramatic speech to the Congress of People's Deputies, Shevardnadze announced that he was resigning, but he avoided any criticism of Gorbachev, directing his barbs at the "lads in Colonel's epaulettes" who had been sniping at him. "Dictatorship is on the way; I state this with full responsibility," the white-haired foreign minister declared in his thick Georgian accent, dismissing attempts to interrupt him with a wave of his hand. "No one knows what kind of dictatorship this will be and who will come—what kind of dictator—and what the regime will be like. I want to make the following statement. I am resigning. Let this be— do not interrupt me, do not insult me—let this be my contribution, if you like, my protest against the onset of dictatorship."

Shevardnadze clearly felt that Gorbachev was on the wrong path and surrounding himself with the wrong people—a view that was to be proved correct in August 1991. But he was too loyal to undermine his chief by saying so in public.

Gorbachev was surprised and discomfited by the sudden resignation of the man with whom, as he had told the writers at the end of November, he had walked on the beach at Pitsunda, in 1985, and discovered a common hatred for the old system. Shevardnadze had been considering resignation for months, ever since it became clear that Gorbachev would not protect him wholeheartedly against the attacks of the military. Shevardnadze felt humiliated by the discovery that the Soviet defense ministry had undermined the agreement he had negotiated on reducing conventional forces in Europe, by shipping some of its weaponry east, beyond the Urals. He disclosed some of his worries about a looming dictatorship, back in November, to Latvian Foreign Minister Janis Peters.[11] Sensing that Gorbachev was beginning to take the military's side, he was not prepared to defend the new line to a Western audience.

Where were Yeltsin and the democrats? Shevardnadze, in

his resignation speech, accused them of scattering. "The reformers have fled into the bushes," he remarked bitterly. The accusation was harsh but not unjustified. Many of the democrats were grappling with trying to keep their cities supplied with food. In the Supreme Soviet, the Interregional Group was caught in a dilemma between its function as an all-Union alliance and its support for shifting power to the republics. Many democrats were reluctant to oppose the growing calls for tighter maintenance of law and order. Meanwhile the centralizing Soyuz group, with no inhibitions about its role, was setting the pace.

Yeltsin was preoccupied with steering a major agricultural reform, which would reestablish private farming, through the Russian Congress of People's Deputies, at the end of November, and appeared to be paying little attention to the right-wing offensive. As he argued in his opening speech to the Russian Congress, ensuring food supplies for the winter and warding off famine should take priority over political confrontation.

On December 19, Yeltsin denounced Gorbachev for accumulating powers without precedent in Soviet history: "Neither Stalin nor Brezhnev possessed such a volume of legally formulated power." The new course, he predicted, would reach an impasse and increased pressure on the republics would fail. "It is impossible to halt objective processes with force." Russia, he warned, would not agree to the restoration of a Kremlin *diktat* over the republics. "This does not mean the disintegration of the Union. On the contrary, this is the only way to save it."

But not all democrats shared his opposition to giving Gorbachev extra powers. Many shared the longing for what Migranyan described as a "good dictator" who would prevent the emergence of something worse. Even liberals saw a strong presidency as essential, if democratization and economic reform were to have any chance of succeeding.

When Shevardnadze resigned, Yeltsin dismissed his action as a mistake and implied that the Foreign Minister had been too sensitive to criticism. Interviewed by Russian radio on January 5, Yeltsin said: "I do not think he [Shevardnadze] was justified, despite all the objective factors he mentioned: the circumstances, the difficulties, and the possibility of dictatorship, and so on, and the criticism. What about Yeltsin, who has had to put up with so much criticism?" In late December, Yeltsin had faced a resignation problem of his own, when his young finance minister, Boris Fedorov, walked out, accusing the Russian government of incompetence and excessive spending in a search for easy popularity. The first ten days of January were spent in a complicated wrangle with the central government over how much Russia should contribute to the 1991 budget.

Gorbachev was now abandoned by his reformist allies and advisers Yakovlev, Bakatin, Shatalin, and Shevardnadze. In their place were such men as Marshal Yazov, Boris Pugo, Vladimir Kryuchkov, and the new vice-president, Gennady Yanayev. Gorbachev replaced the head of Soviet television with Leonid Kravchenko, who was to tighten the screws on the increasingly freewheeling reporters and news teams. Ryzhkov, who had suffered a heart attack, was eventually replaced as head of government by his portly, crew-cut finance minister, Valentin Pavlov. (Pavlov was also to join the August coup, as a member of the Emergency Committee, while Kravchenko was the man who acted as its messenger, personally delivering to Tass news agency the Committee's announcement of its assumption of power.) By January, Gorbachev was even suggesting the press should be put under legislative supervision.

The real test of Gorbachev's new course and of Shevardnadze's warning of dictatorship was to come not in Moscow, but in the wayward Baltic states. The hard-liners wanted, above all, to see Gorbachev take firm steps to end the Baltic march toward independence.

They Fought for the Motherland

"**I** learned about what happened on Monday morning. The report about the tragedy came as a surprise to all," Gorbachev told journalists, the day after soldiers of the Soviet army stormed the television tower in the Lithuanian capital, Vilnius, on January 13, killing thirteen civilians.

If true, it was an extraordinary admission. While millions around the world were following news of civilians being crushed under tank tracks, the man supposedly in charge of the Soviet army was sleeping undisturbed. Many found Gorbachev's version to be a transparent attempt to evade responsibility for the bloodshed, by blaming the local military commander. Others saw it as further evidence of his shaky control over the military.

Historians will probably argue for years about who ordered the violence in Vilnius, in the early hours of January 13, and the parallel events in Riga, a week later, when riot police stormed the Latvian Interior Ministry, killing five people.

Was it all part of a master plan approved by Gorbachev, which he only denied when it went wrong? Or was he only the puppet of military and political leaders following their own private agendas? Was it conspiracy or confusion? Like the famous *putsch* of General Lavr Kornilov against the Provisional Government, in 1917, a classic moment of civilian-military conflict, the Baltic crisis provides ammunition for supporters of both theories.

The wide political fallout of the Baltic crisis made it different from previous military actions in the republics. More people were killed by troops in Tbilisi, in April 1989, and in Baku, in January 1990, but the shockwaves at the center were smaller. For the first time, Gorbachev's image outside the Soviet Union, as a great peacemaker, was seriously damaged.

Yeltsin's role in the crisis is easier to assess. He did not detonate the political earthquake, but placed himself deliberately in its epicenter—a risky decision which was to have far-reaching consequences for his own career. It was a kind of dress rehearsal for the role he was to play in August 1991, rallying opposition to the Moscow coup, by defying the Emergency Committee from the Russian parliament.

Yeltsin's intervention on the side of the Baltics had a decisive influence on his relations with Gorbachev, leading to a bitter confrontation that was to last until April. It also made him the target of violent attacks from the Soviet army. Without it, the course of Russian politics would have been different in the first half of 1991.

Yeltsin's close personal ties with the Baltics, particularly with Latvia, dated back to long before the election of independence-seeking governments in 1990. Back in the summer of 1988, during his political disgrace, it was a Latvian newspaper, *Sovietskaya Molodezh*, which first took the risk of interviewing him while he was vacationing in the resort of Jurmala, near Riga.

In late July 1990, after his election as chairman of the Russian parliament, he headed once again for Jurmala. But his agenda included more than tennis and walks along the beach. Yeltsin seized the chance to forge links with the new leaders of the Baltics, a clear gesture of solidarity in the face of pressure on them from Moscow to back away from their search for independence.

Even before Yeltsin's election, the Baltics saw the newly elected Russian Supreme Soviet as a potential ally against Gorbachev. Estonian Supreme Soviet Chairman Arnold Ruutel, in a message to the Russian parliament on May 14, 1990, promised that an independent Estonia would be as good a neighbor for Russia as Finland was. He invited the Russian legislature to struggle against "imperial thinking" and promised that the rights of the Russian minority in Estonia would be fully respected.[1]

News of Yeltsin's election produced "an explosion of applause and a burst of satisfaction and joy" in the Estonian parliament.[2] Not surprisingly, the Estonians, Lithuanians and Latvians courted him from the start, as a potential counterweight to Gorbachev. On July 28, during Yeltsin's brief vacation in Jurmala, he was joined by Lithuania's Vytautas Landsbergis, Latvia's Anatolijs Gorbunovs, and Estonia's Arnold Ruutel and agreed that Russia would sign treaties with them, recognizing their independence. "Our political thinking is very close to Boris Yeltsin's," enthused Andreis Krastins, deputy chairman of Latvia's Supreme Council and chief negotiator.

Addressing the Latvian parliament, on August 1, Yeltsin promised that a treaty between Latvia and Russia would be signed in a month and a half. He hailed the prospect of Russia and the three Baltic republics forming a "fortified chain of defense" against the center.

However, it was not long before the honeymoon was over. During his Latvian vacation, Yeltsin was busy negotiating not only with the Baltics but also with Gorbachev, their persecutor. A day after his speech to the Latvian parliament, he hurried back to Moscow to celebrate his agreement with Gorbachev on economic reform. The Baltic leaders realized that Yeltsin's first priority was a coalition with Gorbachev, and a rapprochement between the two men in Moscow might be at their expense. They were also uncertain how much real power Yeltsin could wield on their behalf. He promised them Russian oil and gas, but could he ensure its delivery, when he exerted no control over all-Union energy supplies?[3] Landsbergis, the musicologist president of Lithuania, took the view that his government would have to wait until the relative powers of the Union and of Russia were defined, before it could decide with whom to talk.[4]

The early enthusiasm on both sides for full-scale political treaties faded when it came to negotiating practical details. Yeltsin was not prepared to acknowledge the Baltic republics' independence on the basis of their prewar statehood, which would have implied recognition of their pre-1940 frontiers and support for their argument that they were "occupied territories." He was also extremely vulnerable to accusations that he was selling out the interests of the Russian-speaking minorities, who made up nearly half the population in Estonia and Latvia. Yeltsin insisted that their representatives should be present during the treaty negotiations and that there should be legal guarantees for their cultural rights.

Yeltsin's deputy, Ruslan Khazbulatov, recounted, in January, why talks with the Baltics came to a standstill. "Because at that stage, the Baltic countries did not want to observe our demands on guaranteeing a legal mechanism of protection. Therefore we brought them [the talks] to a standstill, we stopped them."[5]

Nonetheless, leaders of the Russian minorities took the view that Yeltsin had betrayed them; their views were frequently expressed in the conservative and Russian nationalist press in Moscow. "You have managed not to notice that, in Lithuania, you are supporting an anti-Russian government," wrote a Russian woman engineer from Vilnius.[6]

Yeltsin's second problem was that he could not afford to identify too closely with the Baltic states without offending another powerful lobby with which he wanted to remain on good terms: the military.

His own preference was for keeping the Union together, at least as a loose confederation of sovereign states and a single economic community. The idea of negotiating a network of separate bilateral treaties between republics was to provide a basis for such a Union. But the Baltics did not share this vision, making it clear that they wanted no part of any new Union Treaty, whatever its terms. Yeltsin's view was that by applying pressure, Gorbachev had forced the Baltics into seeking outright independence, when they might have been satisfied with less.

"The Balts did not ask for much at the start. They asked for economic independence. It should have been granted at once: take your economic independence! Have treaty relationships with other republics, as we have now proposed to each republic! Let us conclude a bilateral treaty! I think that the current processes taking place there in the Baltics would have been inevitable anyway. But they would have passed off more easily, significantly more easily, if there had been no resistance." The Baltic desire for independence was not a sign of nationalism but a sign of their desire for a long-suppressed national dignity, he argued.

"Say one, two, or three republics break away. What of it? What of it? We will conclude treaties; we will live; we will be friends; we will talk to each other," Yeltsin told an interviewer in October 1990.[7]

Later, Yeltsin was to voice regret that he had not given higher priority to completing treaty negotiations with the Baltics. The treaties with Estonia and Latvia were finally signed in the middle of the January 1991 crisis, and the Lithuanian treaty, not until late July 1991.

When the January crisis in the Baltics erupted, it had been widely signaled in advance, during weeks of rising tension. By December, the only piece of guesswork was where the crackdown would come—Lithuania or Latvia? But Yeltsin's attention was directed elsewhere. If he did appreciate what was about to happen, he gave no public sign of it, being preoccupied with Russian problems. In early January, he was involved in another public argument with Gorbachev over the size of the RSFSR's contribution to the Union budget.[8]

Meanwhile there were public warnings, from Landsbergis, of the danger of a coup, frequent incidents involving Soviet troops, and complaints from the military that their position in the Baltic states was becoming intolerable. In Latvia, a force of riot police called Special Purpose Militia Units (OMON), also known as the "black berets," operating outside the control of the Latvian Interior Ministry, seized a printing plant claimed by the local pro-Moscow Communists.

The Baltic governments were increasingly suspicious of Moscow's sudden shifts of policy. Latvian president Anatolijs Gorbunovs was promised, by Armed Forces Chief of Staff General Mikhail Moiseyev, that no more troops would be sent to the Baltics, but three days later, on January 7 Defense Minister Marshal Dmitry Yazov ordered thousands of paratroopers in to enforce the draft.

If decisive military action were to happen, it would make sense for it to coincide with the expiration, on January 15, of the United Nations deadline for Iraq to withdraw from Kuwait. The pattern would follow that of 1956, when Soviet intervention, to suppress an anti-Communist uprising in Hungary, coincided with the Suez crisis in the Middle East.

On January 9, Yeltsin made his first public statement, condemning the dispatch of paratroops: "I am against such a decision. Violence leads to further violence. We must, therefore, negotiate," he told reporters, after meeting Japanese parliament members.[9]

On January 10, Gorbachev took a decisive step, warning Lithuania that he might impose presidential rule unless the republic restored the Soviet constitution, a demand he knew would be rejected. "The situation in essence is entering a dead end. . . . The people demand the restoration of the constitutional order, safe guarantees of security, and normal conditions of life. They demand the imposition of presidential rule," he told Tass. "We have to face the truth and see the genuine causes of the present situation. They are rooted in gross violations of the Soviet constitution," he said. Landsbergis and the Lithuanian Supreme Soviet were "trampling on the political and social rights of the people and striving, under the slogans of democracy, to implement a policy aimed at restoring the bourgeois system."

Was Gorbachev cynically using demands from the local pro-Moscow Communists, or did he really believe his own propaganda that the "people" were demanding presidential rule? After the bloodshed around the television tower, he made repeated defensive references to thousands of telegrams from Lithuania, begging him to intervene.

Lithuania seems to have been chosen for the crackdown, rather than Latvia, because of a domestic political crisis there, caused by the resignation of Prime Minister Kazimiera Prunskiene, in a dispute over price rises.

Yeltsin spoke to Gorbachev about the Baltics on January 10, reminding him that, under RSFSR law, Russian conscripts were not to be used in other republics to intervene in domestic conflicts, without the Russian government's consent. The conversation was apparently without result. On January 12, before a meeting of the Federation Council, Yeltsin convened the Presidium of the Russian Supreme Soviet and won their backing for a blistering statement, issued in his name, warning against the use of force:

> In recent days the situation has been considerably exacerbated in the Baltic republics, especially in Lithuania. This has been caused not only by internal political factors but also by the actions of the Union leadership. Under the crisis conditions that the country is currently experiencing, such a development could give rise to extremely dangerous consequences for all Union republics and complicate even further the formation of a Union of sovereign states.
>
> These events are evoking serious concern among the world community. The appeal to the USSR leadership, to refrain from the use of force and to seek a solution to political problems solely through talks, is being heard more and more insistently all the time.
>
> The Presidium of the Russian Federation Supreme Soviet states:
>
> 1. The use of military force against peaceful citizens in the Baltic republics is inadmissible. This could cause an escalation of violence in this and other regions and unleash a large-scale civil conflict.
>
> 2. The interests of the people of the Baltic republics can only be represented with full authority by the organs of power that they have elected.

3. The use of the army against the legal organs of power is unlawful and unconstitutional.

4. The sending of servicemen, conscripted from RSFSR territory for active service beyond the boundaries of the republic, for the performance of tasks for which there is no provision under article twenty-nine of Russia's constitution, is at variance with the 11 December 1990 decision of the Russian Federation Congress of People's Deputies and is, consequently, illegal.

5. In the existing situation, provoking interethnic conflicts and setting various groups of the population against each other is especially impermissible.

The RSFSR Supreme Soviet Presidium calls for the withdrawal of the additional contingents of the Armed Forces from the Baltic republics and for guarantees from the Union leadership that force will not be used to tackle the problems that have arisen. It calls for the Union leadership to begin talks, as soon as possible, with the legal representatives of the Baltic republics and for a way out of the crisis to be sought by means of dialogue and a quest for mutually acceptable compromises with the strict observance of the rights of all citizens irrespective of their nationality.

The RSFSR Supreme Soviet Presidium expresses its confidence that prudence will prevail and that the Baltic republics will not be turned into an arena for civil conflicts and a beachhead for an offensive by reactionary forces striving to establish a dictatorship in the country.[10]

The Federation Council was essentially a consultative body with no decision-making powers. On January 12, it brought together Gorbachev, most of the leaders of the union republics, including Latvia's Gorbunovs, and top security officials. Yeltsin and other republic leaders extracted a promise from Gorbachev that no force would be used in the Baltics. "Everyone spoke out against events in Lithuania," Gorbunovs told reporters. Uzbek leader Islam Karimov quoted Gorbachev as saying, "Until all the circumstances are fully clarified, no pressure will be applied through force." It was agreed that a fact-finding delegation, headed by Armenian President Levon Ter-Petrosyan, should fly to Vilnius to find out what was going on.

Yeltsin briefed reporters: "We are worried that events could develop that could make it essential—as some people already think—for the army also to restore order. We regard this as an unprecedented thing, as an instance of forcible interference, as evidence of pressure on an independent, self-governing state." The risk was not just to Lithuania but for all the other republics, including Russia. "This is the next Afghanistan," Yeltsin warned. "We have already had Tbilisi, Azerbaijan, Armenia, Fergana, and so on. To have yet another bloody wound on our already lacerated body is of course unacceptable."

Yeltsin complained that Gorbachev was being given "rather one-sided information" by military commanders from the Ministry of Internal Affairs, headed by Pugo and General Gromov.

Just as it looked as though a breathing space had been won, the crisis erupted in Vilnius. According to the official version of events, a self-styled "National Salvation Committee" appealed for protection from the local garrison commander, who obligingly sent his troops to break through a human chain around the television tower and stop its "anti-Soviet broadcasts." What did Gorbachev know, and when did he know it? Who gave the orders? Was his promise to the Federation Council not to use force a deliberate deception, or was it sincere? Yeltsin seems to have gone out of his way to avoid blaming Gorbachev personally for the bloodshed. But there is strong evidence from other participants in the Baltic events that Gorbachev had indeed approved some sort of plan that would lead to the overthrow of the Baltic governments and the imposition of presidential rule. To succeed, the intervention would have had to match the singleminded ruthlessness of earlier Soviet operations in Hungary in 1956, Czechoslovakia in 1968, and Afghanistan in 1979.

But as Fyodor Burlatsky wrote, in *Literaturnaya Gazeta*, "History does not repeat itself, and if it does repeat itself, then it is more likely as farce than as tragedy. What happened in Prague, in 1968, cannot happen here. That is all yesterday's news, or rather yesterday's tanks—there is no bringing them back, they are the scrap of history."[11]

In Budapest, Prague and Kabul, the Soviet military followed orders from the civilian leadership without questions. Once started, the operations continued until they were completed, without political hesitations over the spilling of blood. When its vital interests were at stake, the Kremlin leadership showed it was prepared to ignore foreign reaction to its use of force; domestic reaction was virtually nonexistent.

This time, none of these factors applied: civilian control over military operations was, to say the least, uncertain. Much of the time, the military seemed preoccupied with defending its own interests, rather than those of the Kremlin. The operation fizzled out without achieving its political objectives. Not only foreign but domestic reaction was too powerful to ignore. (Eight months later, when tanks were sent onto the streets of Moscow, it appeared that none of these lessons from the failed crackdown in the Baltics had been learned.)

The scenario under which the Kremlin was to intervene to restore order depended on creating at least the semblance of disorder beforehand; this was the role of the mysterious "National Salvation Committees." Their proclamation of power was not intended to become a reality, merely to create the semblance of *dvoevlastie* (dual power) and the excuse for presidential rule. As a statement from the "National Salvation Committee" said, on January 16, "dual power has now been established in Lithuania: the power of the bourgeois-nationalist Supreme Soviet and the power of the Lithuanian National Salvation Committee. This dyarchy [*dvoelastie*] cannot endure and may end at any moment in large-scale civilian bloodshed. To prevent this, the Lithuanian National Salvation Committee, guided by the resolutions adopted at large rallies and meetings of the working people, has appealed to the USSR president to implement the decision of the Third Congress of USSR People's Deputies, on restoring the operation of the USSR and Lithuanian constitutions on Lithuanian territory, by introducing direct presidential rule in the republic."[12]

Colonel Viktor Alksnis, who was in close contact with the Salvation Committee in Latvia, said they told him they did everything Gorbachev had asked them to. He quoted Alfred Rubiks, leader of the pro-Moscow Latvian Communists, as saying "You were right: Gorbachev has betrayed us." Alksnis told a Danish newspaper that the plan was for Gorbachev to resolve the conflict by dissolving both the Baltic parliaments and the National Salvation Committees. "But halfway through he got cold feet and became afraid, and as a result the army is being given the blame for the bloodshed."[13]

After the troops smashed through the human chain of Lithuanians protecting the television tower, Landsbergis tried in vain to call Gorbachev, who refused to come to the phone. But he spoke three times to Yeltsin, who warned Gorbachev the use of troops was unconstitutional. Yeltsin also spoke with Yazov, who denied any order to shoot. Yeltsin decided, with the backing of his Presidium colleagues, to fly to the Baltic region himself, as a gesture of solidarity with the three republics. Rather than Vilnius or a Russian town on the border, they chose Tallinn, the Estonian capital. "The CPSU Central Committee learned about our plans and tried to torpedo the talks. We were warned that an attack was being prepared on Yeltsin's plane," Estonian prime minister Edgar Savisaar recounted later.[14]

Yeltsin flew to Tallinn from Moscow and met Gorbunovs and Ruutel. Landsbergis, holed up behind barricades in his parliament building in Vilnius and expecting a military assault, did not make the journey to Tallinn but agreed to the text of a joint statement by the four republics which was sent to him by fax.

The statement reaffirmed that only legally elected bodies could exercise power and "actions by parallel structures . . . are illegal." It declared the use of armed force inadmissible, promised concrete support in the event of a threat arising to each other's sovereignty, and appealed to the United Nations to hold a conference on the Baltic independence issue. It avoided direct attacks both on Gorbachev and on the Soviet army, sidestepping the issue of who exactly was to blame for the violence in Vilnius.

Yeltsin, however, decided to issue a direct appeal to Russian soldiers in the Baltics, a move which was bound to be seen by the military hierarchy as an encouragement to mutiny. It was broadcast, late in the evening of January 13, on Riga radio:

> Soldiers, sergeants, and officers: our fellow countrymen, drafted into the army on the territory of the Russian Federation and now in the Baltic republics:
>
> Today, when our country is going through an economic and political crisis and the healthy forces of society are seeking ways out of the existing difficult situation, using lawful and constitutional forms, you may be given the order to act against legally created state bodies, against the peaceful civilian population that is defending its democratic achievements. Moreover, you may be told that, with your help, order will be established in society. But is it really possible to regard violations of the constitution and laws as the establishment of peace? It is precisely in this direction that you are being pushed by all those who are attempting to solve political problems with the force of army units.
>
> Before you undertake the storming of civilian installations in the Baltic lands, remember your own homes, the present and the future of your own republic, and your own people. Violence against the people of the Baltics will bring about new serious crisis phenomena in Russia itself and harm the posi-

tion of Russians inhabiting other republics, including the Baltic republics.

The aims of reaction are to thwart the process of democratization and the transition connected with it to economic forms guaranteeing the well-being not of individual privileged groups of the ruling class and *nomenklatura*, but of all the people, and to annul the declarations of sovereignty of the republics, which were fought hard for by the peoples, and in this way to frustrate the emergence of a new Union of sovereign states. Such are the aims of reactionary forces attempting to use you, soldiers and officers, in their political game.

Surely you will not agree to the role which they have assigned you. I draw your attention to the fact that the dispatch of servicemen, called up for military service in the Russian Federation, outside the republic, in order to participate in carrying out tasks not stipulated in article twenty-nine of the RSFSR constitution, contradicts the decision of the RSFSR Extraordinary Congress of Peoples Deputies, adopted on December 11, 1990, and is therefore unlawful.

Today, the army itself needs protection, above all, social protection. The Supreme Soviet of the Russian Federation is preparing for the adoption, in the very near future, of a whole series of legislative acts aimed at solving the social and economic problems which now concern you and your families. We categorically reject the view of the army as a reactionary and antipopular force, because we know that the army is, above all, made up of the citizens of our country, its children, to whom the fate of our country is no less dear than it is to all of us. We are sure that the healthy forces within the army will not allow it to take the antipopular path of supporting reaction.

We believe in you, today's officers and soldiers of Russia, for whom, just as for preceding generations of Russian soldiers, honor, valor, courage, nobility, and loyalty to one's people and country are imperishable and supreme moral values.

We turn to historical experience, from which it follows that a wrong step today could affect not only those who make it, but also the next generations. I wish you success in your service and happiness to your families.

Yeltsin changed his route back to Moscow because of security worries. Before leaving Tallinn, he signed a treaty with Latvia, promising to "halt the activity on their territories of organizations and groups which have as their aim the violent destruction of the independence and sovereign statehood of the other contracting party and the violent seizure of power."

On his return to Moscow, Yeltsin held a news conference stating that the events in the Baltics were the beginning of a "powerful offensive against democracy," and that "serious pressure from the right" was being exerted on Gorbachev.

Asked what measures he was taking to protect Russian sovereignty, Yeltsin said he would take immediate steps to set up a Russian security committee and to subordinate state security bodies to the RSFSR Supreme Soviet. He added: "We are increasingly coming round to the idea—this, of course will be discussed in the Supreme Soviet and I am telling you this in a preliminary manner—that after all, it seems that we will not be able to defend sovereignty without a Russian army."[15]

Yeltsin seemed reluctant to blame Gorbachev directly for what had happened: "It is probably very difficult for him to speak out." The violence had pushed Gorbachev's goal of a new Union Treaty even further away. "No one is likely to sign a treaty who has a noose around his neck. You won't find any takers in our country now, among the leaders of all the republics."

According to Bakatin, who spoke to Gorbachev on the day of the killings, Gorbachev's military advisers were feeding him false information and he seemed to know nothing of what had really happened. "He knew nothing. He did not know about the tanks and he thought they [the Lithuanians] started the shooting. He did not even know the correct casualty figures."[16]

Despite Yeltsin's reluctance to accuse Gorbachev directly of the Vilnius events, Gorbachev showed no such restraint in return. Red-faced and stumbling over his words with anger, he addressed the Supreme Soviet on January 15. Backing Defense Minister Yazov, he denied responsibility for the Vilnius deaths, blaming Landsbergis and the Lithuanians. He accused Yeltsin of violating the Soviet constitution, by his remarks about a Russian army. It was a "deliberately provocative political act." Yeltsin would have to withdraw his remarks: "We will count on his common sense not having totally deserted him."

Meanwhile thousands of pro-Moscow Russians in Riga demonstrated, condemning Yeltsin as a provocateur and a traitor to their cause. From the military barracks in the Baltics came statement after statement, all targeting Yeltsin as the real villain of the Baltic drama.

Yet on the other side of the barricades, there was a surge of support for Yeltsin's position. Intellectuals who had hesitated between him and Gorbachev now gave him their full support. A hundred members of the intelligentsia signed an open letter, condemning the crackdown in the Baltics, and the economist Stanislav Shatalin, a member of Gorbachev's presidential council of advisers, publicly broke with the Soviet President.

On January 20, a crowd of several hundred thousand people flocked into Moscow's Manezh Square, to support Yeltsin and the Baltics. Yeltsin did not take part, but his representative, Gennady Burbulis, read a message from him, which belatedly recognized that Shevardnadze's warnings, a month earlier, had been correct. "The danger of dictatorship, about which key leaders of our society have warned, is becoming a reality."

The following day Yeltsin addressed the Russian parliament, again avoiding any direct personal attacks on Gorbachev by name. Instead, he blamed "reactionary forces in the union leadership" and suggested that Gorbachev could still see the error of his ways.

> Our main task in this question is to arrest and stop the union leadership's slide toward reaction . . . The tactics of dialogue have not yet been exhausted, of course. It is essential to convince the central leadership, by both word and deed, that it is today no longer possible to line the country up into one column and fetter it with chains. Life itself will compel the top leaders to understand this.
>
> I think the reactionary turn at the present moment has not reached the point of no return. I am convinced that this strategic political mistake can be and must be corrected. . . . We are in a critical situation but it is not a hopeless one.

Yeltsin's main conclusion was that the republics would be able to stand up to the center, if they formed a common front. He recommended the signing of a quadripartite treaty, among Russia, the Ukraine, Kazakhstan, and Byelorussia, as the nucleus of such an agreement.

Significantly, he did not repeat his throwaway remark about a Russian army, arguing instead that all the republics should be given a stronger voice in deciding all-Union military policy: "It is inadmissible that Russia and the other republics should be wholly sidelined from control of the activities of the Army, and that the latter should be turned into the tool of a few top leaders."

As a wave of furious attacks on Yeltsin in the military press continued, Khazbulatov reaffirmed that the Russian authorities had no desire to split up the Soviet army and would not alter this policy. Yeltsin's remark about a Russian

army was merely a case of him "thinking aloud." He acknowledged in a television interview, on January 24, that Yeltsin's
appeal to the United Nations was "not completely felicitous,"
but said it was made at a moment when it looked as though
a major shooting war was going to break out.

After about ten days, the Baltic crisis gradually cooled
down, but not without more casualties, this time in Latvia,
where a Salvation Committee announced it was taking over.
On January 20, OMON riot police seized the Latvian Ministry
of Internal Affairs, in central Riga, killing five people and
wounding ten. This time the cover from Moscow was less
solid, and after a few hours, the OMON withdrew. Gorbachev's interior minister, Boris Pugo, said they had launched
the assault "in a state of profound emotional excitement,"
effectively admitting that they were acting without orders.[17]
This was a pattern that was to repeat itself over the next few
months.

On January 22, Gorbachev met Gorbunovs and agreed
with him that there was no justification for introducing
presidential rule in Latvia. Three days later, Gorbachev's
representative in Vilnius, Georgy Tarazevich, ruled out presidential rule for Lithuania, recognizing the full legitimacy of
Landsbergis and his parliament. The National Salvation
Committee, Tarazevich said, was "an illegal and anticonsti-
tutional organization."

The support of the local population for the Baltic govern-
ments was too strong, the foreign reaction too critical, and
the domestic opposition, led by Yeltsin, too powerful. The
Latvian shootings may have been a last attempt to force
Gorbachev's hand, at a moment when he was already, as
Alksnis put it, "getting cold feet."

The balance sheet of the crisis was overwhelmingly positive for the Baltic leaderships: they had faced down the
Kremlin and survived. According to Landsbergis's adviser,
Virgilijus Chapaitis, "What the army has achieved cannot be
described as a half-coup. It is at best a quarter-coup."[18]

Yeltsin's vigorous intervention had helped block the plan
for presidential rule. It strengthened his position as the leader
of the democrats and won him new respect from intellectuals.
But by his throwaway remark about a Russian army, he had
severely damaged his links with the military establishment.
His own position looked much less strong on January 24,
when his own parliament, many of them far less radical in
their views, failed to approve a draft resolution condemning
the military crackdown.

Gorbachev had earned the mistrust of both sides; neither the democrats nor the military hard-liners would ever fully trust him again. Colonel Alksnis quoted members of the Lithuanian National Salvation Committee as telling him: "We have done all that Moscow asked of us. Moscow promised that it would travel the second half of the way—the introduction of direct presidential rule—itself. But Moscow has abandoned us. We have been betrayed by the President." The fiery air force officer predicted there would be a civil war and asserted that the army, furious at being made the scapegoat for the Lithuanian events, could "switch to an autonomous operating mode." He compared Gorbachev to a surgeon who starts an operation, makes an incision on the body of the patient, and then leaves him.[19]

Gorbachev had told Yeltsin, on January 12, "I am moving to the right because society is moving to the right." Yeltsin, recounting the conversation two days later, told Gorbachev, "You are wrong, Mikhail Sergeyevich, society is moving to the left, toward democracy."[20] That conversation was to mark the start of three months of bitter confrontation, during which each man would try, and fail, to oust the other from office.

18

The House on the Embankment

Political events, in the first half of 1991, were to move at a dizzying speed. The old fixed rules of the game had been discarded with the comfortable rituals of the past. Gorbachev liked to think of himself as the referee in the center of a soccer match between the forces of the left and the right, occasionally joining one team or the other to score a goal but never making more than temporary alliances. At the end of the game, he could be certain of being on the winning side. But increasingly it seemed as though there were half a dozen teams on the field at once, all shooting for different goals, and most of them ignoring the referee.

In February, it looked as though the relationship between Yeltsin and Gorbachev had broken down irretrievably. But by late April, they had once again struck a compromise, and by June, Yeltsin was even hinting he would support his rival in a Soviet presidential election.

Yeltsin's changes of heart led to fresh accusations of inconsistency and some of his closest supporters charged that he was making a terrible mistake. But behind the apparent shifts, there was a logical pattern.

The December 1990 Congress of People's Deputies, at which Shevardnadze resigned, had ended with the democrats defeated and more demoralized than ever. The right wing was advancing, the Communist Party was resurgent and Gorbachev no longer, it appeared, saw the democrats as allies.

Other ideas were in the ascendant, notably a kind of non-Communist, authoritarian centrism, a "third force," with which Gorbachev seemed to be flirting.[1] "The idea of authoritarian modernization emerged victorious," commented Sergei Stankevich, Moscow's deputy mayor.[2] And while the Baltic crisis in January enabled the left to rally around Yeltsin, Soviet politics had become polarized as never before.

Many on the left demanded Gorbachev's immediate resignation. If he had definitively thrown in his lot with the right, then what was the point in continuing to give him support? This was the position of Stanislav Shatalin, who told Gorbachev in an open letter, full of withering scorn, "A politician should not stay on beyond the point when people pity him."[3]

Yeltsin was initially more cautious, feeling that Gorbachev, however weak his position, was still a useful buffer against the hard-liners. Without him, there might be a real dictatorship. The argument for retaining Gorbachev was expressed by political scientist Alexei Kiva: "What does it mean in the language of political realism, to demand Gorbachev's resignation? It means to vote for the extreme right to come to power."[4] It was an argument that Gorbachev's own advisers used quite openly. His close aide, Georgy Shakhnazarov, told *Der Spiegel* that, if the President was forced out, "You can be sure the democrats would not come to power. The forces that would not tolerate a collapse are simply stronger. Then we would get military dictatorship—without parliaments, without democratic guarantees, and without the right for the media to criticize the President."[5]

The democrats were stuck: If they did nothing, Gorbachev could ignore them in the political equation; if they tried to force him from office, they might be landed with someone far worse. In other words, Gorbachev could compromise with the right without facing a decisive challenge from the left. As Khazbulatov noted ruefully in an interview, in mid-January, "We cannot force our line upon the President in domestic policy."[6]

But an increasing threat to his own position, in February, forced Yeltsin to radicalize his stand.

A clue to Gorbachev's new mood came from Algirdas Brazauskas, leader of the pro-independence Communists in Lithuania and a wily observer of Kremlin affairs. After seeing Gorbachev, in early February, he told journalists that the Soviet President "kept going back to the role of Boris Yeltsin in the political life of the Soviet Union."[7] Gorbachev was especially worried by Yeltsin's attempts to negotiate a quad-

ripartite treaty with Kazakhstan, the Ukraine, and Byelorussia.

Gorbachev was clearly in no mood to build bridges to
Yeltsin and the other republic leaders. At the end of January,
Yeltsin protested vigorously at the announcement of joint
military and police patrols, put into effect not by Gorbachev
himself but by his defense and interior ministers, by a secret
order, dated December 29. Yeltsin argued that such use of the
military in civilian areas was a double violation of the Soviet
constitution, because it ignored the rights of the republics
and also exceeded the ministers' powers.

"Our declared sovereignty notwithstanding, we are completely unprotected in Russia," Yeltsin complained. "In practice, a state of emergency is being introduced. No one has
consulted or is consulting us." Yeltsin again put the blame
for the Baltic events not on Gorbachev but on "a very conservative group." He continued: "When I spoke with the
President and asked who issued the orders, the answer was,
'I do not know.' When I spoke with the Minister and asked
who issued the orders, the answer was, 'I do not know.' " He
added, "The offensive against Yeltsin has begun. None of this
is a coincidence."[8]

Yeltsin soon had more to complain about. In early February, Radio Rossiya, the Russian republic's radio station and
the main channel for Yeltsin and his supporters to broadcast
their views, was told it could no longer use the same band as
before. Instead, it would have to switch to a channel that
would be audible to only 60 percent of the republic's population. Oleg Poptsov, head of the Russian broadcasting service,
linked the decision to its coverage of events in the Baltics and
of Yeltsin's speeches.[9]

A few days later came news that bugging equipment had
been discovered in two rooms of the Russian parliament
building, just above Yeltsin's office. The KGB denied that any
bugging was involved and insisted that the equipment was to
monitor telephone conversations and prevent security leaks.

At a news conference, on February 6, Yeltsin disclosed that
he had asked Leonid Kravchenko, chairman of the State
Television and Radio Committee, to schedule an hour's live
interview with him on the First Program, the main TV channel. Kravchenko proposed a half-hour recorded interview on
the Second Program. Yeltsin described this as an insult and
refused.

Meanwhile, the attacks on Yeltsin in the press continued.
On a visit to Kaliningrad province, once Königsberg in Ger-

man East Prussia and now part of Russia, he vigorously denied that he had any plan to set up a Russian army. "I did not and do not state that Russia will set up its own army," he declared before an audience made up of officers of the city army garrison and the Baltic fleet. He also denied rumors that the province would be given up to Germany or used to resettle the Volga Germans.[10]

On February 12, Yeltsin's team suffered a further blow with the resignation of deputy prime minister Gennady Filshin, accused of authorizing a financial deal with a British businessman, involving the illegal sale of billions of rubles in exchange for imports. The discovery of the affair, which Yeltsin accused the KGB of staging, to discredit his government, coincided with accusations, by Prime Minister Valentin Pavlov, of a plot by Western banks to destabilize the ruble.[11]

It soon looked as though the real target would be Yeltsin himself. By February 15, moves were under way to summon an extraordinary Congress of People's Deputies of the Russian Federation, at which Yeltsin's job would be on the line. The request came from 270 deputies, who demanded that Yeltsin deliver a report on his conduct of Russia's affairs.

When the agreed date for Yeltsin's live television interview, February 19, finally arrived, he decided that attack was the best form of defense. There was a real chance that the narrow majority which had elected him to the chairmanship of the Russian parliament might fade away, and he would be removed.

Seated between journalists Oleg Poptsov and Vladimir Lomakin, Yeltsin waited until the last five minutes of his hour-long interview before dropping his bombshell. "In the first two years after 1985 Gorbachev inspired a certain hope in many of us. In fact, from that moment on there began his active policy of—I am sorry—deceiving the people." While using *perestroika*, Gorbachev was in fact trying to preserve the old system, Yeltsin charged. Gorbachev's policy was a failure: Instead of *perestroika*, it had brought monetary manipulation, higher prices, a turn to the right, the use of the army against civilians, bloody clashes between nationalities, an economic crash, and lower living standards.

"There is the result of six years of *perestroika* for you. . . ." Yeltsin declared.

> I have done a great deal. I have made many attempts, several attempts, to cooperate with him. . . . I think my personal mistake was excessive trust in the President. By all accounts,

the center is not going to allow the republics to take independent steps. Having carefully analyzed the events of recent months, I declare: I warned, in 1987, that Gorbachev has in his character an aspiration to absolutization of personal power. He has done this already, and has brought the country to dictatorship, eloquently terming this "presidential rule." I distance myself from the position and policy of the President, and advocate his immediate resignation and the handing over of power to a collective body, the Council of the Federation.

I believe in Russia, and I call upon you, esteemed fellow citizens, esteemed Russians, to believe in our Russia. I have made my choice, and everyone must make a choice and determine his position. I want you to hear me and understand me. I have made this choice. I will not turn off this road. I need the trust and I believe in the support of the peoples of Russia, in your support, and I hope to receive it.[12]

Yeltsin's call for Gorbachev's resignation had been deliberately kept a secret even from close colleagues, such as Khazbulatov. He had deliberately not mentioned it at a meeting of the Russian Supreme Soviet Presidium, on the eve of the broadcast. Many Russians felt it was irresponsible for Yeltsin and Gorbachev to be feuding, at a time when the economy was collapsing further each day. The challenge to Gorbachev was therefore a risky move, and Yeltsin wanted to take sole responsibility for his words. The weakest part of his appeal was that there was no constitutional provision under which power might pass to the Council of the Federation, which was composed of the leaders of the fifteen republics. Although Gorbachev had been elected only by the Congress of People's Deputies, not by a national direct vote, he was still the constitutionally elected head of state, with a mandate running until 1994.

A few weeks later, when Gorbachev modified his course and began cooperating with the democrats again, Yeltsin was to drop his call for Gorbachev to resign and enter a new partnership with him. He defended his remarks in February as a final warning to Gorbachev which had paid off. This seems to have been a rationalization, after the fact. Yeltsin was above all defending his own shaky position by taking the political offensive. He knew from past experience that his best ally, in a confrontation with the "center," was the "center" itself.

Yeltsin had triggered a rise in the political temperature. And he was counting on a groundswell of popular sympathy for himself against his attackers, as in the past. He had gambled with one of the few cards he had to play against Gorbachev—his own popularity.

More worrying was the response of the two other republican leaders whom Yeltsin had been courting, with some success, as allies against Gorbachev—Leonid Kravchuk of the Ukraine and Nursultan Nazarbayev of Kazakhstan. Together with the leaders of Uzbekistan and Byelorussia, they had already met as a group, without Gorbachev, to try to agree on the outlines of a new Union Treaty that would shift more power to the republics.

Kravchuk said he categorically disagreed with Yeltsin's "dictatorial" statement calling for Gorbachev to resign, which he described as rash. But he added a warning to Gorbachev that he would finally have to grasp the reality of republican sovereignty.

Nazarbayev was also critical of Gorbachev, but dissociated himself completely from Yeltsin's speech. "There is no way I can agree with what Boris Nikolayevich Yeltsin said on television. At this crucial moment, when we are experiencing an economic crisis, Yeltsin is organizing a political crisis."[13]

For Nazarbayev, a widely respected figure, it would not be in the interests of Kazakhstan for Gorbachev to disappear. If all power passed to the republics, as Yeltsin was suggesting, then Russia's overwhelming size would mean a reduced role for the other republics. "What is he [Yeltsin] proposing? That the country be headed by the Federation Council, to which the constitution has not given this authority—that is the first thing. Second, there would be no leader of the states, there would be no center at all. Then what, is he proposing that all republics become part of a Russian empire?"[14] Neither Yeltsin nor Gorbachev could afford to ignore the interests of Kazakhstan, the Soviet Union's number three republic, and both had to compete for Nazarbayev's support. After Yeltsin's call for Gorbachev's resignation, it was the Kazakh leader he telephoned. "He called me, and was, it seems to me, depressed," Nazarbayev recalled.

The reactions of Kravchuk and Nazarbayev showed that Yeltsin had stepped too far out of line to count on keeping the most powerful of his new allies. By April, it was clear he had absorbed the lesson that it was more important to stay in step with the Ukraine and Kazakhstan than with Lithuania, Latvia, and Estonia. Yeltsin's own political leverage was not strong enough to enable him to take solo initiatives, either with Gorbachev, as in August, or against him, as in February. Gorbachev was a past master at playing off the leaders of the republics against each other, if they continued to act separately. Only if they formed a partnership could they hope to get their way.

What was Yeltsin's mood at this time? He was frustrated by the setbacks and failures he had encountered in the brief nine months since his election. A short postscript to his autobiography, written at this time, betrays a mood of disillusion. "The past year has put an end to many people's illusions, including mine," he wrote. "This past year has been a year of small, insignificant victories and huge, heavy defeats."

It was not much comfort that his popularity in the opinion polls was still around 70 percent, compared with Gorbachev's rating of 15 percent. "I feel burdened, tired, and drained by this totally senseless conflict." Yeltsin had begun to despair of Gorbachev's ability to detach himself from the old power structures. "It's like watching the death throes of some wounded animal," Yeltsin wrote.

After Yeltsin's television broadcast, the campaign to vote him out of office gathered pace. Six top officials of the Russian Supreme Soviet, led by deputy chairmen Svetlana Goryacheva and Boris Isayev, and the speakers of both chambers issued a statement, on February 21, demanding his resignation. Yeltsin had failed to justify the high hopes placed in him when he was elected, they declared. "Authoritarianism, confrontation, and a tendency to make solo decisions on internal and external policy, as well as contempt for the laws and views of constitutional bodies, have started to show more and more clearly through the initial progressive work," Goryacheva told the Russian Supreme Soviet. Yeltsin's position on economic policy was inconsistent and contradictory, and his remarks about a Russian army caused alarm among the people. "The people are tired of promises and games, of the endless settling of accounts with the center." A special congress should be convened urgently to consider Yeltsin's record. The challenge to Yeltsin was supported by 274 deputies, though the resolution they passed sidestepped his call for Gorbachev's resignation and referred only to the worsening economic situation in Russia. The group of six denied that they were following orders from Gorbachev or the Communist Party headquarters, though Yeltsin's allies were certain they did not act on their own initiative. "Important party interests played a role, and those who signed had been worked on at an appropriate level," Khazbulatov said.[15]

In the central Soviet parliament, deputies lined up at the microphone to denounce Yeltsin and passed a resolution, by

292 votes to 29, accusing him of trying to overthrow the country's legitimately elected supreme organs and "creating an emergency situation in the country."

It was once again open season for the Yeltsin-hunters. "He has a great many problems, and when a person has a lot of problems, he himself becomes a problem. In his speech, he probably became such a problem, not only for the Russian parliament and the Russian people—today he became a problem for the whole of our country," said one deputy.

Yeltsin's opponents in the Russian parliament wanted to convene a special Congress of People's Deputies as soon as possible, in early March; his supporters wanted to delay it until April. The difference was crucial because of the all-Union referendum on the Union Treaty, which Gorbachev had called for March 17. Yeltsin's supporters intended to marshal support by asking the voters to endorse the idea of a directly elected Russian presidency. After a long argument, the Supreme Soviet voted to approve the date of March 28, giving the pro-Yeltsin forces more than a month to mobilize to support him.

Almost immediately, it became clear that popular sympathy for Yeltsin was as strong as ever. On February 24, hundreds of thousands of Muscovites poured into the city's Manezh Square, the huge open space on the north side of the Kremlin, to defend him. The crowd numbered at least half a million, according to some estimates. Yeltsin himself did not attend, but the turnout must have exceeded his hopes. Chants of "Yeltsin, Russia" and "Gorbachev, Resign" echoed around the square. Banners demanded "Hands Off Yeltsin!" and "Yeltsin for President."

The impact of the rally was accentuated by the relative failure of a rival meeting the previous day in the same square, called by the conservative Soyuz group of deputies in the all-Union parliament, to support the armed forces. Instead of the forecast two hundred thousand, only forty thousand turned up to wave portraits of Lenin and red communist flags. Some Soviet newspapers said soldiers were ordered to attend, to swell the numbers.

Gorbachev, who had barely left Moscow for more than a year, except to travel abroad, was meanwhile taking a political gamble of his own, with a trip to the conservative western republic of Byelorussia, where he could count on a warm welcome. Largely untouched by the nationalist ferment of the neighboring western Ukraine and the Baltics, Byelorussia looked, from Moscow, like an ideal place to test the political temperature and drum up support for a Yes vote in the March 17 referendum.

Gorbachev's two speeches in Minsk were a mixed bag of appeals to both the right and the left. To an audience of tractor factory workers, he restated his commitment to reforming the Soviet economy, describing it as "the most militarized in the world." But he also reaffirmed the importance of the "socialist choice" and poured scorn on Western ideas of large-scale privatization of the economy. "We want destatization to proceed in our way and not in Western fashion," he said. "Western marketeers throw us bait, and we bite and pass it off as an achievement of scientific thought." He gave China as an example of a country where market economics had led to a slump. Asked about Yeltsin, he replied that it was not a matter of personal animosity, nor even of tactics, but of "two political lines." Yeltsin's political goals were "at odds with the goals of *perestroika*."

Speaking to the Byelorussian Academy of Sciences, Gorbachev made a bitter attack on those he termed the "so-called democrats," whose use of street demonstrations smacked of what he called "neo-Bolshevism." The democrats called themselves left wing but were in fact "a typical opposition of a right-wing kind." Their ideas, he hinted, came from abroad: reformist slogans were being used to cover up "far-reaching intrigues, which in a number of cases have been born in alien scientific centers and in alien heads. That means someone needs them, but it isn't us."[16]

The "democrats in quotation marks," Gorbachev declared, were trying to break up the Soviet Union, by allying themselves with separatists and fascists: they were striving for power, they were against Communism, they were using psychological warfare. Gorbachev was trying to relaunch his long-time strategy of ruling from the center, seeking broad support for a policy which would take a middle course between the extremes of right and left. But he refused to let go of his ideological heritage, the only step that might have made his position credible. "Nowhere am I embarrassed to say that I am a Communist and adhere to the socialist idea. I will go out with this and, as they say, I will go into the next world with it."

Gorbachev nevertheless went on to hint at the possibility of a truce with his critics, "so that things do not get so far as setting our house on fire." It was less an olive branch and more a recognition that the rise in political tension was benefiting Yeltsin rather than himself. It was to be another two months before Gorbachev, this time under heavy pressure from the right, was to lurch again toward the "democrats in quotation marks" and seek their support. But Gorbachev was already keeping his options open, in case he had to do business with Yeltsin once again.

The hint was too vague to mean anything in practical terms. When Yeltsin addressed a meeting of the Democratic Russia bloc, on March 9, he gave them a blunt message— perhaps too blunt: The time for cooperation with Gorbachev was past, and the democrats must organize themselves into a rival political party to the Communists.

Casting aside his prepared text and speaking directly to the audience in Moscow's House of Cinema, Yeltsin relapsed into Stalinist language against his six critics, describing them as "traitors" and "enemies" and calling on his supporters to "take the offensive."

"Yes, we did make some tactical mistakes, including also me, personally. Gorbachev lulled us to sleep with the five-hundred-days program, pretending it was a mutual program. He managed to lull not only me but also an old wolf like Shatalin. He told us that the resulting program was an interesting and constructive one. Let us fight jointly for it. We believed him . . . we should not have done so." Yeltsin accused Gorbachev of constantly misleading the people and especially the democrats. "It was only on February 19 that I finally summoned up the courage to say that I dissociated myself from Gorbachev's policies." Gorbachev's *perestroika* had after all been just a mirage. "We were deceived, and we must now open our eyes to the fact that it was a lie and go down another path." The democrats should "declare war" on the country's leadership and imitate the striking miners: "Roll up our sleeves and raise our fists!"[17]

While Gorbachev saw the March 16 referendum on a Union Treaty as decisive, Yeltsin saw correctly that the real battles would come later at the Congress, which would decide "whether democracy will be victorious or whether it will lose."

Yeltsin revealed a few days later that his advisers had criticized him for the harshness of his impromptu speech. "I wrote it at night, and when I mounted the rostrum, I realized that I couldn't just read out a speech in that auditorium. I said what I felt. And the next day members of my team came to me and told me I had made mistakes in the speech. The word 'enemies' was unnecessary. I agreed. The word 'war' likewise. I agreed. I should perhaps have read out the text after all, and many errors would then have been avoided."[18]

Despite this unusual *mea culpa*, it was clear that Yeltsin's militant tone helped rally the faithful to more big rallies and demonstrations. Vast crowds poured on to the streets of Moscow, on March 10, chanting, "Gorbachev, get out!" and defending Yeltsin. Two hundred thousand marched in Moscow, seventy thousand in Leningrad, and fifty thousand in Sverdlovsk.[19] Television and the Communist Party press weighed in against Yeltsin, as the man who was trying to tear the country apart.

For Yeltsin, the main question in Gorbachev's referendum, asking people to approve a "renewed federation of equal sovereign republics," was so unclear as to be meaningless. "It is aimed at preserving the imperial and unitary essence of the system," he told a radio interviewer, on the eve of the vote. He rejected Gorbachev's warnings that a No vote would lead to chaos and civil war. "I am convinced there will be no civil war. We simply do not have the social conditions for a civil war. . . . The country's leadership might send the army to some individual spot, against the civilian population, but as a whole, the army will not act against the people."[20]

Yeltsin said that whatever the outcome of the referendum, the Union would not disintegrate, but the old structure was dead. "It will not be possible to drive anyone into the Union by force." Yeltsin said each citizen should make up his own mind how to vote. This recommendation disappointed some radicals in Democratic Russia, who were campaigning for a massive No vote, but Yeltsin must have calculated that a majority Yes was the most likely outcome, and he did not want to end up on the losing side.

What counted was to drum up a big Yes vote for the second question on the ballot, the introduction of a directly elected Russian presidency. Here, a majority was vital, as a test of Yeltsin's public support less than two weeks before the battle, at the Congress, over his future.

Yeltsin said the presidency was needed to fill a vacuum of weak executive power and act as a counterbalance to Gorbachev. "The only power that is strong is power that is based on the support of the people. Therefore, we consider that the President of Russia should be elected not by a narrow circle but by all citizens of the republic, by the whole people. Over the whole history of Russia, which is over one thousand years long, this has never happened before."

Even before the referendum, there were signs that the campaign to remove Yeltsin might be losing momentum. At a news conference, on March 5, Goryacheva and her five colleagues denied that they were seeking his resignation, and softened their proposal for Yeltsin to be called to account at the March 28 congress. What they wanted was merely that Yeltsin should deliver a political report. "That statement should not be regarded as our ultimatum," Goryacheva said.[21] They also confirmed that their statement had been prepared before, not after, Yeltsin's February 19 television appearance. It was clear that the campaign to get rid of Yeltsin predated Yeltsin's call on Gorbachev to resign, by several days.

On March 11, the day after the large pro-Yeltsin rally in the center of Moscow, deputies in the Union parliament dropped the idea of issuing a further condemnation of Yeltsin. It was apparent to many of them that the more they criticized him, the more popular he became. "You know that every one of our actions against Yeltsin increases his rating," commented Nikolai Engver, a deputy from the Urals. Another deputy complained, "In the end we become participants in a show for Yeltsin's benefit."

The "historic" referendum came and went. It proved to be far from the political trump card which Gorbachev had hoped to play. Finally the result was something of a draw. Its effects on the Gorbachev-Yeltsin rivalry were neutral, though arguably Yeltsin gained the most. Gorbachev won a 76 percent majority of votes in favor of his carefully worded question: "Do you think it necessary to preserve the Union of Soviet Socialist Republics as a renewed federation of equal sovereign republics, in which human rights and liberties will be fully guaranteed for all nationalities?" But it was a hollow victory: Lithuania, Latvia, and Estonia had already held nonbinding polls at which a clear majority of the population, even many Russians, voted for independence. Only nine republics cooperated with the referendum, making it more apparent than ever that Gorbachev's writ no longer ran throughout the Soviet Union. The Yes vote did nothing to strengthen his position in negotiating the treaty text with the republics, nor to speed up the process.

Meanwhile, Yeltsin won approval of about 70 percent of his voters for the idea of a Russian presidency, something which Gorbachev said was unnecessary and a danger to the Union. A few days later, he stepped up his challenge to Gorbachev with a militant speech to workers in Leningrad's Kirov factory, a symbolic fortress of past Communist Party strength. "Today we need to save the country not from the enemy without, but from the enemy within," he boomed. Yeltsin made clear there could be no compromise and appealed for the workers' support in resisting plans for a "constitutional coup" against him. "Down with Gorbachev," the workers shouted back. After the presidential election in Russia, Yeltsin promised, Russia's new executive authorities would hold local elections, to remove Communists from local government posts if they sabotaged reform plans. It was a threat aimed at what was perhaps the country's biggest political party—the opportunists—that their jobs would be at stake.

Despite the support of the workers, who threatened to strike if Yeltsin was removed, the outlook for the Congress was uncertain. It was conceivable that Ivan Polozkov's Russian Communist Party would marshal enough votes to remove Yeltsin and elect a replacement.

Gorbachev had stopped short of intervening publicly in the battle over Yeltsin's future, though in a television interview, on March 26, he gave a broad nod of encouragement to the anti-Yeltsin forces. The decision to call a special Congress was "a carefully considered and very responsible decision." Things in the Russian Federation could not continue in such a state, especially the situation in the leadership, he commented.

The fact that the Congress ended with the Communists in disarray and Yeltsin's position strengthened was due to another political mistake by Gorbachev, this time one of huge proportions.

Yeltsin's supporters planned to cap their campaign with a demonstration in the capital, on March 28, to coincide with the opening of the Congress. A week beforehand, the Union parliament approved a decree banning it. Holding a demonstration on a working day would create "considerable obstacles to guaranteeing the necessary public order and safety for citizens and . . . normal working conditions for the capital's establishments, enterprises, and transportation, and it would infringe on the rights and interests of a large number of citizens." Moscow authorities took no notice and said the demonstration could go ahead. A government decree on March 25 banned all demonstrations, picketing, or marches from March 26 to April 15, a period that included not just the Russian Congress but a round of consumer price increases on April 2.

It was a measure of how far the rules of Soviet politics had changed; the right to demonstrate freely, unheard of until 1988, was now something which the authorities could not just take away again when it suited them. An earlier presidential decree banning all demonstrations inside Moscow's inner ring road, without express Kremlin permission, was later overturned by the Constitutional Review Committee, a new legal body which Gorbachev had created.

De facto control of the Moscow streets was taken out of the city's hands by a presidential decree, on March 26, that removed the city's police from the control of the Russian government. Large numbers of Interior Ministry troops and police were deployed to seal off the center of the city. The Interior Ministry announced it had prepared the full panoply of antiriot measures, including water cannons, horseback patrols, riot batons, tear gas, and police dogs. For the first time, armored cars were seen in the capital. A Defense Ministry spokesman explained that the vehicles numbered only twenty-three and had been brought to Moscow to give their young drivers experience in city streets. "Writers from certain newspapers who try to link this perfectly ordinary measure to politics cannot be serious."[22]

When the Russian Congress opened, deputies were, predictably, in an uproar. "Can we hold this Congress behind the bayonets of soldiers?" asked one. Yeltsin, speaking to reporters, called the ban "an unconstitutional action, an insult to the Congress and the people's deputies of the Russian Federation." How could they meet surrounded by bayonets? A protest motion was passed, by 532 votes to 286, and Khazbulatov was dispatched to ask Gorbachev to order the withdrawal of the troops. With this vote, Yeltsin and his supporters won the first round, and the idea of removing him lost further momentum.

Khazbulatov returned from his mission, telling the deputies that Gorbachev refused to budge, but promised to remove the troops the following day. The Russian Congress then decided to adjourn.

In the all-Union parliament, Interior Minister Boris Pugo denied that the presence of troops had anything to do with the Russian Congress. They were designed to cope with the "worsening public-political and criminal situation," he declared. The troops were unarmed, and they were needed because of "a large influx of antisocial elements" in Moscow. "Scores of guns have been taken from criminals, as well as explosives, grenades, and gas canisters." Criminal groups were even using machine guns, and there were reports of illegal vodka sales in the capital, Pugo said, reaffirming that the demonstration in Manezh square would not be allowed to proceed.

Reformist deputies warned that enforcing the ban on demonstrations could lead to violent confrontation. From the hard-line Soyuz group, Colonel Viktor Alksnis replied: "If we permit the rally today, tomorrow, demonstrators will be inside the Kremlin, and within a week, they will be inside this hall."

When the rally assembled, the center of the city was sealed off; columns of military trucks took up positions on streets leading to the Kremlin, as if to ward off an armed assault. Water cannons were parked by McDonald's, and announcements on the Moscow metro told passengers to report any suspicious packages. But the demonstrators defied the show of strength and went ahead. "We have crossed the threshold of fear," Nikolai Travkin, leader of the Democratic Party, proclaimed. Unable to cross the lines of riot police equipped with shields and flak jackets, the protesters—many bearing portraits of Yeltsin and red, white, and blue Russian flags— were able to muster their forces not far away, in Pushkin and Mayakovsky Squares. There were only minor incidents. Estimates of the numbers of demonstrators varied vastly from fifty thousand to nine hundred thousand.

The outcome was widely seen as a self-inflicted political defeat for Gorbachev and an unexpected gift for Yeltsin. By deploying fifty thousand troops on the streets of the capital, Gorbachev seemed to have taken another step toward digging his own political grave. "Today is not the end of *glasnost* but the end of Gorbachev," one official of Democratic Russia told a reporter. "He has become a political corpse."[23] It was not so much a show of strength as a show of weakness.

After the March 28 demonstration came the real business of the Russian Congress, the start of a stormy week of confrontations, insults, fights over microphones, and passionate arguments. Yeltsin spoke for more than an hour, telling the deputies that Russia faced a choice between two political lines—further radical reform or the preservation of the old system in disguise.

> The objective outcome of the past six years has shown that we were dealing not with *perestroika*, but with the last phase of stagnation.
> However, there are also positive results. The country is no longer where it was. The main thing that has changed is people; they have recognized the truth about the society in which they live, about its history, about life in other countries. Millions have awakened. The rotten totalitarian system has definitely lost social support. Democratic forces have grown

up and are becoming stronger. A major result of the past few years has been the weakening of the unitary foundations of the state and the acquisition by the republics of their sovereignty.

As Yeltsin described it, the parliaments and governments of the republics, which for decades had played a purely decorative role, had now been transformed by the democratic elections of 1990. "They could no longer play the role of passive conductors of the policy of Union organs; they could not, because there were millions of other voters behind them; they could not, because the policy of the center diverges from people's basic interests." As the demonstration the previous day had shown, the gulf between the center and the people was growing.

Yeltsin defended the Russian authorities against the charge that they were responsible for economic collapse. Russia in fact owned no more than 15 percent of the fixed assets on its own territory. "Just imagine, fifteen percent! The basic industries of fuel and power generation, iron and steel and engineering belong entirely to the Union. The republic owns essentially nothing in such industries as chemicals, power engineering, instrument manufacturing, and radio," Yeltsin added. Russian authority extended only to light industry, the agro-industrial complex, around half of the fixed assets of the construction industry, around a third of the transport industry and one fifth of the timber industry. This was an admission that the Russian declaration of economic sovereignty the previous year was, in effect, not much more than a piece of paper. "The Russian economy remains to this day, in essence, colonial and dependent." The Soviet Union's financial and budgetary crises were, Yeltsin said, the fault not of his government but of the all-Union government, which had no real plan for reform.

Yeltsin had to pitch his speech to draw support as widely as possible, so he avoided attacks on the Communist Party and demands for Gorbachev's removal. Instead, he asked the Russian Congress to endorse the idea of "a dialogue among all political forces, of all republics, on round-table principles." Among other demands, he asked for the formation of "a coalition government of popular trust and national accord." This was linked to the earliest possible signing of a new union treaty, and the immediate formation of new union bodies. In Russia, there would be a new directly elected presidency and a reorganization of executive power. Yeltsin admitted that he personally had made a number of mistakes

in handling the Russian Federation's numerous internal problems, notably by offering too much sovereignty to the autonomous republics. "We dragged ourselves into competition
against the center in handing out sovereignties. But in this
competition, there can be no winners. In the strategic dimension, the center, Russia, and the autonomous entities are
equally losers. It is time to stop."

Before Yeltsin's speech, his chances of winning approval
for the institution of a Russian executive presidency looked
poor. His opponents managed to delete the proposal from the
Congress agenda, agreeing only to discuss the results of the
referendum on the issue.

Vladimir Isakov, one of the six members of the Supreme
Soviet Presidium opposed to Yeltsin, warned the deputies
that approving the presidency would lead to "a new dictatorship" with Yeltsin as the dictator.

"He is doing everything to achieve his main goal—absolutely unlimited presidential power," he argued, accusing
Yeltsin of "legal nihilism" and "imperial manners." It was
increasingly apparent that the Communist group had quietly
abandoned the idea of forcing Yeltsin's resignation and had
set themselves a more limited goal—denying him the executive presidency. An amendment criticizing Yeltsin's record
won only 320 votes. Even fewer supported a proposal to hold
a no-confidence vote. Ivan Polozkov, leader of the Russian
Communist Party, mounted the rostrum to declare, "I feel
that today is not the time to change the leadership." On April
1, the conservative Communists again blocked discussion of
the presidency, prompting Yeltsin's supporters to say they
would seek the dissolution of the Congress and fresh parliamentary elections.

On April 4, Yeltsin won approval for his report, although
the deputies did not support his call for a coalition government. Then he sprung a surprise, asking the Congress for
extra powers until a proper presidency was created. The
request drew parallels with the emergency powers granted to
Gorbachev as USSR president, though in fact they fell well
short. Goryacheva accused Yeltsin of doing anything to
achieve power. "I am horrified," she declared. Khazbulatov
said that without extra powers, Yeltsin and Prime Minister
Silayev were "like individuals with a noose around their
necks and their hands tied." Suddenly, the deadlock was
broken. By 607 votes to 228, the Congress approved his request and also gave the go-ahead for direct election of a
Russian president on June 12. Yeltsin was not yet home and

dry, however, for a further Congress would have to be held to approve details of the election. But his camp scented that the tide had turned. The factor that tipped the balance was a split in the Communist ranks. Colonel Alexander Rutskoy, an air force pilot who became a Hero of the Soviet Union during the Afghan war, broke with Polozkov and formed a breakaway parliamentary group of 170 deputies under the slogan "Communists for Democracy."

"It's a victory, of course," Khazbulatov said. "The fact this plan was accepted means the plotters have failed."[24]

With the Congress over and his position strengthened, Yeltsin was now in a position to forget his calls for Gorbachev's resignation and offer him a deal, but exclusively on Russia's terms. "The President and the Soviet leadership must know that no differences can be an obstacle to business-like cooperation between the Union and the Russian leadership," he said in a final speech to the Congress, on April 6. "The basis for this cooperation must be resolute movement toward a normal market economy and the strengthening of Russian sovereignty."

The round-table solution, which Gorbachev had spurned in November, was now on offer again. But if Gorbachev accepted a new partnership with Yeltsin, the terms would be immeasurably stiffer than six months before. Gorbachev had plenty of reasons for keeping Yeltsin at arm's length; his distaste for his rival was as strong as ever.

But during the winter, the political landscape had changed. The democrats had showed their strength on the street, and the hard-liners seemed to offer no real solutions to Gorbachev's problems. The rebellious Baltic governments were still in office, and the much vaunted referendum had not brought the goal of a new union treaty any nearer. Yeltsin was still in office, more popular than ever and within sight of his goal of a directly elected Russian presidency.

Gorbachev also had to reckon with the arrival of a powerful new army on the political stage. By April, Soviet miners had gone on strike and were demanding his resignation.

19

Dacha Dwellers

I t was not the first time the miners had stopped work. A long strike, in the summer of 1989, ended with the Ryzhkov government making major concessions to demands for improvements in pay and conditions that proved impossible to fulfill.

In 1991, the miners were determined not to be cheated again. Their strike movement was more openly political, and thus far more dangerous to Gorbachev. By the end of March, three hundred thousand miners were on strike in the Ukrainian Donbass, the Siberian Kuzbass, and in Vorkuta, in the Far North. Yeltsin had visited the Kuzbass and Vorkuta in his August tour of the Russian provinces, and the miners were broadly sympathetic to his cause. In many places, they were openly calling for Gorbachev's resignation, a demand Yeltsin had put forward in February but had since dropped.

Their strike had already helped tip the balance at the Russian Congress of People's Deputies in favor of Yeltsin's survival. Anatoly Malykhin, leader of the Kuzbass strike committee, had gone to the rostrum to state their demands: Gorbachev, "who does not have a mandate or the confidence of the people and is waging an offensive against his own people," should resign; the USSR Congress of People's Deputies should be dissolved, as it had lost the people's confidence; Pavlov's government should step down, and central power should be transferred to a federation of sovereign states.

Their revolt could neither be ignored nor suppressed. Because the coal industry was one of the main central ministries, lagely outside Russian control, Yeltsin could argue that its problems would only be solved once the mines came under Russian control. "We do not object to the mines leaving the Ministry of the Coal Industry and coming under the jurisdiction of the Russian Federation," Yeltsin told the Russian Congress on April 1. Without explicitly endorsing all their demands, Yeltsin skillfully gave the impression that he was on the miners' side. Those who questioned the miners' grievances, he said,

> have probably never been down a coal mine or visited a miners' settlement. I have been in both. In Vorkuta I climbed along a drift of about five kilometers, and I have been to the Kuzbass and looked in the barracks—you cannot even call them barracks—in which the miners live, where in the winter the temperature in the housing is ten degrees. Despite the decisions of the union government, those decisions are not being carried out. They have voiced their demands once, twice, three times, four times, and still they are not being carried out. In that respect, one can understand the miners. It is intolerable.

He offered to let the Russian government take part in the talks. "If the miners accept the proposal, we will accept them into the jurisdiction of Russia and remove the economic problems. The political ones will remain." For good measure, Yeltsin reaffirmed that he wanted to raise the producer prices for all raw materials produced in Russia—not only coal but oil, gas, and other minerals—for all outside consumers, to world levels, including the other Soviet republics.

On April 3, the Soviet government backed down on its initial refusal to talk and offered to double the miners' pay over the next year. The gamble failed. Gorbachev personally conducted the talks in the Kremlin, hinting strongly to the miners that they were being manipulated by outsiders "who would like to play the miners' card." He rejected the demands for his resignation as unconstitutional. If he had been interested in personal power, he would have left the system as it was in 1985: "At that time no sovereign in the world, not even a junta leader, had more power than the CPSU general secretary. . . . Whatever stamping, whatever whistling, whatever slogans may be heard, whatever mocking may come from the squares, it will not break my stride. There is a constitutional process. The people will decide." Gorbachev promised a new government "anticrisis program" in April, but at times he sounded as though he himself did not believe it could be carried out.

"We sign an economic agreement. Then, one republic does not comply with it, then another, then one branch of industry, then a third one, and so on. Sovereign princedoms are starting up. If we do it this way, we shall destroy our country. It seems that those who are fighting for the Ukraine, for Russia, for Karaganda, for the Urals, for Sverdlovsk, for Stavropol— I shall not leave it out—all of them are now presenting themselves as populists, working with such zeal for their lands." But this was fatal to the economy. Only a "blood oath" of loyalty to a single policy by all would allow the country to pull through, he argued.[1]

Gorbachev was acknowledging that no government program would succeed unless all the leading republics endorsed it. The much-vaunted return to law and order at the beginning of the year, the joint patrols on the streets, the KGB's much-publicized swoops on food depots and transport bottlenecks and its campaign against "economic sabotage" had done nothing to solve the basic problems. By the end of the year, his Finance Minister warned him, the state budget deficit was likely to explode to 123.1 billion rubles, or almost half of its total revenues, because the republics, led by Russia, were failing to pay their agreed share of income.[2]

Gorbachev told an armed forces party conference the same week that "a return to old methods of repression and violence" was not on his agenda because it might bring another civil war, or a return to the Stalinist purges of 1937. He was increasingly conscious that the hard-liners he had been working with since November did not have all the answers. There were no more mentions of the trenches of Stalingrad.

In early April, Valentin Pavlov's government pushed through a big round of consumer price increases. Because they had been expected for so long and so frequently postponed, the increases went through without open public protests in most places, though the government's popularity fell further. The price increases, like the clumsy confiscation of large-denomination ruble notes earlier in the year, were aimed at reducing the gigantic "ruble overhang," the excess of money over goods that, as many economists pointed out, had largely been caused by the government's lack of control of the money supply. They pointed out that Pavlov was largely to blame for this printing of money during his tenure as finance minister in the Ryzhkov government. Pavlov's measures brought a market economy no nearer and made it far more difficult to end the miners' strike. Despite Gorbachev's offer to double the miners' pay, the strike continued and the stoppages spread, threatening to shut down huge areas of industry. In the first three months of the year, the gross national product fell by 8 percent, compared to the same period of 1990, and foreign trade fell by one third.

By mid-April, the workers were even out on strike in peaceful, conservative Byelorussia, the western republic that Gorbachev had chosen for his first trip outside Moscow, at the end of February. The workers from the giant tractor plant that Gorbachev had visited a few weeks earlier were marching in thousands through the center of Minsk, baying for his removal and bringing the republic's capital to a standstill.

In addition to the miners' strike and the government's problems, Gorbachev had another motive for a deal with the republics that went beyond purely economic matters. Without their consent, there could be no new union treaty. The referendum in March, through which Gorbachev had hoped to win a crushing popular mandate for a quick agreement on his terms, had failed to transform the political situation in the way he hoped. And without a union treaty, there could be no agreement on power-sharing and no meaningful economic policy at all. Any hope of removing Yeltsin from the political stage had evaporated with his victory at the Russian Congress, from which he emerged stronger than before. At a news conference, on April 5, Yeltsin, boosted by the Congress endorsement of a directly elected Russian president, renewed his offer to Gorbachev of a coalition government. Although the Congress had not specifically endorsed his proposal for round-table talks, Yeltsin repeated it anyway, with a hint that he would use his influence to settle the miners' strike, if Gorbachev accepted. What he had in mind was a formula to allow "Gorbachev, Yeltsin, and the chairmen and presidents of other union republics, and the leaders of various parties, movements, workers' movements, and strike movements, to sit down at a round table in order to achieve peace and concord."

Yeltsin and his allies knew that the democrats still needed a deal with Gorbachev, who could act as a buffer, or shock absorber, between them and the conservatives. As Ruslan Khazbulatov said at a round-table discussion in mid-April: "Roosevelt once said about the Nicaraguan dictator Somoza, 'He may be a son of a bitch, but he's *our* son of a bitch.' You can adapt it and say the same about Gorbachev: He's inconsistent but still our man."[3]

The alternative to Gorbachev might be worse, and the

democrats were still disorganized, compared to the CPSU. Anatoly Sobchak, the mayor of Leningrad, told *Moscow News* that both the conservatives and the democrats needed Gorbachev for their own purposes. "The former are afraid that Gorbachev's removal would cause a popular upheaval, or at least the final disintegration of the CPSU. But the democrats still can't form a government and stay in power. They would be washed away by the advance of dictatorship."[4]

Immediate multiparty elections, as demanded by the miners, would come too early for the democrats, in Yeltsin's view.

> They have not yet got themselves together. If the democratic movement were now to set up a real, large-scale people's legislative party, with ten or fifteen million members, which could form an alternative to the CPSU, then of course it would be realistic to talk of such a thing and move to such elections. But as long as there is one party with fifteen million while the other has twenty thousand—well, the correlation of forces is of course too unequal. And then—there is no getting away from it, let us say it frankly—though in formal terms article six may have been removed from the constitution, the CPSU today remains the ruling party, with all its property, and power, and the KGB and the army. Everything belongs to it.[5]

Gorbachev seems to have made the decision, at the end of the first week of April, to seek a new pact with Yeltsin, not just an armed truce, as he had suggested in his speech in Minsk, but a fresh political agreement. So when he met the Federation Council, on April 10, to seek their support for Pavlov's anticrisis package, he responded to Yeltsin's remarks. "I welcome calls that were heard at the recent RSFSR Congress of People's Deputies for cooperation and mutual interaction between the center and the republic." His close adviser Georgy Shakhnazarov told journalists the next day that Gorbachev had always been a supporter of coalition and consensus. If others showed the same approach, "then indeed a stage of agreement and cooperation could open up, drawing on a broad circle of political forces."

Gorbachev had another motive for seeking a new pact with Yeltsin. The hard-liners were on the march again, sensing that he was wriggling out of their embrace, without having carried through the decisive crackdown they wanted. Not only the Baltic states were still demanding independence, but in April, Georgia's new president, Zviad Gamsakhurdia, a former dissident and radical anti-Communist, began to lead his republic in the same direction. On April 9, the Soyuz group of deputies in the union parliament went to see Gorbachev, to propose he summon an extraordinary Congress of People's Deputies and deliver a report. In other words, Gorbachev should face the same kind of public examination by his parliament as Yeltsin had from the Russian legislature.

The threat to convene an extraordinary Congress did not materialize, but it was clear that Gorbachev would face a rough ride from his own Communist Party Central Committee at the end of April. Rather than give in to their pressure, as he had six months earlier, he would this time stand his ground and defy them. But to do so, he had only two weeks to find a new power base among the reformers.

There was still a big gap to be bridged. Gorbachev wanted a kind of legislative agreement, under which the republics would throw their weight behind the shaky Pavlov government's economic squeeze and help cut the budget deficit. He wanted support for a ban on strikes and for the rest of the Pavlov program, which was being dismissed, by such economists as Shatalin and Yavlinsky, as bound to fail. Yeltsin was looking further down the road to a broad political agreement that would open the way to a union treaty on his terms, reducing Gorbachev's role. "We do not need . . . the scale of the center that exists today. We need independent republics and a minimal center, for coordination. Our president does not like this title: coordinating president. Evidently, if a president really is needed for such sovereign states in a union, then it is only as a coordinating president, or else he is not needed at all. All that is needed is a collective body, such as the Federation Council."[6]

Although Gorbachev had told the miners he would not resign as General Secretary of the Party, his insistence on combining this post with that of the presidency was beginning to place him in an impossible position. As Alexei Kiva, the political scientist, pointed out, "The General Secretary serves first and foremost his Party and its structures. The President should serve the citizens, society, the state. . . . Gorbachev thus finds himself in the grip of an insoluble conflict."[7]

The events of the past six months had destroyed the liberal intelligentsia's trust in Gorbachev. He had lashed out at them as "so-called democrats," sneered at them, and ignored their advice. He was still proclaiming his loyalty to communism and to the "socialist choice." If he was to re-emerge as a reformer, then the democrats would no longer give him the benefit of the doubt. Any agreements they made with him would have to be watertight. Gorbachev set out to mend a few fences, bringing back some of the liberal advisers he had spurned during the winter, such as Vadim Bakatin. He also held a relatively cordial telephone conversation with the Lithuanian president Vytautas Landsbergis.

In mid-April, both Gorbachev and Yeltsin journeyed abroad. Gorbachev went to Japan, where his inability to promise his hosts any substantial concessions on the return of the four islands at the south of the Kuriles led to his returning empty-handed. Compared with his other foreign trips, this was an occasion where the Gorbachev magic simply failed to work. And besides, Yeltsin had signaled clearly that Russia demanded an equal voice in any decision affecting Russian territory, telling Gorbachev in effect that the Kuriles were not his to give away. Gorbachev found that the Japanese were far less susceptible to "Gorbymania" than Americans and Western Europeans.

Meanwhile, Yeltsin had embarked on his ill-fated visit to Strasbourg. Expecting to be greeted as the representative of 150 million Russians, he found himself treated by the French either as a clown or as a mere nuissance to Gorbachev. The snub by Jean-Pierre Cot, the minor French Socialist politician, who called him a demagogue to his face, left him irritated and rude. When Sylvie Kauffman, of *Le Monde*, turned up to interview him, she found that this "wall of incomprehension" had put him in an extremely bad mood. "I am tired of having to answer the same question, Gorbachev-Yeltsin, Gorbachev-Yeltsin," he snapped.

He stressed, however, that he was ready to cooperate with Gorbachev. "Gorbachev has not resigned. He is president of the country. One must try to work with those who hold positions of responsibility, including President Gorbachev. Those who hold such high state positions cannot behave like capricious young girls." If Gorbachev was threatened by the right wing, then he would support him, Yeltsin said. His words were another signal that a deal was in the offing.[8]

Though Yeltsin announced at the end of the visit that all his aims had been met, the trip was a rude reminder that the West only had eyes for Gorbachev. At the Elysée Palace, he was given a meeting only with the French secretary-general, Jean-Louis Bianco, with a brief "drop-in" from President François Mitterrand at the end. "There must be no ambiguity. The Soviet Union has one president and that is Mr. Gorbachev," said Mitterrand's spokesman Hubert Vedrine.

This was much the same treatment that President George Bush had given Yeltsin in 1989. During the previous month he had experienced a similar snub from US Secretary of State James Baker, who during a visit to Moscow, invited Yeltsin to dinner as part of a large group but refused to find time for a bilateral meeting. Yeltsin refused to attend the dinner. When Mitterrand and Britain's Prime Minister John Major visited Moscow a few weeks later, both of them were too busy to see Yeltsin at all.

One politician who was not too busy to see him was Richard Nixon. The former US president was impressed by Yeltsin after meeting him in Moscow, perhaps recognizing a kindred spirit, another political outsider victimized by the ruling establishment. "After being led to expect a lightweight and a demagogue, I quickly realized how inaccurate media reports and assessments by establishment diplomats can be. The Russian leader projects steely determination and strength of conviction. He has the physical magnetism that is so important for an effective politician. He is not as intellectual and sophisticated as Gorbachev, but he is still a political heavyweight. Gorbachev appeals to the head, Yeltsin to the heart; Gorbachev dazzles his listeners, Yeltsin moves them. If, as some of his critics claim, Yeltsin were seeking power for his own sake, he could be a very dangerous dictator. Fortunately, his critics are wrong."[9]

For Yeltsin, a man extremely sensitive to personal slights, the experience of being snubbed by foreign politicians was painful. But on a political level, he drew the conclusion that outright opposition to Gorbachev would lead Russia's embryonic foreign policy into a blind alley. Cooperation would produce better results. This was also the approach of Russian Foreign Minister Andrei Kozyrev, plucked from the Soviet Foreign Ministry in 1990, where he was one of the stars of Shevardnadze's "new thinking."

Before Gorbachev returned from Japan, he had already decided to take the plunge and negotiate a new political pact with Yeltsin and the other republican leaders. The date was fixed for April 23, and the venue was to be a state *dacha* at Novo-Ogarevo just outside Mocow, a large yellow building originally built for Stalin's crony Klimenty Voroshilov.

By this time Gorbachev needed an agreement badly. On the following day he was due to face the wrath of the Central Committee where hard-liners were bound to seek his resignation. As his spokesman Vitaly Ignatenko told reporters, "Gorbachev is facing a challenge to his leadership. . . . He is not in an easy position."

News of the agreement at Novo-Ogarevo broke, in *Pravda*, on April 24, in the form of a communiqué signed by Gorbachev, Yeltsin, the presidents of Kazakhstan, Azerbaijan, Kyrgyzstan, Uzbekistan, Tajikistan, and Turkmenistan, and the prime ministers of the Ukraine and Byelorussia. This deal, which subsequently became known as the "nine-plus-one" agreement, was titled: "Joint statement on immediate measures to stabilize the situation in the country and overcome the crisis."

It outlined a series of "resolute measures to restore constitutional order everywhere and the unconditional observance of laws still in force." Economic agreements for 1991, particularly on the budget, would be fulfilled unconditionally, and the signatories promised to support "joint anticrisis measures" in the economy. There would be a "special work regime" in some sectors of industry and transport. The agreement called on miners and others on strike to go back to work, and said that the signatories "view as intolerable attempts to attain political goals by incitement to civil disobedience and strikes or by calls to overthrow the existing and legitimately elected organs of state power." In other words, Gorbachev had, it appeared, won much of what he had been looking for in the short term. Yeltsin and the republican leaders had been forced to give grudging approval to the Pavlov plan of anticrisis measures and to call on the miners to go back to work.

But what had Gorbachev given away in return? Essentially, his concessions were in the long term and were not fully spelled out in the document. The final sentence of the statement said that all the measures to overcome the crisis "would be unimaginable without a cardinal enhancement of the role of the union republics." There was no elaboration on what this meant, however.

The only concrete concessions involved the future of the Union Treaty. All nine republics promised to complete work on the new "treaty of sovereign states" in the immediate future; within six months it would be followed by a new constitution and then by elections to all "union organs of power." In other words, if the timetable were kept, then the Soviet parliament—and probably Gorbachev himself—would face reelection not in 1994 but, in all likelihood, at least two years earlier. Gorbachev had in effect agreed to cut short his own term of office. Given his unpopularity, he was now on the way to becoming a lame duck head of state, with little chance of winning another term through a free ballot.

On the subject of what would happen to the six other republics, there was a divergence. The nine republican leaders, minus Gorbachev, agreed that Estonia, Latvia, Lithuania, Georgia, Armenia, and Moldavia would be free to choose whether or not to sign the treaty. Those republics that did sign would get "most favored nation" treatment within a single economic space. By implication, those that opted for full independence would be outside and would have to take the consequences—possibly tariff barriers or payment in hard currency at world prices for energy. Though Gorbachev did not endorse this formula, the fact that the other republics did so further undermined his attempt to keep a tight control over the terms under which republics might choose to secede from the Soviet Union. The all-out struggle against "separatism," which he had used as a rallying cry six months earlier, had effectively been forgotten. Merely by signing such a far-reaching agreement with only nine republics, Gorbachev was conceding that the other six were heading for the exit.

A number of other points were conceded by Gorbachev in bilateral talks with Yeltsin, though not mentioned in the statement. Among them was his agreement that only union republics, not autonomous republics, would have full right of signature of the new union treaty. This was a point of vital importance for Yeltsin, whose advisers had been warning him for months that Gorbachev, by promising equal status to Tatarstan and other republics inside Russia, was trying to undermine the Russian state. All except Tatarstan were to accept this formula. Gorbachev also gave the go-ahead for the formation of a Russian Republic KGB organization, something that Yeltsin and KGB chairman Vladimir Kryuchkov had agreed to in outline, in the summer of 1990, but which had never been implemented. There were also concessions over control of foreign currency, foreign trade, and gold reserves.

The nine-plus-one agreement gave Gorbachev the vital piece of paper he needed, to wave in the face of his political foes in the Central Committee the next day. Gorbachev told them the agreement with the republics was a breakthrough that would firmly restore "constitutional order" and reminded his conservative critics that there could be no way back to totalitarianism. When they hit back, he threatened to resign, successfully calling the hard-liners' bluff in the knowledge that they had no candidate to replace him. Gorbachev's outburst was made in the heat of the moment, according to participants, but it undoubtedly contained an element of calculation. A recess was called, and the Politburo recommended that the question of Gorbachev's resignation should not go on the agenda. When the Central Committee resumed, it voted overwhelmingly to endorse this decision, by 322 votes to 13.

Meanwhile Yeltsin was coming in for criticism from his own side. Many of his supporters believed he had caved in to Gorbachev, and had made a serious mistake. The historian Yuri Afanasyev, one of the leaders of Democratic Russia, still wanted Gorbachev to resign. The miners, too, were unimpressed, after their eight weeks on strike. Why was Yeltsin endorsing Pavlov's unsuccessful economic policy? If this was the long-promised round table, then where was the coalition government that Yeltsin had been seeking? Alexander Smirnov, a strike leader in the Kuzbass coalfield, said he believed Yeltsin had turned against the strikers. "The strike committee has sent a telegram to Yeltsin demanding an explanation of the joint declaration," he said. "If it turns out Yeltsin gave in to Gorbachev, I can only say that he deceived us."[10]

Yeltsin had, however, extracted from Gorbachev a promise that the coal industry on Russian soil would be transferred to the Russian government. Armed with this argument, he flew to Siberia at the end of the month and met with skeptical miners. He did not try to browbeat them or tell them what to do but left the decision on the strike in their hands, promising that the transfer to Russian control would mean that they would be able to run their own affairs. Before a crowd of five thousand in the grimy city of Novokuznetsk, he borrowed a miner's pen and theatrically signed a resolution on the transfer. A few days later, the deal was confirmed by Moscow, despite the misgivings of the Pavlov government. The last miners trickled back to work in mid-May.

Although both sides were hailing the Novo-Ogarevo agreement as important, there was no agreement on who had won, or even on what had been agreed. Yeltsin's version was that it was a big victory for the republics. In the nine and a half hours of negotiation with Gorbachev, 80 percent of the president's original draft agreement had been rewritten, he told Russian television viewers on May 4. For the first time, he argued, the republics had been recognized by Gorbachev as sovereign states. "Never before has the country's president accepted that formula." Negotiation of the Union Treaty would now take place between the republics, five of whom had already reached agreement on 99 percent of the text. Yeltsin had to sell the agreement to his own supporters and to the miners, so there was clearly a defensive element in his claims. He had to explain why he was now Gorbachev's ally, barely two months after calling for him to resign and ruling out any future collaboration. Yeltsin argued that his February statement had been a warning to Gorbachev not to surrender completely to the conservatives. Now, he explained, the republican leaders had told Gorbachev: "This really is your last chance. If you carry out our coordinated agreements, then fine, let's act. If you don't, then we shall make things happen our way." He also explained why, after previous agreements with Gorbachev that were not implemented, he was now confident of making him stick to the latest accord: "Then there were just the two of us, and here we were ten, including nine top leaders of the republics. So to refuse to carry out our mutual agreements somehow is quite impossible, I think." He added, "If he tries that, we also have our alternative up our sleeve."[11]

He said he had agreed with Gorbachev on what to do about defining functions and property between the center and the Russian republic and about ownership of the Soviet Union's gold reserves. The agreement on transfer of the coal mines would perhaps turn out to be a costly luxury in the long term, but it served as a precedent for winning control over other, more profitable sectors, such as oil and gas.

Khazbulatov explained that the decision to throw Gorbachev a lifeline ahead of the Central Committee meeting had been made because there was a real threat of his being replaced by someone far worse. "We gave the President very strong support, there is no doubt about it. And we would like to think that the statement that was signed is not a maneuver by Gorbachev, that it will be strictly observed." Khazbulatov spelled out the implications of the agreement for Gorbachev: "He will occupy a worthy place in the Union, taking into account the changes that will be fixed in the Union Treaty. It is time for everyone to understand that the Union will be the way the republics wish to see it. And the head of the Union state will have just as much power as the sovereign states will delegate to him. . . . It would be useful if the President began to learn his lesson. But I agree, he doesn't like learning from his mistakes. and he has made more mistakes than all the other union leaders put together."[12]

Yeltsin's close adviser, Mikhail Poltoranin, Russia's information minister, said in an interview: "We picked up Gorbachev like a wounded man on the field of battle." In other words, Gorbachev would from now on be a political hostage, not of the hard-liners, but of Yeltsin and his allies in the other republics.[13]

Gorbachev, of course, was perfectly well aware of this. He was insisting that nothing fundamental had changed. At a news conference with Mitterrand, on May 6, he was asked how the West should conduct its relations with the republics. "Gentlemen, we should all proceed from the fact that the Soviet Union exists. This is first. Second, that it will continue to exist. Third, that it is a powerful state. And fourth, that it will continue to be such . . . the world is going to be dealing with a mighty power."[14] Gorbachev became animated and his irritation showed through when he rebutted Yeltsin's claims to have won a political victory over him. "All this is not serious. I think it is political death for politicians to put their signatures under such a document in order to play cheap political games and cheap tricks."

Despite Gorbachev's protests, it was clear that something in the balance of power had changed. The mood of political tension in Moscow during January and February had eased palpably. Though there was still a stalemate over power, there was a sense that the hard-line offensive during the winter had failed. Gorbachev had made a perilous leap across the abyss to the side of the reformers, leaving his conservative allies—Pugo, Pavlov, Yazov, Kryuchkov, and the others— behind him.

After the nine-plus-one agreement, it was clear that the conservatives could no longer manipulate Gorbachev, who was now in the clutches of Yeltsin and the other republican leaders. If they were to regain control of events and keep the crumbling Soviet Union together, Gorbachev was no longer the ideal instrument. The hard-liners' conspiracy against Gorbachev would only come in August, but its seeds were sown in April. The Novo-Ogarevo pact spelled doom for the old centralized Soviet Union and its structures—not only the Communist Party but the government, the economic planners, the KGB, and the military.

Four months were to elapse between the nine-plus-one agreement and the August coup, which was to bring the events of the summer to a sudden climax. During this period, Yeltsin's domestic position and that of the democrats was to be further strengthened. For the first time ever, the peoples of Russia were to have the chance to elect their leaders in a democratic ballot.

20

The Mandate

By the standards of a US presidential election, the campaign for president of the Russian Republic was remarkably short—a mere three weeks. Even before the final constitutional details were in place, the date of the voting was fixed for June 12, 1991.

Yeltsin had advocated the creation of a directly elected executive presidency for more than a year, calculating that this would give him a far stronger base than his chairmanship of the Russian parliament. The new post would free him from the need for repeated compromises with his Communist critics, who would no longer be able to threaten to vote him out of office. For the first time, he would have real executive power to enforce laws, such as land privatization, which the parliament had passed but which were often ignored or undermined at local level by Communist Party officials. Most of all, a mandate obtained through a popular vote would strengthen Yeltsin in his negotiations with Gorbachev, who had been elected President only by the Soviet Congress of People's Deputies, not by the voters. Direct election of a Russian head of state would mark a further shift of legitimacy away from the central institutions and toward the republics. Other republics were already moving in the same direction, and to delay creating a Russian presidency would mean the biggest republic was lagging behind the trend.

A law creating the new post of Russian President was passed by the Supreme Soviet and then approved without serious challenge by a session of the Russian Congress of

People's Deputies in late May. The final vote was 894 to 6, with 16 abstentions. The powers of the President included the right to appoint ministers and issue decrees but not to veto laws or dissolve parliament. The new powers were to be balanced by the creation of a Constitutional Court, an attempt to create, for the first time, a separation of powers and an independent judicial authority on the Western pattern. The President had to be between 35 and 65 and was restricted to two five-year terms. Asked what he would do in the unlikely event that he lost, Yeltsin replied, "I shall retire and go and dig my garden."[1]

Yeltsin, still Russia's most popular politician, was the overwhelming favorite, but he needed to obtain 50 percent of the vote in the first ballot, in order to avoid a runoff, which would have been seen as a serious setback. Of the five candidates opposing him, former prime minister Nikolai Ryzhkov, by now recovered from the heart attack he had suffered in December 1990, was the most serious challenger. His running mate was 48-year-old General Boris Gromov, the deputy interior minister, who had become a household name, commanding the army's pullout from Afghanistan. Further to the right was General Albert Makashov, an old-fashioned military conservative who had gained attention, in 1990, with a vituperative attack on Gorbachev's foreign policy. Vadim Bakatin, the liberal interior minister, whom Gorbachev had fired under hard-line pressure in December 1990, also agreed to run against Yeltsin and was generally assumed to be the man Gorbachev supported. The two least known candidates were Aman Tuleyev, a local politician, from Kemerovo province in Siberia, who had opposed the miners' strikes and Vladimir Zhirinovsky, a maverick right-winger. Zhirinovsky was leader of the little-known Liberal Democratic Party, which had helped form a so-called "centrist bloc" of minor political parties that had backed demands for the introduction of a state of emergency in late 1990.

Zhirinovsky's campaign was based on a rabble-rousing appeal to Russian imperial feeling, mixing promarket views on economics with an appeal to maintain the Soviet empire intact at all costs. "I am against even a single meter of Soviet territory coming under the jurisdiction of an alien, foreign flag," he declared to the Russian Congress. He warned that the twenty-five million Russians living outside the Russian Republic were in danger of becoming second-class citizens. "Russia, Moscow, the center, and the USSR are all one," he declared. His calls for law and order and the maintenance of a unitary state had much in common with those of General Makashov, though they were expressed in more demagogic terms.

Yeltsin could have picked a fellow radical as his running mate. Instead he chose to balance the ticket by picking a man calculated to cause maximum confusion and divsion among his opponents. This was Alexander Rutskoi, an air force pilot who had won a "Hero of the Soviet Union" award for his exploits in the Afghan war. The son and grandson of professional soldiers, he was shot down and suffered a fractured spine in Afghanistan, in 1985, but returned, in 1988, as deputy commander of air force units there. He was shot down again—by a Pakistani air force fighter according to his own account—and landed in Pakistan and was hunted for five days by Afghan guerrillas. Wounded again in a shootout with the rebels, he spent six weeks in captivity and was then exchanged for rebel prisoners.[2]

The very model of a military hero, with his graying hair and big moustache, Rutskoi was just the running mate needed to draw support to Yeltsin among the officer corps. Before Yeltsin invited him to join the ticket, some press commentators had spotted Rutskoi's potential appeal to the voters and tipped him as a possible candidate to run against Yeltsin. But he had other advantages too; his entry into politics in 1989 had been as a "patriot" or Russian nationalist, as one of the founders of a group known as Otechestvo (Fatherland). At this time, Rutskoi was certainly no liberal and his picture adorned the cover of the Stalinist literary review *Molodaya Gvardiya*. Rutskoi failed to win a seat in the Soviet Congress of People's Deputies in 1989 but won election to the Russian Congress in 1990. Over this period his views underwent a sea change, partly because of his exposure to social problems, as chairman of a parliamentary committee on veterans' affairs. In January 1990, he furiously denounced Gorbachev for evading responsibility for the killings at the Vilnius television tower and for pinning the blame on the local military commander.[3]

During the third Russian Congress of People's Deputies in early April, Rutskoi had been instrumental in blunting the conservative offensive against Yeltsin, by breaking away from the Communist bloc to form his own "Communists for Democracy" faction, backed by nearly two hundred deputies. As a reform Communist, he could be relied on to sow division not only among the military, but in the ranks of the Russian Communist Party, where many were unhappy with the ultraconservative positions of its leader, Ivan Polozkov. Interviewed by Czechoslovakian journalists, on the eve of an official visit to Prague in mid-May, Yeltsin dwelt on the "Rutskoi effect" as the start of a major split in Communist Party ranks. "I think it is extremely interesting," he said. A week later, he announced the colonel would be his running mate. As he told an interviewer during the campaign, "Rutskoi knows the military. This is one of my weak points. He knows the work with war veterans very well, he knows the work with the disabled very well. He went through Afghanistan, which means the Afghan war veterans will follow him."[4]

(Rutskoi proved his value to Yeltsin during the August coup in Moscow, when his presence and that of other senior officers in Yeltsin's camp contributed to the army's reluctance to carry out orders to crush resistance.)

Nikolai Ryzhkov was unambiguously the candidate of the "center"—the interlocking system of state-run industries, the state planners, the defense sector, the army hierarchy, and the collective and state farms. All of these powerful institutions were threatened by Yeltsin's promise of radical market reform and a further shift of power to the republics. Ryzhkov was fighting the same battle in defense of the old institutions as he had fought to emasculate the Shatalin five-hundred-days plan, nine months earlier. The hard-line Russian Communist Party and the Soyuz group of deputies also gave him their backing. Ryzhkov was opposed to private ownership of land, the breakup of the state sector and wide-ranging privatization, and free prices. He warned that there should be no sell-off of the economy to "millionaires and foreigners." He explained, "I will demonstrate categorically that the path he [Yeltsin] proposes is the wrong one." Collective and state farms, not private farming, were the foundation of agriculture. "Private ownership of land cannot be introduced in our conditions." Ryzhkov criticized not only Yeltsin, but his own successor, Valentin Pavlov, and Gorbachev, whom he had served for more than five years. Like so many others, both liberals and conservatives, he felt betrayed by what he saw as duplicity on Gorbachev's part. "Gorbachev has quite a few shortcomings. . . . He needs to draw conclusions from the criticisms." Ryzhkov was still bitter about the way Gorbachev had decided overnight, in mid-November 1990, to downgrade the government, by turning it into a newfangled, foreign-sounding "cabinet." "The Council of Ministers in Russia goes back to 1861; it was established by Alexander II; 130 years later this institution ceased to exist. Gorbachev rushed into this," he complained.[5]

Gorbachev, learning from past mistakes, avoided open intervention in the campaign. His spokesman, Vitaly Ignatenko, told journalists that ". . . the President does not consider it possible and correct to speak in favor of one presidential candidate or another."[6]

In the armed forces and the KGB, Communist Party organizations gave instructions to support Ryzhkov. The Main Military-Political Directorate of the armed forces met on May 14 and agreed to support "the candidate whose position, as regards the unity of our state and armed forces and our socialist choice, is notable for its consistency and firmness." Technically the Directorate was now a state, rather than a party body, but its open partisanship in favor of Ryzhkov illustrated the shallowness of military reform under Gorbachev.

While his opponents complained about the shortness of the campaign, Yeltsin was taking the high road of an incumbent, making what he described as "working visits" rather than campaign stops to different areas of Russia, to bask in public support. His route began in Murmansk, inside the Arctic Circle, and Severomorsk, the nearby base of the navy's Northern Fleet. It continued to Petrozavodsk in Karelia, to the Russian heartland cities of Tula and Voronezh, then to the Urals industrial cities of Perm, Chelyabinsk, Orenburg, and Sverdlovsk.

Following his truce with Gorbachev, his attacks on the President were now played down. As he told a news conference, on May 25, "We have somehow or other moved toward a rapprochement of our positions, and now the atmosphere is businesslike. Yesterday, in eight hours, we did not once say anything unpleasant to each other; this is an exceptional occurrence." Yeltsin credited above all the effect of the miners' strike, which changed the balance of power to make this possible. "The democratic forces are gathering momentum, as it were. They have become better organized. And I think that in future the process will go in precisely that direction." He even gave Gorbachev a few words of somewhat condescending praise for the way he was facing up to the new realities of power: "[The democratic forces] have made the President understand, after all, that if he will not lean on the left shoulder he will be left no chances at all."[7]

Yeltsin's campaign message promised devolution and radical reform, appealing to patriotism rather than ideology. But there were no more ultrademocratic offers of "as much sovereignty as you can swallow" or inverted pyramids. His year in office had taught Yeltsin, like other democrats, that the Russian "ghost-state," with its eleven time zones, would crumble apart, unless it had a strong central executive power. While distancing himself from the messianic, anti-Western aspects of Russian nationalism, he sought to inspire a new kind of Russian pride. "It has become perfectly clear that patriotism lies not only in words about love of the Russian past, not only in empty admiration of the uniqueness of our national character, and not only in fencing ourselves off from the rest of humanity. Today the highest form of patriotism is to serve the cause of Russia's progress, to participate actively in the deep transformations of its life, giving the Russians a real right to be proud of their motherland."[8] There was a populist note in his promise that there would be no more foreign aid to countries such as Cuba and Afghanistan: "Charity begins at home," he told one audience.

Yeltsin was ready to admit the lack of real achievements by the Russian government in its first months in office and the government's mistakes. But the pessimism he expressed in February was replaced by a certain optimism about long-term changes for the better. The Russian parliament had laid a legal basis for reform which could be built on, he argued. Economic reform was at last on track, and the way was clear for a revival of social groups that had been annihilated under Communism, such as private farmers, businessmen, and the intelligentsia. Following the coal mines, other industrial sectors including forestry, chemicals, and steel were now clamoring to be placed under Russian, rather than central, authority. Most of all, the Russian popular mentality was changing. The Russians no longer wanted to be passive spectators in the game of politics. This claim was to be put to a severe test during the August coup but was to be proved essentially correct.

The myths that oppressed millions over many decades have lost their illusory attraction. The dynamic process of removing ideology from the public awareness has been going on throughout this time. Sometimes this is called a moral disaster. I disagree categorically. Renunciation of the false signposts that have led the people into an impasse, ruined the lives of multitudes, and destroyed the centuries-old traditions of a great nation is not a disaster but the first step toward moral rebirth. It is founded not upon the ideology of a superclass to which all is permitted but on universal human values and norms of life.

Yeltsin refused to be drawn into debating the relative merits of socialism and capitalism. "When I am asked during my trips, 'Are you for socialism or capitalism?' I say: I am in favor of Russians living better—materially, spiritually, and culturally. . . . A healthy society is determined by how people live, how they work, and how they are provided for materially, culturally, and intellectually. As for a name, people will think one up."

Whatever his doubts about embracing the concept of capitalism—still a word with strong negative connotations for many Russians—Yeltsin made clear that the old dream of the "shining future" under socialism was dead. The unhappy Marxist experiment had pushed Russia off the path traveled by the world's civilized countries and led to humiliation and poverty, symbolized by ration cards. "This is a constant humiliation, a reminder every hour that you are a slave in this country."

As Yeltsin traveled the land, he strewed around him promises to bring about rapid economic change, particularly land reform and privatization, by destroying the "ferro-concrete bureaucracy" at the union level and the opposition of local bureaucrats to reform at the bottom. His economic program included promises which could only be funded by higher spending—a better minimum wage, a shorter work week, lower rail fares, longer vacations, and other welfare state measures. He gave particular emphasis to the welfare complaints of the army, promising that Russia would organize some form of "social protection" for demobilized and homeless officers and men. The money, he argued, would be found by reducing Russia's payments to the central budget. Final control over monetary affairs should be transferred from the State Bank and Pavlov's government to the republics acting together in the Federation Council. His list of residual functions to be kept by the hated "center" was now much shorter than the one he had given a year ago. Now it was only defense, railways, and power generation, including nuclear energy. The Russian KGB should be autonomous, and the state airline Aeroflot should no longer have a monopoly, Yeltsin said. After his election win, he would make a start on removing Communist Party cells from state institutions, including the armed forces.

In Murmansk, a city so far north that residents spend half the year in darkness, he promised a future free of the central Moscow bureaucracy. The local fisheries industry would be free to dispose of its catch as it chose and given its economic independence, he promised, to thunderous applause. "We love you, Boris Nikolayevich," a flag-waving crowd chanted. Although he acknowledged that "I have not been trained in Hollywood," Yeltsin's campaign was the only one, apart from that of Zhirinovsky, that had any touches of life. Handed a photograph of a woman along with questions from his audience, he read the text on the back and before sliding it into his pocket, declared conspiratorially: "Ah, a declaration of love. . . . I'll put that away."[9]

Severomorsk, one of the Soviet Union's main nuclear submarine bases, was an important campaign stop, in view of his edgy relations with the military establishment. To the senior officers, his calls for lower defense spending and an end to superpower status were an outright threat, but junior officers and conscripts were keenly interested in his views. So sensitive was the issue of the military's support for Yeltsin that when he toured the nuclear-powered cruiser *Kirov*, Soviet journalists were excluded.[10]

Toward the end of the campaign, the strain of too much travel began to show. On a live radio phone-in program, on June 6, Yeltsin took offense at what he considered to be a string of "negative" questions, particularly concerning his planned purchase of a plot of land for a private *dacha*. Yeltsin made it clear that he felt he was being given rougher treatment than the other candidates, who had appeared before him. Television and radio, though officially neutral, were doing their best to help his opponents.

With only a few days to go, opinion surveys showed him in the lead by a large margin. On June 10, *Pravda* fired its last shots against Yeltsin with a "sociopsychological portrait" by three professors, who described him as disloyal, unpredictable, authoritarian, and incompetent. "His ideas change so easily that one can scarcely identify any of his convictions," they wrote. An analysis of his autobiography showed that the main trait of his personality was "excessive need for power" to compensate for feelings of personal inadequacy. Yeltsin was accused of "a messianic vision of himself as a savior" and of "poor resistance to stress."

On June 11, the day before the poll, the hard-line conservative newspaper *Sovietskaya Rossiya*, organ of the Russian Communist Party, published a report by the Soviet prosecutor-general alleging links between Yeltsin and the mysterious "ruble scam" that had led to the resignation of Russian Deputy Prime Minister Gennady Filshin, earlier in the year. This article followed one, three days earlier, in the same newspaper, accusing Yeltsin of links with the Italian mafia because of the allegedly dubious connections of an Italian appointed to be a Russian honorary consul in Italy.

None of this made much difference to the final result. Shortly before the official end of the campaign, thousands of Yeltsin's supporters rallied in central Moscow, bearing his portrait and waving Russian tricolor flags. "Boris Nikolayevich, fate has sent you to us," said one banner. Gorbachev, clearly expecting a Yeltsin victory, came to cast his vote in Moscow and told reporters: "I am ready to cooperate with anyone the Russians elect. There will be no problems on my side on that account." Early results from the Far East showed that Russia's 105 million eligible voters had gone overwhelmingly for Yeltsin, leaving Ryzhkov and the other candidates trailing badly. The final figures showed a 70 percent turnout and a crushing victory for Yeltsin, with nearly 57.4 percent of the vote. Yeltsin, as expected, did best in the industrial cities of Russia, winning almost 72 percent in Moscow and 90 percent in Sverdlovsk. Ryzhkov, who won more support in the conservative countryside than in the cities, took 17.3 percent. Zhirinovsky, the crowd-pleasing outsider, was a surprise third, showing that his Russian nationalist message had registered. He won 7.9 percent, ahead of Tuleyev with 6.1 percent, and General Makashov, with 3.8 percent. Limping in last was Gorbachev's candidate, Vadim Bakatin, with 3.5 percent, whose low-key appeal to commonsense centrism inspired little support. Yeltsin's allies Gavriil Popov in Moscow and Anatoly Sobchak in Leningrad became the first directly elected mayors. Voters in Leningrad further humiliated the Communists by voting to rename their city St. Petersburg, the name given to it by its founder Peter the Great, which it lost in 1914.

The vote further shifted the balance of legitimacy away from Gorbachev, who had never stood in a popular election, and toward Yeltsin, who had now done so three times. But Yeltsin's victory was not just a personal one; it is no hyperbole to say it marked a watershed in Russian history. For the first time ever, the Russians had become not subjects but citizens, able to exercise popular sovereignty in choosing their own leader—a right taken for granted in the West but denied them by the Tsars and their communist successors. It was an event that, in a sense, healed what Solzhenitsyn called the "mortal fracture of the spine" that took place in 1917 for Russian history. It restored the continuity broken when the Bolsheviks closed down Russia's freely elected Constituent Assembly and sent it home. The June 1991 election laid to rest any lingering doubts about the popular rejection of seventy-four years of Communism, of the "socialist choice" that Gorbachev was still defending. The vote, by cementing the position of the Russian republic and helping it shed its "ghost" image, further weakened the legitimacy of the Soviet Union as a state and strengthened that of Russia.

"With a Yeltsin victory, the very nature of the center changes," commented Vladimir Grinev, the Ukraine's top negotiator on the new Union Treaty. "It's going to be very hard for the center to resist a Russia headed by President Yeltsin and a Ukraine bent on its sovereignty."[11]

Only *Pravda* and *Sovietskaya Rossiya* questioned the validity of Yeltsin's victory, describing his margin as "barely sufficient" and doubting the regularity of the poll.

Yeltsin's formal installation as President came four weeks later, on July 10, in a ceremony, before six thousand guests in the Kremlin, that blended old Soviet rituals with newly invented Russian symbolism. Not only Gorbachev was there to give his congratulations but also Patriarch Alexii of the Russian Orthodox Church. Yeltsin swore his oath of office on the Russian Republic constitution, and not on the Bible, as some had expected. An announcement followed that further cemented his legitimacy and symbolized the new arrangements in Moscow. The seat of the new Russian presidency would not be in the "White House," the home of the Russian parliament, but in the Kremlin. Yeltsin would be moving to offices vacated by Pavlov's government.

But before his installation, there was another moment of apotheosis that was just as important for Yeltsin—a trip to Washington to meet President George Bush.

For any foreign politician, being photographed meeting the President of the United States, in Washington, helps the image back home, and Soviet leaders are no exception. Nikita Khrushchev and Leonid Brezhnev managed it once each, Gorbachev twice. Now it would be Yeltsin's turn. Back in 1989, he had rated no more than a brief "drop-in" by Bush at the end of a hurriedly arranged meeting with national security adviser General Brent Scowcroft. Since then he had repeatedly angled for an official invitation from the White House, only to be told that protocol did not allow this. US officials told Yeltsin that as president-elect of Russia he would get a high-profile meeting with Bush, though in protocol terms his visit would have to be hosted by Congressional leaders.

His US trip was designed to wipe away memories of the 1989 visit, with its "Boris's Boozy Bear Hug" headlines and controversy. This time, the Russian bear was to appear smiling, house-trained, and above all, sober before the American public and the political establishment. Yeltsin succeeded in his aim, helped by the professional diplomatic hand of Russian Foreign Minister Andrei Kozyrev. Acting on orders from Moscow, Soviet ambassador to Washington Viktor Komplektov and ambassador to the United Nations Yuli Vorontsov—neither of them natural Yeltsin supporters—smoothed his path. With rare exceptions, Yeltsin managed to be gracious with his interviewers, dignified with his political hosts, and disarmingly witty in his public appearances.[12] Welcomed by Senator Robert Dole, at Andrews Air Force Base, as "the first freely and popularly elected president of the Russian Republic," Yeltsin set the tone by stressing that his election was a strong statement in favor of radical economic reform and democracy. He praised the United States as "the birthplace of democracy" and told congressional leaders that Russia was now setting out on the same path. The Russian people, he told them without referring to Gorbachev by name, did not want "halfhearted measures, halfhearted reform, semidemocracy." Instead they had chosen a market economy and privatization, the path followed by "all civilized countries of the world."

Pressed by television interviewer Ted Koppel to describe himself, Yeltsin at first avoided answering but was finally pinned down. "I am not a simple person; I am rather harsh, rather rigid. Nonetheless, it is possible to do serious political business with me." He promised to support Gorbachev if Gorbachev continued to support reform. "If he holds up reforms, if he stops and goes backward, if he makes halfhearted decisions, if he pressures the republics, including military pressure, I'm his opponent." On Capitol Hill, he donned a cowboy hat he was given as a present. Outside the corridors of power, Yeltsin happily played to the crowd, plunging into a mob of tourists at the Lincoln Memorial and shaking hands, to shouts of "Boris, Boris."

At a dinner with Vice President Dan Quayle, who spoke of differences over self-determination for the Baltic States and Soviet aid to Cuba, Yeltsin hurried to put the record straight. "We do not differ with you," he explained at the ceremony where he was awarded the Center for Democracy's International Democracy Prize.

Talking to the National Press Club, Yeltsin qualified his

support for Gorbachev, speaking openly of the collapse of the Soviet empire as inevitable. "There is no way for one man to preserve the Soviet Union," he said. While the central government was still hesitating about introducing private property, Russia was now firmly committed to it, he argued. Slow, halfhearted change would be fatal. His message of respect for human rights, the rule of law, democracy, and private property got an enthusiastic welcome. Yeltsin even gave a half-apology for not being a religious believer, explaining he had been brought up as an atheist, but his three grandchildren were making amends and had all been baptized.

In the White House Rose Garden, President Bush praised Yeltsin's election victory but went on to deliver an extraordinary hymn of praise to Gorbachev, promising that the United States would maintain the "closest possible official relationship" with his government. It was Gorbachev "who enabled us to end the Cold War and make Europe whole and free," said Bush. Yeltsin, diplomatically taking his cue, promised to support Gorbachev against "forces back home who want to go back to the time of stagnation."

He promised, "Russia, which accounts for 70 percent of the gross national product of the Soviet Union, is strongly and irrevocably committed to democracy and it will not allow any reversal of history." Yeltsin went away happy with Bush's agreement to open direct channels to Russia, though the White House played down its significance. "We will deal with the center as the government of the Soviet Union," Scowcroft said afterwards. The United States would cooperate with Russia and other republics where the new Union Treaty would permit it.

While Bush was constrained by his loyalty to Gorbachev, a fellow member of the club of world leaders, Washington conservatives, such as senators Jesse Helms and Strom Thurmond, felt no such inhibitions and lined up to shake Yeltsin's hand and be photographed with him at a Soviet Embassy reception.

In New York, Yeltsin spoke for an hour to an enthusiastic audience at New York University without once allowing Gorbachev's name to cross his lips. He delighted students by confessing that he had been a "hooligan" during his college years but was now much more responsible. He provoked laughter when he told them he had been faithfully married to the same woman for thirty-five years. "I realize that is quite surprising for you." Most of Yeltsin's day in New York was spent at the Reserve Bank of New York with leading businessmen and power brokers such as Henry Kissinger, but he found time for a gesture toward the American working class with a trip to a garment factory. Surrounded by glitzy turquoise cocktail dresses trimmed with sequins and gold lamé, Yeltsin donned a garment workers' union cap and tried his hand at a sewing machine, promptly losing the stitch and joking with the seamstresses that they earned more than he did as president of Russia.

Yeltsin's trip to the United States capped a string of political successes, starting with his cliffhanger escape, at the end of March, from the attempt to vote him out of office, followed by the Novo-Ogarevo deal with Gorbachev in April, and his election as Russian president in June.

Yeltsin's rise was for Gorbachev an uncomfortable fact of life. For better or worse, he had burned his bridges with the conservatives, and his new relationship with Yeltsin and the republican leaders could leave him as little more than a constitutional monarch. But as a resourceful tactician, he still had some strong cards to play. There was one area where the new equation would leave Gorbachev free to work his old political magic and prove himself essential—foreign affairs. Neither Russia's Yeltsin nor the Ukraine's Kravchuk nor Kazakhstan's Nazarbayev could challenge his status as the man with whom Bush and other world leaders had to do business, particularly in arms control. Not only Bush but Germany's Helmut Kohl and other foreign leaders felt strong personal debts to Gorbachev for his assent to German reunification and the establishment of non-Communist governments in Eastern Europe. This was the moment for him to call in some of those debts. From May onward Gorbachev lobbied for an invitation to the summit of seven industrialized democracies, in London, in July, and tried hard to reestablish his credentials as an economic reformer. Grigory Yavlinsky, architect of the original five-hundred-days plan for the economy, was given Gorbachev's blessing for a semi-official mission to the United States, to draft a new plan under which Western aid would underwrite reform.

This was part of a broader process of ending the chill caused by the Baltic crackdown, which had led Bush to postpone a trip to Moscow that had been on his calendar for February. Other steps were taken to clear the way for better relations with the West. A long-delayed law on free emigration was at last pushed through parliament, and intensive efforts began to resolve outstanding issues holding up the Soviet-American Strategic Arms Reduction Treaty (START).

Gorbachev successfully cleared the way for Bush to visit Moscow in late July, but his renewed enthusiasm for the kind of economic reform the West favored caused increasing strains with Pavlov and the government.

What Gorbachev would have liked most of all was to get the Union Treaty signed, or at least approved in principle, before his trip to London. A new union treaty would end the uncertainty in the West about the division of power in Moscow and reaffirm his position at the center of the new Soviet political system. Speaking in the Kremlin, on July 2, he said: "In London I will have to answer the questions: Is the nine-plus-one agreement working? Will the Union Treaty be signed? Who can one have dealings with in the USSR, if everyone is declaring their sovereignty?"

Although the large Western aid package that he initially envisaged proved out of reach, Gorbachev achieved his political aim simply by getting himself invited to London and the Group of Seven summit. Playing adroitly on foreign fears of chaos and instability, he managed to reaffirm the principle that he, as leader of the Soviet Union, and not the leaders of individual republics, held the key to membership in such institutions as the International Monetary Fund and the World Bank. Whatever the final shape of economic reform in the Soviet Union and whatever the size and shape of Western aid to help it, Gorbachev would retain his role as the trusted broker in the middle.

Since Novo-Ogarevo, negotiations on the Union Treaty had proceeded much faster, though not at the speed Gorbachev would have liked. Yeltsin, now convinced that the center of gravity of the text was tilted toward the republics and away from the Union, joined Gorbachev in pressing for an early signing. He was joined by an increasingly impatient President Nursultan Nazarbayev of Kazakhstan. Ukrainian President Leonid Kravchuk, however, was effectively bound, by a decision of his own parliament in Kiev, to delay debate on the treaty until September, and it was uncertain if he would win immediate support to sign. The Ukrainian parliament had promised hunger-striking students, back in October 1990, that a new Ukrainian constitution would be approved first, before the Union Treaty could be signed. In the last rounds of negotiations, Yeltsin managed to extract some final concessions from Gorbachev over taxation powers, which would now be effectively in the hands of the republics. The text of the treaty was agreed in late July, and the signing date was fixed for August 20.

It was to preempt this that Gorbachev's conservative opponents fixed the date of their attempt to seize power. A look at the Treaty text must have confirmed their worst suspicions.[13]

The Treaty on the Union of Sovereign States was a compromise shot through with legal, political, and diplomatic ambiguities. Its first clause said: "Each republic that is a party to the treaty is a sovereign state. The Union of Soviet Sovereign Republics (USSR) is a sovereign federal democratic state, formed as a result of a merger of equal republics and exercising state authority within the limits of powers voluntarily delegated to it by the parties to the treaty." The new Soviet Union was a sovereign state under international law, but so were its constituent republics, defined as "full-fledged members of the international community." The powers vested in the new center would include defense, foreign policy, state security, and a certain number of economic powers, but most activities would be under "joint jurisdiction" with the republics, who would help define military and foreign policy and share rights over such resources as gold, diamonds, and foreign currency. The republics would have the final say over taxation and the budget.

The treaty solved almost none of the real issues of power and would probably have led to endless confusion, had it been adopted. It was a transitional arrangement on the road to the disintegration of a great empire. For the republics, it would have meant a real enhancement of their previous status, but for the representatives of the center, it heralded the end of the world. For the empire-savers, who believed in the future of the Soviet Union as a unitary state, Gorbachev had capitulated to the forces of destruction. This opinion was particularly strong among the senior military commanders, whose careers had been linked to the achievement of superpower military status.

Ever since April, Gorbachev's conservative opponents had been watching his course with mounting alarm. After flirting with them through the winter, he had deserted their camp and had no plans to come back. Any hope of reversing the political tide at the Russian presidential election had collapsed with Ryzhkov's crushing defeat at the hands of Yeltsin, in June. When the new treaty was signed, the prospects would be bleak for the Communist Party, the army, the KGB, the Soviet parliament, the central government, and the defense industries. None of these structures would have much future in a loose confederation of states. It was time to act.

21

A Hero of Our Time

The August coup against Gorbachev was the political equivalent of the Chernobyl nuclear catastrophe of 1986—an explosion that was both inevitable and avoidable.

Just as Chernobyl was the inevitable product of a nuclear system that ignored worldwide safety standards, the coup was also a disaster waiting to happen. It was the meltdown of a system that was not designed to withstand the stresses and strains of the democratic reforms to which Gorbachev had subjected it.

But it was a coup that could have been prevented. Like the operators in the control room at Chernobyl, who ignored the warning lights that flashed at them and the dials pointing to red, Gorbachev failed to spot the signs of approaching disaster. Gorbachev ignored warnings from Eduard Shevardnadze and Alexander Yakovlev, previously his fellow-architects of reform, that hard-liners were preparing a return to the old ways. So reckless was his overconfidence that he was even suspected, by some, of complicity in his own removal.

It was an example of wishful thinking and political misjudgment ranking with Stalin's disregard of warnings of the Nazi invasion on June 22, 1941. Just as the ever-mistrustful Stalin was betrayed by Hitler, the one man he ever trusted, Gorbachev was betrayed by men he felt would not dare try to remove him. When he discovered their betrayal, it was a shattering blow to his confidence.

For Yeltsin, on the other hand, the coup proved a vindication and a triumph. If Gorbachev was the hapless control room operator who allowed a political Chernobyl to happen, Yeltsin was the leader of the heroic firefighters who put out the blaze.

A blow-by-blow account of the coup, and of its collapse and aftermath, lies beyond the scope of this book. What can, however, be traced with reasonable precision are the warning signals that led up to it.

In May 1991, during the curious lull in tension in Moscow that followed the nine-plus-one agreement, I interviewed the conservative Russian nationalist writer and editor Alexander Prokhanov, to learn his views on Gorbachev and Yeltsin. Prokhanov, a man with close ties to the military establishment, told me a coup that would sweep away both Gorbachev and Yeltsin was quite possible. "It's quite easy to restore order in the country if you remove Gorbachev. . . . As soon as Gorbachev is removed, Yeltsin will be destroyed immediately." In his view, the Gorbachev-Yeltsin rivalry was a phony war between two men who shared the same liberal views and liberal advisers. The real struggle was between the old structures of the unitary state—the army, the KGB, the Communist Party, and the government—and the emerging forces of private businessmen, the "criminal bourgeoisie" and intellectuals who were hoping to replace them. In an agreed division of labor, Gorbachev was holding the old structures in check while Yeltsin was promoting the new ones, Prokhanov explained. He described the old power structures as seething with turmoil and internal strain, as they faced up to the disintegration of the state. The Communist Party, under Gorbachev, was like a plane, hurtling through the air without its wings and about to crash. But he predicted that a coup by the military alone was unlikely. "Our military leaders don't have a real thirst for power. Our soldiers are not Brazilians or Argentinians—it's not in the tradition of the Russian army. When all the other structures collapse and the army has to get in the harvest, cope with disasters, look after refugees, fight crime, even run the railways—at a certain point, it will be easier for them to take total power. But they don't really want it."[1]

Much of what Prokhanov said about the motivation for the coup later proved to be accurate. This was hardly surprising. Shortly before I interviewed him, Prokhanov had been discussing the idea of a coup with two senior officers and Oleg Baklanov, the civilian gray eminence of the Soviet military-industrial complex and one of the eight-man Emergency Committee that was to overthrow Gorbachev some ten weeks later. Their round-table talk—a thinly veiled discussion of the need for a military takeover—appeared, on May 9, in Prokhanov's weekly newspaper, *Den (The Day)*.

The two senior officers joining Baklanov were Admiral Vladimir Chernavin, head of the Soviet navy, and General Igor Rodionov, who had gained notoriety by commanding the troops who had killed unarmed civilians with shovels in the streets of Tbilisi, in April 1989. All of them agreed that the conversion of defense industries to civilian purposes was "criminal." Baklanov indignantly rejected the suggestion that the military share of the economy might be too large, arguing that, on the contrary, it was too small. It was the leaders of the defense industries, with their vast managerial experience, who should be running the rest of the economy, he argued. As for warnings of impending dictatorship, he replied that the Soviet Union was suffering already from several dictatorships—empty shelves, soaring prices, striking miners, and a liberal monopoly on the information media. Though Gorbachev's name was not mentioned at any point, the whole discussion displayed open contempt for his policies. Baklanov said he was optimistic that the Soviet Union would come through its "Time of Troubles" and reaffirm itself as a great power.

Baklanov was no minor official. Though little known, he had built his career supervising the defense industries and had been Communist Party secretary in charge of this sector. In 1991, he was deputy chairman of the USSR Defense Council, under Gorbachev. But despite his open opposition to Gorbachev's policies, he was neither rebuked nor removed, even when Gorbachev moved away from hard-line policies, from April 1991 onward.

His interview was only one of the alarm signals that Gorbachev failed to heed. There were increasing signs that the armed forces and security services were adopting what Colonel Alksnis had once threatened: "an autonomous mode of work." The mysterious military movements of September 1990, carrying out nonexistent potato harvesting duties around Moscow, had been dismissed by many as of no significance. When the crackdown came in the Baltic states, in January, there was at least a chance that the troops were following orders from Gorbachev. But as 1991 proceeded, it became more and more obvious that some units were acting in open defiance of Gorbachev, in order to embarrass him.

The best evidence for this were the attacks, by OMON special police units or "black berets," on Latvian and Lithuanian customs posts. At times even Boris Pugo, the interior minister, to whom the OMON nominally reported, seemed unaware of what they were doing. After denying their role in one such attack, Pugo was forced to admit he was mistaken, when Alexander Nevzorov, an extreme rightist Leningrad television journalist, broadcast film of the incident. The climax came in later July, when seven Lithuanian border guards were shot dead by a professional hit squad, just as Gorbachev was holding a summit with President Bush in Moscow. The attack, which caused outrage in Lithuania, marked the appearance on the Soviet scene of the kind of death squads better known in Latin America or South Africa. Although Lithuania avoided blaming Soviet units for the killing, there were strong suspicions that the raid was a provocation aimed at stirring up an anti-Russian backlash in the republic, to provide an excuse for military intervention.

The same desire to embarrass Gorbachev was detectable in the timing of a report, issued by the Soviet Prosecutor Nikolai Trubin, on the Vilnius killings in January. This document, which exonerated the military of any role in the deaths of civilians and implied that photographs of bodies being crushed by tanks had been faked, was released just as Gorbachev went to Oslo, in June 1991, to receive the Nobel Peace Prize he had won the previous year.

There were good reasons for Defense Minister Yazov and the senior military commanders to be alarmed by Gorbachev's planned Union Treaty. Not only would six republics probably refuse to sign it, but even the positions of the other nine were unclear.

The army had already been ordered to withdraw from territories in Eastern Europe, where soldiers had been stationed for forty-five years. If the Baltic and transcaucasian republics seceded, the army would have to retreat from lands the Russian Tsars had won a hundred or even two hundred years before. Though, on paper, the treaty still provided for a single army, in practice, the devolution of political authority to the republics threatened to make any idea of a single command unworkable. If several "sovereign" states tried to run a single army by committee, the result would probably be paralysis or worse, as was the pattern in Yugoslavia. Individual republics would gain wide powers over what military activities happened on their territories. Kazakstan wanted to stop nuclear tests in Semipalatinsk, and Russia wanted to stop them in Novaya Zemlya. The Ukraine, traumatized by Chernobyl, might demand the complete withdrawal of nuclear weapons from its territory.

The idea of the republics gaining control over the state budget was just as alarming. Yeltsin in particular was threatening big cuts in defense spending, and he was openly saying that Russia did not want to be a superpower.

Back in November, the army had taken its grievances to Gorbachev. Now, it was not afraid to put pressure on him, using a foreign government. Just when Gorbachev was seeking German support for an invitation to the Group of Seven summit in London, the commander of Soviet forces in Germany, General Matvei Burlakov, wrote to the West German Defense Ministry, announcing that the agreed withdrawal of his men would be slowed down and possibly halted because apartments being built for them with German aid were not ready. Although the timetable of withdrawal had been agreed to by Gorbachev, General Burlakov made clear that the army would make its own decisions. "If the special program for the construction of civilian dwellings is not fulfilled, . . . then the Supreme Command of the Western Group of Armed Forces feels it is forced to raise the question of a temporary stop to the planned withdrawal," he wrote.[2]

Throughout the summer of 1991, Gorbachev pursued his new reformist course, in partnership with Yeltsin, largely ignoring his critics. In mid-June, however, he was forced into action to crush a clumsy rebellion by Valentin Pavlov, his prime minister.

Pavlov had a particular reason for picking a fight with Gorbachev. The President's newfound enthusiasm for economic reform and his dispatch of the radical economist Grigory Yavlinsky on a mission to the United States threatened a repeat of the dispute in 1990, over the Shatalin plan. This time the central government could not be sure of winning the argument. Pavlov betrayed his unease by sneering, in public, at the "gentlemen from Harvard" with whom Yavlinsky was working, saying they did not know anything about the Soviet Union. Ever since the nine-plus-one agreement, with its commitment to a new constitution and new elections, Pavlov knew that, in effect, he was heading a lame duck government. If Gorbachev was to embrace radical reform in exchange for Western aid, then both Pavlov's anticrisis program and the very existence of his government were at risk. On June 17, he made a clumsy attempt to persuade the Supreme Soviet to grant him extra powers to issue decrees, as Ryzhkov had done under the old Council of Ministers. He argued that the cabinet was unable to make proper plans for 1992, because it lacked authority. Gorbachev, he said, was too busy to attend to every question—even if he had a forty-eight-hour working day.

Two days of closed-door debate followed. Pavlov did not quite have the courage to attack Gorbachev publicly and tried hard to play down his request, as if it were a piece of routine business. But conservative deputies, such as Evgeny Kogan of the Soyuz group, were keen to snipe at Gorbachev: "Let's strip the president of his powers—he's not using them anyway—and give them to someone who will." The suspicion that Pavlov's intervention was prearranged increased when Pugo, Yazov, and Kryuchkov all turned up with prepared speeches to speak in support of the prime minister. Yazov complained about a lack of housing for officers and troops, a failure to enforce the draft in at least five republics, and the refusal by republican governments to let their conscripts serve outside their home republics. "Soon there will be no armed forces. The armed forces can only exist under a unified command. When everyone is issuing commands, you no longer have an armed forces." Kryuchkov's speech carried echoes of the Cold War, which revealed the yawning political gulf between him and Gorbachev. He said that events in the country were following a 1977 plan by the CIA, to make the Soviet Union collapse. Western credits of between 150 and 250 billion dollars, as sought by Gorbachev, were "a fairy tale, an illusion." Pugo cited the confiscation of 52,000 firearms and 4.5 tons of explosives, since August 1990, as evidence of a breakdown of law and order. One deputy described the revolt as "a coordinated campaign to remove the president of the USSR from power." Some deputies were making open calls for him to be replaced by Anatoly Lukyanov, the chairman of the Supreme Soviet. Despite a forty-year association with Gorbachev, Lukyanov seemed to be siding more and more openly with the criticisms of the Soyuz group and warning that the parliament was being deprived of any role in negotiating the Union Treaty. In August, he too was to be arrested for complicity in the coup. Gorbachev finally appeared before the parliament, on June 21, telling the deputies in an angry speech that they were "completely detached from reality, as though under a bell-jar." He said to Soyuz group leaders Viktor Alksnis and Yuri Blokhin, "You do not understand anything that has happened to us and to society in recent months."

The browbeaten deputies voted, by 262 to 24, to pass Pavlov's request on to the president for further study, effectively killing it off. Smiling broadly, Gorbachev told reporters "the coup is over." Once again, it looked as though a bravura performance had routed his critics. But support for him in the parliament was wearing thin, and Lukyanov was now an uncertain ally.

In the Communist Party, signs of disintegration were gathering pace, with moves by reformers, such as Eduard Shevardnadze, Alexander Yakovlev, and Stanislav Shatalin, to set up a new democratic movement. Yeltsin's allies Alexander Rutskoi and Ivan Silayev were also involved. Gorbachev, previously so keen on maintaining party unity, appeared to see the new movement as a way of scaring the party conservatives. His spokesman, Vitaly Ignatenko, dropped hints that he saw its formation as a positive step. Gorbachev appeared to be maneuvering toward a split, in which the conservatives would be jettisoned and he would steer the remainder of the Party toward a new social democratic future. At the last Central Committee meeting before the August coup, on July 25 and 26, Gorbachev once again showed that his tactical alliance with Yeltsin was more important to him than the Party's complaints. On July 20, Yeltsin had fulfilled his pre-election promise, to curb the Party's influence in Russia, by issuing a decree banning it from all workplaces. But Gorbachev offered only lukewarm resistance, refusing demands that he use his presidential powers to annul Yeltsin's order.

Gorbachev's moves toward the conservatives, in 1990, had been accompanied by a wave of personnel changes, including the appointments of Pugo as interior minister and Yanayev as vice-president. But when he moved away from their policies, in the spring and summer of 1991, he left all the conservatives in place. It is possible he was planning to wait until the signing of the Union Treaty, or even longer, before renewing his team. Or perhaps he had the sort of overconfidence Alexander Kerensky had, in the summer and fall of 1917, half-hoping for a Bolshevik insurrection against his government, so that he could put it down.

When the Bolsheviks began their coup in Petrograd, in 1917, they signaled it with the firing of a single blank shot from the cruiser *Avrora*, moored on the embankments of the Neva. For seven decades the moment was to be immortalized, in official mythology and in films, as the start of a new era.

In 1991, the Moscow coup that ended by ushering seventy-four years of communist rule to a close was, at its start, bureaucratic, prosaic, and unimaginative—like its authors. Unlike the shot from the *Avrora*, it would not have made rich have been neutralized. At that time, Yeltsin was far away from the center of events, in Kazakhstan, holding talks with Nazarbayev. But by August 19, he had returned to his *dacha* on the outskirts of Moscow, ready for the signing of the Union Treaty the following day. The failure to arrest him there, well in advance of the coup announcement, was probably the conspirators' worst blunder. According to some accounts, they missed him by forty minutes.

By seven in the morning, Yeltsin was at his desk in the Russian parliament building, the White House, by the Moscow river. The streets of Moscow were choked with troops, tanks, and armored vehicles, many of them surrounded by angry crowds. It was like the invasion of Czechoslovakia on August 21, 1968, but this time the invaded city was Moscow, and the angry civilians waving their fists were Russians. There was anger and bewilderment on the streets but, at first, no mass resistance. Western correspondents who fanned out into the streets of the capital found many of the old political reflexes at work. It was as if, suddenly, the Stalinist "inertia of fear" had reasserted itself, and the old conspiracy between rulers and ruled had been restored.

Across the Soviet Union, resistance to the coup was also patchy. While leaders of the Baltic states and Moldavia proclaimed their resistance and Leningrad mayor Anatoly Sobchak did the same, others—notably Kravchuk in the Ukraine and Nazarbayev in Kazakhstan—sat on the fence. Even Georgia's president Zviad Gamsakhurdia, usually the first to denounce the machinations of the Kremlin, was suddenly cautious. The leaders of the Soviet government, the Soviet parliament, and the Communist Party all gave either active or passive support to the Emergency Committee. Some, like Foreign Minister Alexander Bessmertnykh, were suddenly unavailable through "illness," the traditional refuge of the scared bureaucrat in time of crisis. Until the tide began to turn, most of the Soviet political establishment lined up to join the "Opportunists' Party," in the hope of being on the winning side. After the coup was over, it would be hard to find anyone who admitted supporting it. While it was in progress, there were not so many who were prepared to stand up and be counted.

So when, in midmorning, Yeltsin marched out of his White House, surrounded by nervous aides, and clambered onto a tank to read a statement denouncing the coup, he was a lonely figure. "Soldiers, officers, and generals, the clouds of terror and dictatorship are gathering over the whole country.

They must not be allowed to bring eternal night," he proclaimed. He appealed for a general strike and announced that the army and the KGB on Russian territory were now subject to his orders. "The reactionaries will not triumph," he boomed. But there was only a small crowd around to hear his defiance. It looked like the courageous final gesture of a doomed man, recorded for the archives, like the home video that Gorbachev was to tape secretly in his Crimean villa, behind the backs of his guards. Soviet radio and television were in the hands of the coup leaders, and there was no certainty that Yeltsin's call to resist would be heard.

It was a moment of what British Prime Minister John Major later described as "sheer raw courage." Yeltsin's defiance proved, if proof was needed, that he was a man who was prepared to risk his life for his beliefs. The image he had helped create of himself, as a hero standing firm against impossible odds, was finally revealed to be more than what the Russians call *vrayno* (bragging). More than a year earlier, the writer Daniil Granin had reviewed Yeltsin's autobiography and had written prophetically that it would force its author to actually become the protagonist described on its pages. The man so aptly described by Vladimir Bukovsky as "a Bolshevik straight out of central casting" was center stage, in the final scene of the drama that began in 1917. Bolshevism—the system of totalitarian rule for which Lenin had staged the first Russian revolution—was in its death agony. By an irony of history it was Yeltsin, the convert to democracy, who looked and sounded more like an old-fashioned Bolshevik than any other Soviet leader, who was now leading the forces on the other side of the barricades.

Yeltsin's conduct during the coup displayed more than just courage; he not only outfaced but outsmarted the coup leaders, with a mixture of bluff and cunning. When the calls began to come in from world leaders offering support, Yeltsin sent shivers down their spines by telling them he had to cut the conversation short because tanks were rolling toward the Russian parliament. On the second day of the coup, he helped promote an image of confusion and disarray among the plotters by leaking unconfirmed reports that some of them had resigned. On the third day, he managed to trick Vladimir Kryuchkov into leaving the Kremlin for the Crimea, paving the way for his arrest.

Although many details emerged later which suggested the coup leaders may have been incompetent, divided, and even drunk, there was little doubt that the threat of an assault on the Russian parliament building was a real one. It was only because key army and KGB units refused to follow orders that a bloodbath was avoided.

As Yeltsin told an interviewer less than a week later, "One cannot say it was badly organized and badly prepared, if only because the Chief of General Staff of the Ministry of Defense knows how to plan combat operations." According to Yeltsin, the KGB's Alpha antiterrorist squad was to have carried out the assault, at six P.M. on the first evening of the coup. "They were armed with very powerful weapons. . . . The ground floor and first floors of the building were to be subjected to a simultaneous hail of fire from all sides. A hail of fire directed at everything, to shoot at every living thing, doors, windows, everything. Then they were to burst into the building through the doors at eighteen hundred hours on the nineteenth." The group was to capture or kill Yeltsin and his top eleven assistants, opening the way for a full assault to clear the building. "They would have destroyed thousands of people here, without batting an eyelid."[3]

Yeltsin's success in dividing the loyalties of the armed forces, particularly at a senior level, was not fortuitous. The failure of the Alpha group to obey orders and the defection of some army units to his side were not just last-minute decisions. They were the payoff for months of patient efforts by Yeltsin to build personal ties with the army and the KGB. The Baltic crisis in January made Yeltsin realize the need to create some kind of military structure for the republic, which would otherwise be totally defenseless against a right-wing coup. While there could be no question of building a separate Russian army, Yeltsin set himself a more limited goal. At every opportunity he tried to visit military units, doing his best to persuade officers and men he had their welfare at heart. Unlike some democrats, Yeltsin avoided criticism of the military as an institution, while supporting reform and a lower budget. He sought advice from people who knew the military, such as the historian of Stalinism General Dmitry Volkogonov. Before recruiting Alexander Rutskoi as his candidate for vice-president, in May 1991, he had already set up the nucleus of a Russian defense command under Colonel-General Konstantin Kobets. Kobets, leader of a group of Russian parliamentary deputies from the armed forces and KGB, was not just any run-of-the-mill general: He was head of communications for the entire armed forces and a deputy chief of the General Staff, under General Mikhail Moiseyev, Yazov's deputy. As such he was a key figure in the military establishment. Back in January, when many senior officers were baying for Yeltsin's head, after his call for soldiers to defy the crackdown in the Baltics, Kobets refused to join the chorus. "I am absolutely convinced that a common language may be found with the leadership of the (Russian) republic," he declared in an interview.[4] Shortly afterwards, Kobets became chairman of the new Russian State Committee on Defense and Security, a position where he was ideally placed to be a bridge between Yeltsin on one side and the top military commanders on the other. During the coup, it was his professional presence, organizing the defense of the Russian parliament against attack, which contributed to the army's divided loyalties.

After the planned assault on the Russian headquarters failed to happen within the first few hours, the tide gradually began to turn in Yeltsin's favor. Although, on the first night, only a few thousand people stayed to defend the barricaded Russian parliament, more and more came to swell their ranks later. Afghan war veterans helped man the defenses. Young Muscovites, so often in the past outnumbered at prodemocracy demonstrations by the middle-aged, suddenly took over. Television and radio pictures from the Russian parliament were beamed around the world. Shortwave broadcasts from abroad carried the news back to the Soviet Union that the outcome of the coup was still in the balance. Yeltsin, shirtsleeved, recorded a dramatic televized appeal to the Russian people for support. Like his call to Russian soldiers, in January, not to take part in repressive actions in the Baltics, this one appealed to Russian patriotism and Russian honor. "I appeal to you, soldiers and officers of Russia. Do not let yourselves be turned into blind weapons to defend privileges. In this difficult hour, distinguish real truth from lies. Do not dishonor Russia by shedding the blood of your own people. The days of the plotters are numbered. Law and constitutional order will be victorious. Russia will be free."[5]

The stirring appeal made no mention of Gorbachev, whose name was hardly likely to bring the crowds out onto the streets in support.

On the second night of the coup, crowds defied a military curfew to defend the makeshift barricades on the roads leading to the parliament. When airborne troops in light tanks tried to clear a barricade of buses on the Moscow ring road, there were confused and violent clashes in the murky drizzle. Three young men were killed, but there was no assault on the parliament itself. By the morning of the third day, the putsch was unraveling, as its support in the army crumbled and republican leaders who had sat on the fence joined in the condemnation. Yeltsin told the Russian parliament, meeting behind the barricades, that the coup leaders were fleeing Moscow. Rutskoi and Silayev were dispatched by plane to rescue Gorbachev and bring him back to Moscow. Within hours, the conspirators were arrested, except for Pugo, who shot himself.

When the shaken Gorbachev landed in Moscow's Vnukovo airport with his family, he was returning, as he himself was to admit, to a different country. The changes he initiated in 1985 had made it impossible to turn the clock back to a totalitarian system. To that extent, he had been vindicated. But on the other side of the balance, he was the one who had appointed the plotters in the first place. His judgment of people was shown to be flawed, his tactics of perpetual compromise mistaken, and his political beliefs a sham. The coup had shown that there was an unbridgeable gulf between communism and democracy. Gorbachev's attempt to marry the two had proved unworkable—"fried snowballs," as Leszek Kolakowski had written, back in the 1970s.

The failed coup acted as an accelerator to political processes which had been under way for months. Statues of Bolshevik heroes, such as Felix Dzerzhinsky, Yakov Sverdlov, and even Lenin himself, were toppled in scenes reminiscent of the overthrow of Communist rule in Eastern Europe. Every single one of the trends which the coup had been aimed at halting continued, but at several times the previous speed. Within days, the crumbling facade of the building Gorbachev was trying to repair had fallen. There was no more Soviet Communist Party, and without it, there could be little future for the Soviet empire it had held together.

If Gorbachev had thought for a moment that he might restore the political status quo, his illusions did not last for long. It was not Yeltsin's Russia but Gorbachev's Soviet Union that was now the "ghost state."

Conclusion

As the dust settles after the explosion of August 1991, it is evident that Soviet politics—if such a term can still be used—will never be the same again. The house that Gorbachev tried so hard to "restructure" finally came crashing down in rubble. As Yeltsin told the Russian Congress of People's Deputies in March 1991, *perestroika* proved to be only the final phase of stagnation. And Gorbachev has been left clinging to the wreckage, a diminished figure whose policy failed, as more farsighted observers in the West correctly predicted. Writing under the pseudonym "Z" in 1989, the American historian Martin Malia summarized Gorbachev's dilemma:

> All these reforms imply that there is a third way, a halfway house between what the ideological call socialism and capitalism, or what the inhabitants of the East think of as Sovietism and a "normal society." But there is no third way between Leninism and the market, between bolshevism and constitutional government. Marketization and democratization lead to the revival of civil society, and such a society requires the rule of law. But civil society under the rule of law is incompatible with the preservation of the lawless leading role.
>
> At some point, therefore, the red line will be reached where reform crosses over into the liquidation of the leading role and all the structures it has created. And both Russia and Central Europe are now reaching that critical line. The false problem of how to restructure Leninism is now giving way to the real problem of how to dismantle the system, how to effect at last

an exit from communism. *Perestroika* is not a solution, but a transition to this exit.[1]

Malia's harsh list of *perestroika*'s contradictions is not quite complete. Democratization led inevitably not just to the end of the Communist system but to self-determination and the break-up of the imperial state. As a leading American specialist on Soviet nationality problems foresaw several years earlier, "A liberalized Russia might be possible, but . . . a significantly liberalized Soviet Union is probably a contradiction in terms."[2]

History's final verdict on Gorbachev is likely to be colored by future events over which he will have little control. If the peoples of what was the Soviet Union find their way through this Time of Troubles to a better and more peaceful future, he will have earned their gratitude, as the man who showed them the road. If chaos and bloodshed follow him, he will be remembered as the emperor with no clothes.

Summing up Boris Yeltsin in 1991 is more difficult. Is he a democrat at all, or is he just a demagogue? Will he install gallows in the streets, as Nikolai Ryzhkov predicted, and lead Russia back into Tsarist autocracy? Or will Russia have a happy future of prosperity and democracy? Will he prove to have been a Bolshevik all along, or will he emerge as a Russian nationalist?

The rise, the fall, and the rebirth of Boris Yeltsin reveal him to be a complex figure: a man with a strong sense of personal destiny, but one who feels dissatisfied with himself 95 percent of the time; a man struggling to reconcile his authoritarian and abrasive personality with the search for a new, democratic political culture; a man who never thought of himself as a Russian who finds himself at the head of a newly aware Russian nation.

Yeltsin's record shows an acute political intuition, an ability to read power relationships, and a populist flair for discerning the mood of the Russian people. He has little use for abstract concepts but his early diagnosis of the flaws in Gorbachev's *perestroika* was vindicated by events. While he has made some errors of judgment, they have been less serious than those made by Gorbachev.

A close look at Yeltsin's turbulent relationship with Gorbachev since 1985 shows mistakes and personal emotion on both sides. When, after the coup, Yeltsin publicly humiliated Gorbachev in front of the Russian parliament, there must have been an element of sweet revenge for the far worse humiliations he had suffered at Gorbachev's hands. On the whole, since 1985 it is Gorbachev who emerges from the story with the worse record of zigzags, broken promises, and vindictive comments. Yeltsin's strategy toward Gorbachev, since 1990, has been not to replace his rival as president of the Soviet Union but, like a leader of the boyars at the Muscovite court, to turn him into a weak autocrat, subordinate to the will of republican leaders.

This strategy initially met with strong resistance from Gorbachev, who saw himself as the legitimate head of a legitimate state. It can be argued that Yeltsin, while sometimes brutal in the tactics of his struggle against the center, grasped intuitively that the logic of history was moving toward the end of the old empire and acted accordingly.

Yeltsin's character flaws—impulsiveness and a prickly sensitivity to real or imagined insults—are well advertised. He has a Reaganesque dislike for detail and a rough, undiplomatic manner. But he has shown an ability to learn from his mistakes and take advice. His strengths, clearly displayed during his resistance to the August coup, include courage, decisiveness, and leadership in a crisis. But then some accused him of overplaying his hand in the days after the coup, in the pursuit of personal power.

Is his record that of a democrat? Those who focus narrowly on personal qualities may argue that an outsize ego and an autocratic personality do not help him pass the test. But those who look exclusively at his personal beliefs, as expressed in his public speeches, will put him squarely in the democrats' camp.

If a democratic politician is one who is prepared to submit to the verdict of the voters in a free ballot, then Yeltsin passes easily, with his three resounding electoral victories in three years. Those who expect him to act like an American or Western European politician rather than as a product of Russian political culture will remain skeptical. But whether he can meet the broader challenge of governing democratically, of making democracy work in Russia, is more of an open question. If Yeltsin, with such great popular support, fails, then the chances of anyone else succeeding are slim. The challenge in making democracy work in Russia lies partly in overcoming the legacy of Russia's own history, so as to create a civil society and the market economy essential to sustain it. For democracy to take root, there has to be not only the election of a legitimate leader but the growth of a new society with democratic movements and parties, to articulate diverse interests.

Like Lech Walesa in Poland, Yeltsin has managed to form a coalition that bridges the traditional gulf between the workers and the intelligentsia, so far apart for most of Russia's recent history. But just as the transition from opposition to power split Walesa's coalition and divided the Solidarity movement, Yeltsin may find it impossible to keep both groups on his side for long. Tough choices will have to be made among the varying interests of industrial workers, emergent businessmen, private farmers, and foreign investors. Like Gorbachev, Yeltsin may lose his way and find himself relying on an unstable coalition of new groups and parties with irreconcilable interests.

This challenge is one faced by all societies emerging from Communism. But in Eastern Europe, the rebuilding of society is made easier by at least some elements of what has been termed a "usable past." In contrast, Russia's past is mostly undemocratic, though this may not be an insuperable problem.

Russia's deeper challenge may be the reconstruction not of society but of the state. Amid the disintegration of the old Soviet Union, Yeltsin has to find a working formula for a new kind of Russian governance. Borders, citizenship, sovereignty, minority rights, and future defense arrangements—the last the most difficult single issue—all have to be negotiated amid economic chaos and a collapsing currency. Even shorn of the other fourteen Soviet republics, Russia may still be too much of an empire, too large and too diverse, to be a democratically run nation-state.

When empires break up, the process rarely stops halfway. Transitional arrangements normally prove to be unstable compromises that sooner or later collapse. Russia's dual history, as both empire and nation-sate, leaves it with a legacy of problems whose solutions will demand extraordinary vision and statesmanship, as the communist past gives way to a future in which nationalism may prove stronger than democracy. The calendar may say 1991, but the unsolved problems are those of 1917, re-emerging to haunt a new generation of political leaders.

More than twenty million Russians live outside the borders of the Russian republic and for the first time in centuries, they risk being unprotected by the Russian mother-state. In newly independent Latvia, Lithuania, and Estonia, the process has already begun. In Moldavia, the Ukraine, and Kazakhstan, it may not be long postponed. If angry Russian minorities demand self-determination and union with Russia, the result could be a reawakening of the ugly side of Russian nationalism, something which Yeltsin has so far held in check. The result could be worsening tension between Russia and the other republics, many of them ruled by Communists who became overnight converts to national "independence" when the coup in Moscow collapsed.

Handling the "Russian question," in cooperation with the other former Soviet republics in the new loose confederation, will require a great deal of finesse and will test Yeltsin's abilities to the limit. Even if he can avoid accusations of a "new Tsarist empire" in Moscow, he also has to massage the bruised egos of the Russians through the difficult postimperial transition.

As de Gaulle reconciled the French, thirty years ago, to a state that no longer included Algiers or Oran, Yeltsin may have to reconcile the Russians to a future in which Kiev, Odessa, and the Crimea are part of an independent Ukraine. Within the arbitrarily drawn borders of the Russian republic, Yeltsin will have to resolve the same contradiction as Gorbachev in the Soviet Union—between democratizing his empire and keeping it together. Even without interference from the "center," it may be almost impossible to find a democratic constitutional settlement that will balance the need for a cohesive Russian nation-state against the striving of Tatars, Bashkirs, and other national groups for enhanced statehood.

No politician is fully tested until he has not only fought for power in opposition but captured power and used it. For a born rebel, the real examination begins when the long passage through the political wilderness is over and there is no one left to rebel against. If Boris Yeltsin fails in his declared aim of leading the rebirth of Russia, he will go down as just another *samozvanets* or pretender. If he meets the challenge, he may join that special category of rebels who, like Churchill and de Gaulle, return from the wilderness in the middle of national collapse with the aura of men who were right before their time.

For such outsize characters, both success and failure occur on a large scale. Such characters have little room for qualified success or mitigated failure. Yeltsin would probably be content to be judged in these terms. As he told an interviewer from *The Times*, in March 1990: "A man must live like a great bright flame and burn as brightly as he can. In the end he burns out. But this is better than a mean little flame."

Source Notes

INTRODUCTION

1. Edward Keenan, "Muscovite Political Folkways," *The Russian Review*, vol. 45 (1986): 116.
2. Pervy Syezd Narodnikh Deputatov SSSR 1989, Stenografichesky Otchet (Transcript of the First Congress of People's Deputy of the USSR, 1989, Stenographic graphic).
3. Alexander Prokhanov, "Tragediya Tsentralisma," *Literaturnaya Rossiya* (Jan. 5, 1990): 4–5.

TWO

1. Keenan, "Muscovite Political Folkways," p. 118.
2. S. Frederick Starr, "A Usable Past," *The New Republic* (May 15, 1989): 24–27. Starr argues that a civil society including tens of thousands of political groups was already in being by the mid-1980s. "All of this ferment began prior to Gorbachev's rise to power in 1985. He neither created it, nor did much to encourage it."
3. Angus Roxburgh, *The Second Russian Revolution* (London: BBC Books, 1991). This book and the six-part television series on which it is based provide valuable material on the role of Ligachev and the Politburo intrigues of this period.
4. Peter Reddaway, "The Quality of Gorbachev's Leadership," *Soviet Economy*, 6 (1990): 127.
5. Roxburgh, *The Second Russian Revolution*.
6. Reddaway, "The Quality of Gorbachev's Leadership," p. 125.
7. *The Washington Post* (Nov. 25, 1990): A20.
8. Alexander Motyl, *Will the Non-Russians Rebel?* (New York: Cornell University Press, 1987).
9. Nikolai Rudensky, interview with the author, Moscow, May 1990.
10. Alexander Yanov, *The Russian Challenge and the Year 2000* (Oxford: Basil Blackwell, 1987). For a more sympathetic view of Russian nationalism before Gorbachev, see the writings of John Dunlop.

THREE

1. Vladimir Bukovsky, "Born Again and Again," *The New Republic* (Sept. 10, 1990).

2. Sergei Shakhrai, interview with the author, Moscow, May 1991.
3. Roy Medvedev, interview in *l'Unita* [Milan] (Nov. 7, 1990): 11.
4. Dmitry Kazakov, "Trudno byt Bogom," *Glasnost* [Moscow] (May 16, 1991). This new-style CPSU weekly is not to be confused with another unofficial magazine whose name it copied.
5. *The Ukrainian Weekly* [Newark, NJ] (March 31, 1991): 3.
6. *Le Monde* [Paris] (April 17, 1991).
7. *U.S. News & World Report* (July 1, 1991).
8. *The New York Times* (June 22, 1991).
9. "Tsel—Obnovlenie Rossii," *Izvestia* (May 1991).
10. *The Times* [London] (March 6, 1990).
11. *Rossiiskaya Gazeta* (April 23, 1991).
12. Reuter Transcript Report (June 20, 1991).

FOUR

1. The book, titled in Russian *Confession on a Given Theme*, was written with the help of Valentin Yumashev, a journalist for *Ogonek* magazine, and based on tape recordings made in the summer and autumn of 1989. References to Yeltsin's account of his early career come from this book, unless indicated otherwise.
2. Hedrick Smith, *The New Russian* (New York: Random House, 1990): 32–44. Smith gives the fullest account I have seen of Gorbachev's highly political family background.
3. Interview with Josef Riedmiller, *Süddeutsche Zeitung* [Munich] (March 9, 1990).
4. Interview with Alexander Olbiks, *Sovietskaya Molodezh* [Riga] Jan. 3–4, 1990.
5. Ibid.
6. Quoted in *Glasnost News & Review* [New York] (October–December 1990).
7. *Pravda* (Feb. 26, 1981).
8. B. N. Yeltsin, *Sredny Ural—Rubezhi Sozidaniya* (Sverdlovsk, 1981).
9. Interview in "Second Russian Revolution," Part 3.
10. Ibid.

FIVE

1. *Moskovskaya Pravda* (Jan. 25, 1986).
2. *Pravda* (Feb. 27, 1986).
3. *Arkhiv Samizdata No. 23* (July 18, 1986).
4. Interview with Yeltsin, "Second Russian Revolution," Part 3.
5. Interview with *Wiener Zeitung* [Vienna] (Sept. 20, 1988).
6. *Moskovskaya Pravda* (April 14, 1987).
7. Interviews with Dolgikh, Yeltsin, Ligachev, "Second Russian Revolution," Part 3.
8. Interview with Alexander Yakovlev, "Second Russian Revolution," Part 3.
9. Mikhail Poltoranin, interview in *Corriere della Sera* [Milan] (May 12, 1988), quoted in Radio Liberty Research (May 20, 1988).
10. Interview in *Moskovskaya Pravda* (April 14, 1987).
11. Ibid.
12. Mikhail Poltoranin, interview by the author, Moscow, May 1991.
13. *Moskovskaya Pravda* (Aug. 21, 1987).
14. Roxburgh, *Second Russian Revolution*, p. 71.
15. Interview with Yeltsin, "Second Russian Revolution," Part 3.

SIX

1. Dusko Doder and Louise Branson, *Gorbachev—Heretic in the Kremlin.*
2. *Izvestia Tsentralnovo Komiteta CPSU*, 2/1989, pp. 239–287.
3. Ibid., p. 279.
4. Interview with Poltoranin, "Second Russian Revolution," Part 3.
5. Roxburgh, *Second Russian Revolution*, p. 78.
6. *Sovietskaya Rossiya* (Nov. 24, 1987).

SEVEN

1. Mikhail Poltoranin, interview by the author, Moscow, May 1991.
2. Roxburgh, *Second Russian Revolution*, pp. 83–87.
3. *Le Monde* (Feb. 2, 1988).
4. Korotich interview in *NRC Handelsblad* [Rotterdam] (Dec. 11, 1987).
5. *Moscow News* 51 (Dec. 20, 1987).
6. Timothy J. Colton, "Moscow Politics and the El'tsin Affair," *The Harriman Institute Forum*, Vol. 1, No. 6 (June 1988).
7. Interview with Peter Snow, BBC Television, May 30, 1988.
8. Interview with Elem Klimov, "Second Russian Revolution," Part 3.
9. Interview with Daniil Granin, "Second Russian Revolution," Part 3.
10. Doder and Branson, *Gorbachev.*
11. Interview with Alexander Olbiks, *Sovietskaya Molodezh* [Riga] (Aug. 4, 1988).
12. Interview with Melita Sunjic, *Wiener Zeitung* [Vienna] (Sept. 20, 1988).

EIGHT

1. Yeltsin's talk to the Komsomol on November 12, 1988, appeared in the unofficial newspaper *Belorusskaya Tribuna*, Nos. 4 and 5 (1989). The version in the Perm newspaper *Molodaya Gvardiya* (Dec. 4, 1988) was quoted in *l'Unita* [Milan] (Dec. 27, 1988). The transcript of a partial recording broadcast by Vladivostok Radio can be found in FBIS: Soviet Union (May 3, 1989).
2. Interview with Ezio Mauro, *La Repubblica* [Rome] (Jan. 7, 1989).
3. Interview with Paolo Garimberti, *La Repubblica* [Rome] (March 19–20, 1989).
4. AFP in English, March 21, 1989.
5. Interviews with Ezio Mauro, *La Repubblica* [Rome] (March 24, 1989) and Martin Sixsmith, BBC World Service, March 24, 1989.
6. Interview with NHK Television [Tokyo], May 2, 1989.
7. Vitaly Tretyakov, "The Boris Yeltsin Phenomenon," *Moscow News* 16 (April 16, 1989).
8. Interview with Shakhnazarov, "Second Russian Revolution," Part 4.
9. Arkady Murashev, "Mezhregionalnaya deputatskaya gruppa," *Ogonek* 32 (August 1990).
10. Arkady Murashev, interview by the author, Moscow, May 1991.
11. Interview with Chernichenko, "Second Russian Revolution," Part 4.
12. Interview with Sobchak, "Second Russian Revolution," Part 4.
13. Interview with Chernichenko, "Second Russian Revolution," Part 4.
14. Interview with Yeltsin, "Second Russian Revolution," Part 4.
15. *The New York Times* (May 30, 1989).
16. *The New York Times* (June 9, 1989).

NINE

1. *Washington Post* (Sept. 11, 1989).
2. *Washington Post*, Style Section (Sept. 13, 1989).
3. A. M. Rosenthal, "Thanks, Boris, But No," *The New York Times* (Sept. 19, 1989).
4. *The New York Times* (Sept. 13, 1989).
5. *Washington Post* (Sept. 18, 1989).
6. *Washington Post*, Style Section (Sept. 13, 1989).
7. *Baltimore Sun* (Sept. 13, 1989).
8. *Komsomolskaya Pravda* (Sept. 27, 1989).
9. "Frontiers of Soviet Democracy: A Report on Boris Yeltsin's Address at the Institute for Soviet and East European Studies," *University of Miami Occasional Papers Series*, Vol. III, No. 3.
10. Yeltsin interview with Alexander Olbiks, *Sovietskaya Molodezh* [Riga] (Jan. 3–4, 1990).
11. Ibid.
12. Quoted in Doder and Branson, *Gorbachev*.

TEN

1. Arkady Murashev, interview by the author, Moscow, May 1991.
2. Ibid.
3. Mikhail Poltoranin, interview by the author, Moscow, May 1991.
4. Yelena Bonner, telephone interview by the author, Moscow, May 1991.
5. Mikhail Poltoranin, interview by the author, Moscow, May 1991.
6. Anatoly Sobchak, *Khozhdenie vo Vlast* (Moscow: Novosti, 1991), pp. 39–41.
7. Nikolai Rudensky, interview by the author, Moscow, May 1991.
8. *The Sunday Telegraph* [London] (July 30, 1989).
9. Yeltsin interview with Alexander Olbiks, *Sovietskaya Molodezh* [Riga] (Jan. 3–4, 1990).
10. *Literaturnaya Gazeta* (June 28, 1989).
11. Yeltsin interview with Alexander Olbiks, *Sovietskaya Molodezh* [Riga] (Jan. 3–4, 1990).
12. Yeltsin interview in *Positsiya* [Moscow] (February 1990).
13. Yeltsin interview in *Berlingske Tidende* [Copenhagen] (Feb. 18, 1990).
14. Yeltsin interview in *Argumenty i Fakty* (March 3–9, 1990).
15. Yeltsin interview with Yegor Yakovlev, *Moscow News* (Jan. 14, 1990).
16. Yeltsin interview with Moscow Radio World Series in Russian, February 17, 1990.
17. Yeltsin interview in *Berlingske Tidende* [Copenhagen] (Feb. 18, 1990).
18. Viktor Lomin interview on "Vremya," Moscow Television, February 9, 1990.
19. Yeltsin interview with Moscow Radio World Service in Russian, February 17, 1990.
20. Yeltsin interview in *Berlingske Tidende* [Copenhagen] (Feb. 18, 1990).
21. Yeltsin interview in *Soyuz* No. 38 (1990).
22. Yeltsin interview in *Pravda* (June 20, 1990).
23. Interview with Alexander Olbiks, *Sovietskaya Molodezh* [Riga] (July 1990).
24. Yeltsin interview in *Soyuz* No. 38 (1990).

ELEVEN

1. Quoted in Marc Raeff, *Russian Intellectual History. An Anthology* (Atlantic Highlands, N.J.: Humanities Press, 1986).

2. Richard Pipes, Introduction to *Handbook of Major Soviet Nationalities*, Zev Katz, Rosemarie Rogers, and Frederic Harned, eds. (New York: The Free Press, 1975).
3. Richard Pipes, *The Formation of the Soviet Union* (Cambridge, MA: Harvard U. Press, 1954), p. 1.
4. Richard Pipes, "Solving the Nationality Problem," *Problems of Communism* (September–October 1967): 125–131.
5. Ibid.
6. Hugh Seton-Watson, *The Russian Empire 1801–1917* (New York: Oxford University Press, 1988), p. 267.
7. Roman Szporluk, "The Imperial Legacy," in *The Nationalities Factor in Soviet Politics and Society* (Boulder, CO: Westview Press, 1990).
8. Pipes, *The Formation of the Soviet Union*, p. 285.
9. Quoted in Roman Szporluk, "History and Russian Nationalism," in E. Allworth, ed., *Ethnic Russia Today: The Dilemma of Dominance* (New York: Pergamon Press, 1980).
10. Roman Szporluk, "Dilemmas of Russian Nationalism," *Problems of Communism* (July–August 1989).
11. Alexander Yanov, *The Russian Challenge and the Year 2000* (Oxford: Basil Blackwell, 1987).
12. Sobchak, *Khozhdenie vo Vlast*, p. 200.

TWELVE

1. Gail W. Lapidus, "Restructuring the Soviet Federation," *Soviet Economy 1989*, pp. 201–250.
2. Interview in *Polityka* [Warsaw] (Nov. 25, 1989).
3. Interview in *Sovietshaya Molodezh* [Riga] (Nov. 23, 1989).
4. *Sovietskaya Rossiya* (July 29, 1989).
5. *Pravda* (Aug. 17, 1989).
6. *Pravda* (Aug. 19, 1989).
7. *Izvestia* (Sept. 2, 1989).
8. *Pravda* (May 12, 1990).
9. *Sovietskaya Rossiya* (May 20, 1980).
10. Interview in *Duma* [Sofia] (May 17, 1990).
11. Interview on Radio Moscow, May 3, 1990.
12. Yeltsin interview in *Soyuz* No. 38 (1990).
13. Roxburgh, *Second Russian Revolution*, p. 181.
14. Interview in *Avanti* [Rome] (May 30, 1990).
15. *The New York Times* (May 27, 1990).
16. *Washington Post* (May 31, 1990).
17. *The New York Times* (July 1, 1990).
18. Leon Aron, "Yeltsin: Russia's Rogue Populist," *Washington Post* (June 3, 1990).
19. Quoted in *Glasnost News & Review* [New York] (October–December 1990).
20. Ibid.
21. Giulietto Chiesa, "The 28th Congress of the CPSU," *Problems of Communism* (July–August 1990).
22. *Rabochaya Tribuna* (Oct. 14, 1990).

THIRTEEN

1. Interview with Khazbulatov, *Komsomolskaya Pravd* (June 17, 1988).
2. Interview with Silayev, *Moscow News* (July 1–8, 1990).

3. "Text of the RSFSR Declaration of Sovereignty," *Sovietskaya Rossiya* (June 14, 1990).
4. Pavel Voshchanov, *Komsomolskaya Pravda* (June 12, 1990).
5. Fedor Burlatsky, *Literaturnaya Gazeta* (July 10, 1990).
6. Alexander Tsipko, *Izvestia* (May 26, 1990).
7. Interview with Andranik Migranyan and Igor Klyamkin in *Literaturnaya Gazeta* (Dec. 27, 1989). Further discussion and reply by the authors in issues 38, 39, 42, and 52.
8. Yeltsin interview on "Vremya," Moscow Television, June 25, 1990.
9. Moscow Television, June 26, 1990.
10. Moscow Television, June 26, 1990.

FOURTEEN

1. Yeltsin interview with Alexander Olbiks, August 3, 1990.
2. Mikhail Berger, *Izvestia* (July 2, 1990).
3. Interview with Nikolai Petrakov, "Second Russian Revolution," Part 6.
4. Yeltsin interview with Soviet Television, August 2, 1990.
5. Anders Åslund, "The Making of Economic Policy in 1989 and 1990," *Soviet Economy* (1990): 65–94.
6. Interview with Nikolai Ryzhkov, "Second Russian Revolution," Part 6.
7. "Transition to Market," report of The Cultural Initiative Foundation (Moscow/Arckhangelskoe, 1990).
8. Interview with Stanislav Shatalin, "Second Russian Revolution," Part 6.
9. Ed A. Hewett, "The New Soviet Plan," *Foreign Policy* (Winter 1990–91).
10. Interview with Nikolai Ryzhkov, "Second Russian Revolution," Part 6.
11. Interview with Vadim Bakatin, "Second Russian Revolution," Part 6.
12. Interview with Nikolai Ryzhkov, "Second Russian Revolution," Part 6.
13. Nikolai Ryzhkov, interview with Austrian Television, September 11, 1990.
14. News conference by Nikolai Ryzhkov and Leonid Abalkin, Moscow Television, September 12, 1990.
15. Shatalin interview in *Trud* (Sept. 15, 1990).
16. Yeltsin interview with Moscow Television, September 13, 1990.
17. Abalkin interview in *Sovietskaya Rossiya* (Sept. 23, 1990).
18. Ryzhkov interview in *Komsomolskaya Znamya* [Kiev] (Sept. 25, 1990).
19. Shatalin interview in *Izvestia* (Sept. 26, 1990).
20. Shatalin interview with Soviet Television, September 28, 1990.
21. Yavlinsky interview in *Komsomolskaya Pravda* (Oct. 18, 1990).

FIFTEEN

1. *Pravda* (Aug. 14, 1990).
2. Moscow Radio, August 11, 1990.
3. Bill Keller, "Boris Yeltsin Taking Power," *The New York Times Magazine*, (September 23, 1990): 80.
4. Richard Pipes, *Russian under the Old Regime*.
5. Sergei Shakhrai, interview by the author, Moscow, May 1991.
6. *Rossiiskaya Gazeta* (March 28, 1991).
7. *Sovietskaya Rossiya* (Dec. 9, 1990).
8. Moscow Television, August 12, 1990.
9. Tass and Moscow Radio, October 11, 1990.
10. Ruslan Khazbulatov, *Izvestia* (Sept. 25, 1990).
11. This account of Yeltsin's journey is based on a variety of Soviet news reports in FBIS: Soviet Union for August 1990.

12. *Krasnaya Zvezda* (Aug. 28, 1990).
13. Moscow Television, September 1, 1990.
14. Ruslan Khazbulatov, *Argumenty i Fakty* 28 (July 14–20, 1990).
15. Rafik Nishanov, *Izvestia* (Sept. 7, 1990).

SIXTEEN

1. Lariss Piyashcheva, *Sovietskaya Estonia* (Aug. 24, 1990).
2. Andranik Migranyan, *Izvestia* (Sept. 21, 1990).
3. Lyubov Shevtsova, *Izvestia* (Oct. 9, 1990).
4. Yeltsin speech to USSR Supreme Soviet, November 16, 1990.
5. Moscow Radio, November 13, 1990; *Izvestia* and *Sovietskaya Rossiya* (Nov. 15, 1990); *Krasnaya Zvezda* (Nov. 16, 1990).
6. *Pravda* (Sept. 6, 1990).
7. Roxburgh, *Second Russian Revolution*, p. 199.
8. Ibid.
9. Moscow Radio, November 29, 1990; *Pravda* (Dec. 1, 1990).
10. Kryuchkov interview in *Pravda* (Dec. 13, 1990); Kryuchkov interview in *Soyuz* 47 (November 1990).
11. Janis Peters interview in *Bild am Sonntag* [Hamburg] (Jan. 20, 1991).

SEVENTEEN

1. *Sovietskaya Estonia* (June 1, 1990).
2. *Sovietskaya Estonia* (June 2, 1990).
3. Kazimiera Prunskiene, interview with Moscow Radio World Service, August 6, 1990.
4. *Soyuz* 31 (August 1990).
5. Khazbulatov interview with Moscow Television, January 19, 1991.
6. Open letter from I. G. Charnetska, Vilnius, *Literaturnaya Rossiya* (Nov. 2, 1990): 9.
7. Interview with TSN News, Moscow Television, October 31, 1990.
8. Yeltsin interview with Moscow Radio, January 9, 1991.
9. Reuters, January 9, 1991.
10. Moscow Radio, January 12, 1991.
11. *Literaturnaya Gazeta* (Jan. 9, 1991).
12. *Pravda* (Jan. 17, 1991).
13. *Berlingske Tidende* (Jan. 22, 1991).
14. *Der Spiegel* (Feb. 11, 1991).
15. Moscow Radio, January 15, 1991.
16. Interview with Vadim Bakatin, "Second Russian Revolution," Part 6.
17. *Izvestia* (Jan. 23, 1991).
18. Reuters, January 20, 1991.
19. *Argumenty i Fakty* 4 (1991).
20. Reuters, January 14, 1991.

EIGHTEEN

1. The authoritarian ideology of the "Experimental Creative Center," founded by Sergei Kurginyan and lavishly funded by the governments of Ryzhkov and Pavlov, was set out in *Moskovskaya Pravda* (March 28, 1991). See also Kurginyan's article "The Financial War," in *Moskovskaya Pravda* (March 1, 1991). For analysis, see Victor Yasmann, "Elite Think Tank Prepares 'Post-Perestroika Strategy,' " Radio Liberty Report on the

USSR, Vol. 3, No. 21 (May 24, 1991); also Paul Bellis and Jeff Gleisner, "After Perestroika, A Neo-Conservative Manifesto," in *Russia and the World* 19 (1991).

2. *Moscow News* (Jan. 6–13, 1991).
3. *Komsomolskaya Pravda* (Jan. 22, 1991).
4. *Izvestia* (Jan. 25, 1991).
5. *Der Spiegel* (Jan. 21, 1991).
6. *Berliner Zeitung* (Jan. 15, 1991).
7. Brazauskas news conference quoted in FBIS: Soviet Union (Feb. 7, 1991).
8. Moscow Radio, January 28, 1991.
9. Radio Russia, February 4, 1991.
10. Tass in English, February 9, 1991.
11. *Trud* (Feb. 12, 1991).
12. Moscow Television, February 19, 1991.
13. News conference by Nazarbayev and Kravchuk, *Krasnaya Zvezda* (Feb. 21, 1991).
14. *Argumenty i Fakty* 9 (1991).
15. Khazbulatov interview with Radio Budapest, February 24, 1991.
16. Moscow Television, February 26, 1991.
17. Radio Russia, March 9, 1991.
18. *Komsomolskaya Pravda* (March 14, 1991).
19. Reuters, March 11, 1991.
20. Radio Russia, March 15, 1991.
21. Moscow Radio, March 5, 1991.
22. *Trud* (March 27, 1991).
23. Reuters, March 28, 1991.
24. Reuters, April 4, 1991.

NINETEEN

1. Moscow Television, April 4, 1991.
2. Letter from V. Kucherenko, Chairman of the Supreme Soviet Budget, Planning, and Financial Commission, V. Orlov, USSR Minister of Finance, and V. Gerashchenko, Chairman of Gosbank.
3. *Rossiiskaya Gazeta* (April 23, 1991).
4. *Moscow News* 13 (1991).
5. News conference, Moscow Television, Second Program, April 5, 1991.
6. Radio Russia, April 13, 1991.
7. *Izvestia* (April 11, 1991).
8. *Le Monde* (April 17, 1991).
9. *Time* (April 22, 1991).
10. Reuters, April 26, 1991.
11. Moscow Television, Second Program, May 4, 1991.
12. *Rossiiskaya Gazeta* (May 5, 1991).
13. Mikhail Poltoranin, interview by the author, Moscow, May 1991.
14. Moscow Radio, May 6, 1991.

TWENTY

1. Reuters, May 24, 1991.
2. Reuters, May 20, 1991.
3. Julia Wishnewsky, "Will the Conservatives Join the Liberals Against Gorbachev?" Radio Liberty Report on the USSR, Vol. 3, No. 6 (1991).
4. Radio Russia, June 1, 1991.
5. *Rabochaya Tribuna* (May 14, 1991).

6. Tass, May 14, 1991.
7. Radio Russia, June 1, 1991.
8. Ibid.
9. Reuters, May 28, 1991.
10. Mayak Radio, May 28, 1991.
11. Reuters, June 13, 1991.
12. Reuters, *Reuters Transcript Report*, eyewitness reporting by the author in Washington and New York, June 19–21, 1991.
13. Tass in English, August 14, 1991.

TWENTY-ONE

1. Alexander Prokhanov, interview by the author, Moscow, May 1991.
2. Reuters, June 26, 1991.
3. Interview with Russian Television, August 26, 1991.
4. *Argumenty i Fakty* 4 (1991).
5. Russian Television and Visnews, August 20, 1991.

CONCLUSION

1. "Z", "To the Stalin Mausoleum," *Daedalus* (Winter 1990): 295–344.
2. Paul Goble, "Gorbachev and the Soviet Nationality Problem," in Maurice Friedberg and Heyward Isham, eds., *Soviet Society under Gorbachev* (Armonk, NY: M. E. Sharpe, 1987), p. 99.

Selected Bibliography

Quotations from Yeltsin's autobiography *Against the Grain* have been taken from the British edition, translated by Michael Glenny (London: Jonathan Cape, 1990). The paperback edition has a seven-page epilogue, written in February 1991 (London: Pan Books, 1991). The Russian edition *Ispoved na zadannuyu temu* was published in 1990 by several Soviet publishing houses.

I have made extensive use of the English translations of Soviet media by the US govenment Foreign Broadcast Information Service (FBIS). Most of the references come from FBIS: Soviet Union, 1981–1991. In places I have altered the translations to read more smoothly. Speeches to the Congresses of People's Deputies and the Supreme Soviets of the USSR and the Russian republic that are not referenced are taken from FBIS reports.

Detailed source material on the top-level intrigues of the Gorbachev period are to be found in a six-part British television documentary, broadcast in 1991, "The Second Russian Revolution," Brian Lapping Associates. Angus Roxburgh, consultant for the series, has published a book with the same title which contains additional material (London: BBC Books, 1991).

I have also relied heavily on the weekly survey of Soviet events "Report on the USSR," published by the Radio Liberty/Radio Free Europe Research Institute in Munich.

Other works consulted have included the following books:

Richard Pipes. *The Formation of the Soviet Union* (Cambridge, MA: Harvard U. Press, 1954).

Rupert Emerson. *From Empire to Nation* (Cambridge, MA: Harvard U. Press, 1960).

Alfred Cobban. *The Nation State and National Self-Determination* (New York: Thomas Crowell, 1969).

V. S. Shevtsov. *National Sovereignty and the Soviet State* (Moscow: Progress, 1974).

Zev Katz, Rosemarie Rogers, and Frederic Harned, eds. *Handbook of Major Soviet Nationalities* (New York: Free Press, 1975).

Hugh Seton-Watson. *Nations and States* (Boulder, CO: Westview, 1977).

Helene Carrère d'Encausse. *L'empire éclaté* (Paris: Flammarion, 1978).

Edward Allworth, ed. *Ethnic Russia in the USSR* (New York: Pergamon, 1980).

Ernest Gellner. *Nations and Nationalism* (Ithaca, NY: Cornell U. Press, 1983).

Anthony D. Smith. *Theories of Nationalism* (New York: Holmes and Meier, 1983).

Alexander Yanov. *The Russian Challenge and the Year 2000* (Oxford: Basil Blackwell, 1987).

Dusko Doder and Louise Branson. *Gorbachev—Heretic in the Kremlin* (New York: Viking, 1989).

Anders Åslund. *Gorbachev's Struggle for Reform* (Ithaca, NY: Cornell University Press, 1989).

Nadia Diuk and Adrian Karatnycky. *The Hidden Nations* (New York: Morrow, 1990).

Lubomyr Hajda and Mark Beissinger, eds. *The Nationalities Factor in Soviet Politics and Society* (Boulder, CO: Westview, 1990).

Hedrick Smith. *The New Russians* (New York: Random House, 1990).